British readers of the eighteenth and early nineteenth centuries eagerly consumed books of travels in an age of imperial expansion that was also the formative period of modern aesthetics. Beauty, sublimity, sensuous surfaces, and scenic views became conventions of travel writing as Britons applied familiar terms to unfamiliar places around the globe. The social logic of aesthetics, argues Elizabeth Bohls, constructed women, the laboring classes, and non-Europeans as foils against which to define the "man of taste" as an educated, property-owning gentleman. Women writers from Mary Wortley Montagu to Mary Shelley resisted this exclusion from gentlemanly privilege, and their writings re-examine and question aesthetic conventions such as the concept of disinterested contemplation, subtly but insistently exposing its vested interests. Bohls's study expands our awareness of women's intellectual presence in Romantic literature, and suggests Romanticism's sources might be at the peripheries of empire rather than at its center.

CAMBRIDGE STUDIES IN ROMANTICISM 13

WOMEN TRAVEL WRITERS AND THE LANGUAGE OF AESTHETICS, 1716–1818

This series aims to foster the best new work in one of the most challenging fields within English literary studies. From the early 1780s to the early 1830s a formidable array of talented men and women took to literary composition, not just in poetry, which some of them famously transformed, but in many modes of writing. The expansion of publishing created new opportunities for writers, and the political stakes of what they wrote were raised again and again by what Wordsworth called those "great national events" that were "almost daily taking place": the French Revolution, the Napoleonic and American wars, urbanization, industrialization, religious revival, and expanded empire abroad and the reform movement at home. This was a literature of enormous ambition, even when it pretended otherwise. The relations between science, philosophy, religion, and literature were reworked in texts such as *Frankenstein* and *Biographia Literaria*; gender relations in *A Vindication of the Rights of Woman* and *Don Juan*; journalism by Cobbett and Hazlitt; poetic form, content and style by the Lake School and the Cockney School. Outside Shakespeare studies, probably no body of writing has produced such a wealth of response or done so much to shape the responses of modern criticism. This indeed is the period that saw the emergence of those notions of "literature" and of literary history, especially national literary history, on which modern scholarship in English has been founded.

The categories produced by Romanticism have also been challenged by recent historicist arguments. The task of the series is to engage both with a challenging corpus of Romantic writings and with the changing field of criticism they have helped to shape. As with other literary series published by Cambridge, this one will represent the work of both younger and more established scholars, on either side of the Atlantic and elsewhere.

For a list of titles published in the series, see back of book.

WOMEN TRAVEL WRITERS AND THE LANGUAGE OF AESTHETICS, 1716–1818

ELIZABETH A. BOHLS

University of Illinois, Urbana-Champaign

CAMBRIDGE
UNIVERSITY PRESS

Published by the Press Syndicate of the University of Cambridge
The Pitt Building, Trumpington Street, Cambridge CB2 1RP
40 West 20th Street, New York, NY 10011–4211, USA
10 Stamford Road, Oakleigh, Melbourne 3166, Australia

First published 1995
Reprinted 1996

Printed in Great Britain by Woolnough Bookbinders Ltd, Irthlingborough, Northants.

A catalogue record for this book is available from the British Library

Library of Congress cataloguing in publication data
Bohls, Elizabeth A.
Women travel writers and the language of aesthetics, 1716–1818 / Elizabeth A. Bohls.
p.   cm. – (Cambridge studies in Romanticism: 13)
Includes bibliographical references.
ISBN 0 521 47458 2 (hardback)
1. Travelers' writings, English – Women authors – History and criticism.
2. Women travelers – Great Britain – Biography – History and criticism.
3. English prose literature – 18th century – History and criticism. 4. English prose
literature – 19th century – History and criticism. 5. Women and literature – Great Britain
– History – 18th century. 6. Women and literature – Great Britain – History – 19th
century. 7. Aesthetics, British – 18th century. 8. Aesthetics, British – 19th century.
9. Landscape in literature. 10. English language – Style.   I. Title.   II. Series.
PR778.T72B64   1995
910.4'082 – dc20   95–43861 CIP

ISBN 0 521 47458 2 hardback

TAG

Contents

Illustrations

Acknowledgments

Many people have generously contributed to the making of this book. I wish to thank those who have read and responded to parts of the text, including Amanda Anderson, Susan Z. Andrade, Nina Baym, John Bender, Bliss Carnochan, Greg Colomb, Syndy McMillen Conger, John Dussinger, Allen Hance, Nely Keinanen, Harry Liebersohn, Deidre Lynch, Janet Lyon, Paul Mattick, Jr., Paula McDowell, Carol Thomas Neely, Clifford Siskin, Jack Stillinger, Zohreh T. Sullivan, David Wellbery, and members of the University of Illinois History Department Cultural Studies reading group. I am grateful to Margaret Bohls, Marilyn Booth, Ramona Curry, Amy Farmer, Sonya Michel, Jane Sherwood, and Charles Wright for specific references, and to my students, especially the members of English 297 and 427 (Fall 1990) and English 463 (Fall 1993), for stimulating discussions. Terry Burke, Leon Chai, Alma Gottlieb and Philip Graham, Charles Kimball, Jonathan Lamb, Bob Markley, Paula McDowell, Robert Dale Parker, Nancy Roberts, Cliff Siskin, and Zohreh T. Sullivan gave me advice and support at crucial moments and over the long haul.

Terry Castle's teaching and scholarship first inspired me to study the eighteenth century, and she encouraged this project in its early stages. I owe another major intellectual debt to John Bender, an astute and dependable mentor. Bliss Carnochan's patient and generous guidance helped me through graduate school and beyond, earning my deepest gratitude. The University of Illinois English Department, in particular its Head, Richard P. Wheeler, Associate Head Jan Hinely, and Business Manager Rene Wahlfeldt, provided support and assistance of many kinds; the Campus Research Board and the Program for the Study of Cultural Values and Ethics at the University of Illinois provided released time and fellowship support. Kurt Austin's help in checking references was invaluable, as was Josie Dixon's editorial guidance. My fellow members of Second Wind Running Club, especially Lezli Austen, Bonnie Friedman, and Jan Seeley, made it easier to combine writing with mental health. My parents, Mary and Allen Bohls, have supported my endeavors since the beginning. Chris Q. Doe makes everything possible; this book is dedicated to him with love.

Versions of various sections of this book have appeared in *Eighteenth-Century Aesthetics and the Reconstruction of Art,* ed. Paul Mattick, Jr. (Cambridge University Press, 1993), *Eighteenth-Century Studies,* 27 (Spring 1994), *Studies in Eighteenth-Century Culture,* 23 (1993), and *Eighteenth-Century Life* [forthcoming].

Introduction

In Jane Austen's *Northanger Abbey*, a pedantic Henry Tilney lectures Catherine Morland on the picturesque. He holds forth in a self-important jargon of "fore-grounds, distances, and second distances – side-screens and perspectives – lights and shades." Conferring on the country girl the social polish of good taste in landscape, he places her firmly in a secondary, mediated relation to knowledge. Though she finds it all quite odd at first – "It seemed as if a good view were no longer to be taken from the top of an high hill, and that a clear blue sky was no longer a proof of a fine day" – the infatuated Catherine is content to absorb Henry's opinions; she proves "so hopeful a scholar, that when they gained the top of Beechen Cliff, she voluntarily rejected the whole city of Bath, as unworthy to make part of a landscape."[1]

Austen embeds her light-hearted satire of the picturesque as pretentious and rigid in a darker view of women's troubled relation to the powerful discourses and institutions of patriarchal culture.[2] Beechen Cliff reminds Catherine of Ann Radcliffe's reams of scenery in *The Mysteries of Udolpho*; Austen's parody pays ambiguous tribute to Radcliffe, who (I will argue) turns a critique of aesthetics into a sublime nightmare of women's manipulation by a powerful man in control of light and information.[3] The banter among Catherine, Henry, and Eleanor in this scene sketches an analysis of women's systematic exclusion from knowledge as cultural power. Talking of *Udolpho* reminds Henry of all the other books he has read: "I had entered on my studies at Oxford, while you were a good little girl working your sampler at home!" This patronizing reminder of women's lack of access to higher education leads to their absence from "real solemn history," which Catherine, famously, cannot bring herself to read – "the men all so good for nothing, and hardly any women at all." Not only are women

I

excluded from educational institutions, they are written out of the
very structure of what is known. Moreover, the social imperative of
courtship and marriage sets knowledge in an inverse relation to
sexual attraction, as Austen's narrator ironically notes: if a woman
"have the misfortune of knowing any thing, [she] should conceal it
as well as she can."[4] She echoes Mary Wortley Montagu's bitter
advice half a century earlier that a girl be taught "to conceal whatever learning she attains, with as much solicitude as she would hide
crookedness or lameness."[5] In such a climate few women were
likely to aspire beyond the safely mediated access to learning
illustrated by Henry's little lesson on the picturesque.

It is no accident that Austen chooses the language of landscape
aesthetics to frame a meditation on gender, knowledge, and power.
Women's relation to aesthetics in eighteenth-century Britain was
an equivocal one. They were not wholly excluded from aesthetic
reception or production; while they did not write treatises, they did
publish picturesque tours.[6] Throughout the century a handful of
women made careers as painters (like Mary Moser and Angelica
Kauffmann, members of the Royal Academy), and increasing numbers of women published works of fiction, poetry, drama, and even
literary criticism. Much more common for the ladies of Britain's
privileged classes, however, was amateur aesthetic activity. The
genteel accomplishments that occupied ladies' enforced leisure and
enhanced their value on the marriage market included drawing
and the appreciation of scenery, as well as music and needlework.
As literate Britons (though denied a classical education), they read
the canonical texts of aesthetics: Addison on the pleasures of the
imagination, Burke on the sublime and beautiful, Gilpin on the
picturesque. Women were included in the practices of taste, but
marginally. They were tolerated as second-class practitioners or
passive consumers, like Gilpin's numerous "lady admirers" and
drawing pupils.[7]

Addison's remarks on women readers point to the conceptual
difficulties in women's relation to the aesthetic practices of polite
eighteenth-century culture. Though *The Spectator* clearly identifies
its primary audience as the "Man of a Polite Imagination,"
Mr. Spectator ambiguously declares that "there are none to
whom this Paper will be more useful, than to the female World."
Like Henry Tilney, he patronizes women beneath a veneer of
respect:

I have often thought there has not been sufficient Pains taken in finding out proper Employments and Diversions for the Fair ones. Their Amusements seem contrived for them rather as they are Women, than as they are reasonable Creatures; and are more adapted to the Sex, than to the Species. The Toilet is their great Scene of Business, and the right adjusting of their Hair the principal Employment of their Lives...Their more serious Occupations are Sowing and Embroidery, and their greatest Drudgery the Preparation of Jellies and Sweetmeats. This, I say, is the State of ordinary Women; tho' I know there are Multitudes...that join all the Beauties of the Mind to the Ornaments of Dress, and inspire a kind of Awe and Respect, as well as Love, into their Male-Beholders. I hope to encrease the Number of these by publishing this daily Paper, which I shall always endeavour to make an innocent if not an improving Entertainment, and by that Means at least divert the Minds of my female Readers from greater Trifles.[8]

For Addison, women cannot finally avoid being positioned as aesthetic objects, rather than aesthetic subjects. Self-adornment is their "principal Employment"; even their intellectual activities enter his text as "Beauties of the Mind" whose primary importance seems to be their effect on "Male-Beholders." The tongue-in-cheek hyperbole of "Multitudes" adds to the passage's condescending tone.[9] Casting himself as women's rescuer from their love of "Trifles," Addison draws them into the cultural projects of Britain's ruling class as he relegates them firmly to the margin of the aesthetic sphere.

Addison and Austen accurately suggest the obstacles facing women who aspired to a more than marginal role in eighteenth-century aesthetics. This study presents a group of women writers who nonetheless broke out of masculine tutelage to make unrecognized contributions during the formative period of modern aesthetic thought. From Montagu in the early eighteenth century to Mary Shelley in the early nineteenth, these women struggled to appropriate the powerful language of aesthetics, written by men from a perspective textually marked as masculine. They certainly aspired to share in aesthetics' authority and prestige, but they also challenged its most basic assumptions. They did not do this cultural work in the usual genres of aesthetic theory – the discourse, treatise, or inquiry – but instead chose genres more accessible to women, travel writing and the novel, in a period when writing and publishing posed particular difficulties for women. Their critiques of aesthetics, for the most part, are not laid out as argument, but

1. Richard Earcom after Johann Zoffany, "The Founding Members of the Royal Academy," 1768. Mary Moser and Angelica Kauffmann cannot be in the room with the nude model; their portraits hang on the wall.

rather emerge from the subtly or blatantly unconventional ways in which they apply the language of aesthetics. Such oblique strategies have been amply shown to be typical of early women writers.[10] They were perhaps especially necessary when women took on a discourse as prestigious as aesthetics.

Defining aesthetics for the purposes of this study is a necessary, but by no means straightforward, exercise. The term itself, as Carolyn Korsmeyer points out, "was coined for academic discourse and does not have a strong history in vernacular usage."[11] The history of the word reflects aesthetics' exclusive and well-defended social location. Recent work on the history of aesthetics, such as that of Terry Eagleton and John Barrell, still assumes a narrowly canonical, academic notion of what counts as aesthetic thought, for which women's contribution remains invisible. Barrell, for instance, has trouble acknowledging even William Blake as a theorist because he expresses his views on art in mere prospectuses and advertisements rather than a more respectable treatise or lecture to the Royal Academy.[12] My feminist analysis must begin with a working definition of aesthetics that can encompass women's innovative ventures. Instead of restricting aesthetics to a narrow, prestigious genre of academic or theoretical writing, I define it more broadly as a discourse, or a closely related set of discourses, encompassing a set of characteristic topics or preoccupations as well as a vocabulary for talking about these. Aesthetic discourse deals with the categories and concepts of art, beauty, sublimity, taste, and judgment, and more broadly with the pleasure experienced from sensuous surfaces or spectacles. Analyzing language as discourse entails understanding it as socially and historically located, taking shape and circulating within specific institutions, practices, and genres of writing. Discourse is spoken or written from particular social positions, and it marks out a position for its speaker. The circulation of discourse, however – its inherently dialogic character – opens these features to contestation, as we will see on the example of aesthetics.[13]

The boundary between "high" theoretical aesthetics and more popular or applied writing on aesthetic topics was not a rigid one in eighteenth-century Britain. Landscape aesthetics, which particularly attracted women writers, occupied a gray area between the "high" and the middlebrow. William Gilpin, for example, set forth his influential ideas on the aesthetics of the picturesque in both

treatises and picturesque travelogues. This gave women writers the
opportunity to engage with philosophical concepts without directly
trespassing on the more forbidding territory of the treatise. The
lexicon of landscape aesthetics found a plausible place in women's
travel writing and novels; their subtly innovative landscape descriptions bear a heavy burden in my argument. Aesthetic discourse
coexists in individual texts with other discourses, from early
Orientalism to the liberal-revolutionary language of the Rights of
Man, with varying degrees of synergy or friction. The terms of aesthetic discourse, like any discourse, though they display a significant degree of coherence, are not static: they can and do shift from
one text or writer to another, and even within the same text. They
are subject to appropriation and reinterpretation, negotiation and
struggle, with important ideological consequences. This makes it
neither possible nor desirable to give a philosophically rigorous
definition of the aesthetic for the purposes of a study such as this.
Struggle, slippage, and even seeming incoherence often speak more
eloquently than order and exactitude. Thus I can describe, but
not really define, since the conceptual entity in question remains
necessarily and productively imprecise.

Aesthetics took its place in the Enlightenment division of experience that shaped and continues to shape modern Western culture.[14]
Its legacy, like that of the Enlightenment generally, is ambiguous –
especially with regard to gender. Analyses of beauty, art, and taste
comprise a rather rarefied tradition that is almost entirely male.[15]
The guiding question of this study is a version of the well-known
call to historians of women to rethink the assumptions of traditional
historiography: "Did women have an Enlightenment?"[16] What hap-
pens, I ask, when a woman speaks as an aesthetic subject? Taking
gender seriously as a category of cultural analysis affords a new perspective on eighteenth-century aesthetic thought. We may define
gender as the socially established meanings attached to physical sexual difference. It is important to keep in mind that these meanings
are always intertwined with other, not obviously sexual meanings.[17]
Of course, feminists cannot simply read culture as polarized along
the axis of gender, but must account for multiple, interconnecting
categories of difference. The discursive and social logic that structures modern aesthetics is an example of such multiple determination. The writers I will discuss are women; they are also aristocratic
or middle-class, as well as very British. Their social and political

commitments vary widely, and all these factors complicate their relation to the language of aesthetics.

Eighteenth-century Europe witnessed the formation of modern aesthetics as a self-conscious theoretical discipline. This holds true whether we date its emergence to the publication of Baumgarten's *Aesthetica* (1750–58), which coined the term, or look a few decades earlier to British writers like Addison and Shaftesbury who promoted the "pleasures of the imagination." Eighteenth-century Britain was awash with an unprecedented flood of aesthetic discourse. The British thought of this period laid part of the groundwork for Kant's influential systematization of aesthetics in the *Critique of Judgment* (1790).[18] The women I will discuss, writing at this formative moment of modern aesthetics, challenged three of its most important founding assumptions. The first is the generic perceiver, the idea that it is possible to make universally applicable generalizations about "the" subject of aesthetic appreciation. The second is disinterested contemplation, the paradigm of reception that strips the subject's relation to the aesthetic object of any practical stake in that object's existence. The third assumption, closely related, is the autonomy of the aesthetic domain from moral, political, or utilitarian concerns and activities.[19]

The subject or perceiver is constructed in mainstream, male-authored eighteenth-century aesthetic writing through a process that entails disqualifying the vast majority of subjects and falsely universalizing the judgment of the remaining few. These moves are especially apparent in various versions of one well-known doctrine of eighteenth-century aesthetics, the universal standard of taste. Hume, Burke, and Kant all arrive at a universal standard by generalizing the response of a particular perceiver or group of perceivers. Hume's difficult task in his essay, "Of the Standard of Taste," is to uphold such a standard as binding on everyone, while deducing it from the response of a select few. Women writers found various ways of exposing the flawed logic behind the idea that aesthetic appreciation could be uniform for perceivers in widely disparate material and social situations. Women were well placed to gauge the harmful effects of this doctrine on those disqualified from full participation in aesthetic culture. The very act of positioning themselves as aesthetic subjects – appropriating a discourse constructed from a masculine point of view – had far-reaching consequences that I will examine in the chapters that follow.[20]

To ask whose judgment supplied the standard of taste is to confront the unabashed elitism of eighteenth-century aesthetics. When
Addison declared in 1712, "A Man of a Polite Imagination, is let
into a great many Pleasures that the Vulgar are not capable of
receiving," he summarized the widespread view of Britain's social
elite that taste, the capacity for aesthetic pleasure, distinguished
them from the "vulgar" rest of the population.[21] Addison helped
expand that elite by inviting rising merchants and manufacturers
to share in genteel enjoyments like literature, music, painting,
architecture, and natural scenery, while maintaining these pleasures' exclusive social cachet. The polite imagination, he says, gives
its owner "a kind of Property in every thing he sees."[22] He promotes aesthetic contemplation as at once "a gentlemanly pursuit, a
marker of social status, and a training in the experience of individual ownership."[23] Addison's forthright use of aesthetics in the service of social distinction recalls Pierre Bourdieu's account of the
bourgeois *habitus:* "an ethos of elective distance from the necessities
of the natural and social world." Such an aesthetic attitude – a
whole way of life organized to display distance from material need
– values most highly those cultural practices or kinds of pleasure
unattainable by people who live in the grip of necessity, without
the education or leisure to master rigorous codes of access to
"high" culture.[24] Though the tastes of Bourdieu's twentieth-century
France differ from those of eighteenth-century England, taste is
organized by the same principles of distinction and exclusion.

It is not just class that excludes individuals from valued cultural
practices. Addison's system of categories, opposing the "Man of a
Polite Imagination" to the heterogeneous, ungendered "Vulgar,"
omits the possibility of a woman of a polite imagination – a female
aesthetic subject. Shaftesbury's 1711 dialogue, "The Moralists,"
presents an early version of the concept of aesthetic disinterestedness, the second target of women's critiques, in a context that
reveals a whole network of gendered assumptions about relations
of social, economic, and aesthetic power: the interests in disinterestedness. A teacher Socratically quizzes his pupil: "Imagine...if
being taken with the beauty of the ocean, which you see yonder at
a distance, it should come into your head to seek how to command
it, and, like some mighty admiral, ride master of the sea, would not
the fancy be a little absurd?" As he contrasts aesthetic contemplation with a utilitarian attitude toward an object, in this case the

sea, Shaftesbury defines the aesthetic – on the face of it – by the absence of the needs, desires, and vested interests connecting subjects to particular objects in the material world.

The pupil replies with a rather startling logic. "Absurd enough, in conscience. The next thing I should do, 'tis likely, upon this frenzy, would be to hire some bark and go in nuptial ceremony, Venetian-like, to wed the gulf, which I might call perhaps as properly my own."[25] He alludes to the traditional "wedding" between the Republic of Venice and the Adriatic, in which the Doge sails out in state and drops a ring in the water. Mary Wortley Montagu, an unusually well-traveled woman, witnessed this rite during her stay in Italy.[26] So did gentlemen like Shaftesbury, for whom the Grand Tour of Europe was the standard finishing touch to an aristocratic education. By assuming an acquaintance with this bit of Grand Tour trivia, this whimsical example takes a great deal for granted. It further assumes a feminine gender for both objects of property ownership – tellingly exemplified by marriage – and aesthetic objects. The owning or contemplating subject is obviously gendered male. Although the principle of disinterestedness declares aesthetic contemplation incompatible with the will to possess, the context marks them both as aspects of class and gender privilege: contemplating, owning, and marrying are relations that masculine subjects can have to feminine objects. Shaftesbury embeds his version of disinterestedness in a context which strongly implies that the aesthetic subject is a property-owning male. Writings by male aesthetic theorists of the period pervasively construct the aesthetic subject or perceiver as not just a man, but a gentleman.[27] Women's aesthetic writing, as it tampers with the gender of the perceiver, tends to expose the interests that inform supposedly disinterested acts of aesthetic appreciation.

The paradigm of disinterested contemplation is closely tied to the emergent understanding of aesthetics' relation to the other disciplines of modern culture. The eighteenth century gave us the "modern system of the arts," the notion that painting, sculpture, architecture, music, and poetry "constitute an area all by themselves, clearly separated by common characteristics from the crafts, the sciences and other human activities."[28] The classification of human endeavor exemplified by d'Alembert's *Preliminary Discourse to the Encyclopedia* (1751) segregates aesthetic experience from other forms of knowledge. Modern theories and practices of art are grounded in this assumption of an autonomous aesthetic sphere – cut off, in particular, from instrumental, utilitarian, and political pursuits. We can gauge the continuing power of this model, for example, on formalism's long-lasting hold over twentieth-century painting and sculpture and the critical discourse about these, as well as over literary criticism, which has spent decades coming to terms with formalism's legacy.[29] The institution of the museum as a setting for disinterested aesthetic contemplation, deliberately sequestered from ordinary life, gives a material location to the quasi-religious faith in an autonomous aesthetic sphere. This is the third assumption that eighteenth-century women's aesthetic writing goes far to undermine. Their revisionary treatments of landscape aesthetics point to the often inhumane consequences of denying the connection between aesthetic practices and the material, social, and political conditions of human existence.

These women writers attack the very foundations of modern aesthetics. As they do so, they reconfigure central problems of aesthetics whose solution by mainstream theorists was narrow and unsatisfying. Terry Eagleton asserts that aesthetics was born as a discourse of the body,[30] but it is striking to recognize the lengths to which male theorists were prepared to go to keep distasteful aspects of embodiment at arm's length. Aesthetic discourse distances its generic subject, or unmarked category, from the body – a body that disreputably clings to subjects marked by class, gender, or race. Women who try to speak as aesthetic subjects confront this conceptual dissymmetry. Aesthetics also privileges the visual: not gratuitously, but as an integral part of its conceptual structure. Sight, as the least "embodied" of the senses (with the possible exception of hearing), was congenial to a discourse for which embodiment marked inferiority. Kristina Straub has commented on eighteenth-century Britain's fascination with the visual as a site for the symbolic enactment of asymmetrical power relations.[31] Female bodies were constructed as spectacles, objects for a masculine gaze; this, too, palpably hinders women's efforts to position themselves as aesthetic perceivers. Woman's conventional status as spectacle furthermore conflates the aesthetic with the erotic – categories compulsively held apart by the ideological imperative of disinterested contemplation. We will see female subjects, faced with these inhospitable features of aesthetic discourse, find ingenious means to disrupt and reconceive them.

Women writers from Mary Wortley Montagu to Mary Shelley register their dissent from powerful doctrines that persisted long after their lifetime, and still persist, despite a rising chorus of critique from historicists, feminists, postmodernists, and practitioners of cultural studies. These early revisionists are especially timely in the context of today's movement to dismantle the aestheticist structures and standards of literary study in favor of interdisciplinary, materially situated methods for studying the history of culture. Their concerns speak to my own as a historicist feminist critic – even though I often find in their writing a somewhat daunting entanglement between what I, from my twentieth-century perspective, would call structures of oppression and impulses toward liberation.[32] How, for example, can Montagu's proto-feminism coexist with her aristocratic bias? How can Janet Schaw be both a proto-feminist and an arrant racist? How can we reconcile Mary Wollstonecraft's sometimes narrow middle-class prejudices with her liberationist political program? The construction of my study does not try to minimize these embarrassments. On the contrary, I have deliberately put together a selection of writers that will not let us be essentialist about gender or simplistic about feminism, that refuses to authorize easy generalizations about the way women think and write. By calling attention to these writers' diversity, as well as their common concerns, I aim to broaden our sense of the scope of women's endeavors in this period and our means of theorizing the articulation between gender and the other factors that inflect identity and subjectivity.

At the head of the procession of women writing the language of aesthetics stands the imposing figure of Lady Mary Wortley Montagu, the subject of Chapter 1. Her eloquent, sarcastic letters were published posthumously in 1763 and achieved long-lasting popularity (Mary Shelley read them avidly in 1816). Montagu is the only writer I will discuss who is not specifically engaged with landscape. She is an indispensable precursor to later women writing the language of aesthetics. She struggles with the fundamental issue they would revisit, if not resolve: the play of social power in the relation between spectator and spectacle. Women's culturally prescribed status as aesthetic objects, spectacles for a masculine gaze, helps explain Montagu's difficulty in claiming the position of the aesthetic subject. Her writing further discloses an uneasy tension between her identities as an aristocrat and as a woman. The class

character of British aesthetic discourse underwent a significant shift
during the century from 1716, when Montagu embarked for Turkey,
to 1818, the eve of Peterloo. Her emphatically patrician aesthetics
contrasts with the middle-class, anti-aristocratic stance of later writers like Wollstonecraft and Dorothy Wordsworth.

Aesthetics' place in British culture was also in part a product of
global expansion and contact with non-European peoples, whether
an Oriental world power like the Ottoman Empire or a dominated
population like the Afro-Caribbean slaves in Janet Schaw's travel
journal. Mary Pratt suggests that European Romanticism may
have originated not in Europe, but "in the contact zones of
America, North Africa, and the South Seas."[33] One might be
tempted to argue similarly about aesthetics in general. Not every
text I discuss thematizes empire, but it will be clear that a dynamics of exclusion by race or nation, as well as gender and class,
structures aesthetic discourse in this period. Aesthetics harbors a
strong presumption in favor of the hierarchies that structured
British society. Its exclusionary logic constructs not only "the
Vulgar" and women, but also non-Europeans, as foils against
which to define the "Man of a Polite Imagination." Montagu
nonetheless manages to turn aesthetics against another discourse of
domination, early Orientalism, whose crude stereotypes populated
seventeenth-century travel writing on Turkey. Her aestheticizing
rhetoric de-eroticizes and dignifies the Turkish women whom
earlier travelers had relentlessly objectified.

Janet Schaw, by contrast, is largely complacent about aesthetics'
tendency to reinforce inequality. Her unpublished journal of
1774–76, the topic of Chapter 2, like most eighteenth-century writing on the West Indies, effectively beautifies colonial slavery. But as
she sketches the island gender system, articulating gender to aesthetics and racial discourse, Schaw distances herself from the creole women whose exaggerated femininity was a cornerstone of
colonial ideology. Positioning herself as aesthetic subject, she holds
the conventions of femininity – in particular those of feminine
beauty – at arm's length. Women's appropriations of aesthetics, we
realize, are not discursively or politically predictable. They are
governed not by some feminine essence, but by specific historical
pressures and rhetorical exigencies that give each text its distinctive
texture. Each proves differently instructive about the possibilities
and limits of women's relation to the aesthetic.

Though she uses the language of aesthetics to describe Caribbean vistas, Schaw is not a full-blown picturesque tourist. It was not until the 1780s and 1790s that the practice of scenic tourism reached a critical mass and its descriptive conventions coalesced. Women writers from Helen Maria Williams to Mary Shelley were closely engaged with these conventions, which Chapter 3 explores in detail. Both scenic tourism and the related practice of estate gardening apply the aesthetics of the picturesque, whose manner of constructing its generic subject shares basic premises with other areas of mainstream aesthetics. Writings by Addison, Shaftesbury, Hume, and Reynolds, as well as Gilpin, Price, and Knight, display a powerful abstracting impulse, a willed distance from particular objects in the world and the needs and desires that propel individuals toward them. The key to understanding this denial of the particular is the symbolic connection between material particulars and groups of people traditionally thought of as trapped in them, defined by their bodies, as opposed to their minds: the laboring classes and women. Discourses and practices that deny the particular work divisively, a familiar effect of ideology,[34] to enforce the distinction between those positioned within the (masculine) "universal," and thus granted the authority of the aesthetic subject, and those whose "particularity" excludes them.

Eighteenth-century estate gardening reconfigured land in a symbolic economy that distinguished the gardenist, as a property-owning man, from a feminine "Nature" and from the landless laborers who dug his lakes and clipped his shrubbery. Both gardening and scenic tourism frame a scene and carefully detach the viewer from it. The tourist became a disinterested aesthetic subject by eliding the traces of the practical relation between a place and its inhabitants. Human figures in the picturesque scene were reduced to faceless ornaments, like Gilpin's ubiquitous banditti. Aesthetic distance thus reinforces the social distance between the aesthetic subject and the "Vulgar." In such a symbolic economy it is no wonder if a woman, who both was and was not "Vulgar," had trouble occupying the position of the aesthetic subject. Chapter 3 concludes with a brief discussion of Ann Radcliffe's picturesque tour, *A Journey made in the Summer of 1794 through Holland and the Western Frontier of Germany,* a text whose abrupt alternation between picturesque scenes and traces of the ongoing war helps focus our attention on the paradox of the female picturesque.

Women writers worked through their vexed relation not just to
the picturesque, but to the other familiar categories of eighteenth-
century aesthetics. The beautiful presented obvious difficulties for
a female aesthetic subject. Burke's influential 1757 treatise on the
sublime and beautiful elaborates an ideal of beauty that involves
weakness and timidity as well as smoothness and gradual variation
– with pernicious implications for actual women.[35] Mary
Wollstonecraft's *Vindication of the Rights of Men* (1790), refuting
Burke's *Reflections on the Revolution in France,* digresses to lambaste
him for the sexual politics of his aesthetics: "you have clearly
proved that one half of the human species, at least, have not souls;
and that Nature, by making women *little, smooth, delicate, fair* creatures, never designed that they should exercise their reason to
acquire the virtues that produce opposite, if not contradictory feelings." *A Vindication of the Rights of Woman* (1792) continues her
polemic against the "libertine notions of beauty" to which
"strength of body and mind are sacrificed" as women's education is
warped by a sexist aesthetics of feminine appearance.[36]

Women writing the language of landscape aesthetics were not
primarily concerned with the beautiful, however, but with the picturesque and the sublime. Despite her passionate hostility to
Burke's politics, Wollstonecraft was unwilling to relinquish the sublime. As a mode of response to natural scenery, the sublime was
primarily an affective category, while the picturesque emphasized
form and composition. Wollstonecraft's travel account, *Letters
Written during a Short Residence in Sweden, Norway, and Denmark* (1796),
manipulates the emotional register of the sublime from gentle
melancholy to daring transcendence as she pioneers the creation of
a female Romantic persona. She was not the first woman writer to
take an interest in sublimity. Samuel Holt Monk superciliously
describes "a group of learned ladies, who seem to have lived a considerable part of their erudite lives wrought up to the high pitch of
the sublime" – the mid-century "Blue Stockings," including
Elizabeth Carter, Anna Seward, Hester Chapone, and Elizabeth
Montagu.[37]

The bluestockings' enthusiasm for the sublime is of great interest
to the student of aesthetics and gender. It has long been a commonplace that eighteenth-century Britain witnessed the rise of
individualism. Middle-class women were evidently incorporated
into individualist ideology, teaching their children self-discipline

and exercising it on themselves. But, as Mary Poovey observes, they "were not encouraged to think of themselves as part of this nation of individuals."[38] Did these female intellectuals seize on the individualistic aesthetics of the sublime in resistance to the reflexive subordination and self-effacement advocated by conduct literature and woven into the texture of women's daily lives? The Burkean dichotomy between the sublime, fueled by the passions of self-preservation, and the beautiful, which channels the sociable emotions, captures a fundamental tension in the structure of experience at this period. If the extremes of solitude and self-absorption demanded by the sublime were regarded with suspicion by a male poet like Wordsworth, as Theresa M. Kelley has argued, one suspects they were exponentially more dangerous – and more exhilarating – to women.[39]

The picturesque and the sublime could function as opposites (linking the picturesque with the beautiful in a Burkean scheme), but this was by no means always the case. Women writers treated these categories opportunistically, exploiting their ambiguities through creative reappropriation and redefinition. Helen Maria Williams, for example, taps the emotional energy of the sublime even as she carefully frames and orders her descriptions of revolutionary spectacles. This politically savvy expatriate, whose multiple volumes of published letters reported on the French Revolution to British readers between 1790 and 1796, mobilizes aestheticized nature as a recurring trope in her effort to make sense of chaotic historical events. Chapter 4 traces the fate of landscape through Williams' massive work. At first a metaphor for utopian political order, it is reframed as an imaginative escape from politics when the revolution turns to Jacobinism and violence, plunging the Girondist Williams from idealism into near despair.

Aesthetics fares more hopefully in Mary Wollstonecraft's *Letters Written During a Short Residence in Sweden, Norway, and Denmark* (1796), the topic of Chapter 5. Even after the Terror, Wollstonecraft's revolutionary politics informs her quiet transformation of the categories of picturesque and sublime in this beautifully crafted travel account. She humanizes the contemplation of nature by grounding it in concern for the needs of people who live on and from the land at the same time as she experimentally poses a feminine, non-distanced version of the aesthetic subject. Wollstonecraft's feminist critique of aesthetics exposes the moral risks a culture runs by separating the aesthetic, as a category of value, from the material circumstances of human life.

Chapter 6 introduces a scenic tourist who shares Wollstonecraft's compassion for the struggles of the rural poor without her overtly political agenda. But Dorothy Wordsworth is also an avid participant in the class-specific discourse and practice of scenic tourism. For her (as for her famous brother) the solitary figure in the landscape is sublime precisely in its absolute distance or inaccessibility. The sublime thus represents an aesthetic and social distance quite similar to that codified by the picturesque. Toward both, Wordsworth nourishes a profound ambivalence. A pattern of metaphors from exploration and colonialism is one way in which her writing colludes with aesthetics' exclusionary project even as it hints at a troubling self-alienation. Both Montagu and Schaw align aesthetic distance with the geographic and cultural distance that separated imperial Britain from its overseas Others. Wordsworth's comparisons between Scottish Highlanders and Hottentots or Indians figure both the marginality of Britain's internally colonized Celtic fringe, and the intimate distance that fractures the female aesthetic subject.

I will conclude with two influential novels that use aesthetics to explore the consequences of structuring the self, the community, and knowledge itself through processes of exclusion. Ann Radcliffe and Mary Shelley take advantage of the novel's formal potential for incorporating and critiquing socially situated languages to dramatize the insights won by women travel writers beginning with Montagu. The protagonists of Radcliffe's *The Mysteries of Udolpho* (1794) and Shelley's *Frankenstein* (1818) – a demure heroine and a hideous monster – share their painful exclusion from the power of knowledge. Radcliffe introduces her heroine, Emily, as a female aesthetic subject who exercises the authority of taste as a class privilege and spends hundreds of pages appreciating picturesque scenery. But once she is locked in Montoni's castle, deprived of light, knowledge, and power, her privilege collapses into a nightmare of gendered oppression that both extrapolates and travesties the Burkean sublime. Radcliffe sets sublime and picturesque in an unstable counterpoint that puts pressure on both categories as it sketches a radically decentered female subjectivity.

In *Frankenstein,* aesthetic sensibility binds the little communities of the Frankenstein and De Lacey families. These microcosms of

Western civilization need to banish Frankenstein's creature, a being whose appearance inspires universal disgust, but whose eloquent voice subverts the standard of taste that condemns him. Many feminists read the creature as projecting Shelley's sense of women's cultural exclusion. I understand her project as a broader one. The indeterminate otherness of this universally excluded being becomes a lightning rod for the multiple fears of excluded Others that galvanized early nineteenth-century British society: colonized peoples abroad and the working class, as well as unruly women, at home. Shelley's modern myth assesses the cost of distanced contemplation as it questions the very principle of constructing self and community through exclusion.

These women were not just writers, but travelers as well. (Each of the two novelists also published a travel account.) Travel – always a source of knowledge and power – informed Enlightenment investigations of human nature and civilization. Explorers went in search of trade routes or potentially docile populations and brought back raw materials for working through the terms of Europe's global consciousness. Then, as now, travel was marked by class and gender, race and nation, as we glimpsed in Shaftesbury's Venetian allusion. The travel writer, like the aesthetic subject, was normatively male in an age when the home was literally and symbolically woman's place. The imaginary topographies of Western travel, its stagings of self and other, were systematically gendered and powerfully institutionalized.[40] Women did not fit the traveler's image as heroic explorer, scientist, or authoritative cultural interpreter. A woman like Mary Wortley Montagu, who was lucky enough to be mobile, was forced to experiment with unconventional modes of travel. She turned, as we will see, to the aesthetic.

For these women, travel is destabilizing in ways that generate both anxiety and, at times, exhilaration. Geographic displacement seems to loosen the grip of familiar cultural orderings just enough to let them glimpse alternatives. They become traveling theorists, bending the alien intentions of aesthetic discourse to their own.[41] Sometimes they use aesthetics for rhetorical purposes that resist the conservative tendency of the discourse, as when Montagu uses it to neutralize early Orientalism or Helen Maria Williams yokes it in the service of the French Revolution. Their texts are marked by ambivalence and strain. Seeming incongruities open a window onto the social logic of mainstream aesthetic thought. Through the language of aesthetics they explore their own relation, as privileged women, to individuals and groups variously marginalized by aesthetic discourse and European society: the rural laboring classes of Scotland and Scandinavia as well as the revolutionary French, the women of Turkey and the slaves of colonial Antigua. The representations they produce are by no means uniformly tolerant or liberating. Nonetheless, at their best, these women writers challenge and creatively reconceive the conventions of aesthetic discourse.

Clearly, travel does not always entail openness to unfamiliar cultures. In fact one suspects this is rarely the case. Most travelers carry with them an entire apparatus for assimilating their new experiences to comfortable systems of belief. In the case of eighteenth-century British travelers, part of this baggage was the language of aesthetics, specifically landscape aesthetics. Landscape description was an established convention in eighteenth-century travel writing, though the specialized genre of the scenic tour did not take off until the late 1770s. But a deeper cultural logic helps explain the intensity of women's response to this particular subset of aesthetics. The implied subject of mainstream aesthetic discourse, I have already suggested, was a gentleman: a privileged man, educated and leisured, an actual or potential property owner. Landownership as a source and sign of power was the traditional heart of the British political system – the essence of the gentleman. Even when the growing clout of a moneyed bourgeoisie began to shift the political center of gravity, those who made their fortunes in the City hurried to buy country estates and assimilate aristocratic manners. Women writing the language of landscape aesthetics work through their exclusion from the political, social, and cultural privileges of the gentleman. As their travels put distance between them and the gentleman's home turf, they seem emboldened to experiment with aesthetics' symbolic encoding of a social world viewed from the top down.

My study of these women's writings is shaped by some fairly familiar terms and assumptions. I use the term "subject" in three main, related senses. First of all, the subject of a given text or discourse is the position which that discourse marks out for the one who reads, writes, or speaks it – a place that can be occupied by different concrete individuals who use the discourse in particular social, institutional, or literary settings.[42] Mainstream eighteenth-century aesthetic theory constructs its implied subject as both masculine and property-owning. Secondly and more generally, I assume that we are constructed as subjects or selves in and by discourses, or we may say in and by ideology, if ideology is understood as the historically specific, differential relation of discourses, practices, and institutions to structures of power in a given society.[43] We are thus subjected to configurations of language and relations of power that pre-exist us, giving form and content to our consciousness. But the very character of this subjection leaves it open to realignment, as I will demonstrate in the case of eighteenth-century women writers. Neither discourse nor ideology is monolithic; it would be better to speak only of discourses and ideologies. Subjectivity (or we may call it "experience") is a process, "an ongoing construction, not a fixed point of departure" – a continual engagement in practices, discourses, and institutions that bestow meaning on perceptions and events.[44] As Joan Scott puts it, "Subjects are constituted discursively, but there are conflicts among discursive systems, contradictions within any one of them, multiple meanings possible for the concepts they deploy."[45]

The literate eighteenth-century British woman is caught in just such a conflict: she is entitled by class, but not by gender, to the authority of the aesthetic subject. But conflict can be productive. This realization leads to the third and importantly different sense in which I understand the term "subject," as not entirely subjected after all – possessing a crucial, if limited, room to maneuver. One source of this latitude, John Frow points out, is the "discontinuity between discursive [subject] positions and the actual social position of the speaker." It is not easy to pin down the relation between describing the general tendency of a discourse (itself a necessarily inexact endeavor) and accounting for the forms which that discourse takes in specific texts. It seems clear that writers respond to the position of speaking subject implied by an established discourse, genre, or idiom. It also seems intuitively likely that concrete individuals with social identities at a distance from this ideal speaker (along various axes, in varying degrees) will have trouble adapting the discourse to their needs. Every speaker or writer occupies any number of discursive positions, in the course of a lifetime and even in the space of a single text, many of which do not correspond especially well to the predominant social construction of his or her identity.[46] We can try to identify the textual traces of such an ill fit; our efforts will be complicated by the unpredictable interweaving of the multiple social languages that co-inhabit any given text. Circulating through the texts of "improper" speakers like the women I will discuss, the language of aesthetics often emerges mutated in revealing ways.

Middle-class women bear a rather paradoxical relation to the language of aesthetics. Their membership in Britain's "polite" classes apparently entitles them to speak as aesthetic subjects, yet their feminine gender forms part of the symbolic complex of "the particular," the constitutive background from which the subject implied in mainstream aesthetic discourse needed to differentiate himself. My remaining chapters explore the varieties of textual disruption and significant reconfiguration that attend several women's appropriation of this idiom. By no means do I want to be understood as claiming that women writing the language of aesthetics necessarily or automatically resist or refuse its inscription of its subject as masculine; neither do all men writing on aesthetics automatically uphold its discursive conventions and all aspects of the social agenda that those conventions advanced. I have chosen to discuss women writers largely because of the way women have been written out of literary and cultural history since the eighteenth century. Their socially constructed disadvantage, not any supposed essential difference, is my concern. My observations are not and could not be categorical or absolute; their status must remain historical, local, and provisional. I am constructing explanations for textual phenomena by reading a chronologically and thematically limited set of texts with and against one another, describing a significant pattern of convention and variation.

These women's texts offer disrupted, disjunctive, or openly revisionary renditions of aesthetic discourse that register in various ways the problematic position of the female aesthetic subject. Analyzing writings by women of this period demands a combination of caution and daring. Early women's writing discloses typical strategies of obliqueness, conditioned by restrictive cultural definitions of femininity that made it nearly impossible for women to articulate certain meanings directly. Meaning may emerge from gaps or juxtapositions; appropriated discourses (like the language of aesthetics) may be "italicized," as Nancy K. Miller calls it – inflected with a peculiar intonation, a certain intensity or stress. Teasing out such muted gestures of dissent demands what Miller elsewhere calls "a poetics of the *underread* and a practice of 'over-reading.'" Taking up this suggestion, Carol Thomas Neely urges feminist critics "to over-read, to read to excess, the possibility of human (especially female) gendered subjectivity, identity, and agency, the possibility of women's resistance or even subversion. A feminist critique should be able to over-read text with history, and expand history into histories which must include the history of women."[47]

The texts in which women write the language of aesthetics share with a great deal of women's writing a peculiar relation to mainstream literary aesthetics, the values by which works of art have traditionally been judged. Their texts tend to lack the unity prized by critics since Aristotle. Many of them are fundamentally disjunctive, even self-contradictory, marked by a profound ambivalence traceable to the contradictions of middle-class womanhood in eighteenth-century Britain. Contradictory messages about femininity began with the very trajectory of a woman's life. Was it a rising path toward the status of the romantic "treasure" and the fulfillment of marriage, as romantic fiction promised? Or did it peak with the excitement of being young and "out" in society, only to decline to a static, powerless female maturity, as conduct books warned? In a society where literate women's two staple types of reading matter conveyed opposite expectations, the "ability to sustain and express contradiction [was] both a response to ideological conflicts in the culture and a strategy for female psychic survival."[48]

A woman writing the language of aesthetics is already caught in a contradiction, as we have seen. Entitled by her class, excluded by her gender, she is predisposed to produce a deeply divided text. To appreciate such texts I have gone through a long process of relinquishing ingrained habits of interpretation. In particular, I have had to rethink the impulse (quite deeply internalized, I believe, despite deconstruction, in most of us with literary training) to resolve an interpretation into a coherent argument. Is Dorothy Wordsworth or Ann Radcliffe a secret feminist, or a failed one? Is not to decide to abdicate one's responsibility as a critic? Rather than dismissing inconsistency and disunity as mere aesthetic flaws, evidence of poor skill or limited vision, I have learned to value their negotiation of cultural conflict. Ambivalence need imply neither vagueness nor deficiency; it can speak both richly and precisely, once we have re-learned to read. Although literary evaluation as such is not my primary concern, work like mine can contribute indirectly to the ongoing overhaul of literary value by proposing new ways to understand the seriousness of marginalized authors' projects and new contexts in which to gauge the effectiveness of their writing.

The ongoing crisis in literary aesthetics is one aspect of a larger cultural crisis involving the aesthetic as a category of experience – the category that emerged from the cultural upheavals of the Enlightenment. Postmodernism presents itself as "anti-aesthetic," repudiating the Kantian aesthetics that have shaped theories and practices of the arts, and in particular the ideology of the autonomous aesthetic sphere. Feminism, cultural studies, post-marxism, and new historicism have joined the attack on aestheticism as a smokescreen for a conservative cultural agenda.[49] An incident from recent history, the political struggle during the Bush administration over government funding of controversial artists through the National Endowment for the Arts (NEA), found the ideology of the autonomous aesthetic sphere alive and well, if somewhat ironically enlisted in the NEA's defense against its conservative critics. The 1989 Senate protest of Andres Serrano's *Piss Christ* led by Jesse Helms paid a backhanded tribute to art's political explosiveness, its ability precisely not to stay neatly contained but to agitate across categorial boundaries. The entire NEA debate exemplifies the continuing tension surrounding the relation between the aesthetic and the practical, artistic activity and political struggle, prominently including struggle over gender and sexuality in the homoerotic photos of Robert Mapplethorpe or Karen Finley's nude, chocolate-smearing performance art.[50] Women writers started this controversy when modern aesthetics was in its formative stage. They initiated a counter-tradition of aesthetic thought especially valuable to those of us concerned to challenge the present-day legacy of this powerful discourse.

CHAPTER I

Aesthetics and Orientalism in Mary Wortley Montagu's letters

> I confess I am malicious enough to desire that the World shou'd see to how much better purpose the LADYS Travel than their LORDS, and that whilst it is surfeited with Male Travels, all in the same Tone, and stuft with the same Trifles, a *Lady* has the skill to strike out a New Path, and to embellish a worn-out Subject with variety of fresh and elegant Entertainment.[1]

Lady Mary Wortley Montagu (1689–1762) was well educated for a woman of her day, though largely self-taught. Her incisive intellect was attuned to the nuances of art, literature, and criticism in Augustan England. She was a contemporary of Congreve, Shaftesbury, and Addison, whose tragedy *Cato* she was asked to critique in manuscript, not to mention her vexed relationship with Pope. The letters she wrote throughout her long, adventurous life persistently thematize aesthetic concerns: the visual allure of sensuous surfaces as well as the hierarchies of power that complicate the relations between spectator and spectacle, aesthetic subject and aesthetic object. We have glimpsed the assumptions held by Montagu's male peers about these matters. Addison reserves the "Polite Imagination" to privileged men, dismisses "the Vulgar" and relegates "Fair ones" to the margins of the aesthetic sphere, while Shaftesbury implicitly aligns aesthetic contemplation with property ownership as masculine prerogatives. Such attitudes are the context for Montagu's innovative approach to both travel and aesthetics.

Montagu's husband was appointed British Ambassador to the Ottoman Empire in 1716, affording her a rare opportunity for contact with a distant and misunderstood culture. I will be centrally concerned with her portrayal of the Turkish women whose hospitality and beauty she enjoyed during her eighteen-month stay, women whom male travelers had already written up as exotic-erotic Orientals. Reporting on her journey through Europe en route to Turkey, Montagu stakes out a distinctive territory for herself as a woman traveler by subtly but persistently appropriating the aesthetic domain. Her encounters with the women of Europe and Turkey reveal the tensions generated by a female aesthetic subject in a culture that constructs woman overwhelmingly as object, rather than subject, of the aesthetic gaze. Her famous description of the women's baths boldly turns the language of aesthetics as a rhetorical weapon against Orientalist stereotypes, but cannot leave aesthetics' troubling power dynamics entirely behind.

Montagu's unorthodoxy led to increasing isolation during her lifetime; she spent the final decades of her life in Italy in self-imposed exile. A strong sense of propriety led her, as a woman and an aristocrat, not to publish any of her writings under her own name.[2] She nourished a fierce and bitter ambivalence toward her own activity as a female aesthetic producer. When the Turkish Embassy letters appeared in print in 1763, the year after their author's death (by her own arrangement, it appears, and against her family's wishes), they were an immediate sensation. They went through multiple editions, inspired imitations and at least one spurious sequel, and were praised by such figures as Smollett, Gibbon, Voltaire, Samuel Johnson, and Hester Thrale Piozzi. The letters' popularity endured for decades; they were read avidly in the early nineteenth century by both Byron and Mary Shelley.[3] Working at the same time as the men who founded modern aesthetic theory, Montagu launches an alternative tradition of aesthetic thought.

WOMAN AS AESTHETIC TRAVELER

Writing from Holland in 1716, Montagu compares a Dutch castle to one in Nottingham. Her remarks suggest a gendered division of labor among travelers: "'Tis true the fortifications make a considerable difference. All the learned in the art of war bestow great Commendations on them. For my part that know nothing of the matter, I shall content my selfe with telling you tis a very pritty walk on the Ramparts, on which there is a Tower very deservedly call'd the Belvidere, where people go to drink Coffee, Tea, etc., and enjoy one of the finest prospects in the World" (1:251–52).

Holland, of course, rivaled Britain as a military and economic world power. By this time the Grand Tour of Europe was an institution with an established itinerary; it retained a militaristic dimension from its Tudor origin as training for diplomats. The patriotic traveler (presumptively male) was expected to collect useful information for country and sovereign, to note geography and fortifications.[4] But Montagu leaves such pursuits to "learned" men and turns instead to pretty walks and fine prospects, the beauty of visible surfaces – in short, to aesthetics. She steps mock-apologetically into the position of the aesthetic subject. Stereotypical feminine ignorance or superficiality becomes a tongue-in-cheek pretext for suggesting a new perspective.

Her scorn for traditional, masculine modes of travel is more explicit in her later letters. Living in Italy from 1739 to 1761, she was often visited by teenaged British aristocrats, whom she labels "the greatest blockheads in nature" (II:177). Here she lectures her daughter, Lady Bute.

I find you have many wrong notions of Italy, which I do not wonder at. You can take your Ideas of it only from Books or Travellers. The first are generally antiquated or confin'd to Trite Observations, and the other yet more superficial. They return no more instructed than they might have been at home by the help of a Map. The Boys only remember where they met with the best Wine or the prettyest Women, and the Governors (I speak of the most learned amongst them) have only remark'd Situations and Distances, or at most Status and Edifices.
(II:494–95).

Montagu decries conventional travel writers as well as Grand Tourists. Men, we realize, are the truly superficial travelers. The tutors' quantitative or monumental approach is as worthless as their charges' pursuit of women and wine. Passages like this suggest that her aesthetic approach may have been part of a conscious search for an alternative mode of travel.

As she tours European capitals and courts, Montagu persistently attends to matters of surface display and sensuous pleasure. She regales her correspondents with rich descriptions of dress, food, buildings, and furnishings, the glitter of relics in churches and curios in noblemen's homes; she is stirred by the grand spectacles of theater and opera. Local customs are judged from an aesthetic perspective. In a letter written from Nuremberg she argues in favor of sumptuary laws, citing the "agreable Effect to the Eye of a

Stranger" of a society that distinguishes rank by dress (1:255). Connecting aesthetic pleasure to a legally enforced code of social–sartorial hierarchy, Montagu firmly anchors such pleasure in class privilege. This view from the top continues as she visits the Austrian aristocracy's magnificent Vienna apartments and suburban villas, like Count Schönborn's: "the Furniture all rich brocards, so well fancy'd and fited up, nothing can look more Gay and Splendid…through out the whole House a profusion of Gilding, Carving, fine paintings, the most beautifull Porcelane, statues of Alablaster and Ivory, and vast Orange and Lemon Trees in Gilt Pots" (1:261). The Viennese "Fauxbourg" becomes an extravagant, operatic spectacle of glittering profusion. The aesthetic sphere, and specifically the realm of the visible, emerges as an arena for conspicuous consumption. The aristocrat's position entails not just the right, but seemingly the obligation, to visibility as a flaunting display of privilege and power − a display underwritten by this aristocratic woman traveler's polite imagination.

Another type of spectacle, however, moves Montagu to consider the relation between aesthetic pleasure and social power from a different perspective. We can sense throughout her letters an uneasy tension between her social rank and her gender as interpenetrating dimensions of her subjectivity. Generally conservative on matters of class, she can be surprisingly subversive when speaking as a woman rather than, primarily, an aristocrat. Traveling through Europe, she notices the aesthetics of female appearance, the ways in which women of different nations produce themselves as objects of the gaze. She lampoons types of artifice that she finds degrading, from her hilarious account of Viennese court dress − "more monstrous and contrary to all common sense and reason than tis possible for you to imagine" (1:265) − to her description of the heavily made-up women of Paris, "these grotesque Dawbers" (1:440). Montagu herself nonetheless takes part in the process of feminine self-objectification. She is presented at the Emperor's court, "squeez'd up in a Gown and adorn'd with a Gorget and the other implements thereunto belonging," presumably with a fashionable hairdo "too large to go into a moderate Tub" (1:265). Suspicious of women's conventional status as spectacles, she cannot avoid making a spectacle of herself. The cheerful sarcasm of her self-observation deflects the coercive overtones of words like "squeez'd" and "implements."

In Saxony a female aesthetic subject confronts a female object in a distorted mirror as Montagu recounts the misdirected artifice of Saxon ladies, who "would think it a mortal sin against good breeding if they either spoke or mov'd in a natural manner. They all affect a little soft Lisp and a pritty pitty pat step, which female frailtys ought, however, to be forgiven 'em in favour of their civility and good nature to strangers" (1:282–83). But directly following these remarks on female frailty we get an elaborate account of a Saxon woman's strength and determination. The Countess of Cosel, mistress of the Elector of Saxony, defies her powerful lover until he locks her up (1:283–84). The spectacle of women producing themselves as frail, dependent objects triggers – as if in protest – a violent assertion of female will. This juxtaposition points to a recurring tension in the letters: a difficulty reconciling women's objecthood (whether aesthetic or erotic) with their status as independent subjects or agents. Power and visibility stand in a different relation under the sign of gender than under that of social rank. The visibility of gender displays not power, but conventional weakness; the mincing Saxon beauties seem to warn Montagu that her position as an aesthetic subject is a compromised prerogative. Already these letters go far to expose the fallacy of a generic or universal model of aesthetic perception in a culture where looking and being looked at are so deeply implicated in relationships of social power.

"NOT THE LEAST WANTON SMILE OR IMMODEST GESTURE"

Montagu was a uniquely privileged woman traveler. Arriving in Turkey as the wife of the British Ambassador gave her access to the upper echelons of Ottoman society. Her gender admitted her to distinctive institutions off limits even to privileged men. Harems and women's baths were already topics of prurient speculation by male travel writers, several of whom claimed to have visited them, though as Montagu points out, "'Tis no less than Death for a Man to be found in one of these places" (1:315). These fabricated portrayals of Turkish women were a key element of early Orientalist discourse. Though Edward Said's study gives no detailed account of Orientalism before Napoleon, late seventeenth- and early eighteenth-century British and French accounts of travel to the

Ottoman Empire are consistent with later representations of the Middle East. The Orient is discursively feminized and eroticized; West stands to East in a relation of proto-colonial domination that takes on a seemingly inevitable sexual character.[5] Oriental women carry a disproportionate symbolic burden in this discourse. Doubly other and doubly exotic, they become a synecdoche for the Orient itself. Their supposedly insatiable sexual appetites offer an excuse for the sexualized domination that these travelogues underwrite.

Montagu was familiar with at least some of these writings; she remarks with characteristic sarcasm, "'Tis a particular pleasure to me here to read the voyages to the Levant, which are generally so far remov'd from Truth and so full of Absurditys I am very well diverted with 'em. They never fail giving you an Account of the Women, which 'tis certain they never saw, and talking very wisely of the Genius of the Men, into whose Company they are never admitted, and very often describe Mosques, which they dare not peep into" (1:368). But she seems genuinely concerned to correct the falsehoods spread by previous travel writers, especially those about Turkish women. Debunking fantasies extremely attractive to readers – especially male readers – is Montagu's difficult task as she describes the women's baths.[6] How do you describe a room full of naked Turkish women without repeating their double objectification as women and as "Orientals"? A key element of the rhetorical strategy she develops to meet this challenge is an appeal to aesthetics, setting it against the offensive idiom of early Orientalism. By comparing the bathing women to works of European art, I will argue, she attempts to de-eroticize and de-exoticize them, neutralizing Orientalist stereotypes. But to accomplish this, she must present herself as someone capable of perceiving and judging aesthetically: a female aesthetic subject.

Sara Suleri is one of those who have recently expressed concern that much scholarship on travel and colonialism is still structured, like Said's book, by a "rhetoric of binarism" between self and other, West and East, which may subtly nourish the colonial mentality it intends to attack. "Even as the other is privileged in all its pluralities, in all its alternative histories, its concept-function remains too embedded in a theoretical duality of margin to center ultimately to allow the cultural decentering that such critical attention surely desires." Suleri calls for the "productive disordering" of this duality.[7] The historian Billie Melman finds representations of external cultural Others produced by Europe's internal Others, especially women, useful for uncovering what she calls "polyphony" in travel writing.[8] Montagu's polemic against male travelers is an instructive example of such polyphony, reminding us that neither Orient nor Occident is monolithic. Internal diversity and dialogue are vital principles of her approach to both travel and aesthetics. Until quite recently, analyses of colonial discourse followed Said's example by avoiding women's writing, and thus evading the theoretical challenge presented by the unpredictable difference that gender makes.[9] As we watch Montagu challenge the male Orientalists of her day, we may succeed in complicating the theoretical paradigms of our own.

Portrayals of male and female Turks in writings by travelers like Robert Withers, Paul Rycaut, Aaron Hill, and Jean Dumont ("that worthy author Dumont," jeers Montagu (1:368), "who has writ with equal ignorance and confidence") bear out Said's description of a discursively feminized and sexualized Orient.[10] Turkish men are feminized, as in Dumont's 1705 assertion – repeated if not plagiarized by Hill in 1709 – that the "Turks are opposite to us in almost all respects." They wear long, dress-like habits and "crouch down to Piss, like Women" (149). They are ignorant, covetous, lazy, and sensual, according to Dumont (261ff.). Rycaut claims they are inclined to sodomy, echoed by Hill who euphemistically calls it "the strange and curs'd Pollution of *inverted Nature*" (80). Rycaut even blasphemously insinuates that the Prophet shared this "carnal and effeminate inclination" (153).

These travelers unanimously present Turkish women as wanton or hypersexual: "they are accounted the most lascivious and immodest of all Women, and excel in the most refined and ingenious subtilties to steal their pleasures," summarizes Rycaut (153). The custom of segregating women from men, he says, sharpens their desires. The inventive Hill imagines a gang of these sexual predators getting hold of a hapless man:

so lascivious are their Inclinations, that if by the ingenuity of their Contrivances they can procure the Company of some Stranger in their Chamber, they claim unanimously an equal share of his Caresses, and proceed by Lots to the Enjoyment of his Person; nor can he be permitted to leave them, till having exerted his utmost Vigour in the Embraces of the whole Company, he becomes incapable of further Service, and is dispatch'd with the Thanks and Presents of the oblig'd Family. (111)

Dumont tells of a Frenchman who does not get off so easily. Summoned by a noble lady, he obliges her to near exhaustion, but is forbidden to leave. Her last twenty lovers have been strangled to ensure their silence, confides her maid, who agrees to help him out by way of the chimney if he will sexually service her as well (269–70). Rycaut claims lesbianism is rampant in the harems: "they die with amorous affections one to the other; especially the old Women court the young" (34).[11] Withers hints at other sexual outlets for harem women: "if they have a will to eat radishes, cucumbers, gourds, or such like meats, they are sent in unto them sliced, to deprive them of the means of playing the wantons" (55). These stereotypes were obviously in current circulation. Pope echoes Withers in a letter he wrote to Montagu as she traveled toward Turkey, salaciously warning that she would soon arrive in "the Land of Jealousy, where the unhappy Women converse with none but Eunuchs, and where the very Cucumbers are brought to them Cutt."[12]

Another point of consensus is Turkish women's confinement, even outside the Sultan's palace. According to Dumont, "There is no Slavery equal to that of the Turkish women" (268). "'Tis but very rarely that they go abroad, and then to no Place but the publick Bagnio's, or the Funeral, or Marriage, of some near Relation," claims Hill, adding a description of their veils (95). But their strict confinement, the writers agree, does not always keep these wily and insatiable creatures from fulfilling their desires.

Montagu's letter to "Lady —" dated April 1, 1717, describing the women's baths in Sophia, is a clear response to such crude stereotypes of Turkish women. She carefully counteracts previous travelers' eroticized fabrications with a rhetoric founded on her appropriation of the aesthetic domain to the woman traveler. She narrates her first interaction with the bathers in a manner that affirms the women's independent subjectivity while exposing the delusions of Eurocentrism. Arriving at the baths in her riding habit, she is received with surprising tolerance.

I know no European Court where the Ladys would have behav'd them selves in so polite a manner to a stranger. I beleive in the whole there were 200 Women and yet none of those disdainfull smiles or satyric whispers that never fail in our assemblys when any body appears that is not dress'd exactly in fashion. They repeated over and over to me, Uzelle, pek uzelle, which is nothing but, charming, very charming. (1:313)

Already Montagu has reversed the usual relation between traveler and inhabitant. She is obviously a curiosity that the Turkish women inspect with a lively interest modulated by their extremely good manners.[13] In refined politeness, the pride of European courts, these Easterners surpass Western aristocrats. Their tactful conduct reveals them as intelligent and sensitive individuals with whom the visitor may reasonably aspire to some kind of rapport.

Next, using the male travel writers' own language, Montagu bluntly refutes them by asserting that these women do not present themselves erotically. She describes them in the baths,

in the state of nature, that is, in plain English, stark naked, without any Beauty or deffect conceal'd, yet there was not the least wanton smile or immodest Gesture amongst 'em. They Walk'd and mov'd with the same majestic Grace which Milton describes of our General Mother. There were many amongst them as exactly proportion'd as ever any Goddess was drawn by the pencil of Guido or Titian, and most of their skins shineingly white, only adorn'd by their Beautifull Hair divided into many tresses hanging on their shoulders, braided either with pearl or riband, perfectly representing the figures of the Graces. (1:313–14)

Likening the bathers to prestigious European works of art – Milton's Eve, the nude paintings of Guido and Titian, and the frequently painted classical motif of the Three Graces – is the crux of Montagu's ingenious strategy. These comparisons reinforce her claim that the Turkish women are neither "wanton" nor "immodest."[14] They do so by invoking contemporary aesthetic thought, and in particular the developing concept of disinterested aesthetic contemplation, which we have glimpsed in Shaftesbury's rather eccentric explication. If aesthetic objects, especially works of art, are by definition not objects for prurient regard, then Montagu's aesthetic comparisons should have the effect of de-eroticizing her readers' imaginary gaze and thus blocking the crass fantasies of Withers and Dumont's lascivious crew.

I am not arguing that her use of aesthetic discourse could entirely, unambiguously desexualize the scene, nor that this was what she necessarily hoped. Her letters' nineteenth-century reception makes clear that they retained the potential to titillate. Victorian women readers were shocked,[15] while a French Romantic like the painter Ingres in *Le Bain turc* (1862), a painting based on his reading of Montagu, could re-activate the latent sensuality of the scene and ironically reproduce the Orientalism that was the target

2. Titian, "Danae."

3. Raphael, "The Three Graces."

of her polemic. But these later readings neglect the important counterweight that qualitatively transformed the eroticism of this highly charged scene, lending it a productive ambiguity. The language of aesthetics does not just mute the baths' erotic appeal, but, more important, raises its tone to a refinement commensurate with the status of these Turkish aristocrats. Montagu, speaking as an aristocrat and a woman, brings to bear not just the paradigm of disinterested aesthetic contemplation, but also – and somewhat paradoxically – aesthetics' exalted social level. Invoking disinterestedness, she simultaneously invokes the class interest that informed this concept from its inception. Her language, then, does not

4. Ingres, "The Turkish Bath."

wholly de-eroticize, but primarily dignifies and de-exoticizes the bathers. They are recast from oversexed houris playing with cucumbers into Venus, Eve, and the Graces, bringing them closer to upper-class European sensibilities. Aesthetic distance helps defuse the degrading potential of their corporeality within Orientalist discourse (which feeds on other entrenched Western discourses about women's bodies[16]) to let Montagu present them as human individuals potentially deserving of interest and respect, rather than essentially non-human Others.

This aesthetic strategy is obviously not without its problems. Presenting them as works of art may rescue the Turkish women from their representation as exotic sex objects, but such a comparison still casts them as objects, rather than subjects. Aesthetic contemplation may elevate them, in a sense, where a purely erotic regard was taken as denigrating. Both types of gaze nonetheless risk leaving the women looked at rather than looking, acted on rather than acting, despite Montagu's initial concern to establish their independent subjectivity. We noted the tension in her letters from Europe between women's culturally prescribed status as objects – whether aesthetic or erotic – and their culturally discouraged aspiration to subjecthood, in particular her own claim to the status of aesthetic subject.

The art historian John Berger discusses this gendered imbalance in Western culture with reference to the European tradition of nude painting. He coins a distinction between nudity and nakedness, or object and agent: "To be naked is to be oneself. To be nude is to be seen naked by others and yet not recognized for oneself. A naked body has to be seen as an object in order to become a nude . . . Nakedness reveals itself. Nudity is placed on display."[17] In these terms we might understand Montagu as reaching toward a means of representing the Turkish bathers' undress as a dignified nakedness, seeking to evade modes of representation that would render them as merely nude, mere objects. But Berger helps us understand the cultural blind spot that hinders her by demonstrating that most (though not all) aesthetic representations of women finally do pander to male desires for sexualized appropriation. Invoking the emergent paradigm of disinterested aesthetic contemplation, Montagu cannot avoid invoking the entire complex of interests that already underwrite it. In one sense these serve her rhetorical aim, as we have seen; but in another they contravene it. Her introduction of the nude painting tends to break down rather than uphold the distinction, so important to her rhetoric, between an aesthetic and a certain type of erotic gaze. (Among the paintings Berger classes as representing nudity rather than nakedness – the vast majority – are Titian's nudes.) This attempt to turn aesthetic disinterestedness against male travelers' crude sexism nonetheless proves highly instructive in the context that the letters have already established: the problematic relations of power between gendered subjects and objects. Montagu's rhetoric at once deploys and debunks the paradigm of reception that would later come to dominate European aesthetics.

By comparing the bathers to works of art produced by men, representations of women through men's eyes, Montagu imports the imaginary eyes of Milton, Guido, and Titian into the all-female enclave of the baths. She repeats this move more explicitly with the popular London portrait painter Charles Jervas:

> To tell you the truth, I had wickedness enough to wish secretly that Mr. Gervase could have been there invisible. I fancy it would have very much improv'd his art to see so many fine Women naked in different postures, some in conversation, some working, others drinking Coffee or sherbet . . . In short, tis the Women's coffée house, where all the news of the Town is told, Scandal invented, etc. (1:314)

This bit of wickedness highlights the persistent ambiguity in Montagu's portrayal of her aestheticized bathers, the titillating charge the images retain. But another possibility lurks beneath her risqué wit. Could the imagined male gazers be surrogates onto whom Montagu displaces her homoerotic attraction to the beautiful bathers? This possibility raises interesting questions about the gender dynamics of aesthetic experience, not easy to answer for this historical period.[18] If a masculine subject's experience of a feminine object is one of erotic appropriation, how might this change with a feminine subject and same-sex eroticism?

Turning from speculation back to historical fact, we are reminded that the painters of Montagu's day were almost all men. The privilege of looking and representing aesthetically was gender-restricted, just as those represented in European nude paintings were (as Berger points out) practically all women. The allusion to coffee-houses rather wistfully calls attention to another privilege reserved for men in Montagu's England: gender-specific public space. London's coffee-houses, sites of political, economic, and cultural ferment during the early eighteenth century, were off limits to genteel women, and there existed no equivalent type of all-female public space.[19] Women's problematic access to the discursive position of the aesthetic subject is clearly linked to the absence of institutions supporting their participation in public cultural exchange. The idea of a women's coffee-house must have been profoundly empowering for an English woman, hinting at a society where women might claim space and power in the public realm. Part of the harem's ambivalent fascination for Western men no doubt lay in its threat of untrammeled free association between women.[20] By introducing symbolic male surveillance, however, Montagu undercuts this illusion of power and recalls the real gendered power imbalance in cultural production, as in other areas of British public life.

The next rhetorical turn develops the role reversal that opened the letter. Again Montagu is a spectacle, a curiosity the Turkish women now comically misconstrue.

The Lady that seem'd the most considerable amongst them entreated me to sit by her and would fain have undress'd me for the bath. I excus'd my selfe with some difficulty, they being all so earnest in perswading me. I was at last forc'd to open my skirt and shew them my stays, which satisfy'd 'em very well, for I saw they beleiv'd I was so lock'd up in that machine that it was not in my own power to open it, which contrivance they attributed to my Husband. (1:314)

The corset/chastity belt – an everyday object suddenly made strange – becomes a witty allegory for Montagu's oppression as an English woman. She neatly overturns earlier travel writers' clichés about Turkish women's slavery. In the process, however, she calls attention to her own ambiguous position in relation to the women whose dignity her rhetoric seems intended to save. The scene is reminiscent (to turn again to painting) of Manet's *Déjeuner sur l'herbe*, with its men formally clad in top hat and tie, picnicking with nude women in a blatant juxtaposition of social power and sexual vulnerability. As the bathers inspect her underwear, Montagu becomes a show. Through most of the sequence, though, she is the privileged spectator, observing other women's unclothed bodies while hers remains concealed.[21] Her rhetoric dignifies their nakedness; for her part, she prefers to keep her clothes on.

In this letter a woman boldly occupies the privileged position of the aesthetic subject, a position culturally inscribed as male. The move appears less daring to the degree that it imports the power dynamics of masculine aesthetic discourse into the all-female preserve of the women's baths. Though we may understand this partly as a defense against homoerotic desire, another sharp anxiety seems to underlie Montagu's witty turn about her corset. As the women urge her to undress, she is on the brink of the peculiarly vulnerable condition of female nudity – a vulnerability of which her language proves her well aware. Keeping her clothes on, Montagu preserves the distance between herself and a group of people who are women, but also "Orientals." The gendered relation of aesthetic contemplation is not the only axis of unequal power distribution in this scene. Though Montagu takes aim at demeaning stereotypes, her solidarity with their targets reaches its limit when they invite her to mingle naked, to "go native." Her clothing is a multivalent symbol. It defends her as a woman, but it also maintains her Occidental privilege. Montagu sweating in her riding habit in the Turkish bath poignantly epitomizes a Western woman's conflicted, multiply determined relation to the women of a non-European culture.

The letter's close re-emphasizes the ambiguity of Montagu's position. Inside the baths she has the power of the aesthetic spectator; outside this all-female zone she is subordinated to her husband's commands.

I was charm'd with their Civillity and Beauty and should have been very glad to pass more time with them, but Mr. W[ortley] resolving to persue his Journey the next morning early, I was in haste to see the ruins of Justinian's church, which did not afford me so agreable a prospect as I had left, being little more than a heap of stones.

Adeiu, Madam. I am sure I have now entertaind you with an Account of such a sight as you never saw in your Life and what no book of travells could inform you of. 'Tis no less than Death for a Man to be found in one of these places. (1:314–15)

The mention of Wortley, holder of the key to his wife's "machine," signals her departure from the Utopian enclave of the baths. At the same time, though, she reasserts her privilege as a woman traveler with access to aesthetic pleasures – including the beauty of the Turkish women – much more rewarding than the sterile pursuit of "a heap of stones."

A SHINING FIGURE

Montagu's later encounters with Turkish women recapitulate the dynamics of the baths letter, in particular its self-conscious use of aesthetics to derail sexualized stereotypes. In a tone less distanced and controlled (indeed almost unbearably effusive) she recounts her two visits to the beautiful Fatima, wife of the Kahya, or second-in-command to the Grand Vizier, in letters to her sister, the Countess of Mar:

I have seen all that has been call'd lovely either in England or Germany, and must own that I never saw any thing so gloriously Beautifull, nor can I recollect a face that would have been taken notice of near hers...I was so struck with Admiration that I could not for some time speak to her, being wholly taken up in gazing. That surprizing Harmony of features! that charming result of the whole! that exact proportion of Body!

that lovely bloom of Complexion unsully'd by art! the unutterable Enchantment of her Smile! But her Eyes! large and black with all the soft languishment of the bleu! every turn of her face discovering some new charm! (1:349–50)

The erotic undertones of her pleasure in Turkish women's beauty rise closer to the surface here. Describing a dance by Fatima's maids, she comments, "I am very possitive the coldest and most rigid Prude upon Earth could not have look'd upon them without thinking of something not to be spoke of" (1:351).

Nonetheless, Montagu's description of Fatima disclaims prurient interest by using the language of disinterested aesthetic perception. The terms "Harmony" and "proportion" are prominent, amplified by this remark: "I think I have read somewhere that Women allways speak in rapture when they speak of Beauty, but I can't imagine why they should not be allow'd to do so. I rather think it Virtue to be able to admire without any Mixture of desire or Envy" (1:350–51). As we have seen, Shaftesbury and others defined aesthetic contemplation precisely as a regard for beauty unmixed with desire. Again, the detached position of the aesthetic subject extricates Montagu from erotic involvement and Fatima from degrading stereotypes of the wanton Turkish woman. She goes on to compare Fatima to a work of high art, repeating the rhetorical tactic of her baths letter. "The Gravest Writers have spoke with great warmth of some celebrated Pictures and Statues. The Workmanship of Heaven certainly excells all our weak Imitations...I am not asham'd to own I took more pleasure in looking on the beauteous Fatima than the finest piece of Sculpture could have given me" (1:351). As earlier, the apparent effort to de-eroticize the representation of a Turkish woman puts Montagu in the position of aesthetic subject over against Fatima as exquisite aesthetic object.

This impression is modified, however, if we consider their second meeting almost a year later. Montagu, having meanwhile improved her Turkish, forgoes further description of Fatima's beauty to emphasize her "politeness and good breeding": "now I understand her Language, I find her Wit as engaging as her Beauty" (1:386). Taken together, the two letters sketch an ambiguity in Montagu's relation to Fatima, similar to the one we saw in the baths letter. Her apparent concern to present "Oriental" women as peers of Europeans is partially undercut by her aesthetic strategy. Blocking their portrayal as erotic objects, she renders them instead as another kind of object – aesthetic objects to her own aesthetic subject. Again, it is as though she hesitates to put herself on the same level with these doubly objectified, doubly vulnerable beings.

The letters' treatment of Turkish women is thoroughly ambivalent, doubtless tangled up with Montagu's ambivalence about women's status in her own culture. Her assertions at various points approach outright self-contradiction. Women are "the only free people in the Empire," she declares (I:329), denying previous travelers' reports of their confinement. "They go abroad when and where they please" (I:406), clad in the all-concealing costume of the veil and baggy cloak (ferigée), a "perpetual Masquerade" (I:328) that frees them from masculine eyes.[22] Among the advantages of this outfit, Montagu fantasizes, is control over one's sexuality: "entire Liberty of following their Inclinations without danger of Discovery" (I:328). Turkish women's other freedoms, she points out, include married women's right to own property (a right not granted English women until 1857) and absolute privacy within their apartments, or harem.[23] The connection between the privilege of being the looker, rather than looked upon, and controlling one's own property and space is at the heart of early British aesthetic theory. The prerogative of the "Man of a Polite Imagination" both depends on the class and gender privilege of property ownership, and mimics it: aesthetic contemplation emerges as a kind of visual appropriation. Upper-class Turkish women's privileges match those of Addison and Shaftesbury's aesthetic subject, exceeding the cultural limits of British womanhood.

Elsewhere, however, Montagu reports that Turkish culture compels women to be baby factories (I:372). According to Muslim doctrine, she writes, "the End of the Creation of Woman is to encrease and Multiply, and she is only properly employ'd in the Works of her calling when she is bringing children or takeing care of 'em, which are all the Virtues that God expects from her; and indeed their way of Life, which shuts them out of all public commerce, does not permit them any other" (I:363). Turkish women's vaunted freedom is on balance merely negative, a freedom from, rather than freedom to. The veiled woman in the street moves about in a kind of portable harem, a sacred space exempt from harassment, but effectively isolated from "public commerce," in Montagu's resonant phrase. According to the historian Ian C. Dengler, though eighteenth-century Turkish women probably did enjoy relative freedom of movement, they were certainly shut out of the public economic, political, and cultural life of the Empire. "Turkish women...lived within a system of restrictions that made it improbable they would have either the need or the ability to interact with males outside the network of kin, family, and household unit."[24]

This is the gist of Montagu's sociological observation when she comments on a Turkish graveyard. "They set up a pillar with a carv'd Turbant on the Top of it to the memory of a Man, and as the Turbants by their different shapes shew the Quality or profession, tis in a manner putting up the arms of the deceas'd...The Ladys have a simple Pillar without other Ornament, except those that dye unmarry'd, who have a Rose on the Top of it" (1:362–63). Men are memorialized by the public attribute of rank or profession; women are classified by the private one of marital status. English women, though they could interact socially with men in public, were excluded just as certainly as Turkish women from the really significant "public commerce" – the transactions that created and sustained the *res publica*, including the cultural production to which Montagu's own talents were ideally suited.

At several points during her residence in Turkey, Montagu dons Turkish women's clothing for her own personal masquerade. She takes advantage of the public anonymity (if not the sexual license) afforded by "asmak" and ferigée to visit bazaars and mosques and cross the straits to Pera unmolested (1:354, 358, 397). "The asmak, or Turkish vail, is become not only very easy but agreeable to me," she declares (1:397). Claiming the freedom to see the city without being seen parallels Montagu's bold rhetorical tactic of positioning herself as an aesthetic subject. The other Turkish costume she puts on, however (in which she later had her portrait painted more than once), seems to gratify a different impulse. In the ornate indoor dress of an upper-class Turkish woman, described in loving detail in a letter to her sister, she is the consummate spectacle. She remarks complacently, "I beleive you would be of my Opinion that 'tis admirably becoming" (1:326). The two costumes epitomize the contradictory impulses that traverse these letters: woman as spectacle, eagerly cooperating with the cultural imperative to feminine self-display; and woman as subject, evading the burden of the gaze to become a gazer herself. But even Montagu's description of her magnificent indoor outfit uses language whose transvestite overtones ("drawers" instead of a petticoat, a "wastcoat" instead of a gown) hint at a social status beyond that of ordinary women (1:326). Does decentering herself as a British subject give her access to new ways of imagining a female self?[25] Dressing up in Turkish costume is a safer, more culturally sanctioned means to this end than undressing in the steamy baths.

The bathing women's tactful, then amused regard as they look back at their Western guest realigns Montagu's perception of herself and her society. Her vacillation between privilege and oppression as she represents the women of Turkey projects her ambivalence about her own situation as an English woman, bearing out James Clifford's dictum that "every version of an 'other'...is also the construction of a 'self.'"[26] But if I were to rest content with reading her representation of Turkey as mere veiled self-exploration, I would risk lapsing into the kind of unbridgeable self–other, West–East binarism that I have undertaken to try to move beyond. These letters are perhaps most valuable for their apparent attempt (however partial and intermittent) at actual cultural exchange – a condition of intersubjectivity whose precondition is acceptance of the other as an intelligent, sensitive, acting self.

Montagu's polemic against earlier travelers' degrading portrayals of Turkish women is clearly a conscious intervention. Post-colonial critics like Gayatri Spivak and Aihwa Ong warn us to view with suspicion attempts by Westerners to rescue non-Western women from their own culture or from other Westerners. Believing that feminist goodwill alone can bridge the cross-cultural abyss would be either naively essentialist or merely disingenuous; Spivak elsewhere targets the fallacy of assuming an automatic congruence between feminism and anti-imperialism.[27] Montagu is at least as vulnerable as later Western feminists to this type of critique. We have noted the way she substitutes for the crass power differential of Orientalism the subtler inequalities of aesthetic discourse. But her decision not to undress, to preserve a certain distance between herself and them, is susceptible to more than one interpretation. Distance, as Ong suggests, can sometimes connote respect, recognizing a difference that it may not be either possible or desirable to alter.[28] Only on the basis of such a recognition can a tentative, necessarily partial mutuality be built.

Reading this early feminist intervention can help us interrupt Orientalist binaries if we attend with care to the complicated

5. Charles Jervas, "Lady at the Clavicytherium." Subject is Lady Mary Wortley Montagu in at least partly Turkish dress.

interplay of social categories – sexuality and ethnicity or nationality as well as gender and class – in Montagu's shifting relation to
her Turkish counterparts. She re-carves more than one categorial
boundary as she dons the veil or her embroidered "wastcoat." It is
no coincidence that the nascent language of aesthetics can play
such a key role in this type of cultural work. As it crystallizes eighteenth-century Britain's preoccupation with the symbolic economy
of spectator and spectacle, the power of the directional, non-reciprocal gaze, aesthetic discourse incorporates the society's hierarchical fabric of power relations. Encounters between individuals
excluded from power in various ways, like women and "Orientals,"
could test that fabric. We will see later women travelers use the
language of aesthetics to work through their relation to other
excluded groups: the laboring classes, Addison's "Vulgar," as well
as non-Europeans like these bathing women.

Montagu's later letters from Italy revisit the charged issues of
social power in visual perception that inform her representations of
Turkish and European women in 1716–18. The aging expatriate is
relieved to be past the age of self-display. She reaffirms her taste
for public anonymity, praising the Venetian custom of wearing
masks in public (II:159). "I...am not sorry," she remarks, "to have it
in my power to hear an Opera without the Mortification of
shewing a wrinkled face" (III:194). One of the joys of her country
retirement is freedom from critical eyes, in this case those of other
women:

I have had this morning as much delight in a Walk in the Sun as ever I
felt formerly in the crouded Mall even when I imagin'd I had my share of
the admiration of the place, which was generally sour'd before I slept by
the Informations of my female Freinds, who seldom fail'd to tell me it was
observ'd I had shew'd an inch above my shoe heels, or some other criticism of equal weight, which was construe'd affectation, and utterly
destroy'd all the Satisfaction my vanity had given me. (II:446–47)

The feminine aesthetic object's vain satisfactions emerge in retro-
spect as self-canceling, deflated by catty sniping in this depressing
satire of female friendship.

In another charged juxtaposition, Montagu moves in this same
letter from one kind of attention, which she has escaped, to another
kind that continues to evade her. Her late letters abound with joking
references to her suppressed desire for literary fame. "I have now
no other [satisfaction] but in my little Huswifery, which is easily

gratify'd in this Country, where (by the help of my receipt Book) I make a very shineing Figure amongst my Neighbours by the Introduction of Custards, Cheesecakes and mince'd Pies, which were entirely unknown in these Parts, and are receiv'd with universal applause, and I have reason to beleive will preserve my Memory even to Future ages" (II:447). Her witty burlesque evokes the classical topos of reputation: "a shineing Figure," "universal applause," "preserve my Memory even to Future ages." Throughout the Italian letters she compulsively displaces ambition, conventionally gendered masculine, onto the comically humble feminine pursuits of "Huswifery," cooking and gardening. Her wit darkens with pathos when we read it in the context of the lifelong frustration of her own well-justified ambition. "I am realy as fond of my Garden as a young Author of his first play when it has been well receiv'd by the Town" (II:407). "I expect Immortality from the Science of Butter makeing" (II:485), which she has taught to her Italian neighbors. No longer a shining figure, an object on display, the aging writer still cannot be an aesthetic subject in the fullest sense of the word, publicly circulating her writings like an Addison or a Pope.

Beneath their witty veneer, these letters convey an embittered acquiescence to the pressures excluding women from the "public commerce" of British culture. We sense Montagu's mounting anger at British culture for denying women the full power and prestige of the aesthetic perceiver, and *a fortiori* the aesthetic producer. Her oblique commentary on aesthetics reads as an even more oblique political comment. The most painful, deeply repressed, inarticulate and virtually inarticulable longings of eighteenth-century British women were, I suspect, not sexual but finally political. In the course of her life Montagu's bold claim to the privilege of the aesthetic subject came to seem increasingly quixotic. Her insight and intellectual daring nonetheless broke ground for later women who aspired to share in the cultural power of the aesthetic domain.

CHAPTER 2

Janet Schaw and the aesthetics of colonialism

Antigua is beautiful. Antigua is too beautiful.
Sometimes the beauty of it seems unreal.[1]

Janet Schaw traveled and wrote more than half a century after
Montagu's trip to Turkey, though just a decade after the publication of her letters. The circumstances of the two women's journeys
were quite disparate. While Montagu went to Turkey as a member
of a diplomatic mission between Occidental and Oriental world
powers, Schaw paid a private visit to British colonists, her friends
and fellow Scots, the owners of sugar plantations dependent on
slave labor. Montagu sets the language of aesthetics against
Orientalism to dignify Turkish women; Schaw, on the other hand,
aligns aesthetics with discourses of race to beautify colonial slavery.
Despite these differences, the two women's writings yield complementary insights into the social logic of aesthetics. Writing the language of aesthetics in the contact zone, using it to work through
encounters with non-European Others, both expose (intentionally
or not) the tension between the putative disinterestedness of the
aesthetic gaze and its actual implication in hierarchies of social
power.[2] Positioning themselves as aesthetic subjects, both display a
mistrust of woman's conventional status as spectacle. Their appropriations of aesthetics differently exemplify women's multiply
determined, conflicted relation to the powerful languages of the
dominant culture.

Schaw was a single, middle-aged woman from a well-to-do
Scottish family who traveled to the islands of Antigua and St. Kitts
in the British West Indies in 1774 and 1775.[3] Her unpublished epistolary journal aestheticizes the West Indian sugar plantation as it
echoes the racist apologetics that helped rationalize Britain's
presence in the Caribbean, the cornerstone of its pre-Industrial

Revolution colonial system, whose economy depended on African slave labor. She juxtaposes the beauty of these lush islands with glimpses of the ugliness and violence underlying plantation culture, demonstrating the power of aesthetic discourse while revealing its collusion with colonial exploitation. The journal is eminently readable, at times gripping, with a distinctive narrative voice. At the same time it is representative of a variety of writings on the West Indies by both women and men in the eighteenth and early nineteenth centuries which draw on the cultural power of the aesthetic to legitimize colonial plantation culture.[4] These range in genre from histories and natural histories to less formal "accounts" or unpublished journals. As I discuss Schaw I shall invoke these other writers to suggest the pervasiveness of such aestheticizing during this period. Writers of both genders responded to the cultural pressure that channeled the prestige of aesthetics to harmonize discordant elements of colonial society.

Schaw's text departs significantly from these other writings, however, in its much fuller exploration of the West Indian gender system. Nature as figured in the aestheticized plantation is gendered female; both gender and "race" are textually articulated with aesthetics. Studying this intersection complicates our grasp of women's relation to aesthetics, as well as their position within colonialism. In the *Journal of a Lady of Quality* a subtle, critical ambivalence toward the West Indian gender system and toward women's culturally prescribed status as aesthetic objects coexists with a disturbing complacency toward slavery. After working through the textual symbiosis between aesthetics and colonialism I will go on to explore the vexed status of gender and the conflicted position of the woman observer.[5]

ENCHANTING SCENERY AND RICH PROSPECTS

The literature of travel, trade, and colonization possessed an aesthetic dimension before eighteenth-century developments in aesthetic theory. Though Montagu managed to turn aesthetics against "Oriental" stereotypes, Westerners' sensuous infatuation with the Orient nonetheless amounts to a proto-aesthetic regard. Tributes to British mercantile imperialism frequently capitalize on what Laura Brown calls "the romance of empire." Aphra Behn's *Oroonoko, or the Royal Slave* (1688), set in the South American colony of Surinam, unfolds enticing catalogues of exotic commodities.[6] In 1711 Addison's *Spectator* extols the London Stock Exchange as the center of global trade, which "gives us a great Variety of what is Useful, and at the same time supplies us with every thing that is Convenient and Ornamental...our Eyes are refreshed with the green Fields of *Britain*, at the same time that our Palates are feasted with Fruits that rise between the Tropicks."[7] The distinction between aesthetic and practical, useful and ornamental, structures the panegyric as both categories converge in support of merchant adventure. Richard Blackmore's 1712 poem *Creation* celebrates the wind,

> Which thither wafts *Arabia's* fragrant Spoils,
> Gemms, Pearls and Spices from the *Indian* Isles,
> From *Persia* Silks, Wines from *Iberia's* Shore,
> *Peruvian* Drugs, and *Guinea's* Golden Oar[.][8]

The Rape of the Lock appeals to the romance of empire as Pope describes the exotic commodities, the "various Off'rings of the World," on Belinda's dressing table: "*India's* glowing Gems," Arabian perfumes, and ivory and tortoise-shell combs.[9] The world-wide trade that Addison, Blackmore, and Pope extol was closely linked with actual colonial settlements like those in the British West Indies. The Atlantic Triangle Trade, moving European manufactured goods to African markets, African slaves to the Caribbean and North America, and returning to Europe with cargoes of sugar and tobacco, was vital in raising eighteenth-century Britain to prosperity and power and accelerating the development of a world economy.[10]

Aesthetic discourse disclosed a heightened potential for contributing to the colonial project later in the century as travelers began to inscribe the concept of disinterested contemplation on the landscape through scenic tourism. This peculiar practice, which I will examine in greater detail in Chapter 3, visually and verbally framed natural scenes. The effect was to distance spectators from their surroundings and obscure the connection between topography and people's material needs. Eighteenth-century landscape aesthetics thus promoted what Bourdieu calls a "moral agnosticism": a habitual distance of consciousness from both practical and ethical considerations.[11] At the time Schaw wrote, the flood of picturesque travelogues and guidebooks that began with West's

Guide to the Lakes (1778) was still in the future. She was not a full-blown, self-conscious "picturesque traveler" of the type common in the 1780s and 1790s. Her representation of the West Indies nonetheless serves to introduce aspects of landscape aesthetics with which later women travelers like Helen Maria Williams, Mary Wollstonecraft, and Dorothy Wordsworth would engage more extensively.

A literate gentlewoman like Schaw would have come into contact with aesthetic discourse through polite conversation, if not through her own reading. She had probably read at least some theoretical writings, such as Addison's *Spectator* or Burke's treatise on the sublime and beautiful, widely known among those with pretensions to gentility. During one of the terrifying gales that punctuate Schaw's sea journey from Scotland to the Caribbean, her young cousin Fanny picks up a book and reads aloud, trying to calm her mind. At the time neither frightened woman understands a word. Afterward they discover that, as Schaw says wryly, "we were meeting death, like philosophers not Christians: with a Lord Kaims in our hands in place of a Bible" (45).[12]

By the time Schaw arrives in the West Indies after an eventful seven-week passage, her journal has established an engaging *persona*: an adventurous, vivacious, brave, and compassionate woman with a resilient, often self-deprecating sense of humor. Though I will not emphasize these aspects of her writing, it is important to keep in mind that her aesthetic argument for slavery is embedded in a narrative calculated to captivate its audience. Schaw finds material for humor as the party (her brother Alexander and herself, two young nephews and a teenage cousin as well as a male and a female servant) adjusts to life on shipboard. Her maid, Mrs. Mary Miller, lazy, contrary, and infatuated with a faithless sailor, plays the comic lead. During the storms Schaw recites psalms and comforts the frightened boys. At their height the ship "broaches to" – meaning "that the Vessel fairly lies down on one side" (50) – then rights itself, sending furniture and passengers flying: "amongst many other things a barrel of Molasses pitched directly on me, as did also a box of small candles, so I appeared as if tarred and feathered, stuck all over with farthing candles" (52).

Schaw displays compassion in her account of a group of poor emigrants packed into steerage. On first sight they look "like a Cargo of Dean Swift's Yahoos newly caught" (28), an epithet conflating class and racial otherness.[13] But sailing past the Orkney Islands, "gazing fondly on the dear spot they were never more to behold," they become "hapless exiles . . . forced by the hand of oppression from their native land" (33). Schaw abandons the language of class prejudice for a patronizing discourse of sensibility. "Where are now the Cargo of Yahoos? they are transformed into a Company of most respectable sufferers, whom it is both my duty and inclination to comfort" (36). Her talk of duties and social virtues echoes the moral philosophy of the Scottish Enlightenment; she continues to deplore the steerage passengers' sufferings throughout the voyage (47, 49–50, 53, 54–55, 71–72).

Sailing into St. John's Bay in December 1774, Schaw applies an aesthetic vocabulary to describe her first view of the island of Antigua. She includes without comment glimpses of the island society's economic base and the military power needed to defend it, simultaneously presenting and masking visual evidence of the institution of plantation slavery.

[W]hen we got into the bay, which runs many miles up the Island, it is out of my power to paint the beauty and the Novelty of the scene. We had the Island on both sides of us, yet its beauties were different, the one was hills, dales and groves...the sugar canes cover the hills almost to the top, and bear a resemblance in colour at least to a rich field of green wheat; the hills are skirted by the Palmetto or Cabbage tree, which even from this distance makes a noble appearance. The houses are generally placed in the Valleys between the hills, and all front to the sea. We saw many fine ones. (74)

She sets out to "paint" the island "scene" in words – the typical visual trope of landscape aesthetics – applying terms familiar from Addison's 1712 *Spectator* essays on the pleasures of the imagination. He divides the pleasure arising from the "View and Survey of outward Objects" into greatness, novelty or uncommonness, and beauty ("noble" is a synonym for "great" or "grand").[14] Fields of sugar cane, the mainstay of the island economy, are aestheticized with the adjective "rich," whose double meaning applies figuratively to their color, but literally to their productivity. We begin to recognize how aesthetic discourse works to naturalize a colonial system based on the sugar plantation.

Schaw's description continues to interweave the language of aesthetics with revealing glimpses that connect the island's visual surface to its social structure.

The other side exhibits quite a different scene, as the ground is almost level, a long tongue of land runs into the Sea, covered with rich pasture, on which a number of cattle feed. At the farther end of this Peninsula is a fort...[W]e saw some very rich plantations, all inclosed by hedges...The next object that engaged our attention, was a high rock, on the sides of which grew a vast number of Oranges and lemons. At the top is a large building, which, our Pilot tells us, is the Old Barracks. This Barracks is able to contain a thousand Men...We saw a number of the officers walking among the Orange-trees and myrtles, and I own I thought the prospect was mended by their appearance. (75)

On an island where white Europeans were a tiny minority, vastly outnumbered by their slaves, fort and barracks were necessary installations. The British West Indies' transition during the 1640s to a sugar monoculture based on imported African slave labor (the indigenous population had died out or been exterminated on most islands) determined the islands' social structure and racial composition. By the 1780s their total population, including Jamaica and Barbados as well as several smaller islands, was estimated at about 540,000, including 65,300 whites, 20,000 of mixed race, and 455,000 blacks. Thus overwhelmingly outnumbered, faced with the ever-present danger of slave revolt, the colonial society was necessarily militarized.[15] As Schaw paints this scene, fort and barracks are prominent features; their aestheticized presentation attempts to neutralize the violence they signify.[16]

The institutions and apparatuses of colonial power can be so visible, Homi Bhabha points out, precisely because the manner in which this power is exercised through colonial discourse "makes their *relationship* obscure, produces them as...spectacles of a 'natural'/racial pre-eminence." Colonial discourse is peculiarly at home in the register of the visible – predisposed to paint pictures with words – since colonial rule bases its legitimation on that most visible and seemingly "natural" of signs, the color of skin. But the superficially natural, stable relations between colonizer and colonized, master and slave, white and black, posited by colonial discourse reveal themselves as inherently unstable, ambivalent, self-contradictory, haunted by constant anxiety.[17] We shall see below how Schaw incorporates skin color into a scheme of contrast and chiaroscuro in her most spectacular tableau of island life. Throughout her journal, aesthetic discourse collaborates with colonial power, exploiting the visible to obscure or naturalize the relationships between the island "scene" and the violence which that scene both reveals and conceals, as in her matter-of-fact inclusion of fort and barracks in her scenic tableau. The last line of the description exemplifies this kind of double consciousness: the "prospect was mended" by the officers' appearance. Couched in the aesthetic language of the "prospect," the painterly framing of a view, the comment presents the red-coated figures among the trees as elements of artistic composition, appropriate ornaments for a verbally sketched landscape.[18] But the technical aesthetic meaning barely camouflages a white woman's expression of relief at the soldiers' presence in the face of the constant danger of slave revolt.

The lexicon of landscape aesthetics informs a wide range of eighteenth-century writings on the West Indies. William Smith, for example, sailing from Nevis to St. Kitts, is "all the way agreably entertained, with a most beautiful Prospect of both the Islands...the finest Pencil does not presume to paint out in Perfection so lovely a Landskip." Even the practical planter Edward Long waxes poetic about Jamaica's "romantic scenery," which affords "a succession of elegant objects." His parish-by-parish descriptions are as good as a guidebook, noting each romantic spot and picturesque landscape (II:185, 205, 208, etc.). Like Schaw, Long tends to conflate beauty with productivity: "the face of the country...appears truly beautiful from the continued succession of well-cultivated sugar-estates and rich pastures" (II:193). Maria Nugent comments, "Nothing, certainly, can exceed the beauty and enchanting scenery of this country."[19] Throughout these writings on the West Indies the vocabulary of scenic tourism plays a key role in mediating or "enchanting" Caribbean reality for the European eye.

THE AESTHETICIZED PLANTATION

When Janet Schaw leaves St. Johns to visit a series of plantations we see her fully succumb to the sensuous allure of island life. She announces her shift into an aesthetic register, boldly casting herself as artist − at once aesthetic spectator and aesthetic producer: "I have heard or read of a painter or poet...that when he intended to excell in a Work of Genius, made throw around him every thing most pleasing to the eye, or delightful to the Senses. Should this always hold good, at present you might expect the most delightful epistle you ever read in your life, as whatever can charm the senses or delight the Imagination is now in my view" (90). Ensconced at the plantation "The Eleanora," Schaw revels in the vivid color and scent of the flowers outside her bedroom window: they "glow with colours, which only the western sun is able to raise into such richness, while every breeze is fragrant with perfumes"(90). She feasts on turtle soup and tropical fruit, an instant epicure. This usually matter-of-fact Scotswoman presents herself in a state of sensory overload, her rational faculties semi-paralyzed: "the beauty, the Novelty, the ten thousand charms that this Scene presents to me, confuse my ideas. It appears a delightful Vision, a fairy Scene or a peep into Elysium; and surely the first poets that painted those retreats of the blessed and good, must have made some West India Island sit for the picture" (91). Bestowing moral overtones on the beauty of the plantation – a retreat of the blessed and good – she protests a hint too much.

Schaw's aestheticized plantation becomes a site for taking stock of the island's natural bounty. She catalogues exotic fruits (97–98), trees and flowers (101–2), incorporating into her journal features of the popular-scientific genre of natural history, increasingly favored throughout Europe during this period of accelerating colonial expansion. "The Carnation tree, or as they call it the doble day is a most glorious plant...The leaf is dark green, the flowers bear an exact resemblance to our largest Dutch Carnation, which hang in large bunches from the branches. The colours are sometimes dark rich Crimson spotted or specked with white, sometimes purple in the same manner" (102). Schaw assimilates aesthetic appreciation for the beauty of exotic species to the proto-scientific striving toward exact description and classification. Besides Smith and Hughes, whose main project is natural history, other writers on the West Indies also incorporate catalogues of flora and fauna.[20] Both natural history and landscape aesthetics are "transformative, appropriative" ways of seeing that distance or detach the observer while asserting the dominance of an eye that is European, male, and urban or literate. Both discourses share a peculiar capacity "to subsume culture and history into nature." The human figures that can ornament a landscape, losing their individuality and their material connection to the places they inhabit, can, alternatively, be classified by Linnaeus or his disciples, rewriting cultural differences as subspecies differentiae.[21] The racist diatribes of Edward

Long, which we shall examine shortly, take the form of a natural-historical survey of Jamaica. In Janet Schaw's journal and contemporaneous writings about the West Indies, natural history collaborates with aesthetics to underwrite the colonial status quo.

Another visual feature of Schaw's aestheticized plantation is the elision of labor. The only place we see slaves for almost fifteen pages after her arrival at the plantation is in church, dutifully praying (94). Prefacing a six-page description of a lavish feast she editorializes, "Why should we blame these people for their luxury? since nature holds out her lap, filled with every thing that is in her power to bestow, it were sinful in them not to be luxurious" (95). Raymond Williams observes a similar tactic in seventeenth-century country house poems. To achieve the discursive reproduction of Paradise, one must magically extract the curse of labor, man earning his bread in the sweat of his brow.[22] This is done by extracting the existence of the laborers – the actual men and women who pick the fruit, catch the turtles, raise the animals, kill them and prepare them for dinner, and above all, till the fields in the labor-intensive methods of agriculture demanded by cane cultivation. Schaw's aestheticized presentation depends for its effect on her reader's ability to ignore for long stretches the practical structure of the plantation. Nature, holding out her lap, mystifies the human-created social order in which some feast while others toil.

When we finally see slaves at work it is through the lens of a benevolent paternalism: "a large troop of healthy Negroes, who cheerfully perform the labour imposed on them by a kind and beneficent Master, not a harsh and unreasonable Tyrant" (104). The beneficent master is Colonel Martin, the "loved and revered father of Antigua" as well as of his own twenty-three children, and head of the local militia for forty years (103). He has freed his household staff, who serve with such alacrity "[y]ou would have thought [they] were inspired with an instinctive knowledge of your wishes" (105). But a plantation tour confronts Schaw with visible evidence that slaves' wishes are different from their masters': the scars of the overseer's whip.

Every ten Negroes have a driver, who walks behind them, holding in his hand a short whip and a long one. You will too easily guess the use of these weapons; a circumstance of all others the most horrid. They are naked, male and female, down to the girdle, and you constantly observe where the application has been made. But however dreadful this must appear to a humane European, I will do the creoles [island whites] the justice to say, they would be as averse to it as we are, could it be avoided, which has often been tried to no purpose. When one comes to be better acquainted with the nature of the Negroes, the horrour of it must wear off. It is the suffering of the human mind that constitutes the greatest misery of punishment, but with them it is merely corporeal. As to the brutes it inflicts no wound on their mind, whose Natures seem made to bear it, and whose sufferings are not attended with shame or pain beyond the present moment. (127)

Schaw, the "humane European," describes "the nature of the Negroes" on the analogy of animals or "brutes," deflecting the horror of the corporal punishment needed to perpetuate the system of forced labor. Her reaction needs to be understood in the context of contemporary eighteenth-century discourses of race.

The structure of knowledge or belief required to implement colonial power and slave labor was both broad and flexible. The debate on race ranged from the more liberal environmentalist view that differences in color were gradually produced by climate, to a biological determinism maintaining that racial differences were innate, created by God. Most of the environmentalists were also so-called monogenists, holding, like the influential French naturalist Buffon, that all humanity shared a common ancestry with Adam and Eve. Polygenists, on the other hand, the worst of the racists, believed that Africans were a separate species, perhaps closer to apes and orangutans than to European man.[23] But even liberal thinkers like Buffon often compare Africans to monkeys or apes. Soon after Janet Schaw arrives on the island she mistakes a group of naked black children running down a lane for "a parcel of monkeys" (78) – a predictable error within this discourse.[24]

Late eighteenth-century writings on the West Indies all address the issues of race and slavery in some fashion, tellingly appended to their praise of the islands' beauty. Though their tone ranges from baldly racist to humanely reformist, all agree in their fundamental acceptance of slavery as an institution. Several, notably Long and Stewart, defend it at length, presumably in response to the growing abolitionist movement. Long's chapter entitled "Negroes" presents a strongly stated apology for slavery with which other, superficially more liberal writers have a great deal in common. He disagrees with Buffon, defending at length and with considerable erudition (citing Linnaeus, Hume, and Shakespeare as

well as travel literature) the idea that blacks and whites are indeed
different species. Long portrays Africans as a degenerate group
without a single redeeming feature, "a brutish, ignorant, idle,
crafty, treacherous, bloody, thievish, mistrustful, and superstitious
people" (II:354). They lack everything Europeans value most about
themselves: art, science, morality, technology, self-discipline, and –
significantly – the ability to appreciate beauty.

In general, they are void of genius, and seem almost incapable of making
any progress in civility or science. They have no plan or system of morality among them. Their barbarity to their children debases their nature
even below that of brutes. They have no moral sensations; no taste but
for women; gormondizing, and drinking to excess; no wish but to be
idle...Their houses are miserable cabbins. They conceive no pleasure
from the most beautiful parts of their country, preferring the more sterile...They use neither carriages, nor beasts of burthen. They are represented by all authors as the vilest of the human kind, to which they
have little more pretension of resemblance than what arises from their
exterior form.[25] (II:353)

Here we can glimpse the pervasive instability of colonial discourse
in the form of the peculiar mimesis or mirroring (to paraphrase
Michael Taussig) between the brutality that slaveholders like Long
attributed to Africans, and the brutality they themselves per-
petrated in the name of civilization, meaning business.[26]

Long delights in retailing lurid anecdotes of cannibalism and
reports of sex between black women and orangutans. He is especially preoccupied with the nature of the Negro mind. Black
people, he argues, on the analogy of the orangutan, cannot be said
to have minds or to think in the same way that white Europeans do
– a powerful contention in an Enlightenment climate of thought
that valued rationality as the primary distinction between man and
beast. In the passage cited above, Janet Schaw applies a similar
principle to justify whipping slaves: their minds are different, therefore they don't suffer the way we do. Observing the scars on the
slaves' stripped trunks, she interprets away the visual evidence of
pain by resorting to a claim about invisible mental difference. This
is a crux in her text: the one moment when the visible surface
alone is not enough to accomplish the aim of reconciling people
who think of themselves as "humane Europeans" to the brutality
of the plantation system. Schaw's evasive maneuver exemplifies
the self-contradictory, shifting foundations that characterize

colonial discourse. This moment also tells us something about the relationship between Long's account of racial difference and the less openly vitriolic comments of Schaw and others, who casually ensconce remarks on race amid alluring descriptions of tropical beauty. In all these texts the aesthetic donates legitimacy to racism and the institution of plantation slavery.[27]

Schaw's aesthetic glorification of slavery is at its height in a remarkable passage, which I will quote at length, describing slaves on their way to market on the day after Christmas. In this pictorial *tour de force* the slaves come to embody the island's bounty and aesthetic appeal. Again the violence of the slaveholding system and the pervasive fear of plantation culture are simultaneously acknowledged and anxiously neutralized.

We met the Negroes in joyful troops on the way to town with their Merchandize. It was one of the most beautiful sights I ever saw. They were universally clad in white Muslin: the men in loose drawers and waistcoats, the women in jackets and petticoats; the men wore black caps, the women had handkerchiefs of gauze or silk, which they wore in the fashion of turbans. Both men and women carried neat white wicker-baskets on their heads, which they ballanced as our Milk maids do their pails. These contained the various articles for Market, in one a little kid raised its head from amongst flowers of every hue, which were thrown over to guard it from the heat; here a lamb, there a Turkey or a pig, all covered up in the same elegant manner, While others had their baskets filled with fruit, pine-apples reared over each other; Grapes dangling over the loaded basket; oranges, Shaddacks, water lemons, pomegranates, granadillas, with twenty others, whose names I forget. They marched in a sort of regular order, and gave the agreeable idea of a set of devotees going to sacrifice to their Indian Gods, while the sacrifice offered just now to the Christian God is, at this Season of all others the most proper, and I may say boldly, the most agreeable, for it is a mercy to the creatures of the God of mercy. At this Season the crack of the inhuman whip must not be heard, and for some days, it is an universal Jubilee; nothing but joy and pleasantry to be seen or heard, while every Negro infant can tell you, that he owes this happiness to the good Buccara God [white men's God], that he be no hard Master, but loves a good black man as well as a Buccara man, and that Master will die bad death, if he hurt poor Negro in his good day. It is necessary however to keep a look out during this season of unbounded freedom; and every man on the Island is in arms and patrols go all round the different plantations as well as keep guard in the town. They are an excellent disciplined Militia and make a very military appearance. (107–9)

This extravagant tableau presents the visual sign of racial difference, the slaves' black skin, as part of a pleasing composition, contrasting with their white clothing and the brilliant colors of fruit and flowers. Again the fruits of nature offer themselves in profusion with labor nowhere in sight. We see laborers, but we see them freed from work and punishment by the religious mandate of Christmas, dressed not in filthy work clothes but in spotless, festive garb. Ironically, the cause of the joy that Schaw attributes to the slaves is a temporary halt to the full functioning of the slaveholding system.[28]

Orlando Patterson's *Sociology of Slavery* describes Christmas festivities on Jamaica. He does not specifically mention a ban on whipping, but notes "the remarkable change that overcame the Negroes in their dress, their manner, and, most significant, their relationship with their masters which assumed the character of a kind of ritual license." Patterson suggests that this temporary, cathartic "world upside down" reinforced the system of slavery by offering temporary relief.[29] In Schaw's description the Christmas reversal offers an aesthetic argument in favor of slavery. But the suspension of violence is as fragile as this vulnerable idyll, at whose margins we glimpse the armed colonists of "a very military appearance" patrolling streets and plantations to prevent slaves from taking advantage of their masters' benevolence. Again, Schaw's aesthetic framing of island life draws into its composition visible signs of the violence and threat that underwrote the plantation system. These signs are naturalized by the beauty of the foregoing images and the power of the category of experience upon which they draw: the aesthetic, cut off by definition from practical concerns of money and power in a discourse well established in Britain by 1774. The very autonomy of the aesthetic, its supposed segregation from practical matters, makes it especially well suited to advancing a range of practical agendas, as in Schaw's journal it reinforces the West Indian system of racially based exploitation.

ELEANORA AND THE HURRICANE

Aesthetic discourse, as we have seen, was predisposed to uphold different types of social stratification. Schaw's account of West Indian colonialism turns aesthetics to an implicit defense of racial domination. Her aestheticized plantation further reveals a close articulation between class, gender, and race. Genteel femininity, the white "lady" – symbolically aligned with the plantation's aestheticized Nature – becomes crucial to upholding the structure of racial domination.[30]

A dead white woman bears the heaviest symbolic burden in Schaw's text. One of the plantations she visits is "The Eleanora," owned by her fellow Scot Dr. John Dunbar and named after his first wife, who perished in the hurricane of 1772.

Every body has some tragical history to give of that night of horror, but none more than the poor Doctor. His house was laid in ruins, his canes burnt up by the lightening, his orange orchyards, Tammerand Walks and Cocoa trees torn from the roots, his sugar works, mills and cattle all destroyed; yet a circumstance was joined, that rendered every thing else a thousand times more dreadful. It happened in a moment a much loved wife was expiring in his arms, and she did breath her last amidst this War of Elements, this wreck of nature; while he in vain carried her from place to place for Shelter. This was the Lady I had known in Scotland. The hills behind the house are high and often craggy, on which sheep and goats feed, a Scene that gives us no small pleasure, and even relieves the eye when fatigued with looking on the dazzling lustre the other prospect presents you. (91)

Schaw's dramatic narrative of the death of "a much loved wife" positions Eleanora as the final item in an inventory of destroyed or damaged property, a suggestion borne out by Dunbar's naming the plantation after her. When Eleanora is stricken, nature goes awry. The death of woman and the "wreck of nature" are closely intertwined, suggesting an identification – heavily fraught in this colonial context – between Woman and Nature. Dr. Dunbar's sentimental gesture, naming his plantation after his departed wife, adds a further link to the signifying chain: the feminine, and hence the natural, is equated with the plantation system. White womanhood is an indispensable part of this symbolic construction.

Its role is crucially mediated, however, by the category that presides over Janet Schaw's representation of West Indian life: the aesthetic. Schaw brackets the narrative of Eleanora Dunbar's death between two characteristic passages applying the vocabulary of aesthetics to the plantation. The first, Schaw's gushing over the plantation's concentrated aesthetic appeal, has been quoted above: "the beauty, the Novelty, the ten thousand charms that this Scene presents to me, confuse my ideas. It appears a delightful Vision…" (91).

The vision is juxtaposed with its antithesis, the "War of Elements" that wrecked Elysium in a radical but temporary skewing of the "natural" order. Schaw delivers a noteworthy break in tone from sentimental melodrama to measured aesthetic appreciation as she returns to her description of the "Scene" behind the plantation house. The craggy hills (suggesting the Burkean sublime) provide a welcome contrast to the "lustre" of the other "prospect" (evoking Burke's concept of beauty). The white woman whose name the plantation bears is ensconced between assertions of its aesthetic value. The cultural cachet of Woman as prized possession joins forces with aestheticized Nature to assert the beauty and value of the plantation way of life.

While white ladies are presented as natural, black women bear the stigma of unnaturalness and the blame for the quintessentially "unnatural" phenomenon of miscegenation. Gender differences among black men and women are downplayed. We recall field hands of both sexes stripped to the waist for work, their trunks scarred by the whip, in the passage cited above (127).[31] To the extent that black "wenches" have a separate sexual character, they are "licentious" (112). In a familiar stereotype, they are represented as overwhelmingly physical, corporeal beings, parading the streets and plantations with "little or no clothing...they are hardly pre-vailed on to wear a petticoat" (87). Their flaunting sexuality draws on them the blame for miscegenation, which Schaw views with horror, resulting in "the crouds of Mullatoes, which you meet in the streets, houses and indeed every where" (112).

The young black wenches lay themselves out for white lovers, in which they are but too successful. This prevents their marrying with their natural mates, and hence a spurious and degenerate breed, neither so fit for the field, nor indeed any work, as the true bred Negro. Besides these wenches become licentious and insolent past all bearing, and as even a mulattoe child interrupts their pleasures and is troublesome, they have certain herbs and medicines, that free them from such an incumbrance, but which seldom fails to cut short their own lives, as well as that of their offspring. By this many of them perish every year. (112–13)

These "wenches" will do anything to avoid the "natural" role of motherhood. When they do bear offspring they are "degenerate," unfit for their destiny of servitude. Race mixing and abortion are equated as vile, unnatural practices. Black women threaten the "natural" order of which white women are the cornerstone.

The black male appears in Schaw's text only as a stripped, scarred field hand or an unnamed threat to white women's safety in public places. Only one non-white man is further individualized: "Black Robert," the "Indian" servant of Schaw's brother Alexander, introduced as "a handy good fellow." Though he moves with "the dignity of a slow-stalking Indian Chief" (25), Robert is cast in the role of nurturer. We see him holding the ladies' parasols, fishing for their dinner on shipboard, and fanning them as they nap (117–18). He shops for pickles and sweetmeats at an island bazaar (138) – efficient, indispensable, and emphatically feminized, an essential fiction, perhaps, for a non-white man serving white women at such close quarters, but consistent with portrayals of indigenous men in a colonial setting such as India. Their feminization justifies their subordination to the only truly masculine men, the white colonists.[32]

Black Robert is the most individualized of the servitor figures who make quiet appearances at the margins of Schaw's text. Memboe, the "swarthy waiting maid" lent to the visitors by their Antiguan landlady, is "extremely well qualified for the office" (86), "most exact in her duty" (107), but never given a voice. Equally silent is the five-year-old mulatto girl kept "as a pet" by Schaw's friend Lady Isabella Hamilton, "dressed out like an infant Sultana," her "brown beauty...a fine contrast to the delicate complexion of her Lady" (124). Again, skin color forms part of a pleasing chiaroscuro whose aesthetic value reinforces the rightness of enslaving and silencing racial others.

Gender distinctions among whites, unlike blacks, are sharply emphasized, even exaggerated. The more manly the creole men appear, the more obviously they are entitled to dominate both women and slaves. "The sun appears to affect the sexes very differently," Schaw comments (113). It brings out the planters' energy, exuberance, and especially their sexual desires. Schaw collectively cathects these men, "the most agreeable creatures I ever met with" (111). She declares, "the woman that *brings a heart here* will have little sensibility if she carry it away" (112). The one "failing" she admits in the handsome, gallant islanders – their "licentious and even unnatural amours" with female slaves (112) – she excuses by blaming it on black women, not the white men. The planters show their masculinity by publicly protecting their women: "No Lady ever goes without a gentleman to attend her" (87), an oblique reference to the fear of black male sexuality that has such rich potential for exploitation in the colonial setting.[33]

These chivalrously protected ladies are praised for conventionally feminine qualities that approach an ideal of womanly perfection. They are paragons of modesty, gentility, reserve, and temperance, in pointed contrast to the black "wenches'" licentiousness as well as their own husbands' lusty appetites. They "make excellent wives, fond attentive mothers and the best house wives I have ever met with...I never admired my own sex more than in these amiable creoles," declares Schaw, herself neither wife nor mother (113–14).[34]

Visiting the plantation of her friend Lady Isabella Hamilton on the island of St. Kitts, Schaw uncovers another function of the idealized white woman in the symbolic economy of colonialism. Touring the Hamiltons' vast operation, the ladies visit a boiling house to observe this key stage in the sugar-making process. They are "much entertained" by the exertions of the stripped, sweaty slaves (129). But, Schaw observes, "My Lady had another design, besides satisfying my curiosity in this visit... There were several of the boilers condemned to the lash, and seeing her face is pardon. Their gratitude on this occasion was the only instance of sensibility that I have observed in them" (129). A gendered division of labor governs the psychological manipulation of the slaves. While white men (planters, overseers, and drivers) administer the physical punishment that drives the system, a white woman metes out the occasional, symbolic pardon, which seems to function similarly to the ritual Christmas world-upside-down, temporarily dissipating frustration and warding off revolt. Justice and mercy cynically complement one another in the moral economy of the slave plantation, the two virtues gendered as they appear in the *Theory of Moral Sentiments* of Schaw's fellow Scot, Adam Smith.[35]

In addition to gender, Schaw also emphasizes the other dyad defining white woman's identity, that of race. Island ladies, she comments, "want only colour to be termed beautiful...Yet this I am convinced is owing to the way in which they live, entirely excluded from proper air and exercise. From childhood they never suffer the sun to have a peep at them, and to prevent him are covered with masks and bonnets, that absolutely make them look as if they were stewed" (114). Pointing out the whiteness of the women's skin emphasizes the visible sign or "fetish" of racial difference, skin color, as it naturalizes colonial domination in the register of the visible – the same domain colonized by the language of aesthetics.[36] Again, as in Schaw's tableau of slaves going to market, the aesthetic value of skin color forms part of a visual argument for the legitimacy of slavery. Schaw's teen-aged relative Fanny, anxious to fit in, dons a mask and loses her rosy cheeks within a week. But Schaw herself significantly refrains from this practice: "As to your humble Servant, I have always set my face to the weather; wherever I have been. I hope you have no quarrel at brown beauty" (115).

This casual remark complicates our sense of Janet Schaw's relation to the island culture she has entered as guest and observer. Her self-deprecating reference to her suntanned features calls attention to her status as an outsider. She implicitly distances herself from the island women whose unhealthily pale skin is a sign of both racial superiority and the feminine qualities Schaw so fulsomely praises. Unmarried and childless, she cannot share in the virtues of housewife and mother. Her comment underlines her status, so unusual for a woman of her day, as a traveler – an adventurer who has been places and endured hardships, setting her face to the weather. We imagine her on the deck of the *Jamaica Packet*, her hair blowing in the Atlantic breeze. I sense a certain restrained satisfaction in Schaw as she projects this self-image. Her obliquely expressed relief at being, to some degree, outside the restrictive gender role of the West Indian lady carries with it an inchoate criticism of the island gender system. This type of complicated ambivalence – an unstable tension between explicit homage to conventional femininity and unstated resistance against it – will be familiar to readers of texts by eighteenth-century women. Severe cultural constraints could mute women's resistance into unobtrusive gestures like this one of Schaw's.

The phrase "brown beauty" also brings us back to aesthetics. Beauty, the conventional category applied to women and associated with the feminine, sorts oddly with the adjective "brown."[37] A suntanned complexion was outside the pale, so to speak, of ladylike beauty in late eighteenth-century Britain. Schaw chooses to portray herself not as a rosy-cheeked, healthy Scottish lass, but as downright bronzed by the tropical rays. She underscores her self-exclusion from contemporary standards of femininity with this

culturally oxymoronic phrase, as she opts out of womanhood
specifically in its capacity as aesthetic object. Did she feel the
ambiguous self-positioning revealed in this loaded self-description
to be a necessary step in taking up the position of the aesthetic subject? Her gesture accords with various moves by other eighteenth-
century women writers attempting to speak as aesthetic subjects.
Montagu aestheticizes the Turkish bathers, but distinguishes herself from the beautiful naked women by staying strategically
clothed. Helen Maria Williams, promoting the beauty and
sublimity of the French Revolution, establishes her authority as an
aesthetic perceiver by aligning aesthetics with a "feminine"
language of sensibility, as we will see in Chapter 4. Their strategies
point to the strain involved for women in speaking a discourse that
tended to position women as objects rather than subjects.

If we pursue this line of thought in the case of Janet Schaw,
however, we quickly confront a political dilemma. Her proto-
feminist gesture emerges in the course of a paean to the slave
plantation, combining positions that look incompatible from a
twentieth-century perspective. Mary Louise Pratt encounters a similar paradox in Anna Maria Falconbridge's *Narrative of Two Voyages
to the River Sierra Leone* (1802): proto-feminist overtones in what turns
out to be a pro-slavery tract.[38] Laura Brown finds an interpretive
challenge in Jonathan Swift, some of whose poems disclose a troubling misogyny, while other writings position him as an early
anti-colonialist. Such seeming paradoxes, she argues, ought to be
fertile for historical critics, whose methodologies may be enriched
as their political dogmas are challenged by coming to terms with
"the necessary intimacy of structures of oppression and liberation
in...eighteenth-century culture."[39]

In the *Journal of a Lady of Quality* we find this intimacy mapped
onto a woman writer's multiply determined, conflicted subjectivity.
As she engineers a collaboration between the discourse of aesthetics and that of "race," Schaw sidesteps identification with the white
womanhood epitomized by the dead Eleanora Dunbar, whose
name adorns the aestheticized "nature" of her husband's sugar
plantation. Her brown beauty places her ambiguously between
genders – not stationary, pale, and protected like a West Indian
lady, but mobile and robustly tinged. If we push this casual remark
even further, we notice that it blurs a second, crucial duality: the
visual poles of "black" and "white" whose apparent naturalness

anchors colonial discourse. Her suntanned face moves Schaw closer to the skin color of the slaves she denigrates and fears. It suggests a connection that the weight of her practice resolutely contravenes: the link between women's oppression and that of "racial" groups like the West Indian slaves. This strange suggestion is by no means intended to excuse her participation, like countless other white "ladies," in the imperial endeavor, but it certainly highlights the complexity and historical irony of women's position in the culture of empire.

Janet Schaw's remarkable journal is an especially instructive example of the way aesthetics lent itself to knitting together categories of social domination. In her insistently visual prose, aesthetics' pictorial logic strains to reconcile antagonistic forces in West Indian society. Anchored by that most "natural" of visible signs, the color of skin, her account of colonial life encompasses fort and barracks, the creoles' luxury and the suffering of their slaves, within well-ordered "prospects." Aesthetics argues without arguing. Its vocabulary of visible surfaces represents power relations as natural and unchallengeable precisely by casting them as irrelevant to the compelling business of the quest for beauty through the senses and imagination. In Schaw's journal the visible signs of beauty collude with those of "race" to clothe in seductive appeal the relations of power and brutality that marked this colonial system.[40]

CHAPTER 3

Landscape aesthetics and the paradox of the female picturesque

The verdure of the flower-motleyed meadow; the variegated foliage of the wood; the fragrance and purity of the air, and the wide spreading beauties of the landscape, charm not the labourer. They charm only the enlightened rambler, or affluent possessor. Those who toil, heed them not.[1]

The rich prospects of Britain's Caribbean colonies inspired Janet Schaw and her contemporaries to paint verbal pictures of West Indian landscapes. By the mid-1770s scenic tourism was gaining momentum among Britons with the means and leisure to travel in search of the perfect view. The scenic tour peaked in the 1790s and the first decade of the nineteenth century as a practice and a genre of writing. At this point it is worth examining in some detail the conventions of this peculiar practice – conventions that women writers would disrupt and creatively redefine. Good taste in landscape was a widely accepted means of displaying one's polite imagination (remember Austen's Henry Tilney strutting his cultural capital for Catherine Morland as he initiates her into the picturesque). Like the other pleasures valued by the man of taste, proper landscape appreciation took a good deal for granted: a high degree of literacy; an acquaintance with writings on aesthetics and works of literature; access to paintings, or at least engravings; and the mobility to examine and compare different views. Such stringent requirements obviously limited this species of taste to a relatively tiny elite. Women of the aristocracy and middle classes had the means, mobility, and to some degree the education needed to develop a taste in landscape. A few wrote and even published scenic tours.[2] But one suspects the average woman tourist took up the position of Austen's Catherine or Gilpin's lady drawing pupils – subject to tutelage from better educated, more authoritative men.

Women's relation to landscape aesthetics was fundamentally compromised, I will argue, by the discursive logic of the language of landscape appreciation. This chapter will situate the conventions of landscape aesthetics within the larger field of eighteenth-century aesthetic thought. Theorists of the picturesque like Gilpin and Richard Payne Knight share with aestheticians like Shaftesbury, Hume, and Reynolds a distinctive manner of constructing the subject: a strategy of willed distance from particular objects in the world and the needs and desires that connect or cathect individuals to them. This denial of the particular is grounded, I will suggest, in the symbolic connection between material particulars and groups of people thought of as trapped in them, defined by their bodies rather than their minds: specifically, women, the laboring classes, and non-Europeans. The aesthetic subject depends on these categories of the "vulgar" as a foil – that from which he is distinguished. The polite imagination, in other words, cannot do without vulgarity. Once we recognize this conceptual pattern in mainstream, male-authored aesthetic discourse, we can better appreciate the significance of the specific kinds of textual disruption and reconfiguration that mark women writers' appropriation of aesthetics.

Before taking up the discourses and practices of gardening and scenic tourism at greater length, I will consider three areas of aesthetic theory that best exemplify what I call denial of the particular: pre-Kantian versions of aesthetic disinterestedness, Hume's doctrine of the universal standard of taste, and Sir Joshua Reynolds' civic humanist theory of painting. All three unfold seemingly contradictory tendencies. They distance the subject from particular things and desires with an abstracting or universalizing strategy, while marking out a very specific social location for that subject. Casual remarks and examples chosen by various aestheticians disclose aesthetics' close affinity, not just to class and gender hierarchy, but also to systems of racial classification. John Barrell's persuasive reading of Reynolds' *Discourses* in the context of the political discourse of civic humanism will help me to elucidate the systematic cultural logic that aligns the familiar, powerful duality of mind and body with the conceptual oppositions between abstract and concrete, general and particular, form and matter – but also with the structuring dualisms of eighteenth-century society: polite/vulgar, man/woman, civilized/savage. The second terms are subordinated as the foils against which the aesthetic subject defines himself.

This context affords considerable insight into aesthetic discourses about land, as well as the material practices of estate gardening and scenic tourism. The gardenist and the picturesque tourist are constructed along the same lines as Addison's man of a polite imagination or Hume's true judge in the fine arts: presumptively, they are gentlemen, distinguished by clear textual cues from the unpropertied and the feminine. Gardening and scenic tourism share a paradigm of imaginative appropriation and manipulation that inscribes social hierarchy on the face of the land. I will close with a brief discussion of a scenic tour authored by a woman. Ann Radcliffe is best known as the author of *The Mysteries of Udolpho*, the topic of Chapter 7. Her *Journey made in the Summer of 1794, through Holland and the Western Frontier of Germany* (1795) records the tour that she and her husband took, presumably financed by the profits of her Gothic best-seller. To a reader familiar with the cultural logic of landscape aesthetics, *A Journey* discloses a thought-provoking pattern of textual disruption. I will read it as an idiosyncratic, but in some ways exemplary version of what can happen when a privileged woman occupies a discursive position for which she both is and is not an appropriate speaker. Sometimes she finds herself (in Teresa de Lauretis' phrase) in "the empty space between the signs."[3]

DISINTERESTEDNESS AND THE UNIVERSAL STANDARD OF TASTE

Let us begin with disinterested contemplation, certainly an essential tenet of eighteenth-century aesthetics' legacy to the modern era. The concept is most familiar from Kant's *Critique of Judgment* (1790). Truly aesthetic contemplation, according to Kant, is a state of mind defined by the absence of any vested interest or practical stake in the aesthetic object. To regard an object aesthetically, one cannot desire to eat it, embrace it, own it, or otherwise draw worldly benefit from it. One must be entirely indifferent to the object's material existence, regarding it solely as ideal form. The disinterested aesthetic subject is the mirror image of the autonomous aesthetic sphere into which modern art increasingly retreated: a domain conceptually severed from all practical, utilitarian, or political activities and concerns, which found institutional embodiment in the hushed and sterile halls of that secular temple, the museum. We can scarcely overestimate the persistent influence of this model of aesthetic reception in post-Enlightenment Western culture. Aesthetic autonomy, with its hand-maid formalism, adopted by high modernists as a weapon against philistinism, in due course became "a staple of the status quo" whose mystique helped legitimize bourgeois cultural hegemony. As formalism came to dominate twentieth-century art and criticism, autonomy and self-referentiality became indispensable marks of prestige by which artists strove, and still strive, to distinguish their valuable art from mere craft or popular trash.[4] When postmod-ernism declares itself "anti-aesthetic," it is art's autonomy – its putative aloofness from the practical realities of everyday life – that is its primary object of attack.[5]

Disinterestedness was not Kant's invention. Versions of this key concept were advanced by a succession of British writers, begin-ning with Addison and Shaftesbury and continuing through Francis Hutcheson, Hume, Kames, and Alexander Gerard to Kant's contemporary, Archibald Alison.[6] These writers also share an unabashed acknowledgment that aesthetic reception is a class privilege. They are fully aware that comfortable material circum-stances are needed to appreciate art, beauty, or sublimity in the specially valued ways they describe. Addison, for example, as he distinguishes the pleasures of the imagination from both the "grosser" pleasures of sense and the more "refined" ones of the understanding, is especially concerned (as I noted in the Introduction) to distinguish the "Man of a Polite Imagination" from the "Vulgar."[7] We also saw how Shaftesbury's quirky medita-tion on the sea, as it frames an important early version of disinter-ested contemplation, embeds this in a matrix of social assumptions about the rank and gender of the aesthetic perceiver, making clear that the aesthetic subject is none other than a property-owning man.

Alison follows Shaftesbury and others in excluding the useful, the agreeable, and the convenient from the specifically aesthetic qualities of objects. He emphasizes leisure as a primary condition of aesthetic reception: the mind must be "vacant and...unem-ployed," not pursuing any practical aim, in order to be "open to all the impressions, which the objects that are before us, can create."

This helps explain why we find "only in the higher stations...or in the liberal professions of life...men either of a delicate or comprehensive taste."[8] The aesthetic attitude explicitly depends on the luxury of idle time. The point of this brief survey is not to endorse a teleology marching toward Kant's more rigorous account of disinterestedness. Rather, I am concerned with the consistent pairing in these texts between a distancing or abstracting impulse, nominally disconnecting aesthetic reception from practical affairs, and a careful specification of the aesthetic perceiver's social identity.

The self-contradictory tendency of this coupling emerges more fully in the writings of David Hume, who employs a model of disinterested reception in pursuit of that favorite fantasy of eighteenth-century aestheticians, the universal standard of taste. Hume's scattered remarks on aesthetic judgment in the *Treatise of Human Nature* (1739–40) treat it as analogous to moral judgment: what distinguishes an aesthetic sentiment, or a moral one, from a feeling of merely private satisfaction is that the object or character is "considered in general, without reference to our particular interest." We need to correct for the limitations of our individual points of view in order to "arrive at a more *stable* judgment of things." Hence "we fix on some *steady* and *general* points of view; and always, in our thoughts, place ourselves in them, whatever may be our present situation."[9] A process of abstraction or generalization becomes a means of escaping the threatening instability caused by particular commitments.

In his later essay, "Of the Standard of Taste" (1757), Hume elaborates this train of thought in the service of an aesthetic axiology – a claim to objective validity for certain norms, standards, and judgments, a project of intense concern to aestheticians from Hume and Samuel Johnson to Kant (and still an object of struggle in the US "culture wars" of the 1990s). Hume's argument in this essay, as Barbara Herrnstein Smith and others have noted, is "deeply at odds with itself" and not especially successful *qua* argument as it proceeds in an "infinite regress" of assertion and qualification, advance and retreat.[10] He begins by acknowledging the obvious variety and inconsistency of tastes and then labors heroically to prove that a universal standard nonetheless exists. Though this standard applies to everyone, only very few are qualified to recognize it. A "true judge in the finer arts" is a "rare...character:

Strong sense, united to delicate sentiment, improved by practice, perfected by comparison, and cleared of all prejudice, can alone entitle critics to this valuable character; and the joint verdict of such, wherever they are to be found, is the true standard of taste and beauty."[11] The most important requirement for the critic is to overcome his prejudices: "considering myself as a man in general, [I must] forget, if possible, my individual being and my peculiar circumstances" (276). Taste must rise above "the different humours of particular men" as well as "the particular manners and opinions of our age and country" (280).

Hume does not specify the socioeconomic profile of the true judge. He does indicate that such critics need the opportunity to compare large numbers of art works, which clearly entails education, leisure, and travel – the familiar prerogatives of the aesthetic subject, taken for granted by writers from Shaftesbury to Alison. No worthwhile aesthetic judgment can be made without extensive experience in judging. "The coarsest daubing," scoffs Hume, "would affect the mind of a peasant or Indian with the highest admiration" (276). Striving to standardize taste through rigorously disinterested reception, Hume paradoxically succeeds in revealing aesthetics as a discourse of distinction that serves to elevate a few privileged men. His casual coupling of peasant and Indian as the antithesis of the true judge of taste affords further insight into exactly who is barred from this exclusive gentlemen's club. "Peasant" is no surprise; we are familiar with social rank or class as an assumed qualification of the aesthetic subject. It is worth dwelling at greater length on the implications of the Indian as aesthetic incompetent.

Paul Gilroy has noted the importance of racial concepts to Enlightenment aesthetic thought.[12] Hume's views on race emerge most clearly from a footnote that he added in 1754 to his 1748 essay "Of National Characters," where he argues against Montesquieu's theory of the influence of climate on national character, but makes an unsubstantiated exception based on race. "I am apt to suspect the negroes, and in general all the other species of men...to be naturally inferior to the whites. There never was a civilized nation of any other complexion than white, nor even any individual eminent either in action or speculation. No ingenious manufactures amongst them, no arts, no sciences...Such a uniform and constant difference could not happen, in so many countries and ages, if nature had not made an original distinction betwixt these breeds of men."[13] Edward Long's *History of Jamaica* (1774) takes a similar tactic in describing Africans: "they are void of genius, and seem almost incapable of making any progress in civility or science...They conceive no pleasure from the most beautiful parts of their country."[14] Lack of aesthetic capacity is offered as proof of incapacity for civilization. Hume's casual remark about peasants and Indians reads as the inverse of Long's circular claim: people who are uncivilized and inferior cannot be expected to appreciate beauty.

Hume's aesthetics share fundamental features with his beliefs on race. Both generate value through systems of hierarchical distinction or classification, sanctioned by "nature"; both brand non-Europeans as non-participants in the practices of civilization. A similar conceptual structure informs an aesthetic proclamation by the natural historian Buffon: "The most temperate climate lies between the 40th and 50th degree of latitude, and it produces the most handsome and beautiful men. It is from this climate that the ideas of the genuine colour of mankind, and of the various degrees of beauty, ought to be derived. The two extremes [tropical and subarctic] are equally remote from truth and from beauty."[15] A Eurocentric aesthetic standard takes on moral overtones as it co-opts the seemingly neutral, mathematical marks of latitude to a value-laden triage of humankind. Non-Europeans are reduced to aesthetic objects to be judged by a European subject.

A final telling example of the intersection between aesthetics and race occurs in Burke's treatise on the sublime and beautiful. In order to anchor our response to the sublime in nature, rather than learned associations, he invokes the case of the boy who was born blind and cured at the age of fourteen by the famous surgeon Cheselden. "Cheselden tells us, that the first time the boy saw a black object, it gave him great uneasiness; and that some time after, upon accidentally seeing a negro woman, he was struck with great horror at the sight."[16] Horror or terror, of course, is the wellspring of the Burkean sublime. Since the boy had had no time to accumulate associations, Burke reasons, his fear must have been caused by the nature of the senses themselves. Once again a non-European becomes the object of an aesthetic judgment. Value emanates from the perception of a European subject whose very senses are imagined as instinctively repulsed by the African's physical characteristics. We will later see Mary Shelley dismantle such a racist aesthetics by imagining a being who is at once universally repulsive in appearance, and eminently human.

Hume's essay on the standard of taste exemplifies the peculiar logic and anxious texture of arguments that attempt to reconcile these two potentially divergent agendas: abstraction or generalization – distance from particular, practical objects and desires – and social stratification. Sir Joshua Reynolds' theory of painting shares both these linked concerns. Considering his *Discourses on Art* in their political and philosophical contexts helps to clarify the rationale behind their linkage, while affording further insight into the least explicit criterion of disqualification, that of gender.

REYNOLDS: DETAILS AS DEFORMITY

The relation between general and particular was an urgent problem in the theory and practice of art for a diverse group of eighteenth-century figures from Dryden to Goethe (sometimes labeled "neoclassical").[17] Reynolds wrestles with the issue in his *Discourses on Art* (1769–90). A deep-seated mistrust of material specificity in the visible universe manifests itself in the *Discourses* as a striking repugnance for the particular – the detail – in painting. As president of the Royal Academy, Reynolds' view of art carried considerable cultural weight.[18] The Third Discourse begins its discussion of Beauty and the Grand Style by urging young painters toward a more conceptual approach. They need to move beyond real models and paint according to abstract mental ideals. Reynolds asserts that "the power of discovering what is deformed in nature, or in other words, what is particular and uncommon, can be acquired only by experience; and the whole beauty and grandeur of the art [painting] consists, in my opinion, in being able to get above all singular forms, local customs, particularities, and details of every kind."[19]

Eccentrically particularized natural objects, especially (for the portraitist) human bodies, arouse Reynolds' disgust. His "metaphorics of the detail," notes Naomi Schor, makes use of "the vocabulary of teratology, the science of monsters."[20] The term "deformity" or "deformed" is repeated seven times within three pages of the passage cited above. In his early *Idler* essay, Reynolds pronounces an especially forceful version of his anathema on the detail: "if...the painter, by attending to the invariable and general ideas of Nature, produce beauty, he must, by regarding minute particularities, and accidental discriminations, deviate from the universal rule, and pollute his canvas with deformity."[21] "Deformity" stands opposed not just to beauty but to the idea of form itself. Deformity is more than just formlessness, the anarchy of random particulars ungoverned by ordering abstractions; the detail becomes a positive "pollution," a monstrosity.

We can begin to understand the urgency of Reynolds' preoccupation by placing his thought, as John Barrell has persuasively done, within an influential tradition of political theory: the discourse of civic humanism.[22] The historian J. G. A. Pocock has traced civic humanism from its classical antecedents through the republican experience of Renaissance Florence and thence to eighteenth-century Britain and America. I will summarize, at the risk of oversimplifying this rich and resilient tradition.[23] Civic virtue, or disinterested commitment to the public good, which preserves the body politic against the strains of time and contingency and the push and pull of competing individual interests, can only survive under certain conditions. One of these is limited citizenship. Those who are occupied in their daily lives with the material particularity of the world of craft or trade, the "mechanical arts," pursuing the demands of economic survival or the lure of acquisition and luxury, will never achieve the generalizing, rational habits of thought needed to move beyond private interest, to grasp and act on the idea of the public good. The man of independent means, in this line of thought, has the potential (somewhat paradoxically) to free himself from experiencing the world as material. Only he may arrive, with effort and study, at the "liberal," "comprehensive," or "disinterested" point of view that is the basis of virtuous political action. As Terry Eagleton puts it in another context, "Only those with an interest" – in the eighteenth-century sense of property ownership – "can be disinterested."[24]

Property, however, had long been in a state of transition by the time Reynolds wrote; his version of civic humanism is a relatively belated one. The increasing importance from the 1690s onward of mobile rather than landed property, based on a national debt and a system of public credit, accompanied the emergence of a new ruling elite, the "moneyed interest." To traditional civic humanists this state of affairs endangered virtue and threatened widespread national corruption. Economic modernization thus made it necessary to redefine the concept of virtue with the aid of a concept of manners. Instead of corrupting, commerce could be viewed as making possible leisure, cultivation, and diverse social relationships that would refine citizens' passions and polish their manners.[25] Reynolds situates the art of painting within this aesthetic dimension of citizenship. Writing at a time when heroic political action seemed increasingly irrelevant to a modern market society, he shifts his emphasis from action to comprehension. The ability to grasp one's relation to the idea of the public, depending in turn on the ability to abstract general ideas from sense data, now defines the liberal mind. Painting must foster this capacity by pursuing ideal objects, which address the intellect and cannot be possessed, rather than actual, material objects in the world, which appeal to the senses and excite the acquisitive urge. Understood this way, painting – as Reynolds repeatedly insists – is a liberal art and not a "mechanical" trade.[26] The liberal mind is different in its fundamental economy, the very ordering of its faculties, from a "mechanic" mentality.[27]

The Ninth Discourse contains Reynolds' most sweeping account of "the progress of the mind," a progress that quickly leaves some minds behind.

Man, in his lowest state, has no pleasures but those of sense, and no wants but those of appetite; afterwards, when society is divided into different ranks, and some are appointed to labour for the support of others, those whom their superiority sets free from labour, begin to look for intellectual entertainments...As the senses, in the lowest state of nature, are necessary to direct us to our support, when that support is once secure there is danger in following them further; to him who has no rule of action but the gratification of the senses, plenty is always dangerous: it is therefore necessary to the happiness of individuals, and still more necessary to the security of society, that the mind should be elevated to the idea of general beauty, and the contemplation of general truth;...the mind...obtains its proper superiority over the common senses of life, by learning to feel itself capable of higher aims and noble enjoyments. (169–70)

Foremost among these enjoyments is, of course, the art of painting. Social stratification is an informing principle in Reynolds' theory of painting. He presents his art as produced and consumed by "those whom their superiority sets free from labour," relying on an analogy between social groups and the faculties of the mind: the "high" intellect versus the "common" senses. The capacity to abstract from the particular to the general – developed, for example, through a taste for the right kind of art – "elevates" citizens' minds. Good painting helps overcome differences between private interests by leading toward a consensual apprehension of the world at the fundamental level of perception itself. The "security of society" depends on this kind of solidarity among the governing elite against all of those who, because their views are confined to sense gratification and private interest, pose a constant danger to the state.

An important classical antecedent for the analogy that underpins this passage is Plato's *Republic*. Critics generally recognize Platonic elements in the *Discourses*, though they disagree as to the extent of Reynolds' Platonism.[28] The analogy between the well-ordered mind and the well-ordered state is elaborated in Book IV of the *Republic*. The "just" hierarchy in which the rational soul governs the desires of the base senses parallels the warrior Guardians' rule over craftsmen, money-makers, women, children, and slaves.[29] The homogeneous, self-disciplined class of enfranchised citizens is associated with reason, while the diverse and potentially disorderly throng of the ruled is linked to the "lower" faculties of sense. In Book X Plato adds a third term to the analogy as he justifies his wish to expel all imitators (such as poets and painters) from the city. By imitating the appearance of particular material things and appealing to the senses, he claims, the imitator "awakens and nourishes and strengthens" the base, irrational elements of the soul and thus "impairs the reason." Imitative art threatens proper hierarchy in the state by subverting the hierarchy of faculties within the human soul: "As in a city we cannot allow the evil to have authority and the good to be put out of the way, even so in the city which is within us we refuse to allow the imitative poet to create an evil constitution indulging the irrational nature" (605).[30] Reynolds joins a long tradition of European painters and critics in resisting this particular dictum of Plato's, just as he resists Plato's closely related classification of painting as a craft or trade. Instead, Reynolds uses the Platonic analogy between mind and state to assert painting's political inoffensiveness – indeed, its usefulness to the state – by aligning it primarily with reason, rather than sense. Concerned to establish painting as a liberal art, he maintained that "properly pursued, painting did not threaten the good order of the mind or of the state, but rather confirmed the grounds of the distinction, between reason and the senses, the franchised and the unenfranchised, on which good order was based."[31]

Reynolds' concern for good order in the work of art pervades the *Discourses*. The Fourth Discourse instructs students in applying to every facet of painting the guiding principle "that perfect form is produced by leaving out particularities, and retaining only general ideas" (57). As he translates his subject, an incident from history or myth, into an image on canvas, "the Artist should restrain and keep under all the inferior parts of his subject" (59). The moral and political overtones of such "restraint" are palpable. They are confirmed by reading the *Discourses*, as Reynolds' classically educated audience certainly would have, in the context of Platonic psychology-politics. The "inferior parts" of the painting (details that capture the senses); of the mind (the senses themselves); and, most crucially, of the state (the laboring classes and women) must be "restrained" or "kept under" so that they do not threaten proper hierarchy in the respective wholes. "Particularities" are divisive. The painter of talent, Reynolds asserts, will not "waste a moment upon those smaller objects, which only serve to catch the sense, to divide the attention, and to counteract his great design of speaking to the heart" (50). Division in the painting fosters division in the mind or soul of its viewer, which both figures and encourages division or subversion in the state.

In another section of the Ninth Discourse (perhaps his most Platonic), Reynolds says more explicitly that upholding the hierarchy of the faculties is the painter's contribution to proper political order.

Our art, like all arts which address the imagination, is applied to somewhat a lower faculty of the mind, which approaches nearer to sensuality; but through sense and fancy it must make its way to reason... and without carrying our art out of its natural and true character, the more we purify it from every thing that is gross in sense, in that proportion we advance its use and dignity; and in proportion as we lower it to mere sensuality, we pervert its nature, and degrade it from the rank of a liberal art; and this is what every artist ought well to remember. Let him remember also, that he deserves just so much encouragement in the state as he makes himself a member of it virtuously useful, and contributes in his sphere to the general purpose and perfection of society. (170–71)

The political context of the *Discourses*, delivered in an institution of royal patronage to an audience with everything to gain from George III's "encouragement," underscores the political content of Reynolds' message. The "purification" of painting to address the "higher" faculties, using the "lower" ones merely as stepping-stones, is clearly related to painting's usefulness to the state. By suppressing "gross" sensory particulars, the painter contributes by analogy to the "perfection of society," namely the continued rule of its "higher" over its "lower" members.

Reynolds' reliance on the Platonic analogy between the hierarchy of faculties and that of persons suggests that his social concerns are not limited to class alone. Women were prominent among those whom classical philosophy associated with the body and the senses, and who therefore needed restraint. For Reynolds, as for Plato, it went without saying that women were among the ruled and not the rulers. There was no question of female citizenship. Other classical thinkers develop the chain of association between woman, the body, the senses, and material particularity.[32] As Schor points out, citing Aristotle's *Physics,* Greek theories of reproduction "mapped gender onto the form–matter paradigm, forging a durable link between maleness and form (*eidos*), female-ness and formless matter... 'matter longs for form as its fulfillment, as the female longs for the male.'"[33] Reynolds' gendered language replicates this Aristotelian scheme by casting nature, the painter's raw material, as feminine and in need of discipline. The painter "corrects nature by *herself, her* imperfect state by *her* more perfect. His eye being enabled to distinguish the accidental deficiencies, excrescences, and deformities of things, from their general figures, he makes out an abstract idea of their forms more perfect than any one original" (44, emphasis added). He treats excessive details in a finished painting as uncorrected remnants of an "imperfect," form-less or deformed, feminine nature. Details are "deformities" when they are "accidental" rather than essential, not properly subordinated to "general figures" or abstract ideas of form. These ideas can only be "made out" by the painter's form-providing masculine eye. Nature's feminine substrate must be subject to discipline by a masculine intellect in order for painting to contribute "to the general purpose and perfection of society."

The antipathy to details that pervades Reynolds' *Discourses* can thus be understood as rooted in the powerful analogy between the state, the individual mind, and the work of art. Good form in painting subordinates objects and figures to ideas; each figure is formed through a process of comparing and abstracting from actual things. Details not subordinated to form symbolically threaten proper order in both mind and state. They are associated with "low," potentially unruly elements in each: the senses and their disorderly desires, in need of regulation by the intellect; and groups of people – workers and women – more susceptible to those desires and hence likely to foment political subversion if not ruled by citizens in whose minds, in turn, the senses are firmly under the control of reason. For Reynolds, the primacy of form in painting both represents and promotes right rule in mind and state.

Understanding Reynolds' aesthetics in this manner as socially situated obliges us to rethink standard narratives of the history of aesthetics. The accepted periodization separates "neoclassical" theories like Reynolds', grounded in a mimetic conception of art, from a "Romantic" paradigm of reception in which disinterested subjects contemplate autonomous or intransitive, internally coherent works of art. Thinking about aesthetics in the way I propose casts doubt on such a division. Not only did disinterestedness originate at the chronological height of British neoclassicism, but its de-particularizing impulse directed at the subject also mirrors Reynolds' de-particularized aesthetic object, the painting. A work that is in theory mimetic, but purged of particular content as Reynolds demands, moves decisively in the direction of the autonomous work and of formalism.[34] We can begin to recognize the interconnections between the three founding assumptions of eighteenth-century aesthetics: universality, disinterestedness, and autonomy. The generic perceiver's claim to universality may be founded, as in Hume's "Of the Standard of Taste," on a paradigm of disinterested aesthetic perception that abstracts or generalizes by disengaging the perceiver from particular objects in the world. This self-enclosed model of the aesthetic subject in turn mirrors the autonomy of the artwork and the aesthetic domain, supposedly cut off from practical or utilitarian and especially from political concerns.

Landscape aesthetics incorporates this set of linked assumptions in specific discourses and practices that women writers would find ingenious ways to disrupt. Women's ambivalent assaults on these powerful fictions expose them as cultural constructs serving the interests of a dominant group at the expense of everyone else. There is no such thing as disinterested aesthetic contemplation. Aesthetic discourse circulates in contexts and is used for ends that are inextricable from the intricately articulated interests, conscious or unconscious, of the individuals who use and modify symbol systems even as they are produced as subjects in and by them. These interests have a great deal to do with power, and in particular with various types of social stratification. To this extent my analysis is congruent with Bourdieu's description of the aesthetic as "an ethos of elective distance from the necessities of the natural and social world," a set of cultural practices that reinforce social distinction – rather paradoxically – precisely by means of denying the social.[35] But Bourdieu's sociological account needs to be amplified by understanding aesthetics as a discursive technology of self-fashioning, or subject formation, a line of analysis pursued by certain strands of cultural studies.[36]

Aesthetics' production of a few individuals as aesthetic subjects, I have shown, rests on its elaborate disqualification of the rest. In the words of Peter Stallybrass and Allon White, the "high" bourgeois subject constitutively depends on a "low-Other" – that which is "despised and denied at the level of political organization and social being whilst it is instrumentally constitutive of the shared imaginary repertoires of the dominant culture."[37] Judith Butler describes this prevalent mode of subject construction in Western culture as "an exclusion and differentiation, perhaps a repression, that is subsequently concealed, covered over, by the effect of autonomy." Subjects "are constituted through exclusion, that is, through the creation of a domain of deauthorized subjects, presubjects, figures of abjection, populations erased from view."[38] Aesthetics finds its figures of abjection in the laboring classes, in non-Europeans like Hume's Indian and Burke's negro woman, and – most pertinent for women writers – in the feminine. My discussion of Reynolds is not meant to imply that all of eighteenth-century aesthetics is rooted in civic humanism and Platonic psychology. Rather, the *Discourses* exemplify especially well the way in which British culture of this period pervasively aligned women, the laboring classes, and non-Europeans with body as opposed to mind, matter rather than form, and the particular rather than the universal, and the way in which these dualities govern the construction and disqualification of aesthetic subjects.

This conceptual structure is by no means limited to aesthetics. Since aesthetic theorists operated in the broader intellectual context of political and economic liberalism, it is no surprise to find similar conceptual structures in influential works of liberal thought. I have elsewhere discussed Locke's *Second Treatise of Government* (1690) and Adam Smith's *Theory of Moral Sentiments* (1758) in this connection.[39] Smith's regulatory concept of the impartial spectator is of special interest in relation to the aesthetic subject. Conceptualizing the ethical subject as a spectator or observer moves Smith's ethics (like Shaftesbury's half a century earlier) in the direction of aesthetics. The position of the impartial spectator is achieved through a process of distancing oneself from particular, material circumstances: to make an ethical judgment on someone's action, one becomes an impartial spectator by stripping away all biases pertaining to one's own specific situation or that of the moral actor being judged. Prominent among the particulars that must be set aside are the body and its desires. Since bodily appetites are transient as well as idiosyncratic, they are difficult or impossible for others to enter into. "When we have dined, we order the covers to be removed; and we should treat in the same manner the objects of the most ardent and passionate desires, if they were the objects of no other passions but those which take their origin from the body." Behind the amusing image of the sated libertine ordering the "covers removed" lies the historically charged association of such "objects" – women – with particular, material bodies as well as with aspects of our moral being that require restraint under a civilized moral code. Again, even more explicitly than in Reynolds, we recognize the link between women and bodily or material nature. Women do not make good impartial spectators, says Smith, because of their particularism. "Humanity is the virtue of a woman, generosity of a man...Humanity consists merely in the exquisite fellow-feeling which the spectator entertains with the sentiments of the persons principally concerned." Generosity, by contrast, is a "higher" virtue mediated by the impartial spectator.[40] Smith aligns the feminine with all that must be superseded on the way to higher morality, as Reynolds aligns it with everything that is inimical to high art.

Twentieth-century theorists point out the importance of denying the particular, at many levels, to the formation of a post-Enlightenment civic public and, more broadly, of the modern nation state. Iris Marion Young summarizes this paradigm:

"Because virtues of impartiality and universality define the public realm, it precisely ought not to attend to our particularity. Modern normative reason and its political expression in the idea of the civic public, then, has unity and coherence by its expulsion and confinement [in the domestic sphere] of everything that would threaten to invade the polity with differentiation: the specificity of women's bodies and desire, the difference of race and culture, the...heterogeneity of the needs, the goals and desires of each individual."[41]

The de-particularized artwork and its mirror image, the disinterested aesthetic subject, in spite of – or more accurately by virtue of – their overtly apolitical stance, thus contribute to sustaining political unity. Such a de-particularizing drive played a prominent role in the historical formation of the English state, which Philip Corrigan and Derek Sayer have traced from the Middle Ages into the nineteenth century. States, they point out, "attempt to give unitary and unifying expression to what are in reality multi-faceted and differential historical experiences of groups within society, denying their particularity. The reality is that bourgeois society is systematically unequal, it is structured along lines of class, gender, ethnicity, age, religion, occupation, locality. States act to erase the recognition and expression of these differences." Such systematic, institutionalized denial of particularity is inevitably painful, for some much more than others. Aesthetic discourse is among the "universalizing vocabularies" that mediated the complex interaction between the emergence of a modern British nation state and the making, so to speak, of its ruling class – an elite of subject-citizens suited to govern and sustain that state.[42]

LANDSCAPE GARDENING

It is now time to consider at greater length the subset of aesthetic theory and practice with which women writers were most closely engaged: the applied aesthetics of natural scenery, which burgeoned in theory and practice throughout the eighteenth century. The conventions of landscape appreciation exemplify aesthetics' central tension between affirming and denying material and social particularity. The aesthetic appreciation of land counted as an indispensable social grace in polite British society. Expensively landscaped estates by designers like William Kent and "Capability" Brown became coveted signs of material power and social prestige.

The closely related practice of scenic tourism spread during the last decades of the century; the scenic tourist imaginatively re-created landscape by viewing, sketching, and describing it according to models derived from painting. Landscape appreciation thus trickled down to those who lacked the enormous resources to create their own private scenic preserves, but aspired to the sensibilities of their social betters. Scenic tourism was not seamlessly continuous with gardening, however. The less lofty class position of the average tourist lent the aesthetics of the picturesque a submerged ambivalence that women writers would exploit.

Landownership as both source and sign of power was the traditional heart of the British political system. William Marshall writes as late as 1804, "Landed property is the basis on which every other species of material property rests; on it alone mankind can be said – to live, to move, and have its being."[43] Even as the political center of gravity began to shift to the moneyed bourgeoisie, a merchant prince's career was crowned by the purchase of a landed estate, certainly the prerequisite for attaining a knighthood and *a fortiori* a peerage in Britain's system of limited social mobility. Women writing the language of landscape aesthetics thus aimed straight at the center of material and symbolic power in their society.

Women's relation to landed property was not the same as men's. Susan Staves analyzes the legal dimension of this relation at length in *Married Women's Separate Property in England, 1660–1833*. "In the property regimes of patriarchy," she summarizes, "women function as procreators and as transmitters of inheritance from male to male." The British legal system's intricate thicket of arrangements for regulating women's severely limited access to property – including marriage settlements, pin money, and separate maintenance agreements – functioned together in the service of this imperative. Ideologies of femininity, as well as legal codes, increasingly contributed to prevent women from exercising control over land. Women, Staves reports, "were seen to lack not only the rationality required for citizenship but also the rationality required for the active management of property...So long as the owner was male, to own even a moderate-sized estate meant not only to be entitled to use the land as a capital resource but also to be entitled to a degree of social prestige and a degree of political power." But an estate, as one historian puts it, "needed a man" to own and administer it. A woman could not perform easily, or at all, the

6. J. Taylor, "Fences Called Invisible." Humphrey Repton, *Fragments on the Theory and Practice of Landscape Gardening* (1816). The gentleman and his garden.

range of political, economic, and social functions incumbent on the landowner.[44] Where these primary dimensions of individuals' relation to land differed by gender, we will not be surprised to find the aesthetics of land inflected by gender as well.

Aesthetic discourse about land both assumes and reinforces the status of land as the foundation of sociopolitical power. This discourse constructs its subject along the same lines as the aesthetic discourses we have already surveyed: presumptively, he is a gentleman. A variety of textual cues distinguishes him from both the unpropertied vulgar and the feminine, or woman. The theory and practice of landscape gardening in the early part of the century appeared to be moving in the direction of the greater freedom and flexibility that became the hallmark of the English garden, as opposed to the geometric precision of the Continental style. Symmetrical beds or parterres studded with topiary gradually gave way to the idea of artful artlessness that Pope (an influential figure in gardening whose Twickenham estate was much admired) expounds in the familiar lines of his "Epistle to Burlington":

> To build, to plant, whatever you intend,
> To rear the Column, or the Arch to bend,
> To swell the Terras, or to sink the Grot;
> In all, let Nature never be forgot.
> But treat the Goddess like a modest fair,
> Nor over-dress, nor leave her wholly bare;
> Let not each beauty ev'ry where be spy'd,
> Where half the skill is decently to hide.
> He gains all points, who pleasingly confounds,
> Surprizes, varies, and conceals the Bounds.[45]

Such an illusion of boundlessness rhetorically invokes British political freedom in contrast to Continental servitude.[46] Underlying this supposed return to nature, however, is the gendered power relationship that this passage clearly poses between an active, masculine aesthetic subject and a passive feminine object, the "Goddess" Nature.

Carole Fabricant, in an important essay, analyzes the "paradoxical combination" of "freedom and constraint, abandonment and discipline" that characterizes Augustan gardening discourse from Addison and Pope to William Shenstone and Horace Walpole.[47] Like a woman, Nature was expected to be sensuous and pleasing, but only within bounds defined by her male owner: "Both women and landscape were continually being judged for their ability to titillate the imagination and satisfy the senses while at the same time remaining within carefully prescribed moral, aesthetic, and territorial limits" (III). The "magnificent fantasy of power" (123) conjured by the muscularly active (and vaguely sexually suggestive) verbs in the passage cited above ("Build," "plant," "rear," "bend," "swell," "sink") culminates with the poem's final lines, which praise Burlington as quasi-omnipotent engineer:

> Bid Harbors open, public Ways extend,
> Bid Temples, worthier of the God, ascend;
> Bid the broad Arch the dang'rous Flood contain,
> The Mole projected break the roaring Main;
> Back to his bounds their subject Sea command,
> And roll obedient Rivers thro' the Land (lines 197–202)

Again expansion vies with containment as Pope completes the analogy between Burlington the gardener and Burlington the mastermind of "Imperial Works" (line 204). The aesthetic subject as landscape gardener appears here and throughout these Augustan writings as emphatically masculine, his gender signified through intertwined "aesthetic, economic and sexual forms of possession" and manipulation performed on the feminine substrate of "Nature" (Fabricant, 117).

Pope's poem shares with Reynolds' theory of painting its subordination of Nature's formless, feminine raw material to the painter's form-giving masculine mind. Indeed, in this period the landscape gardener began to be described as a kind of painter, as when Pope proclaims that "all gardening is landscape-painting."[48] The analogy persisted throughout the century, culminating with Uvedale Price's and Richard Payne Knight's theories of the picturesque garden during the 1790s. For example, Horace Walpole praises William Kent in 1771 as "painter enough to taste the charms of landscape, bold and opinionative enough to dare and to dictate...the pencil of his imagination bestowed all the arts of landscape on the scenes he handled. The great principles on which he worked were perspective, and light and shade...he realised the compositions of the greatest masters in painting."[49] The garden was thought of as a kind of outdoor gallery, "a natural extension of the picture galleries constructed indoors, in the great halls and salons, where both landscapes and women were commonly framed and placed on display." Arthur Young, in his agricultural surveys of England's great estates, routinely pairs a description of the landscaping with a catalogue of the picture gallery.[50] Here we discover an important conceptual link between two characteristic activities of the eighteenth-century Man of Taste. He was a connoisseur of both painting and gardening. The relation between the gardener and the feminized landscape was conceived similarly to that between painter and model: the active framing, composing subject with his passive object or substrate. These conceptual operations of framing and composing, essential (as we will see) to the aesthetics of the picturesque, were integral to landscape gardening before Gilpin, whose first published work was *A Dialogue upon the Gardens of the Right Honourable the Lord Viscount Cobham, at Stow in Buckinghamshire* in 1748.

The idea of appropriation, actual or imaginative, links the period's conceptualizations of gardening, painting, and merely contemplating a natural scene. Addison's remarks on natural scenery connect it to property. The man of a polite imagination "often feels a greater Satisfaction in the Prospect of Fields and Meadows, than another does in the Possession. It gives him, indeed, a kind of Property in every thing he sees, and makes the most rude uncultivated Parts of Nature administer to his Pleasures."[51] Looking at landscape becomes a paradigmatic mental exercise in ownership. The art historian John Berger finds in the European tradition of painting, with its institutional context of patronage, commission and collection, a persistent theme of "metaphorical appropriation": "Just as [the painting's] perspective gathers all that is extended to render it to the individual eye, so its means of representation render all that is depicted into the hands of the individual owner-spectator."[52] The process of framing and composing constitutes an exercise of power, a non-reciprocal mode of vision whose effect is to display and reinforce mastery.[53] Recent feminist film theory posits the gaze as a culturally constructed form of non-reciprocal power. I understand the recent technology of cinema as extending, in an important sense, this European tradition of gendered aesthetic domination through vision.[54] Eighteenth-century landscape aesthetics leaned on the analogy with painting as it institutionalized a dominative, appropriative vision in a range of cultural practices that distinguished the aesthetic subject from those not entitled to own and dispose.

As the century wore on, estate gardeners' display of the power of taste and the taste of power strove to exceed all previous bounds. Britain's demographic, scientific, and economic transformations increasingly colluded with these "improvers." Ann Bermingham points to landscape gardening's symbiotic relationship with its material base in the later eighteenth century. As urban growth demanded dramatically increased food production, breakthroughs in agriculture made greater efficiency possible. Implementing new techniques, however, called for economies of scale. With the help of Parliament, aspiring agrarian capitalists stepped up the process of enclosure: consolidating common lands, formerly used by the rural poor for grazing and gardening, under private ownership. Besides cutting off these resources and helping create a miserably dependent agricultural proletariat, this trend provided raw material for the increasingly admired luxury of the large-scale, natural-looking estate garden. "As the real landscape began to look increasingly artificial, like a garden, the garden began to look increasingly natural, like the preenclosed landscape." Landowners flaunted their new prosperity through the conspicuous display of "a completely nonfunctional, nonproductive use of land" – an imaginative compensation that the privileged few granted themselves for the aesthetic cost of the agricultural revolution.[55]

Landscape gardening by the late eighteenth century thus projected power along both axes, gender and class. Beginning early in the century, the aesthetic subject as gardenist was discursively constructed in terms of a gendered power relation between a male subject and a feminine object, "Nature." The practice of estate "improvement" symbolized socioeconomic power by defying the practical considerations of land use that were its material conditions of possibility. The gardenist was symbolically distinguished both from a feminine "Nature" and from the laborers who dug his lakes and trimmed his shrubs. Tastes in landscaping evolved in the course of the century from the statue-studded grottoes of Cobham's Stowe to "Capability" Brown's sleekly shaven parks, and later the luxuriant shagginess endorsed by Price and Knight. However, a more important continuity underlay these shifts: a shared paradigm of imaginative appropriation and manipulation that inscribed class and gender on the landscape.

An evocative scene from Ann Radcliffe's *Romance of the Forest* (1791) dramatizes the gendered power relation inscribed in the landscape garden. Radcliffe was immersed in aesthetic theory and extraordinarily sensitive to its ideological dimension, as we will see in her travel narrative and *The Mysteries of Udolpho*. *The Romance of the Forest* features her standard scenario of a sensitive, moderately self-assertive heroine persecuted by a power-obsessed villain. The Marquis de Montalt kidnaps the orphan Adeline, intending to force her into marriage; she is deposited in his "magnificent saloon" amid his other possessions, the rich furnishings, paintings, and busts that establish him as a prototypical Man of Taste.[56] Withstanding his advances, she is finally left alone and takes the opportunity to jump out of the window into "an extensive garden, resembling more an English pleasure ground, than a series of French parterres" (164). (Radcliffe's fictional France resembles eighteenth-century England in more than just garden design.) At first Adeline, hoping to escape, "trip[s] lightly along" in the moonlight. The park is "a scene of tranquil beauty" with its typical features of alleys, lawns, groves, and "a lake overhung with lofty trees." Its "every object seemed to repose," in contrast to the heroine's growing agitation as she finds herself running in circles (165). "To her imagination the grounds were boundless; she had wandered from lawn to lawn, and from grove to grove, without perceiving any termination to the place" (166). The English garden's artful disarray stymies and traps her more effectively than symmetrical French-style hedges. Radcliffe gives us landscape theorists' idyll of containment and achieved serenity from the anything but serene perspective of a feminine object who does not consent to be contained: an aesthetic nightmare of boundless power.

SCENIC TOURISM

Tourism as an institution might be said to begin with the Grand Tour of Europe, the standard finishing touch to the male aristocrat's education from at least the late seventeenth century onward. Certainly the Grand Tour had an aesthetic component. Witness the trunkloads of paintings and other art objects carted home by aspiring connoisseurs, collections that would later feed the fashion for picturesque nature. The first reports of scenic tourism – traveling in search of aesthetically pleasing natural scenery – date from mid-century. It took three decades to reach a critical mass; the many tours and guidebooks published from the late 1770s into the first decade of the next century testify to scenic tourism's coming of age.[57] Travel within England became more practicable during the last decades of the century with better carriage design, road-building, inns, and other services.[58] Scenic areas such as the Wye Valley, the Lake District, Wales, and the Scottish Highlands, more affordable than Europe, attracted a class of tourist not quite so grand, though Thomas West exaggerates in the preface to his popular *Guide to the Lakes:* "Since persons of genius, taste, and observation began to make the tour of their own country, and to give such pleasing accounts of the natural history, and improving state of the northern parts of the kingdom, the spirit of visiting them has diffused itself among the curious of all ranks."[59] The ranks of middle-class tourists had certainly swelled by the 1780s and 1790s, but tourism's indispensable prerequisites of means, leisure, and education still restricted it to a comparative elite. Not until the advent of the trains that William Wordsworth fought against in the 1840s can we begin to talk of anything resembling modern mass tourism.

Thus, considerable social distance still separated the late eighteenth-century tourist from the average inhabitant of Britain's beauty spots. Tourists sometimes idealized country dwellers, praising their modesty and simplicity. The inhabitants of a working countryside, too busy with subsistence to dream of elaborate leisure activities, were likely to regard tourists with attitudes ranging from bewilderment or amusement to resentment, suspicion, and contempt (unless they were among those profiting from the influx of money into the area: innkeepers, shopkeepers, guides, proprietors of excursion boats and museums). William Wordsworth – himself an avid if not average tourist – quotes a "shrewd and sensible" Lake District woman: "'Bless me! folk are always talking about prospects: when I was young there was never sic a thing neamed.'"[60]

The relation between the scenic tourist and the inhabitants who became figures in the landscape, ornaments to the imagined scene, is a charged site in the discourse of applied landscape aesthetics which I will discuss at length in subsequent chapters. This relation is complicated by the class position of the average scenic tourist. He or she is in the middle: not a landowner, at least not on the scale ideally needed to transform the landscape in the service of aesthetic aims; but still set apart by means, leisure, and education from members of the laboring class like the Wordsworths'

Grasmere neighbors. Kim Ian Michasiw posits an antithesis, conditioned by this class distance, between William Gilpin's picturesque, conceived by a clergyman of modest means and directed to an audience of tourists, and the landowner picturesque of Sir Uvedale Price and Sir Richard Payne Knight, aimed at men like themselves with the power physically to create picturesque vistas on their vast estates. I am not willing to go nearly as far as Michasiw in this respect. It does stand to reason that the middle-class traveler had a somewhat different relation to land than the aristocratic proprietor. But a middle-class man could at least aspire to own land in his own right and enjoy the social perquisites of landownership, as women, for example, could not. Gilpin's picturesque seems primarily driven by wistful emulation of his social betters. He was part of the ongoing process, beginning with Addison, of extending the prerogative of the aesthetic subject downward in the social scale from the aristocracy into the moneyed bourgeoisie and professional classes. Gilpin's picturesque tourist substitutes imaginary for real ownership and manipulation of land; Carole Fabricant's argument that country house tourism imaginatively appeased desires which might otherwise threaten landowners provides a relevant model for this conservative tendency in Gilpin's picturesque.[61] Only very occasionally is this dominant impulse disrupted in his writings by a lurking potential for subversion. The women writers who appropriate and revise the picturesque primarily target Gilpin's composition-driven version, attracted perhaps by these undertones of conflict; my discussion will focus on his writings.

One woman writer whom I will later discuss in detail, Dorothy Wordsworth, exemplifies the scenic tourist's situation in the middle, somewhere between lavishly entitled aristocrat and objectified peasant. Wordsworth had the unusual experience of occupying both positions: that of the tourist during her trip to Scotland, and that of the inhabitant at home in Grasmere, where she became an object for the tourist's gaze. "A coronetted Landau went by when we were sitting upon the sodded wall. The ladies (evidently Tourists) turned an eye of interest upon our little garden and cottage," she writes in her journal.[62] A complicated ambivalence underlies this seemingly neutral remark. Wordsworth's experience at home in Grasmere becomes a fulcrum for criticism when she herself takes up the position of the tourist, the aesthetic subject.

Her class position at a distance from both aristocrats and working inhabitants makes her well situated to gauge tourism's effect on those whom it constructs as human ornaments to the pastoral scene.

Scenic tourism did not remain a domestic affair. Travelers at England's commercial and colonial frontiers took along its familiar aesthetic mode of vision and descriptive vocabulary. The relation between traveler and inhabitant was again a site of tension when explorers turned an aesthetic gaze on exotic scenes for which no guidebook existed. Mary Pratt analyzes landscape aesthetics' collusion in the projects of empire when the colonial representative John Barrow travels into the South African interior in 1797–98. Barrow carefully segregates his remarks on the "manners and customs" of the African inhabitants from his descriptions of "the face of the country," in effect emptying the African landscape to ready it for European possession. "Where, one asks, is everybody?" Pratt's study of travelers in southern Africa documents the "fantasy of dominance and appropriation that is built into" the stance of the aesthetic traveler as he takes verbal possession of colonial "prospects." The superficial passivity and innocence of the aesthetic attitude – just looking – obscures its aggressiveness in an ideological strategy that she calls "the anti-conquest."[63] Janet Schaw's journal demonstrates landscape aesthetics' susceptibility to colonial use; later women writers, notably Dorothy Wordsworth and Mary Shelley, would approach the relation between aesthetics and empire more critically.

Late eighteenth-century landscape aesthetics had its roots in a tradition of estate gardening that, as we have seen, constructed its subject as masculine and property-owning, "improving" a feminized land in a tasteful display of power and privilege. The picturesque substitutes imaginative for real possession as a central principle in aestheticizing land. The analogy with painting situates both discourses in a long-standing cultural nexus of vision, power, and possession. But painterly framing as a mode of conceptualizing land also helps to uncouple aesthetic perception from that land's material particularity, and especially from the use value that connects it with its working inhabitants, who dwindle to abstract, sanitized figures in the landscape. The aesthetics of the picturesque, like those of Hume and Reynolds, thus combines the contradictory impulses toward social specificity – marking the position and power of the aesthetic subject – and detachment, or denial of the particular.

The social historian Keith Thomas situates the new taste for natural scenery as a reaction to the unprecedentedly rapid social, economic, and demographic changes of the eighteenth century: a nostalgic clinging to the undeveloped land that grew ever scarcer with urbanization, expanding cultivation, and rising population. Scenic tourism feeds "fantasies which enshrine...values by which society as a whole cannot afford to live."[64] But this nostalgia takes a paradoxically modern form, as critics like Ann Bermingham and Alan Liu suggest. Land that was supposedly valued precisely because untouched by the "hand of art" must, to become a proper object of value, be touched and transformed in a manner that standardized, even commodified landscape.[65] Liu finds in the picturesque "a deep imagination of the economic institutions then transforming feudal notions of property into the new sense of exchangeable proprietorship that [Raymond] Williams has called the 'rentier's vision.'"[66] Scenic tourism as an expanding cultural institution was no doubt fueled by these concrete possibilities of ownership and upward social mobility.

Making land a commodity called for an attractive package. The very usage of words like "landscape," "prospect," and "scene" incorporates the basic principle of the picturesque: visually "packaging" land into compositional units, like paintings.[67] Taste, as Knight puts it in his poem *The Landscape,* will lead "the prying sight / To where component parts may best unite, / And form one beauteous, nicely blended whole, / To charm the eye and captivate the soul."[68] Knight is addressing fellow estate gardeners, but his preoccupation with form applies equally well to scenic tourism and underscores the continuity between the two practices. Gilpin proposes a new objective for travel: "examining the face of a country *by the rules of picturesque beauty:* opening the sources of those pleasures which are derived from the comparison."[69] The scenery seeker set off in pursuit of "that kind of beauty which *would look well in a picture,*" equipped with principles or guidelines concerning pictorial composition, light and shadow, color and texture.[70] Often tourists went equipped with a Claude glass, a concave mirror on a dark foil that reflected a scene over the viewer's shoulder, framed and mellowed like an old oil painting. This quaint device catered to scenic tourism's tendency to detach the viewer from the scene, and the scene, neatly packaged, from its surrounding environment. Such willed distance from the actual, particular place before the tourist's eyes was of course prototypical for the aesthetic subject.

This valued cultural practice declared its distance from material necessity, first of all, by demanding the investment of time and study in a painstakingly acquired familiarity with paintings. Seventeenth-century French and Italian traditions of landscape painting by such artists as Claude Lorrain, Salvator Rosa, Nicolas Poussin, and Gaspard Dughet were especially valued. Many works by these painters had been brought to England during decades of acquisitive connoisseurship; if they could not view paintings in the original, students of the picturesque should at least have access to them in the form of prints or engravings. Borrowing the technical jargon of the painter and art critic (the "fore-grounds, distances, and second distances – side-screens and perspectives – lights and shades" that Austen mocks in *Northanger Abbey)*, the tourist then faced the task of bringing real places into line with the formal ideals abstracted from painting.[71]

This active, even aggressive procedure enacted the symbolic appropriation that was the tourist's substitute for the landscape gardener's actual ownership.[72] The picturesque had in common with landscape gardening the mentality of the "improver," always trying to determine "what would amend the composition; how little is wanting to reduce it to the rules of our art."[73] Of the town of Newport Gilpin comments hopefully, "A few slight alterations would make it picturesque."[74] The picturesque tourist was encouraged to see and sketch, not what was in front of him, but what made the most interesting scene. Latitude was permitted in moving, deleting, and even adding a rock here, a tree there. Essential to this mode of perception was the opportunity to compare different places or views. Of course, such mobility was only available to those with the means and motivation for travel, unlike most of the population at this time. At Tintern Abbey improvement takes a violent turn. Disgusted by overly regular gables, Gilpin observes, "A mallet judiciously used (but who durst use it?) might be of service in fracturing some of them" to achieve picturesque irregularity (49). This famous fantasy of the mild-mannered cleric betrays the destructive undercurrent in his nomadic version of the picturesque – a subversive strain coexisting uneasily with its dominant conservative tendency.[75]

The net effect of this complicated apparatus of perceptual mediation was to detach the viewer from the concrete particularity of the place he saw. The aesthetics of the picturesque thus achieves, by a different route, an effect quite similar to that of Reynolds' anathema on the detail. Like the *Discourses*, picturesque tourism de-particularizes the aesthetic object in order to assert the subject's distance from those social groups associated with the senses and their disorderly desires: the laboring classes and women. When later theories of the picturesque like that of Uvedale Price focus on eccentric objects, they do so (as W. J. Hipple points out) only to insist on such objects' aesthetic qualities of shape, texture, and color taken "abstractly from the concretes in which they occur."[76]

It should also be evident by now how much the picturesque has in common with aesthetic disinterestedness. Both are modes of contemplation divested of any stake in the existence of a particular object. The picturesque takes disinterested contemplation out of the picture gallery and on the road. Here too we have a carefully delimited mode of perception that distances the subject from the practical implications of what he sees. One especially important way in which picturesque aesthetics displays disinterestedness is in its refusal to recognize, in looking at land, the ways the topography of a specific place reflects the material needs of its inhabitants, the people living on and from it. Land shaped by people and serving their needs through agriculture, or even industry, is not the stuff of picturesque description. The picturesque keeps its distance from this kind of necessity; in Malcolm Andrews' phrase, it is "aggressively anti-utilitarian" and specifically "anti-georgic."[77] It emphasizes purely visual qualities and deemphasizes associated ideas of any kind, whether intellectual, emotional, historical or moral. In effect, scenic tourism fostered the "moral agnosticism" that Bourdieu attributes to any aesthetic attitude.[78]

The clergyman Gilpin openly confesses the amorality of the picturesque. Excessive traces of human habitation, industry, or commerce are undesirable intrusions on a picturesque scene. An isolated cottage or hamlet may add a certain charm, "but when houses are scattered through every part, the moral sense can never make a convert of the picturesque eye" (12). Social agendas like sheltering the lower orders are extrinsic to picturesque aesthetics; cultivation too is undesirable. "Furrowed-lands, and waving-corn, however charming in pastoral poetry, are ill-accommodated to painting. The painter never desires the hand of art to touch his grounds," Gilpin declares with a peculiar logic, his associations ranging from poetry to painting while studiously ignoring the extra-aesthetic value of plowed and planted fields (46). Elsewhere he observes the effect of charcoal smoke which, "issuing from the sides of the hills, and spreading its thin veil over a part of them, beautifully breaks their lines, and unites them with the sky" (22). He aestheticizes a trace of grimy human industry until its source is quite forgotten. In tour after tour, imposing "the rules of our art" on the unruly idiosyncrasies of what he actually sees, Gilpin elides materially conditioned meaning from the English countryside. Choosing or producing landscapes innocent of the traces of contemporary civilization and economic struggle, he uncouples aesthetic perception from the practical use value of land.

Gilpin's doctrine on human figures in a landscape is in keeping with both the resolutely formal attitude of picturesque vision and its anti-utilitarian bias. Since their primary concern is with landscape, the picturesque tourists and amateur landscape artists whom he addresses cannot afford to divide their attention by focusing too closely on human beings. These are and must remain "mere / Appendages, & under-parts" of the composition: staffage, accessories or ornaments, as carefully grouped as the cows, horses, and goats that served the same formal functions. These were three: "to characterize a scene, to give it life and animation, and lastly they often prove a mechanical necessity" to break harsh lines, give an idea of scale, or lead the eye along a path or toward the horizon. Figures are viewed from a distance, with a casual eye. Hence they need not and should not be portrayed with anatomical exactness or precise attention to facial expression: "we merely consider general shapes, dresses, groups, and occupations." Lastly, people should preferably not be shown in productive interchange with the land. Work is unpicturesque. "Milk-maids…ploughmen, reapers, and all peasants *engaged in their several professions*, we disallow…in the scenes we here characterize, they are valued, for what in real life they are despised – loitering idly about, without employment. In wild, & desert scenes, we are best pleased with banditti-soldiers…and such figures, as coalesce in idea with the scenes, in which we place them."[79] Readers of Ann Radcliffe will recall the ubiquitous dancing peasants and lurking banditti that ornament the margins of her novels in homage to Gilpin.

The ideological implications of positioning human beings as faceless ornaments in a landscape are not far to seek. Aesthetic distance reinforced the social distance that was becoming more visibly marked in the English countryside, giving genteel tourists an appealing way to visualize their separateness from the laboring-class figures in the landscape.[80] Landowners in this period withdrew from public view behind the wrought-iron palings of their mansions, well defended from trespassers and poachers and insulated from villagers by acres of tastefully landscaped grounds.[81] Country-house architecture added back stairs and separate servants' quarters to make servants' distasteful work and vulgar persons increasingly invisible. The aesthetics of the picturesque gave middle-class tourists an analogous means of affirming their distance from vulgarity. Eighteenth-century landscape aesthetics, Fabricant remarks, gave the perceiver "a definite 'frame' in every sense (a framework of values, a frame of reference) which comprehended within its bounds certain kinds of objects, arranged in particular configurations, while it exiled others to a precarious and nebulous existence beyond the frame, where things became not only invisible but in a very real sense inconceivable as well."[82]

The other thing made inconceivable by the picturesque is people's practical connection to the land they live on and from. By declaring work and its traces unaesthetic, this way of seeing refuses to recognize the use value of land to its inhabitants. This aligns the tourist with the proprietorial classes' increasing refusal to acknowledge or take responsibility for agricultural laborers' struggles during rural Britain's momentous transformation from a "moral economy" — the bonds of mutual obligation between landowners and their dependents — to an agricultural capitalism that connected employers and laborers only through a cash nexus and an inadequate system of poor relief. While enclosure ended grazing or gardening on common lands as supplemental forms of subsistence, cash-hungry proprietors (who spent more and more time in London, less and less in the country) rack-rented and evicted with growing frequency, reducing tenant farmers to day laborers or forcing them to seek their fortunes among the rapidly growing urban working class.[83] Picturesque aesthetics' carefully deindividualized treatment of human figures needs to be understood within this changing social landscape.

Although the picturesque was the predominant aesthetic category

7. S. Alken, aquatint, "Corfe Castle." William Maton, *Observations relative chiefly to the Natural History, Picturesque Scenery, and Antiquities of the Western Counties of England made in the years 1794 and 1796* (1797). Picturesque composition with laboring-class figures, not laboring.

in scenic tourism, it was not the only one. I mentioned in the Introduction women writers' attraction to the sublime, and their opportunistic juxtapositions or combinations of the two categories. Possibilities for their convergence are best illustrated by one scenic feature highly prized by the later eighteenth century, the ruin. The ruined castle or abbey evoked from about the 1740s sentimental responses, the ubiquitous "pleasing melancholy" or "agreeable horror." This emerging taste for ruins (signaling the erosion of British intellectuals' confident neoclassicism) came to be linked after 1757 to the Burkean sublime. Malcolm Andrews usefully classifies the period's wide-ranging responses to ruins under five major rubrics: sentimental, antiquarian, aesthetic, moral, and political.[84] Burke's description of an instinctive aesthetic response to a vast, shadowy, craggy edifice full of obscure recesses incorporated sentimental reactions while moving away from the associationist ranges of response, the moral – the ruin as *memento mori*, symbol of the Vanity of Human Wishes – and especially the political, ruins as symbols of England's liberation from feudalism, popery, and superstition. As a feature in a landscape, the ruin could work at two levels. Its formal features of irregularity in outline and texture (aided by moss and vines, the agents of its return to nature) perfectly answered the criteria of picturesque composition. But affective responses to the ruin's combination of sublimity and decay could also contribute to the mood of a scene, diffusing the atmosphere or "effect" that was the key to a landscape's unity.[85]

Moral and political responses to ruins persisted throughout the century (as Helen Maria Williams' treatment of the Bastille will testify). The increasing prevalence of aesthetic response, however, is consistent with Alan Liu's closely argued interpretation of the history of the picturesque as, first of all, a forgetting of history. The classic seventeenth-century landscapes of Claude Lorrain, so prized in eighteenth-century England, contain "motives" – figures that evoke historical, mythological, or religious narratives. Lorrain's paintings are characterized by the much-admired quality of repose, an emotional tone or atmosphere of arrest, stasis, otherworldly stillness, arising, Liu speculates, from an aversion to post-Reformation religious conflict. Protestant England adapted Lorrain's repose, his hypostatization of form, to a non-narrative mode of representing landscape. Forgetting the stories, painters, theorists, tourists, and poets focused on topographical motifs (like

Lorrain's famous bridge in the middle distance) and effects like roughness, intricacy, and variety. Picturesque landscape, in other words, elides or sublates the conflicting interests of history in favor of pure form. The picturesque and the sublime collude to aestheticize the exemplary reabsorption of history into nature that is the architectural ruin. But as Liu insists, "If form arrests motive within the frame of a literary or pictorial text, there must be a larger, cultural context motivating and supervising the arrest."[86]

THE PARADOX OF THE FEMALE PICTURESQUE

Let us test this hypothesis on a picturesque tour written by a woman: Ann Radcliffe's *Journey made in the Summer of 1794 through Holland and the Western Frontier of Germany*. The cultural context of gender is the primary focus of my study. We have examined the ways in which texts of mainstream aesthetic theory distance their subject from the concrete particulars of the body and the material world. These are symbolically linked to social groups denied the privilege of aesthetic judgment: the laboring classes, non-Europeans, and women. But the middle-class woman has an ambiguous place in this conceptual scheme. Excluded by her gender, she is nonetheless entitled by her class to a membership, if liminal, in the tasteful elite. Before examining a woman writer's bid for her share in landscape aesthetics' authority and prestige, we must pause to consider a further complication in women's relationship to aesthetics. This concerns the "culture of sensibility," in G. J. Barker-Benfield's phrase – a culture (or cult) increasingly prevalent in late eighteenth-century Britain. Barker-Benfield has traced the elaborately nuanced gendering of sensibility through the century. This powerful nexus of discourses and practices opened a potential justification for women to lay claim, despite the powerful structure of exclusion I have discussed, to the privilege of the aesthetic subject.

Of course, sensibility shares with aesthetics its genesis in sense. The empiricist philosophy of Locke and Hume, making the senses the fountain of knowledge, supports the high value that both these discourses placed on sense experience. Scientific research on the nervous system suggested that women's nerves or "fibers" – along with those of male artists and intellectuals – were more delicate than ordinary men's, legitimating women's claim to the refined sensibility or taste that was increasingly prized (but also making them supposedly more prone to nervous disorders).[87] Hume, for example, asserts that "women, who have more delicate passions than men, have also a more delicate taste of the ornaments of life, of dress, equipage, and the ordinary decencies of behaviour." The aesthetic, understood in its broadest sense, could encompass not only fine art, but also self-adornment, manners and mores, the social graces of everyday life.[88] This goes along with the Scottish Enlightenment commonplace that the company of women civilizes men, reforms their manners, and improves the quality of public life. Heterosocial mingling was believed essential to the progress of civilization.

Women's finer nerves could make them more moral than men, because less prone to excess; on the other hand, they lacked men's firmness or self-command. Conversely, too much softening through sensibility put men in danger of effeminacy. Thinkers from Shaftesbury to Adam Smith worried over a finely calibrated "gender gauge," seeking to balance sensitivity with strength in a troubled redefinition of masculinity; "masculine" qualities retained pride of place in the hierarchy of virtues (recall Smith's dismissal of women as too fixated on particulars to achieve impartiality), but an array of moral-aesthetic attributes under the rubric of sensibility became indispensable auxiliaries. To the extent that sensibility encompassed the aesthetic capacities of taste, delicacy, and refinement, the aesthetic thus took on an ambiguously feminine gender.[89] This entire range of associations potentially contravenes the powerful discursive structure I have called denial of the particular, which constructs the aesthetic subject as gentleman through a process of exclusion or differentiation. Women writers like Radcliffe, Helen Maria Williams, and Mary Wollstonecraft, aiming to make the language of aesthetics their own, found support in the differently gendered but intersecting discourse of sensibility.

Middle-class women's everyday duties gave them another kind of connection to the aesthetic domain. The ongoing economic shift away from the self-sufficient household economy entailed a shift in women's primary activities from production to consumption.[90] Their increasing responsibility for choosing commodities to satisfy home demand, the backbone of eighteenth-century economic growth, was another way in which women became identified with taste, beginning at the literal level of "groceries." Upwardly mobile dietary preferences for white bread, sugar, tea, coffee, and chocolate displayed a family's social standing on its dining table. The domestic space of the home became an increasingly feminized locus of consumption and display. The material objects accumulating in domestic space, from furnishings and dishes to fashionable clothes and decorations, were invested with emotion coded as sensibility or taste. Manufacturers like Josiah Wedgwood and Matthew Boulton were certainly aware of women's tastes and the changing fashions that fed them. They had to be; women presided over the aesthetic decisions – everyday judgments of taste – that gave the household its social, emotional, and moral tone.[91]

The leisured wife, herself a family status symbol, marker of upward mobility, occupied her time with symbolic practices. Many of these fall under the umbrella of the aesthetic: not only home decoration, including needlework, japanning, and related crafts, but also the other "accomplishments" that were such a prominent (and controversial) part of women's education, such as music and drawing. Self-adornment was a time-consuming and much-satirized feature of privileged women's daily routine (witness Belinda's toilet or the less savory self-fashioning of Swift's Celia and Corinna). Laura Brown has discussed the importance of the upper-class female body as aesthetic icon of empire, displaying the luxuries brought from the ends of the earth to bedeck her.[92] Mary Wortley Montagu's letters reveal the potential for conflict between woman's conventional role as aesthetic object and the potential for power and self-expression opened by women's access, even if dubious and partial, to the position of the aesthetic subject.

Women's rapidly spreading literacy extended their participation in aesthetic practices to reading and writing sentimental fiction and scenic tours. Radcliffe's novels, for example, present their heroines as paragons of sensibility and taste. We meet Emily St. Aubert of *The Mysteries of Udolpho* in her room with "her books, her drawings, her musical instruments, with some favourite birds and plants. Here she usually exercised herself in elegant arts, cultivated only because they were congenial to her taste." Outside her window, of course, is the first of the novel's numberless picturesque views. Radcliffe was prominent among the women authors who worked to assimilate taste to sensibility "as the expression of women's literate and consumer culture. Sentimental fiction held up a specific range of objects with implicit aesthetic value: artfully produced informal and irregular gardens, wild landscapes, melancholy poetry, romance, the poetry of Ossian or paintings of Salvator Rosa, Gothicism, peasants, and banditti…Like sensibility, 'taste' expressed distinction, not only from 'the world' but above 'the vulgar.'"[93] One polemical function that taste assumed in the context of women's leisure activities was to help restrain their pursuit of "outdoor" consumer pleasures, from shopping and visiting to opera, gambling, and masquerades. The language of sensibility and taste gave an important channel to the profound ambivalence of British culture's response to consumer capitalism. A delicate taste could supposedly discipline or spiritualize excessively worldly consumerism – though even the most refined taste often ironically depended on the production and distribution of commodities, like novels or scenic tours.[94] Both tourism and writing for publication took women into the public realm in potentially transgressive ways. Sensibility and taste helped legitimize a woman like Radcliffe in her pursuit of these dubious endeavors.

We have seen how the discourse and practice of landscape aesthetics "packaged" the countryside, negotiating between aesthetic distance and appropriative desire. As scenic tourism inscribed disinterestedness on the landscape, constructing scenes through its process of detachment from the material specificity of land and people's practical connection to it, one thing that was elided (as Liu makes clear) was the unruly contingency of history. In Radcliffe's *Journey* the traces of history return to disrupt the serene aestheticized surface of the travelogue. Radcliffe's expansive and uneven narrative of her Continental excursion combines elements of the report on manners and conditions abroad with the genre of the picturesque tour as popularized by Gilpin and others. Manners and conditions prevail in scenically unrewarding regions like Holland, while Germany, especially the Rhineland, inspires elaborately aestheticized landscape descriptions. Along the Rhine Radcliffe and her husband also encounter more frequent traces of the ongoing war between Austria and its allies (including England) and the revolutionary French. The timing of their picturesque tour may seem strange given the French army's ongoing occupation of the east bank of the Rhine (the allies continued to hold the west bank). No major battles took place in the vicinity that summer, though skirmishes were frequent. Radcliffe reports that they went equipped with a map of military positions.[95]

Her descriptions of picturesque and sublime scenery, however, ignore such practical considerations. This description of castles on the Rhine combines panoramic pictorial composition with the affective contribution of the ruin to dehistoricize scenic Nature.

The Rhine no where, perhaps, presents grander objects either of nature, or of art, than in the northern perspective from St. Goar. There, expanding with a bold sweep, the river exhibits, at one coup d'oeil, on its mountainous shores, six fortresses or towns, many of them placed in the most wild and tremendous situations; their antient and gloomy structures giving ideas of the sullen tyranny of former times. The height and fantastic shapes of the rocks, upon which they are perched, or by which they are overhung, and the width and rapidity of the river, that, unchanged by the vicissitudes of ages and the contentions on its shores, has rolled at their feet, while generations, that made its mountains roar, have passed away into the silence of eternity, – these were objects, which, combined, formed one of the sublimest scenes we had viewed. (305)

Form comes to the fore in the pictorial delineation of river and cliffs through height, breadth, "bold sweep" and "fantastic shapes." Wildness and gloom join to diffuse an atmosphere of sublimity, while the historical referents of these feelings are carefully generalized or distanced. "Sullen tyranny" hints at a political response to the ruins, only to displace it into a distant past (not a safe assumption in eighteenth-century Germany, as Radcliffe knew). Nature diverts our attention from history – aesthetics leads us away from politics – in a powerful ideological pattern so familiar that it still rings like a platitude.[96]

Human contentions do not stay silent, however. They reassert themselves, as the Radcliffes travel down the Rhine, in an almost eerie alternation with stylized scenic descriptions. Radcliffe records the sights of war in language both realistic – conscious of material detail – and sympathetically engaged.[97] Here she describes hospital wagons full of wounded soldiers in Cologne:

They were all uncovered, so that the emaciated figures and ghastly countenances of the soldiers, laid out upon straw in each, were exposed to the rays of a burning sun, as well as to the fruitless pity of passengers; and, as the carriages had no springs, it seemed as if these half-sacrificed victims to war would expire before they could be drawn over the rugged pavement of Cologne. Any person, who had once witnessed such a sight, would know how to estimate the glories of war. (327–28)

She observantly notes not only the disturbing effects of war on the bodies of the "half-sacrificed victims," but their painful interaction with their physical surroundings: the sun burns, the cobblestones jolt the wagons. But on the same page the text recovers its composure. Its surface closes like still waters over the momentary disturbance as Radcliffe goes on to praise the "venerable and picturesque character" of the city of Cologne viewed from the water.

As the travelers move south the traces of war remain obtrusive. In Mainz they view the damage from the siege of 1793. The Elector's palace is being used as a barracks and hospital, and Radcliffe glimpses "half-dressed soldiers" in its windows (182). Nearby Oppenheim is scarred by much earlier conflicts: "Louis the Fourteenth's fury has converted it from a populous city into little more than a picturesque ruin" (236). Here violence and the picturesque manifest an uncommented relation (we think of Gilpin's mallet): present scenic attractions result from past battles. The Radcliffes ride along, passing more mountains, castles, and quaintly costumed peasants. At one point they are within earshot of a battle (240). Other times they expect to hear gunfire but do not; the peasants go on cutting their harvest, and "nothing but the continuance of patroles and convoys reminded us of our nearness to the war" (268). One day at dinner they are told that the French have tried to cross the Rhine fifteen miles upstream. Marching Austrian battalions keep them awake all night in their inn; the blare of military music at dawn seems "like a dream" (271).

Shortly after this rough night appears a long description memorializing Radcliffe's ride along the Bergstrasse:

Our way lay along the base of these steeps, during the whole day; and as we drew nearer to Switzerland, their height became still more stupendous, and the mountains of Alsace seemed advancing to meet them in the long perspective; the plains between, through which the Rhine gleamed in long sweeps, appeared to be entirely covered with corn, and in the nearer scene joyous groups were loading the waggons with the harvest. An harvest of another kind was ripening among the lower rocks of the Bergstrasse, where the light green of the vines enlivened every cliff, and sometimes overspread the ruinous walls of what had once been fortresses. We passed many villages, shaded with noble trees...their spacious street generally opening to the grandeur of the mountain vista, that extended to the south. In these landscapes the peasant girl, in the simple dress of the country, and balancing on her large straw hat an harvest keg, was a very picturesque figure. (272–73)

Again formal features dominate Radcliffe's presentation as she works with the "long perspective" between the mountains, artfully using color and contrast, light and shade, to compose her scene. Appealingly overgrown ruins ornament the background; carefully grouped human figures, the foreground. Radcliffe lets the peasants work, despite Gilpin's preference to exclude work from the picturesque scene, but she keeps their figures distanced and deindividualized. Their only expression is an attributed joy at the harvest – part of a natural cycle that transcends ephemeral events like the war, just as the peasant girl in her country costume embodies timeless class and ethnic stereotypes, rather than denoting a historical individual living in an actual place. How joyous, if we think about it, are these laborers likely to be with a French invasion on the horizon? Their joy is as purely conventional as that of the dancing peasants in Radcliffe's fiction. It underscores the disjunction in *A Journey* between the ahistorical idylls dictated by the discourse of scenic tourism and the traces of historical conflict that, banished from set-piece descriptions like this one, return as incongruous breaks in the travelogue's placid tone.

To give Radcliffe her due, she is not insensitive to the material condition of Germany's laboring classes. Traveling through Prussia she describes the poor in a different register, attributing their misery to "arbitrary" government: "From almost every cluster of huts barefooted children run out to beg, and ten or a dozen stand at every gate, nearly throwing themselves under the wheels to catch your money, which, every now and then, the bigger seize from the less" (85). Even in the wine country near the Rhine the peasants' situation is, she acknowledges, bleak. Significantly, she couches her comment in terms that directly connect the inhabitants' means of subsistence, their practical relation to the land, with her own pleasure in viewing it: "the bounteousness of nature to the country is very little felt by the body of the inhabitants...How much is the delight of looking upon plenteousness lessened by the belief, that it supplies the means of excess to a few, but denies those of competence to many!" (152–53). To suggest a friction between the "delight of looking" and the suffering of the laboring class flies in the face of mainstream landscape aesthetics' concern to distance the viewer from the scene, and especially from the figures in the landscape.

This comment is the exception amid *A Journey's* hundreds of pages of "interesting pictures" (157). I read it, however, as beginning to articulate the disjunction that my hindsight can recognize between aesthetic discourse and the practical traces of history in the making. Passing through "Wetteravia," the domain of the Elector of Treves (a region marked by "misery and savageness"), Radcliffe again seems obliquely to question the politics of aesthetic distance. "These are the mountains of Wetteravia, the boundaries of many a former and far-seen prospect, then picturesque, sublime, or graceful, but now desolate, shaggy, and almost hideous; as in life, that, which is so grand as to charm at a distance, is often found to be forlorn, disgustful and comfortless by those, who approach it" (170). Do we hear, couched in the eighteenth-century moralist's stately generalities and balanced antitheses, an incipient demystification of aesthetics' reliance on distance to generate charm and erase disgrace? Can we sense in the awkward transitions and sometimes almost comic incongruities of Radcliffe's travelogue the difficulty of sustaining that distance for a writer who lacked the implied qualifications of the aesthetic subject as Man of Taste? Her membership in England's wealthy, literate classes would seem to authorize her aesthetic pronouncements, but as a woman she was implicated in the complex of meanings that aesthetic discourse needed to exclude. Feminine gender was presumed "particular" in relation to the masculine universal; British women's everyday lives were certainly limited by the fact of their gender. This helps us recognize the awkward breaks and seeming incongruities in Radcliffe's text, and those of her contemporaries, as oblique means of questioning the assumed mental freedom or spurious universality of the aesthetic attitude.

CHAPTER 4

Helen Maria Williams' revolutionary landscapes

> Posterity...will contemplate the revolution in the same manner as we gaze at a sublime landscape, of which the general effect is great and noble, and where some little points of asperity, some minute deformities, are lost in the overwhelming majesty of the whole.[1]

Helen Maria Williams arrived in France in July 1790, just in time to witness the Festival of the Federation on the anniversary of the storming of the Bastille. She was twenty-eight, already a published poet and novelist; she would live in France for most of the rest of her life. During the next turbulent six years, Williams published eight volumes of letters reporting on the French Revolution to British readers. They gained considerable circulation and were excerpted in magazines and miscellanies. According to Robert D. Mayo, she was "for more than ten years the principal interpreter and popular spokesman [*sic*] for political changes in the neighboring republic."[2] In her letters two seemingly disparate 1790s phenomena converge: the fashionable "rage" for landscape, which peaked during this decade, and the historic raging of the Revolution. An open advocate of revolutionary ideals, Williams was also immersed in the language of landscape aesthetics. Landscape description insistently recurs as a metaphor and structuring principle throughout her letters, which mobilize aestheticized nature in a sustained if increasingly strained effort to make sense of the historic events in France and naturalize them for British readers.

Putting aesthetics in the service of politics clearly transgresses the autonomy of the aesthetic domain, its separation from practical and political interests, posited by the dominant strain of eighteenth-century aesthetic theory and inscribed on the face of the country by the conventions of landscape aesthetics. Unlike

Radcliffe's *Journey through Holland and Germany*, with its uneasy disjunction between aesthetic and practical, scenic description and social observation, Williams' letters confidently take aesthetics' political relevance for granted. She shares this assumption with her friend and fellow radical, Mary Wollstonecraft, and with another unlikely bedfellow, Edmund Burke, the influential aesthetician and statesman against whose conservative politics both women fought. Burke's politics, as Wollstonecraft points out in *A Vindication of the Rights of Men*, were thoroughly aestheticized. His aesthetics of the beautiful and sublime turns on hierarchical relations of power, a feature Radcliffe's *Mysteries of Udolpho* exploits, as we will see. *Reflections on the Revolution in France* is informed by the aesthetic categories its author had expounded decades before; even more fundamentally, it is shaped by the conviction that aesthetic response is an integral and desirable component of political life. Burke was isolated in these beliefs from most other aestheticians of his day. It is ironic that he shared them with women whose politics he found abhorrent.

Helen Maria Williams lived in Paris in close contact with those who shaped the Revolution. She hosted a salon attended by leading deputies of the National Assembly, both Girondins and pre-radical Jacobins. A list of her intimates is a roll of revolutionary leaders, including Vergniaud, Grégoire, Barère (later "lacquey of Robespierre") and the Rolands, as well as British republicans and expatriates including Paine, Wollstonecraft, Thomas Christie, and John Hurford Stone. She visited Madame Roland in prison and eulogized her after her execution. Many other friends of Williams' would lose their heads; she came close to losing her own when Robespierre learned that she had published criticisms of him in England (she fled to Switzerland in June 1794, just before his fall). M. Ray Adams avers that "no Englishman, except Thomas Paine, ran as great a risk of the guillotine as she."[3] Her politics, as well as her long-lasting collaboration and cohabitation with Stone, who was indicted for treason in connection with plans for a French invasion of Britain, made her ripe for libel by anti-Jacobins even as she was hounded out of France as a counterrevolutionary.[4]

Twentieth-century critics have not taken Williams as seriously as did the Jacobins and anti-Jacobins. Until recently her letters were read as stereotypically feminine, sentimental, politically naive, and historically inaccurate.[5] Analyses by Mary Favret and Matthew

Bray break away from this dismissive pattern to praise Williams' political daring and literary innovation.[6] I aim to amplify their tribute, but also to test the limits of Williams' revolutionary vision, by paying careful attention to her changing deployment of aesthetic discourse. As we chart through these copious volumes the shifting relation between revolutionary politics and the aestheti-cized "nature" of scenic tourism, we can begin to take the measure of just how far this courageous woman of letters could and could not go in her departure from the mainstream political and cultural values of her nation and class. Like the rest of the women writers I will discuss – and like Gilpin, the prototypical picturesque tourist – Williams was middle-class: privileged by comparison with the majority of Britons, yet by no means a member of the ruling elite. Though she enthusiastically supported France's bourgeois revolu-tionaries, the Girondins, in their fight against aristocratic privilege, she eventually came to reject the Revolution's more radical Jacobin turn (as did all but the most hard-core British sympathizers). In Williams' case this suspicion seems driven by visceral suspicion of the proletarian *sans-culottes* as well as principled condemnation of their leaders' violent tactics. The vicissitudes of her ambitious project can teach us a great deal about the possibilities and limits of a middle-class woman's difficult relation both to the language of aesthetics, with its conservative masculine bias, and to national revolution.

The French revolutionaries' preoccupation with language and symbolism is well known. From modes of dress to forms of address, from the calendar to playing cards, revolution meant reinventing and renaming the world. Leaders gave a high priority to the design of the festivals and monuments that would commemorate the Revolution's achievements and pass on its lessons. Lynn Hunt has called attention to the flood of discourse – newspapers and broad-sides as well as orations, plays, festivals, political clubs, and con-versations – that accompanied the dissolution of the French state.[7] Recent historiography attaches increasing significance to such discursive and symbolic manifestations of revolution. Historians have rejected interpretations that privilege a socioeconomic "base" as the determining instance to recognize political action as pivotal to the course of the Revolution. Keith Baker locates political action precisely within political discourse: politics is "about making claims...the activity through which individuals and groups in any society articulate, negotiate, implement, and enforce the competing claims they make upon one another and upon the whole. Political culture is, in this sense, the set of discourses or symbolic practices by which these claims are made." Social interests are discursively defined and contested in a political arena archaeologically layered with heterogeneous languages and symbols. These coexist in every-day life and in individuals' consciousness, superimposed or intersecting in combinations that are unpredictable and finally uncontrollable.[8]

A prominent feature of the political culture of the revolutionary period, on both sides of the Channel, was the rhetorical deploy-ment of various complementary and competing versions of "Nature." Such appeals characterized both revolutionary and counterrevolutionary positions. Perhaps the most bizarre was the Egyptian-style statue of Nature erected for the Festival of Republican Reunion, held August 10, 1793, her breasts gushing water that was ceremoniously quaffed by revolutionary officials. The revolutionary calendar took advantage of the happy accident that the Republic was declared on the precise day of the autumnal equinox to lend political change the inevitability of celestial motion. Revolutionary festivals incorporated pastoral elements, fol-lowing Rousseau's call to abandon the theater for the great out-doors; they built artificial mountains and decked them in a "vegetal exuberance" that did away with the historically saturated space of the city as it strove to erase history itself and recapture the state of nature as *tabula rasa,* a zero point for the utopian future of Revolution secured.[9]

British observers of the Revolution, whether sympathetic or fear-ful, did not hesitate to harness nature to their respective political agendas. We think of Burke's famous contrast between an organi-cally conceived British constitution and the mechanical rationalism of the revolutionaries (years before their large-scale deployment of the guillotine, the ultimate revolutionary machine).[10] He gives "our frame of polity the image of a relation in blood," knitted together by natural instincts and affections, to naturalize unequal property and social hierarchy. The French become unnatural children of their good king-father.[11] For other British observers, the Revolution, epitomized by the storming of the Bastille, unleashed long-suppressed natural forces as fearsome as those that drove London's Gordon Riots in 1780. Images of tempests or hurricanes conveyed this destructiveness, but could also mask the more disturbing human face of revolutionary violence.[12]

Early sympathizers with Revolution, by contrast, conveyed their sense of regeneration in natural metaphors like Wordsworth's blissful dawn or Thomas Paine's spring. Paine's Revolution, like Rousseau's, partakes of a pastoral nature viewed through the aesthetics of the beautiful. The final paragraph of *The Rights of Man* gives revolution the inevitability of seasonal cycles. Strolling in February, Paine casually plucks a twig and observes a swelling bud: "though the vegetable sleep will continue longer on some trees and plants than on others, and though some of them may not *blossom* for two or three years, all will be in leaf in the summer, except those which are *rotten*. What pace the political summer may keep with the natural, no human foresight can determine. It is, however, not difficult to perceive that the spring is begun."[13] Refuting Burke, Paine appropriates nature for republicanism, appealing to natural feelings in his turn and claiming equal natural rights and dignity for all. For him aristocracy is the unnatural "monster." Letitia Barbauld, too, aligns the metaphor of light or enlightenment with irresistible natural forces: "We appeal to the certain, sure operation of increasing light and knowledge, which it is no more in your power to stop, than to repel the tide with your naked hand, or to wither with your breath the genial influence of vegetation."[14]

Landscape aesthetics presented itself as an already well-elaborated discourse of nature. Eighteenth-century writings on the West Indies, like Janet Schaw's journal, turned aesthetics' cachet to the defense of colonial slavery. Helen Maria Williams set out to use aesthetics' rhetorical power to attack rather than defend an oppressive status quo. She was not the only writer to couch her impressions of Revolution in landscape metaphors, though none does it so extensively. Sir Samuel Romilly, for example, rhapsodizes in 1790 on "the bright prospect of universal freedom and universal peace...just *bursting on* [France's] *sight.*"[15] Mary Wollstonecraft's *Vindication of the Rights of Men* uses landscape aesthetics to comment on British politics. It becomes an example of everything that is wrong with English society, the callous attitude that Burke's conservative manifesto defends. The rich retreat to their tastefully landscaped estates, turning their backs on the poor and neglecting their social duty. "Every thing on the estate is cherished but man."[16] Wollstonecraft's condemnation of aesthetics as abetting social injustice suggests the difficulty Williams will face in turning this fundamentally conservative discourse to revolutionary ends. Her challenge is twofold. First, to legitimize the Revolution, she must legitimize herself as a female aesthetic subject in the face of aesthetics' marginalization of women. Furthermore, she is trying to put aesthetics in the service of an anti-hierarchical political vision running directly counter to the conservative politics in which it had its roots. Williams' means of meeting these challenges were canny and creative. Tracing the fate of landscape through her monumental reportage affords an unusual perspective on the cultural semiotics of revolution.

TOURING THE REVOLUTION

Williams' first two volumes of letters, covering the years 1790 and 1791, incorporate elements from the fashionable genre of the scenic tour. She conducts her readers through a landscape transformed by the Revolution; her letters package national renewal as a loose string of tourist attractions, focused by a series of scenes or tableaux that incorporate the aesthetic elements of ordered composition and artful lighting. Williams' persona – though deeply sympathetic, even enthusiastic toward the Revolution – retains an almost paradoxical detachment as she deliberately transmutes political sentiment into the terms of aesthetic emotion. A reflective passage sets forth the aesthetically grounded paradigm of historical contemplation that informs these early letters. "Posterity will not demand, contrary to what appears the law of our nature, 'universal good,' unmixed with 'partial evil'; but will contemplate the revolution in the same manner as we gaze at a sublime landscape, of which the general effect is great and noble, and where some little points of asperity, some minute deformities, are lost in the overwhelming majesty of the whole" (1.2.23). Williams' rhetoric applies aesthetic distance and the formal relation of part to whole to the ends of political persuasion, giving the spectacle of revolution the static grandeur of a well-composed painting. We can predict the trouble such a paradigm will have in accounting for the inevitable messiness of historical change, and especially revolution. "Minute deformities" will loom rather larger in subsequent volumes.

The first and most awe-inspiring sight to be seen is the Festival of the Federation, "the most sublime spectacle, which, perhaps, was ever represented on the theatre of this earth" (I.I.2). The term "spectacle," emphasizing the separation of observer from observed, is recurrent in Williams' revolutionary travelogue. "Half a million of people assembled at a spectacle, which furnished every image that can elevate the mind of man...which addressed itself at once to the imagination, the understanding, and the heart" (I.I.5–6). She presents herself as a model spectator for her readers' imitation: "it required but the common feelings of humanity, to become in that moment a citizen of the world...my heart caught with enthusiasm the general sympathy; my eyes were filled with tears" (I.I.14). As she enlists "the common feelings of humanity" under the banner of constitutional revolution, she insists on grounding the Festival's grip on the hearts and minds of its audience in the "admirable order" with which it is conducted (I.I.16).

The details of Williams' description repeatedly link this order – the painstaking artifice of its composition – with its ability to evoke emotional response. She carefully records the spatial configuration of the Champ de Mars: at one end the royal pavilion; in the middle the "Autel de la Patrie," flanked by priests with tricolor sashes; at the other end triumphal arches "adorned with emblems and allegorical figures" (I.I.8). Her description of the procession to the arena juxtaposes sentimental images of old men kneeling in the streets, "blessing God that they had lived to witness that happy moment," and mothers holding their infants aloft, with a two-page catalogue of the order of marching contingents, including groups of deputies from the departments "arranged alphabetically" (I.I.11).[17] We learn where each group sits or stands and by what protocol the national oath was taken. The description culminates with a carefully composed, painting-like tableau, complete with lighting effects. "At the moment the consecrated banners were displayed, the sun, which had been obscured by frequent showers in the course of the morning, burst forth; while the people lifted their eyes to heaven, and called upon the Deity to look down and witness the sacred engagement into which they entered" (I.I.13). Nature, God, and humanity collaborate to stage this emblematic moment, its cast of hundreds of thousands outdoing the most lavish history painting, freeze-framing the solemn joy of revolutionary commitment. Pictorial composition mediates between emotion and discipline.

This somewhat contradictory combination of emotional closeness with the aesthetic distance connoted by Williams' emphasis on order and form seems to be her way of negotiating the fundamental tension that Mona Ozouf has traced through the historiography of the revolutionary festival, from contemporary accounts to the twentieth century. Historians are divided between seeing orchestration and spontaneity, planning from above and unbridled release from below. Williams wants both. The crowd, she maintains, can be enthusiastic without being orgiastic. Their exuberance is not the dangerous, motiveless license portrayed by so many observers, beginning with Burke; it is both nobly motivated and safely contained by a disciplined revolutionary people.[18]

Aesthetics in its formative period functions for Williams in a way with which twentieth-century literary critics will be familiar. Accommodating ambiguity by subsuming it in formal unity, Williams neutralizes fears of the revolutionary crowd, her readers' as well as her own. Her formal devices endow the aesthetic object – the crowd – and the aesthetic subject – Williams herself, and, by extension, her reader – with a mutually mirroring unity as reassuring as it is fragile. The act of representation involves the willed production of a unified self whose artificially static relation to the unified spectacle is distant yet close, effervescently emotional yet safely controlled. The energy generated by holding opposites in tension is contained within the formal and psychological frame of aesthetic experience. Experimentally harnessing aesthetics in the service of politics, Williams confines the political impulses of the revolutionary populace within an ideologically colored means of representation. The affinity for order that governs her description of the Festival – and her choice of landscape as a predominant metaphor throughout her letters – links her to the social hierarchies that structured the language of aesthetics. The Revolution's relentless escalation would threaten both its spectacular unity and the buffering distance between spectator and crowd. We will see how the language of aesthetics holds up under the onslaught of history.

National celebration does not end with the crowd's dispersal from the Champ de Mars. The following Sunday evening Lafayette reviews the National Guard, followed by "a scene of general rejoicing." Again lighting effects are prominent in Williams' description: "The whole city was illuminated, and crowds of company filled the gardens of the Tuilleries, from which we saw the beautiful façade of the Louvre lighted in the most splendid

manner. In the Champs Elysées, where a fête was given to the
Deputies, innumerable lamps were hung from one row of trees to
another, and shed the most agreeable brilliance on those enchanting walks; where the exhilarated crowd danced and sung"
(1.1.19–20). Paris by night becomes a carefully lighted, static back-
drop for revolutionary festivity, incorporating elements of both
painting and theater. The centerpiece is that master symbol of
Revolution, the ruined Bastille, which Williams describes not once
but twice in the course of her tour: once under the rubric of each
aesthetic category, the picturesque and the sublime. Her general
approach to these categories is opportunistic, treating conceptual
boundaries loosely in order to mine them all for maximum rhetorical effect with the "pragmatic stylistics," or rhetorical opportunism,
that Julie Ellison has noted in Williams' political prose.[19] "The
French revolution is not only sublime in a general view, but is often
beautiful when considered in detail," she elsewhere asserts (1.2.22),
confounding Burke's insistence that the sublime and the beautiful
are mutually exclusive.

The Bastille – "the spectacle of all others the most interesting to
my feelings" – first appears in a curiously schematic urban picturesque. "The ruins of that execrable fortress were suddenly
transformed, as if with the wand of necromancy, into a scene of
beauty and of pleasure. The ground was covered with fresh clods
of grass, upon which young trees were placed in rows, and illuminated with a blaze of light. Here the minds of the people took a
higher tone of exultation than in the other scenes of festivity"
(1.1.21). Turf and saplings stand in for rural nature, complementing
the ruin, another standard element of the picturesque view. The
composition is unified by lighting, artificial rather than natural.
Williams lines up with pundits of the picturesque like Gilpin and
Radcliffe when she incorporates the ruin's traces of violence into a
"scene of beauty and of pleasure," elevating picturesque repose
with overtones of sublimity.

Her next visit to the Bastille dwells at greater length on sublime
violence. "Before I suffered my friends at Paris to conduct me
through the usual routine of convents, churches, and palaces," she
demands a full tour of this new attraction with its "horrid secrets":
hooks for securing shackles, "subterraneous cells" where skeletons
have been found "with irons still fastened on their decaying bones"
(1.1.22–24). These Gothic effects combine terror with fascination,

lurid emblems of revolution for a British readership used to fictional dungeons and chains.[20] Williams reshuffles aesthetic categories to present the Revolution as the transition from the false sublime of despotism to a picturesque idyll.

If the splendor of a despotic throne can only shine like the radiance of lightning, while all around is involved in gloom and horror, in the name of heaven let its baleful lustre be extinguished for ever. May no such strong contrast of light and shade again exist in the political system of France! but may the beams of liberty, like the beams of day, shed their benign influence on the cottage of the peasant, as well as on the palace of the monarch! May Liberty, which for so many ages past has taken pleasure in softening the evils of the bleak and rugged climates of the North...diffuse her blessings also on the genial land of France, and bid the husbandman rejoice under the shade of the olive and the vine! (1.1.25–26)

Again she works with light and shade, lending political concepts an aesthetic form as she abjures despotic chiaroscuro for the soft natural light of liberty. She enlists British patriotism by linking freedom to northern climes before marshaling a southern pastoral for the closing "scene of beauty and of pleasure," reminiscent of her pastoralized Bastille. Landscape metaphors anchor Williams' revolutionary travelogue; the prestige of aesthetic discourse casts an aura of legitimacy on her political agenda.

The nation's touristic topography undergoes a political transformation. Ancient monuments like cathedrals and royal tombs are displaced by the newly invented iconography of revolution. In France, Williams declares, "it is not what is *ancient*, but what is *modern*, that most powerfully engages attention" (1.1.104). At the Maison de Ville she contemplates *la lanterne*, the site of impromptu lynchings. She laments the violence. "But alas! where do the records of history point out a revolution unstained by some actions of barbarity?" (1.1.81). Versailles forms part of a moralistic photomontage as she imagines its image superimposed on the dungeons of the Bastille; the thought "prevented my being much dazzled by the splendour of this superb palace" (1.1.83). She views the bedchamber and balcony, sites of the "October days," the "memorable night when the *Poissardes* visited Versailles" to take the royal family back to Paris. Her narration of the events retains an edge of menace: the crowd's pikes, though bloody, hold bread rather than heads; they are "incensed" but easily mollified by Lafayette's tactful efforts (1.1.84–5).[21] A remark during a visit to the National Assembly epitomizes Williams' aesthetic rhetoric. The deputies' "tumultuous" meetings, their "impetuosity in debate," are of "little consequence," she remarks, "if the decrees which are passed are wise and beneficial, and the new constitution arises, like the beauty and order of nature, from the confusion of mingled elements" (1.1.44–45). The profound newness of these historic events calls for a cultural politics that can simultaneously mask and celebrate absolute innovation by assimilating it to nature's "beauty and order."

POLITICIZING THE PICTURESQUE

In her second volume of letters Williams leaves the capital for the countryside, the conventional milieu of scenic tourism. The grape harvest near Orleans inspires a verse epistle to her friend Dr. John Moore, another revolutionary sympathizer, in which Williams creatively reconfigures the standard pastoral–picturesque idyll (1.2.10–13). The epistle that Moore has written her from Wales (a standard destination for picturesque tourists) describes the "landscapes of my native isle" (line 4) to the homesick expatriate:

> Her cultur'd meadows, and her lavish shades,
> Her winding rivers, and her verdant glades;
> …[W]here frowning on the flood below,
> The rough Welsh mountain lifts its craggy brow;
> Where nature throws aside her softer charms,
> And with sublimer views the bosom warms. (lines 5–10)

Moore's familiar descriptive vocabulary, from "verdant" to "craggy," delivers a composition artfully blending picturesque and sublime, but devoid of human life. The Loire Valley that Williams goes on to describe is full of people, a "joyful band" of harvesters. She departs from Gilpin's stricter picturesque by portraying them at their labor, as does Radcliffe's *Journey*. Even less conventional is the emphatically human-centered character of her scene.

Figures in picturesque landscape are typically peripheral, faceless, grouped as carefully as trees or cattle, and included solely as ornaments. These harvesters, by contrast, have distinct subjectivities. They show and satisfy their needs, from the most basic (a "gay meal" after a morning's work, line 24) to less tangible needs for information and self-respect. Her third stanza presents the Revolution from the agricultural laborer's point of view.

> Delightful land! Ah, now with gen'ral voice
> Thy village sons and daughters may rejoice.
> Thy happy peasant, now no more a slave,
> Forbad to taste one good that nature gave,
> Views with the anguish of indignant pain
> The bounteous harvest spread for him in vain.
> Oppression's cruel hand shall dare no more
> To seize with iron gripe his scanty store;
> And from his famish'd infants wring those spoils,
> The hard-earn'd produce of his useful toils;
> For now on Gallia's plain the peasant knows
> Those equal rights impartial Heav'n bestows.
> He now, by freedom's ray illumin'd, taught
> Some self-respect, some energy of thought,
> Discerns the blessings that to all belong,
> And lives to guard his humble shed from wrong. (lines 27–42)

Here we have another before-and-after picture, like the one Williams had painted of the Bastille. She contrasts the pre-revolutionary peasant's "anguish" with his new self-awareness. He "knows...equal rights" and "discerns...blessings"; members of the laboring classes take the initiative in her active verbs. The conventional allegory of "freedom's ray," the "spreading light" or "philosophic day" of liberty (lines 45, 48), contrasted with the "night" of despotism, gains added significance in her aesthetic context. Lighting is indispensable to the aesthetics of the picturesque; Williams' rhetorical deployment of the language of aesthetics charges even this most seemingly abstract of formal elements with political meaning. Her human-centered landscape foregrounds the practical connection between land and its working inhabitants, flouting picturesque convention's resolute denial of particular, practical interests – deliberately transgressing the conceptual boundary between aesthetic and practical. We will see both Mary Wollstonecraft and Dorothy Wordsworth use similar tactics as they rewrite the language of landscape aesthetics.

Williams goes on to reject another treasured element of picturesque convention, the pleasure of ruins. Picturesque gardeners and tourists favored ruins as a compositional element with formal qualities of irregularity and shadowiness, as well as melancholy associations that lent atmosphere to a scene. Burke's

Reflections on the Revolution, however, brought back the political associations that his treatise on the sublime and beautiful had held at a distance in favor of intuitive response. Throughout his attack on the Revolution, the ancient edifice embodies the tradition or "precedent" his conservative philosophy reveres. Progressives like Williams and Wollstonecraft responded by reversing the valence of the castle or ruin. Their emblem was the Bastille, the castle-prison demolished by the revolutionary crowd; they drew on the Gothic novel's repertoire of massive, crumbling buildings as sites of unjust imprisonment. Williams is attacking the foes of liberty, those "reasoners who pretend that each abuse, / Sanction'd by precedent, has some blest use" (lines 49–50), a fairly explicit reference to Burke. She expostulates,

> Does then some chemic power to time belong,
> Extracting, by some process, right from wrong?
> Must feudal governments for ever last?
> Those Gothic piles, the work of ages past;
> Nor may obtrusive reason boldly scan,
> Far less reform the rude mishapen plan;
> The winding labyrinths, the hostile towers,
> Whence danger threatens, and where horror low'rs;
> The jealous draw-bridge, and the moat profound,
> The lonely dungeon in the cavern'd ground;
> The sullen dome above those central caves,
> Where lives one tyrant, and a host of slaves?
> Ah, Freedom, on this renovated shore,
> That fabric frights the moral world no more!
> Shook to its basis, by thy powerful spell,
> Its triple walls in massy fragments fell;
> While, rising from the hideous wreck, appears
> The temple thy firm arm sublimely rears;
> Of fair proportions, and of simple grace,
> A mansion worthy of the human race. (lines 49–70)

One way in which the aesthetics of the ruin abetted the conservatism of the picturesque was by downplaying human agency. Ruins "were admired," as Ian Ousby puts it, "as witnesses to the triumph of time and nature over man's handiwork."[22] This fits well with Burke's conservative message of humility: no individual or group, not even an entire generation, was qualified to pull down the "noble and venerable castle" (40) of the constitution, or to put up a new one; "it is with infinite caution that any man ought to venture upon pulling down an edifice which has answered in any tolerable degree for ages the common purposes of society, or on building it up again without having models and patterns of approved utility before his eyes" (70).

Wollstonecraft, recognizing the politicized aesthetics that underlies Burke's rhetoric, rejects it wholesale in *A Vindication of the Rights of Men:* "These are gothic notions of beauty – the ivy is beautiful, but, when it insidiously destroys the trunk from which it receives support, who would not grub it up?" An aesthetic that would have us "reverence the rust of antiquity" perverts morality to find pleasure in parasitism.[23] Williams, like Wollstonecraft, rejects Burke's aesthetics and the conservative politics they helped justify. Her politicized landscape levels the "Gothic piles" of conventional picturesque scenery. "Rude," "mishapen," "hostile," "jealous," "sullen," "hideous wreck[s]" like the Bastille should be not idealized, but demolished. In their place she imagines a "temple…Of fair proportions, and of simple grace," suggesting the neoclassical aesthetics adopted by revolutionary cultural politicians like the painter Jacques-Louis David. Her credo calls for structures, architectural or political, "worthy of the human race." Her human-centered version of the picturesque scene emphasizes the dignity of the laboring men and women who inhabit the landscape. Infusing the picturesque with revolutionary politics, she self-consciously modifies aesthetic discourse to bring its politically dubious elements in line with her utopian vision.

A further vignette from Williams' provincial travels exemplifies her drive to conflate the aesthetic with the political. At the same time, like her descriptions of the Festival of the Federation, it hints at the limits of aesthetic radicalism. As with the ruin, she appropriates a conventional element of picturesque composition as a political symbol. This time it is the tree that is ceremonially planted as a symbol of liberty in the town square of Montreüil sur Mer.[24] Once again her aestheticized presentation showcases the self-discipline of the revolutionary people as they put on a carefully ordered spectacle.

A flag, from which streamed the national colours, was fastened to the highest branches, crowned with a bonnet rouge. When this cherished tree was firmly rooted in the earth amidst the acclamations of the multitude, an officer of the national guard mounted on a chair beneath the shade of the tree, and read a paper of instruction to the people, who formed a circle round him, and listened with the most respectful attention. After descanting upon the blessings of the constitution, the orator enforced the necessity of the most absolute submission to the laws. – The tree of liberty, with its green branches, and waving streamers; the orator placed under its shade; and the circle which surrounded him, formed altogether a most picturesque groupe. (I.2.195–96)

The decorated tree becomes the centerpiece in a tableau of ideal civic communication, celebrating the rule of law. Williams continues to emphasize the participants' self-awareness, putting them at the center of the scene; revolution takes on the attractive guise of an orderly transition to popular self-rule. Gilpin's concept of the group as the most pleasing arrangement for people, animals, or trees in a picturesque scene gives this peaceful political assembly an aesthetic rationale. Pictorial composition harmonizes the scene, subordinating one element to another to reinforce the orator's message of submission to the law. The picturesque reveals itself as the perfect means to package this comforting image of a "respectful" revolutionary people for middle-class consumption. Transgressing the conceptual boundary between the aesthetic and the political to put landscape aesthetics' prestige in the service of revolution, Williams absorbs aesthetics' class bias into her revolutionary rhetoric.

PARTICULARISM, OR THE POLITICS OF THE HEART

Williams' scenic tour of the early Revolution negotiates with impressive rhetorical acumen between diverse bodies of discourse as she works to legitimize herself as a female aesthetic subject. Like Ann Radcliffe and other women writers of the late eighteenth century, Williams took advantage of the ambiguously gendered intersection between sensibility and taste as a fulcrum for prying the language of aesthetics loose from its masculine bias. The more conventionally feminine vocabulary of sentiment mingles with that of scenic tourism in her descriptions of Parisian spectacles.[25] She punctuates the first two volumes of her *Letters* with inserted narratives of aristocratic parental tyranny that downscale *ancien régime* oppression to an emotionally accessible family melodrama, ensconcing the love match and middle-class domesticity at the heart of revolution. The stories of the du F— family and of Auguste and Madelaine evidently appealed to contemporary audiences; they were the selections most often reprinted in magazines and miscellanies.[26] But the language of heightened feeling also enters descriptive passages to amplify the aesthetic effect of the sublime spectacle or picturesque idyll. Again, Ellison's point about Williams' rhetorical opportunism in combining sentiment with the sublime is well taken. Opportunistically, she cultivates the almost paradoxical mixture of engagement and detachment that we saw in her account of the Festival of the Federation. The culturally clichéd feminine gendering of emotion helps legitimize a woman who claims the privileged position of the aesthetic subject. Like other women writers, notably Montagu, Williams stands in a deeply ambivalent relation to aesthetic discourse and its cultural power. Aspiring to share in that power, she is nonetheless critical of fundamental aspects of aesthetics – most notably the doctrine of disinterestedness, aesthetics' segregation from the practical or political domain. We have already glimpsed potential pitfalls in her efforts to turn aesthetics to political ends. The risks and the stakes would increase as the Revolution intensified.

Williams' use of the language of sentiment is closely connected to a central rhetorical feature of the *Letters From France* that demands further scrutiny. I will call this her particularism: her insistence that, as she puts it, "my political creed is entirely an affair of the heart" (1.1.66), grounded in affective connections to particular individuals rather than abstract or generalized reasoning. This seems initially designed to cover her intrusion into the masculine arena of politics. Closer scrutiny discloses an intricate interweaving of discursive alliances and oppositions centered around this overdetermined feature. Its affective content helps Williams speak as a female aesthetic subject. Particularism subtly reconceptualizes the aesthetic domain, blurring the boundary between the aesthetic and the practical or political. She distances herself simultaneously from the masculine cultural politics of the revolutionary French and from those of the reactionary British, led by the redoubtable Burke. Her friends' fears "that I shall return to my own country a fierce republican" (1.1.66) draw a self-deprecating response: "it is very difficult, with common sensibility, to avoid sympathising in general happiness. My love of the French revolution is the natural result of this sympathy; and therefore my political creed is entirely an affair of the heart; for I have not been so absurd as to consult my head upon matters of which it is so incapable of judging" (1.1.66). This kind of language exploits as a strength what was frequently counted a feminine weakness. The appeal to "common sensibility" lets her sidestep formal argument and move to higher ground. At the same time, her maneuver aggressively stakes out for the Revolution the rhetorically fertile territory of the heart. Disarmingly, if disingenuously, she asks, "Did you expect that I should ever dip my pen in politics, who used to take so small an interest in public affairs...?" (1.1.108). As she elaborates her "politics of the heart," however, she expressly sets aside the conceptual boundary between the private and the public or political, the heavily gendered opposition that prevented a woman from speaking as a political subject: "in my admiration of the revolution in France, I blend the feelings of private friendship with my sympathy in public blessings; since the old constitution is connected in my mind with the image of a friend confined in the gloomy recesses of a dungeon, and pining in hopeless captivity; while, with the new constitution, I unite the soothing idea of his return to prosperity, honours, and happiness" (1.1.71–72).

The young aristocrat du F— was in reality Augustin Thomas du Fossé, husband of the Williams sisters' French teacher in London, the friend who first invited them to France. Much of the first volume (1.1.122–194) is devoted to an account of the tyranny of du F—'s father. The heartless aristocrat blocks his son's marriage and uses a *lettre de cachet* to have him imprisoned, but is luckily foiled by the Revolution. Williams' stories of individual injustice relinquish logical "arguments and inferences" to harness a different, extralogical type of argument: the exemplary power of narrative. Her "politics of the heart" has a further effect especially germane to our concern with aesthetics and gender. Mingling the language of aesthetics with that of sentiment helps legitimate her use of the former; but sentiment is premised on affective connections between specific, socially situated individuals. As she appropriates aesthetics' cultural authority, Williams thus resists its imperative to deny the particular – the distancing, abstracting impulse that I examined in Chapter 3 – by insisting on the specificity, the social situatedness, of her own perceptions and affiliations. By representing the Revolution in the language of aesthetics, but doing so from such an emphatically particular, engaged position, she implicitly rejects the dominant paradigm of the disinterested aesthetic subject. Practicing an aesthetics that is openly interested, in the sense of being politically committed, she maneuvers toward a subject position with a specific gender, class, and political agenda, all of which intensify rather than hinder aesthetic appreciation. In the place of the generic, universalized perceiver of mainstream aesthetic theory, she suggests a universe of particular perceivers linked by a web of practical ties. The rhetorical constraints she faced as a female aesthetic subject thus pushed Williams in the direction of significant theoretical innovation.

Her particularist approach consciously diverges from the cultural politics of the French revolutionary intelligentsia. Joan Landes has analyzed the revolutionaries' reliance on a "formalist and universalist rhetoric" rooted in the "bourgeois liberal principle of abstract equality." Landes makes use of Jürgen Habermas's account of the early bourgeois public sphere, though it fails, as she points out, "to acknowledge the way the symbolic contents of the bourgeois public sphere worked to rule out all interests that could not or would not lay claim to their own universality...He ignores the strong association of women's discourse and their interests with 'particularity.'"[27] In Enlightenment France, even before the Revolution, gender and class were imbricated in a cultural politics that valorized as "natural" a masculine neoclassicist rhetoric of the abstract and universal. Such a rhetoric set itself explicitly against the rococo, "precious" or particularist, aristocratic, and feminine style of expression associated with the powerful *salonnières* of the absolutist public sphere.

Salons and their female proprietors occupied an ambiguous position: neither entirely bourgeois nor aristocratic, associated with the court, but also competing with it from their urban location. As arbiters of a limited upward social mobility, *salonnières* were attacked by the traditional aristocracy, while the men whose careers they fostered (men like Diderot and Rousseau) joined the clamor of antifeminist attacks on these public women. Something of a *salonnière* herself, Williams was certainly a public woman by virtue of her voluminous publications. Her prose style is closer to *preciosité* than to the universalist rhetoric of Revolutionary reason. Her calculated refusal to take part in abstract political discourse ironically aligns her with a pre-revolutionary French type of the powerful public woman. She was already something of an anomaly within the restrictive gender roles favored by the revolutionaries, which would rigidify during the radical Jacobin phase. Landes notes the ban on the Society of Revolutionary Republican Women (October 1793), the beheading of the outspoken feminist Olympe de Gouges (November 1793), and the triumph of the ideology of republican motherhood that pushed French women decisively back into a private, domestic sphere.[28] In a later volume Williams reports the banning of "a certain class of the women of Paris, who gave themselves the title of revolutionary women," defensively distancing herself from these "female politicians" (II.1.139–40).

Her rhetorical task in the British context is rather different: reclaiming the rhetorical turf of particularism, staked out for the right by Burke's *Reflections on the Revolution*, for the liberal side. Particularism informs Burke's defense of an idealized British constitution and his assaults on the French revolutionaries. Early in the *Reflections* he proclaims, "I cannot stand forward and give praise or blame to anything which relates to human actions, and human concerns, on a simple view of the object, as it stands stripped of every relation, in all the nakedness and solitude of metaphysical abstraction ...The circumstances are what render every civil and political scheme beneficial or noxious to mankind" (8). Scorn for French intellectuals' abstract reasoning generates hyperbolic effects: "Is it because liberty in the abstract may be classed amongst the blessings of mankind, that I am seriously to felicitate a madman, who has escaped from the protecting restraint and wholesome darkness of his cell, on his restoration to the enjoyment of light and liberty?" (8). Elsewhere he fumes, "They despise experience...They have 'the rights of men'" (66). His defense of the particular rings similarly to Williams'. "To be attached to the subdivision, to love the little platoon we belong to in society, is the first principle (the germ as it were) of public affections. It is the first link in the series by which we proceed toward a love to our country and to mankind" (53). With unintended irony, he generalizes about particularism, where she is content to state her own predilection. But the rhetorical force of her insistence on the particular, in the wake of the *Reflections*, is clear. Aligning herself with Burke's other liberal denouncers, including Paine and Wollstonecraft, Williams sets about reclaiming this valuable tactic in support of the Revolution.

Burke's particularism is nostalgic. He famously glorifies the feudal allegiances of the "age of chivalry." The age "of sophisters, economists, and calculators has succeeded, and the glory of Europe is extinguished forever" (86). Williams revises his chronology to announce a new age of chivalry, "not indeed in its erroneous notions of loyalty, honour and gallantry…but in its noble contempt of sordid cares, its spirit of unsullied generosity, and its heroic zeal for the happiness of others" (1.2.5). Re-situating chivalry in the revolutionary future, she relegates calculation to the *ancien régime* past. The story of Auguste and Madelaine blames aristocrats for sordid calculation in matters of marriage. Auguste, son of a Count, arrives at the resort of Barèges and meets Madelaine, daughter of a retired officer. The ladies of Barèges don't bother envying Madelaine: "Although the French revolution had not yet happened, these ladies were aware that, with respect to marriage, the age of *calculators* was already come, and therefore no rival was to be feared in Madelaine" (1.2.163). This somewhat clumsy allusion to Burke reverses his narrative of decline for one of revolutionary progress. Despite the Count's machinations, the lovers are united as Williams pits her version of particularism against Burke's rhetoric. The early volumes of *Letters From France* mark out a speaking position at the intersection of seemingly incompatible discourses as they conflate the de-particularized aesthetic subject with the particular sentimental self. The synthesis is predictably unstable. We will watch it come apart as the Revolution intensifies.

DISRUPTED LANDSCAPES

With the third and fourth volumes of *Letters From France*, published in 1793 and covering events that occurred early that year, Williams' struggle to represent the unprecedented enters a new stage. Violence warps the spectacular order of the Revolution and its events swiftly transcend the framing capacity of her aesthetic model. The static spectacles and pictorial metaphors that punctuate the first two volumes, with their distanced observing subject, give way to a perspective less stable, less detached, and more open to the dynamism of historical change: "Upon the whole, the French revolution is still in its progress, and who can decide how its last page will finish?" (1.3.19). The shift is incipient at the opening of volume 1.3 as Williams reiterates her aesthetic model of spectatorship. "While you observe from a distance the great drama which is acting in France, I am a spectator of the representation. – I am placed near enough the scene to discern every look and every gesture of the actors, and every passion excited in the minds of the audience. I shall therefore endeavour to fill up the outline of that picture which France has presented to your contemplation since the memorable epocha of the tenth of August" (1.3.2). A distance that is relative, rather than absolute, subtly disrupts a static model that would relegate the viewer (like a picturesque guidebook) to a precisely designated "station." Williams is closer to "actors" and "audience" than her correspondent, yet identical with neither. This suggests the possibility of multiple perspectives on the same events. We gradually realize that no whole exists to be grasped by a spatial aesthetic perspective. Events unfold in an unpredictable temporal sequence that stubbornly resists such totalizing. Williams gradually relinquishes her attempt, couched in the vocabulary of scenic tourism, to freeze-frame the chaotic flux of history.

The shift is accompanied by a new mode of authorship. These volumes, Williams explains in her "Advertisement," are the product of a three-way collaboration. None of the authors is named on the title page of the first edition; the second was probably Williams' companion, John Hurford Stone, and the third Thomas Christie. Additionally appended to volume 1.3 is the war correspondence of General Dumouriez, who by the time of publication had defected to Austria.[29] Events are refracted through several lenses: Williams' observations appear side by side with war reports, political comment, and the General's letters unfolding a plot of intrigue and betrayal. She embraces multiple authorship as she lets go the single, fixed consciousness of the safely distanced aesthetic spectator. History is no longer linear, but multiperspectival – subject to interpretation by, or negotiation among, any number of writers and readers. Favret praises this as a thought-provoking innovation through which Williams stimulates her readers to challenge any one "official" version of events. Williams' heterogeneous epistolary history, Favret claims, is truly revolutionary in contrast to a linear narrative like Burke's: "the discontinuities of the narrative call attention to the obstructing barriers of law, government, social convention, national identity and language...time, place and identity lose their clear definitions and surrender to the epistolary movement...[they] cannot rest secure in a period of revolution."[30]

Favret's interpretation throws into relief the dramatic shift beginning with volume 1.3 from the static, highly ordered, individual viewpoint of the aesthetic spectator to a mode of presentation more sensitive to the increasing disorder of revolutionary change. This view needs to be qualified, however, by noting a counter-movement in Williams' capacious and increasingly chaotic volumes. As she draws revolutionary disorder into her text, she also betrays a growing discomfort with the radical direction revolutionary politics are taking. This erupts most dramatically in her organizing metaphor of the landscape. Political trauma registers in a series of disrupted landscapes that dramatize a widening disjunction between aesthetics and politics.

Ah! what is become of the delightful visions which elevated the enthusiastic heart? – What is become of the transport which beat high in every bosom, when an assembled million of the human race vowed on the altar of their country, in the name of the represented nation, inviolable fraternity and union – an eternal federation! This was indeed the golden age of the revolution. – But it is past! – the enchanting spell is broken, and the fair scenes of beauty and of order, through which imagination wandered, are transformed into the desolation of the wilderness, and clouded by the darkness of the tempest. (1.3.6)

Linking the euphoria of the Festival of the Federation with the language of landscape aesthetics, the utopian "fair scenes of beauty and of order," she looks back on both with a bitter nostalgia. By her final four volumes, published in 1795–96 and recounting the events of the Terror leading to the fall of Robespierre, the aesthetic domain has become the antithesis of a sinister and chaotic political arena. The threat and tragedy of dictatorship and Terror generate a survival strategy that involves a return to the conventional conception of aesthetics and politics as mutually exclusive. Landscape offers an imaginary escape from a nightmare reality.

Williams' historiographical practice registers her belief in the Revolution's liberatory potential at all levels of human perception and interaction. Her letters do retain this sense at some level, in spite of everything, through the darkest days of the Terror. In the later volumes this guarded, severely qualified optimism projects itself outward onto the far-flung armies of the Republic, which become repositories of uncorrupted revolutionary zeal, the last refuge of a nation battered by cynical power-hounds like Robespierre. Her perspectivism stretches to encompass opposite views of "the People" as contemptible tools of the demagogue and as his innocent victims. Hope contests with despair through her polyvocal presentation as an account of expansionist war and international intrigue jostles for space with a highly personalized melodrama starring Robespierre as chief villain.

The factor of class, in particular, seems strongly to inflect the nature and scope of Williams' political radicalism. Her emphatically bourgeois, Girondist allegiance is accompanied by a deep suspicion of the urban *sans-culottes* mobilized by the Jacobins of Robespierre's Mountain – "that swarm of idle and profligate elements which infest great capitals," those "dangerous instruments of party rage and faction," imprudently armed by the Legislative Assembly.[31] The letters shift from their initial utopian–spectacular mode into a vocabulary reminiscent of the Gothic novel at a time when the crowd assumes a higher profile in Revolutionary politics with the insurrection of the Paris Commune, the August 10, 1792 attack on the Tuileries, and the ensuing September massacres.[32] Williams paints these events in a stark chiaroscuro. The actors take on a savage, subhuman quality as she describes "the inhuman judges of that night wearing the municipal scarf which their polluting touch profaned, surrounded by men armed with pikes and sabres dropping with blood – while a number of blazing torches threw their glaring light on the ferocious visages of those execrable judges, who, mixing their voices with the shrieks of the dying, passed sentence with a savage mockery of justice, on victims devoted to their rage" (1.3.4–5). Stock phrases like "ferocious visages" and "devoted victims" smack of the novelistic discourse of Gothic horror. The proletarian figures loom as threatening Others.

The pictorial juxtaposition of bloody darkness with "glaring light" suggests the manichean moral opposites that characterize melodrama in Peter Brooks' influential definition. Williams' commentary makes this view explicit: "That conflict which after the King's acceptance of the new constitution existed in this country between the executive and legislative powers, between the court and the people, has since the tenth of August been succeeded by a conflict far more terrible; a conflict between freedom and anarchy, knowledge and ignorance, virtue and vice" (1.3.2–3). The dualities are stark: the Commune are "demagogues," their rule a sheer "usurpation" in which power is "shamefully abused" (1.3.3). Brooks suggests that melodrama as a facet of modern sensibility reacts to "the vertiginous feeling of standing over the abyss created when the necessary center of things has been evacuated and dispersed." To Williams, whose Revolution had been the orderly utopia imaged by the Festival of the Federation, this period must have felt vertiginous and decentered indeed.[33]

The melodrama continues with a series of disrupted landscapes that register the emotional impact of the Terror on the poet and political idealist. One of these landscapes incorporates human figures whose distortion is a thinly veiled allusion to the low social status of the urban revolutionaries. Williams is quoting "a Frenchman of my acquaintance" as he gives his rationale for withdrawing from politics at this stage of the Revolution. He elaborates, "'Our revolution...reminds me of the works of a celebrated Italian painter, who drew the most charming scenery, enriched with the most beautiful prospects and delicious walks – but the groups of figures which were seen in those delightful regions, were grotesque and hideous. – Such...appears our revolution in my eyes. The theory is beautiful, the principles are sublime, but many of the actors are detestable; and it is a system of which the present race is not worthy'" (I.3.25–26). Troping the disparity between principles and actors as that between a landscape and the human figures in it, Williams returns to the aesthetic–ideological problem of the relation between figure and landscape, human beings and their material or cultural environment. Her poetic reworking of the picturesque harvest scene had already tackled this problem. There we saw human figures move from margin to center, from facelessness to dignity. Here, rather than dignified, the lower orders are distorted. They are individualized, but in a "grotesque and hideous" manner. Williams throws together incompatible categories, violating aesthetic doctrines as well as the principles of social stratification that inform eighteenth-century aesthetic discourse. As she laments the violence, she mourns the decisive violation of a social order that she had wished modified, but not abolished.

Her use of aesthetic theory, with its social assumptions, is a sensitive barometer to the degree of social change she can tolerate. She presents Robespierre's Mountain as anti-aesthetic: "This faction have declared war against every improvement, and every grace of civilized society – all that embellishes human life – all that softens and refines our nature. – They desire to send the arts and sciences into everlasting exile, to throw down all the monuments of taste and genius, and to destroy all literature in one impious conflagration" (I.3.23–24). Her bourgeois bias moves increasingly to the foreground. The protagonists of her inserted narratives, Auguste and the young Baron du F—, combine revolutionary allegiance with aristocratic birth (even when they renounce their privileges). The story of du F— presents a revolution in which despotism is superseded by an aestheticized paternalism, a "charming society at the *chateau*" (the estate young du F— inherits from his cruel father) where "the peasants dance under the shade of the old elms, while the setting sun pours streams of liquid gold through the foliage" (I.1.213). We begin to wonder how much Williams' new age of chivalry might actually have in common with Burke's idealized feudalism. At this point the class content of aesthetic discourse no longer seems to pose such a difficulty for Williams. Aesthetics, with its conservative ideological inflection, gradually evolves into a defense against the troubling shift in the class composition of the revolutionary "People."

LANDSCAPE AS REFUGE

By Williams' fifth volume the relation between aesthetics and politics is completely transformed. Rather than conflated, the aesthetic and the political are now conventionally posed as mutually exclusive. Escape into imaginary landscapes becomes a survival strategy for a narrator who opens her fifth volume with the report of her own arrest in October 1793 as the Committee for Public Safety rounds up all the English living in Paris. Her first morning in the Luxembourg palace, now a jail, she climbs on a table to look at the garden.

Its tall majestic trees had not yet lost their foliage; and though they were fallen, like our fortunes, "into the sear, the yellow leaf," they still presented those rich gradations of colouring which belong to autumn. The sun gilded the gothic spires of the surrounding convents, which lifted up their tall points above the venerable groves; while on the back-ground of the scenery arose the hills of Meudon. It seemed to me as if the declining season had shed its last interesting graces over the landscape to sooth my afflicted spirit; and such was the effect it produced. (II.1.16–17)

The discourse of the picturesque governs her concern with light, color, foreground, and background. Emily St. Aubert, the heroine of Ann Radcliffe's *Mysteries of Udolpho* (published in 1794, the year before this volume) repeatedly gazes out of the window of the Gothic castle that is her prison, seeking consolation in scenery.

Chapter 7 will trace Emily's sense of comfort to the class privilege that aesthetic discourse reinforced. Williams, threatened by the "extraordinary malignity" (I.3.7) of the Montoni-esque Robespierre, may be reaching for a similar kind of solace. Like Emily, she dwells on the contrast between the beauty and order of her aesthetic vision and a grim reality, in Williams' case that of factional politics run amok. The tapestry on the wall of her prison apartment provides another escape.

The walls of that apartment were hung with tapestry which described a landscape of romantic beauty. On that landscape I often gazed till I almost persuaded myself that the scenery was alive around me, so much did I delight in the pleasing illusion. How often, while my eyes were fixed on that canvas which led my wounded spirit from the cruelty of man to the benignity of God – how often did I wish "for the wings of a dove, that I might flee away and be at rest!" To be seated at the foot of those sheltering hills which embosomed some mimic habitations, or beneath a mighty elm which rose majestically in the fore-ground of the piece, and spread its thick foliage over a green slope, appeared to me the summit of earthly felicity. (II.1.36–37)

The landscapes of the early volumes advanced the vision of a new political order, an ideal harmony like a well-composed scene. Now landscape is a temporary escape from the baffling anarchy of revolutionary politics. After her release from prison, Williams – her published attacks on Robespierre having come to his attention – leaves the country.[34]

Appropriately, she flees to Switzerland, a country that "nature seems to have created more for ornament than use" (II.1.37). She has physically escaped the Terror. Intellectually, she reflects, the historian has no refuge.

At the fearful climax of revolutionary government which we have now reached, we find no soothing objects which can repose the weary eye, or cheer the sinking heart. An historical sketch of this period is no common picture of human nature, tinctured with the blended hues of vice and virtue: it is like the savage scenery of Salvator, where all is wildly horrible, and every figure on the canvas is a murderer. We are forced to wander through successive evils; to turn our eyes from the popular commission of Orange to the revolutionary tribunal of Arras, from the crimes of Maignet to the atrocities of Lebon. (II.3.112)

The dreamlike landscape metaphor inverts to nightmare as the "savage scenery" of Salvator Rosa tropes revolutionary horror. The sublime Festival is superseded by the grisly theater of death she has witnessed in the Place de la Révolution: "we saw...the crowd assembled for the bloody tragedy, and the gens d'armes on horse-back, followed by victims who were to be sacrificed, entering the square. Such was the daily spectacle which had succeeded the painted shows, the itinerant theatres, the mountebank, the dance, the song, the shifting scenes of harmless gaiety, which used to attract the cheerful crowd as they passed from the Thuilleries to the Champs Elisées". (II.2.7)

Dystopic violence seems entirely to have displaced the early vol-umes' aesthetic utopia when Williams once again invokes the Festival of the Federation. The occasion is Robespierre's Festival of the Supreme Being, held June 8, 1794, a month and a half before his fall on 9 Thermidor (July 27). This event exemplifies to Williams all that has gone wrong with the Revolution: a "polluted festival insti-tuted by a tyrant" (II.2.86), imposed from above rather than gener-ated from below and starring Robespierre in "all the littleness of his vanity" (II.2.92), rather than "the people."[35] Williams inserts a long digression on the Girondist martyr Brissot, whose "perfect disinter-estedness" (II.2.79) pointedly contrasts Robespierre's self-display. She sarcastically decries his attempt to reconcile the irreconcilable: beauty and violence.

She is especially outraged by the role of the painter Jacques-Louis David in designing the Festival – "he, whose mind the cultivation of the finer arts has had no power to soften" (II.2.74). The artist traves-ties his role when he presumes to dictate how the people shall mani-fest their political sentiment. "At this spot, by David's command, the mothers are to embrace their daughters – at that, the fathers are to clasp their sons – here, the old are to bless the young, and there, the young are to kneel to the old – upon this boulevard the people are to sing – upon that, they must dance – at noon they must listen in silence, and at sun-set they must rend the air with acclamations" (II.2.86–87). Williams contrasts this with her memory of a very differ-ent festival.

What was become of that sublime federation of an assembled nation which had nobly shaken off its ignominious fetters, and exulted in its new-born freedom! What was become of those moments when no emotions were pre-ordained, no feelings measured out, no acclamations decreed; but when every bosom beat high with admiration, when every heart throbbed with enthusiastic transport, when every eye melted into tears, and the vault of heaven resounded the bursts of unpremeditated applause! (II.2.87)

Sublime nostalgia prompts her to reaffirm her own commitment to revolution. She does so in a landscape metaphor: "Let us not abandon a fair and noble region filled with objects which excite the thrill of tenderness or the glow of admiration, because along the path which France has chosen serpents have lurked beneath the buds of roses, and beasts of prey have issued from the lofty woods: let us discover, if we can, a less tremendous road, but let us not renounce the land of promise" (II.2.87–88). Again she tropes the Terror with the grotesque disjunction between figures – this time not human beings, but snakes and "beasts of prey" – and the landscape they inhabit.

Commanded to decorate their houses, the Parisians achieve a "gay and charming spectacle" by creating an ecological disaster. "Woods had been robbed of their shade, and gardens to the extent of some leagues rifled of their sweets, in order to adorn the city" (II.2.88). On this "profusion of gay objects" Williams luridly superimposes the Terror. "The scent of carnage seemed mingled with these lavish sweets; the glowing festoons appeared tinged with blood; and in the back ground of this festive scenery the guillotine arose before the disturbed imagination. I thought of that passage in Mr. Burke's book, 'In the groves of *their* academy, at the end of every vista I see the gallows!'" (II.2.89–90). Robespierre's "festive scenery" marshals nature to the banner of Terror, but it is haunted by the ghost of the deadly machine. Williams' pastoral utopia is incompatible with the gruesomely mechanical methods of the Committee of Public Safety. Her near-concession to Burke hints at a temptation to despair.

The last four volumes of *Letters From France* feature "Scenes Which Have Passed in the Prisons of Paris" as well as "Scenes Which Passed in Various Departments of France During the Tyranny of Robespierre" – a catalogue of executions, last words, and scaffold demeanor. Despite the pathos and heroism that punctuate these volumes, the accumulated atrocities are finally numbing. Williams and her family leave Paris when the Committee proscribes aristocrats and foreigners from the city. In the country, aestheticized nature releases the emotions that had been blocked by the sheer magnitude of the slaughter.

We reached our little dwelling at the hour of sun-set. The hills were fringed with clouds, which still reflected the fading colours of the day; the woods were in deep shadow; a soft veil was thrown over nature...The tears which the spectacle of the guillotine had petrified with horror, now flowed again with melancholy luxury. Our habitation was situated within a few paces of the noble park of Marly; and the deserted alleys overgrown with long grass – the encumbering fragments of rock, over which once fell the mimic cascades, whose streams no longer murmur – the piles of marble which once formed the bed of crystal basons – the scattered machinery of the jets d'eaux, whose source are dried – the fallen statues – the defaced symbols of feudality – the weeds springing between the stone steps of the ascent to the deserted palace – the cobwebbed windows of the gay pavilions, were all in union with that pensiveness of mind which our present circumstances naturally excited. (II.2.8–10)

"[M]elancholy luxury" and "pensiveness" replace sublime elevation as the dominant emotions of Williams' aesthetic response to the Revolution. She embraces the aesthetic of ruins that her epistle to Dr. Moore had earlier rejected. Is she endorsing the sense of human helplessness, the determinist overtones of such an aesthetic? The picture of the ruined chateau and landscape garden, with its "scattered machinery" and "defaced symbols," conveys a fragmentation that threatens to paralyze her political will. The ruins' theme of mutability provides her only comfort: "It was impossible that this state of extreme violence could be permanent" (II.3.151–52).

She is right, of course; it ends with the fall of Robespierre. Her final volumes circle restlessly around this key occurrence with a refusal of linear narrative that conveys a deep sense of discontinuity. The conclusion of vol. II.1 summons a landscape metaphor to reassure readers that

the dark picture which you have been contemplating is relieved by a bright and soothing perspective. The past seems like one of those frightful dreams which presents to the disturbed spirit phantoms of undescribable horror, and "deeds without a name"; awakened from which, we hail with rapture the cheering beams of the morning, and anticipate the meridian lustre of the day...the whole nation, roused into a sense of its danger by the terrible lesson it has been taught, can be oppressed no more. (II.1.257–58)

Williams' attempt to put aesthetics in the service of narrative closure is unconvincing. The "hideous contrast" between the "dark picture" and the "bright...perspective" that "relieves" it figures an inexplicable break between the Terror and its aftermath. As she leaves unexplained how such violence could arise out of lofty ideals, she makes no attempt to account for the nation's return to relative tranquillity. The unresolved contrast between the aestheticized dream of revolution and the nightmare of the Terror confronts us again with the inadequacy of the spatializing discourse of aesthetics to the temporal vicissitudes of historical change.[36]

Successive variations on the trope of aestheticized nature forgo argument in favor of sheer repetition, desperately seeking a way to put paid to the Terror. "Upon the fall of Robespierre, the terrible spell which bound the land of France was broken; the shrieking whirlwinds, the black precipices, the bottomless gulphs, suddenly vanished; and reviving nature covered the wastes with flowers, and the rocks with verdure" (II.3.190). The broken spell substitutes romance for history – an unworldly, utopian vision of revolution. Again: "Like the weary traveller, who having passed along paths beset with danger, where bare and horrid precipices frowned above, and deep and dark abysses yawned below, gains at length some fair summit, from whence, while he shudders to look back, the prospect opening before him presents scenes cheered by vegetation, and softening into beauty" (II.4.2). The travel simile naturalizes the juxtaposition of idealism with violence; again, temporal continuity skirts the issue of causation. The overall movement of Volumes II.1–3 could be described as centripetal, gesturing toward the corrupt center, the "malignity" of Robespierre (I.3.7).

The final volume supplements centripetal with centrifugal movement. As Williams reports France's defense against the allies and early offensive forays into Belgium and Holland, the army becomes the refuge of uncorrupted revolutionary sentiment: "the honour of the French name, sinking beneath the obloquy with which it was loaded by the crimes of its domestic tyrants, was only sustained by the astonishing achievements of the French armies. They alone remained pure and unsullied by the contagious guilt which overspread their country" (II.4.206). More and more, the armies stand in for that elusive entity, "the people." At home "the people" increasingly appear as passive victims:

we should beware of the injustice of accusing the French people of those crimes of which they are the mourners, and of which they only have been the victims. They, who have seen their fields ravaged, their vineyards stained with blood, their cities reduced to ashes; they, who have lost their fathers, their husbands, their children, their friends…to charge that people with the enormities under which they have groaned, would be indeed to arraign the oppressed for the guilt of the oppressor. (II.4.175–76)

Only armed and on the move, it seems, escaping the tainted center, can "the people" retain their political initiative. The center of gravity of Williams' Revolution has radically shifted from the "private" domain of sentimental romance and domesticity to the conventionally public and masculine military arena. But as she heralds France's military achievements, Williams is haunted by the evil her narrative has failed to explain or exorcise: "The French republic had now arrived at a pitch of glory unequalled in the annals of modern history…The only enemy that France had to dread, was that spirit of savage misrule and anarchy which the daemon of Jacobinism had raised, and which had transformed the cradle of infant liberty into a den of desolation and carnage" (II.4.127–28). The language of the supernatural again points toward the Gothic melodrama at the center of Williams' epistolary history: the manichean allegory of moral absolutes that obscures the vertiginous, decentered character of revolutionary political change.

These volumes lay no claim to historical objectivity. The personal motives Williams gives for loving the Revolution correspond with her emphatically situated perspective. Although she supplements her own impressions with those of others situated elsewhere in France, she does not pretend to totalize. Perhaps by frustrating readers in this way – offering aesthetic impressions instead of causal explanations, letting discontinuity be – her letters engender respect for the difficulty of the leap from situated impressions to any supposedly impartial interpretation. She is an ambivalent revolutionary: committed to ideals of liberty, but disillusioned when it leads to disorder and violent license; sympathetic to the disadvantaged until they take politics into their own hands. Nonetheless, she deserves our respect. To our backward gaze she looks like something of a moderate; in her lifetime she was reviled in England as a Jacobin whore. *Letters From France* stages a prolonged textual encounter between aesthetics and politics, categories then in the process of being constituted as mutually exclusive. Williams succeeds in speaking as a female aesthetic subject only to confront aesthetics' manifest inadequacy to represent revolutionary change. As the stratified society that underwrote aesthetic discourse was violently challenged for the first time in history, she turned to aesthetics to legitimize the challenge. Not surprisingly, her strategy broke down. The manner in which it did so pays tribute to the immense cultural power of aesthetics. As Williams tries to persuade her readers of the beauty of revolution, she seems to persuade herself instead of the naturalness of social hierarchy. In this sense her attempt can be said to fail, but to fail in a highly instructive manner.

CHAPTER 5

Mary Wollstonecraft's anti-aesthetics

> If the aesthetic is to realize itself it must pass over into the
> political, which is what it secretly always was.[1]

Mary Wollstonecraft was a controversial figure in her own time.
Like Helen Maria Williams, she was reviled by England's
anti-Jacobin backlash, called an "unsex'd female" and a "hyena in
petticoats."[2] A few years after the bicentennial of her best-known
work, *A Vindication of the Rights of Woman*, she is still controversial.
Hailed in the 1970s as a feminist heroine, during the 1980s she drew
less sanguine scrutiny by critics who believed her feminism had
fallen prey to the crippling limitations of a liberal Enlightenment
discourse of reason.[3] Such assessments are part of the ongoing
exploration of the multiple suppressions and exclusions that accompanied the Enlightenment's projects of emancipation and progress.[4]
Wollstonecraft seized on a key exclusion when she confronted the
French revolutionaries with their failure to include women in the
Rights of Man. But this most recent pendulum swing in her reception overlooks her assault on a key Enlightenment category: the
aesthetic.

The language of aesthetics, as we have seen, strongly tended to
reinforce the systematic inequalities that structured eighteenth-
century British society. This comes into sharp focus when
Wollstonecraft takes aim at Burke in what Frances Ferguson calls
"one of the shrewdest political insights of late eighteenth-century
writing."[5] Her *Vindication of the Rights of Men* (1790), the first
published reply to his *Reflections on the Revolution in France*, reveals his
aesthetics of the sublime and beautiful to be inextricable from his
anti-egalitarian politics, which she scaldingly condemns. The very
first paragraph of the first *Vindication* polemically redefines the
concepts that made Burke's reputation as an aesthetician: "truth, in
morals, has ever appeared to me the essence of the sublime; and, in

taste, simplicity the only criterion of the beautiful."[6] For
Wollstonecraft, Burke's total lack of truth and simplicity were
predictable consequences of his aristocratic bias, which she fought
from the explicitly middle-class standpoint that she announces in *A
Vindication of the Rights of Woman*. She writes not to aristocratic ladies,
she says, as had earlier conduct books, "but, addressing my sex in a
firmer tone, I pay particular attention to those in the middle class,
because they appear to be in the most natural state." Inherited rank
and wealth keep their owners from developing the habitual activity
and independence of body and mind that Wollstonecraft believed
essential to real virtue. Like Helen Maria Williams and Dorothy
Wordsworth, she positions herself as proudly middle-class against
an aristocracy she viewed as corrupt and vulgar – as incapable of
either virtue or taste as conservatives held the laboring classes to be,
and for similar reasons. Both rich and poor are mired in depen-
dence on particular material things, whether from necessity or
addiction to luxury. The material conditions of their lives prevent
them from gaining any broad moral or political perspective.[7]

Wollstonecraft's travel account, *Letters Written during a Short
Residence in Sweden, Norway and Denmark* (1796), carries forward in a
subtler, less polemical fashion what the first *Vindication* had begun:
a politically motivated revision of aesthetic discourse. Instead of
proscribing pleasure, as Cora Kaplan sees her doing to women's
sexual pleasure in *A Vindication of the Rights of Woman,* she sets out
to re-imagine one culturally central, ideologically fraught kind of
pleasure. The alternative aesthetics that emerges from these writings would situate aesthetic pleasure in a practical, material
matrix extending from the body and its sensations to political
engagement. This ambitious revision of aesthetics must be understood, I will argue, as part of Wollstonecraft's liberal political project of extending rights and reducing social inequality.[8] Her
emphasis on the body and material needs importantly stretches
the parameters of liberalism. Standard critiques of liberalism
target what the philosopher Alison Jaggar calls its "normative
dualism": the assumption that body and mind are fundamentally
separable, combined with "the belief that what is especially valuable about human beings is a particular 'mental' capacity, the
capacity for rationality."[9] Liberal political thought values the mind
and devalues the body, leading it to emphasize procedural rights
and freedoms like free speech and voting rights rather than

substantive entitlements like freedom from starvation, home-lessness, or unemployment. This influential tradition of thought thus obscures the ways in which material obstacles keep human beings from unfolding their mental or spiritual capacities.

Terry Eagleton reads the early Marx as an aesthetician whose Utopian social thought strives to reconnect aesthetics with politics by understanding the body and its practical activity of labor as the root of both. Wollstonecraft's revisionist aesthetics shares a great deal with the Marx of the 1844 manuscripts – most importantly the belief that the only way to "restore to the body its plundered pow-ers" is to change the discourses and institutions that construct our bodies and senses.[10] Both writers sketch out an emancipatory or utopian aesthetics that depends on political change to change the way we see, hear, feel, smell, and taste. Resisting the aversion to bodies, material particulars, and vested interests that pervades mainstream eighteenth-century aesthetics, Wollstonecraft, like Marx, seamlessly subsumes the aesthetic in the practical as she works toward a corporeally and politically situated mode of perception. Rather than following the repressive tendency of Enlightenment rationalism, as her critics charge, in these writings we see her resist one of the period's more repressive discourses. Portrayed as hostile to bodies, especially female ones, here she shows a profound concern that the body get its due.[11]

REBUTTING BURKE

The 1790 publication of Burke's *Reflections on the Revolution in France*, the opening salvo of counterrevolution, galvanized the British left as the book's massive popularity made clear the power of the political and cultural forces arrayed against change. Prominent among these was the language of aesthetics.[12] The somewhat frivolous connota-tions of Burke's reputation as an aesthetician gave Wollstonecraft a rhetorical springboard for *ad hominem* attacks. But aesthetics was far from frivolous, as they both knew. Indeed, it occupies the very center of Burke's vision of civilization. Her achievement in *A Vindication of the Rights of Men* is to expose the political consequences of Burkean aesthetics. Wollstonecraft's reaction to his thought helps her work toward her own aesthetics – no less politicized than his, but in the opposite direction.

When Burke mourns the passing of the "age of chivalry" and the arrival of that "of sophisters, economists, and calculators," he is lamenting the bourgeois revolutionaries' rejection of the aesthetic dimension of political life. "All the pleasing illusions which made power gentle and obedience liberal, which harmonized the different shades of life, and which, by a bland assimilation, incorporated into politics the sentiments which beautify and soften private society, are to be dissolved by this new conquering empire of light and reason. All the decent drapery of life is to be rudely torn off." This "barbarous philosophy," he sums up, "is as void of solid wisdom as it is destitute of all taste and elegance."[13] Aesthetic response is the social glue of the Burkean commonwealth, the lens through which our country is supposed to appear lovable, because lovely (88). What Burke is invoking, of course, with his self-consciously aesthetic vocabulary of pleasing illusions, harmonized shades, beautifying sentiments, elegance, and taste, is the well-established political valence of taste. He is in line with aestheticians from Addison to Archibald Alison, for whom taste was a litmus test to distinguish the genteel, who have it, from the vulgar, who do not. The hierarchy of taste upholds the hierarchical structure of Burke's ideal state. He inventories its ranks, from monarchy and aristocracy through the commons down to "a protected, satisfied, laborious, and obedient people, taught to seek and to recognize the happiness that is to be found by virtue in all conditions; in which consists the true moral equality of mankind" (42). When the people grow dissatisfied and disobedient he reviles them, famously, as "a swinish multitude" (89), giving radical pamphleteers opportunities for titles like *Hog's Wash, or A Salmagundy for Swine*.[14]

Wollstonecraft's fiery, hastily written pamphlet, published less than a month after *Reflections*, sets out to expose Burke's aestheticized politics: "to shew you to yourself, stripped of the gorgeous drapery in which you have enwrapped your tyrannic principles" (37). She is attacking not the connection that he assumes between aesthetics and politics – this assumption, as we will see, she shares – but his reactionary political beliefs. Mitzi Myers convincingly argues that this *Vindication* (which other critics call disorganized) is organized around the fundamental connection between its two main lines of attack, its "socioeconomic and moral-aesthetic arguments" (121). Wollstonecraft identifies the central principle of the Burkean state as "the demon of property" (9), glossing phrases like "true moral equality" as doublespeak for a system that makes individuals, as Frances Ferguson puts it, mere "epiphenomena of property in land" (58) and makes the existing distribution of property look natural. She expostulates, "I beseech you to ask your own heart, when you call yourself a friend of liberty, whether it would not be more consistent to style yourself the champion of property, the adorer of the golden image which power has set up?" (13).[15]

Power is the central principle of the aesthetics that Burke elaborated thirty years earlier in his *Philosophical Enquiry into the Origin of our Ideas of the Sublime and Beautiful* (1757). Wollstonecraft's critique reveals the *Reflections* to be structured by the same aesthetic categories.[16] In Burke's scheme, the position of the aesthetic subject relative to the aesthetic object in a power hierarchy determines that object's effect: "we submit to what we admire, but we love what submits to us" (113). Admiration or awe is the aesthetic response evoked by the sublime; love is our response to the beautiful. Burke's aesthetic power relations are notoriously gendered. Large, dark, rough, craggy, intimidating sublime objects are masculine; small, bright, smooth, curvy, weak, beautiful objects are feminine. *A Vindication of the Rights of Men* seizes on this dimension of Burke's aestheticized politics, using women as a key example of the harmful effects of his views.

Burke divides the women of the French Revolution into two antithetical groups. An aristocratic woman like Queen Marie Antoinette embodies his concept of beauty as idealized passivity and supports his paean to chivalry. Proletarian women, like the ones who marched on Versailles on October 6, 1789, are excoriated as "the furies of hell, in the abused shape of the vilest of women." Wollstonecraft drily glosses, "Probably you mean women who gained a livelihood by selling vegetables or fish, who never had had any advantages of education" (30). Deflating his rhetoric, she points out his exaggerated hatred or fear of politically active women who fail to fit his category of beauty as weakness. He pities the French queen's distress, but not the "vulgar sorrows" of laboring-class English mothers whose husbands are kidnapped by government press gangs. "Misery, to reach your heart, I perceive, must have its cap and bells" (15). Such distorted responses are the result of Burke's system, which "would undermine religion and virtue to set up a spurious, sensual beauty, that has long debauched your imagination, under the specious form of natural feelings" (48). "Spurious" aesthetic response perpetuates political injustice.[17]

Elsewhere in *A Vindication of the Rights of Men* Wollstonecraft explores the bad effects of an aesthetics articulated with power relations along another axis: that of class. As she lambastes Burke's open contempt for the poor, she draws illustrations from landscape aesthetics, beginning the critical reconsideration of this discourse that *Letters Written...in Sweden* will extend. While not a central pre-occupation of Burke's *Enquiry*, landscape aesthetics was a fashionable topic familiar to any educated Briton. The representation of land, as Chapter 3 made clear, bore an extraordinary ideological charge in late eighteenth-century England. Landed property was still the organizing principle of the British political system; land use and distribution were the objects of ongoing political struggle as Parliament approved the enclosure of common land for private agriculture or landscape gardening. The language of landscape aesthetics promoted a way of seeing that effectively encouraged such land use policies.

Wollstonecraft's excursion into landscape aesthetics takes off from one of Burke's patronizing pronouncements about "the people," which she cites: "'the people, without being servile, must be tractable and obedient...They *must* respect that property of which they *cannot* partake.'...This is contemptible hard-hearted sophistry," she indignantly exclaims: the poor "have a right to more comfort than they at present enjoy...if an intercourse were established between [rich and poor], it would impart the only true pleasure that can be snatched in this land of shadows" (55). This comment leads her into estate landscaping in what at first seems a digression:

I know, indeed, that there is often something disgusting in the distresses of poverty, at which the imagination revolts, and starts back to exercise itself in the more attractive Arcadia of fiction. The rich man builds a house, art and taste give it the highest finish. His gardens are planted, and the trees grow to recreate the fancy of the planter...Every thing on the estate is cherished but man; – yet, to contribute to the happiness of man, is the most sublime of all enjoyments. But if, instead of sweeping pleasure-grounds, obelisks, temples, and elegant cottages, as *objects* for the eye, the heart was allowed to beat true to nature, decent farms would be scattered over the estate, and plenty smile around. (56)

Wollstonecraft frames the disgust, or imaginative revulsion, that makes the rich turn their backs on the poor and escape into

tasteful artificial enclaves specifically as a negative aesthetic
response.[18] Landscape aesthetics, with its emphasis on distance and
detachment, fends off real contact between people of different
social ranks. A more humane system of aesthetic value and social
organization would overcome that distance. The italicized "*objects*
for the eye" conveys her sophisticated grasp of the effect of aesthetics' objectifying mode of perception on perceiver as well as
perceived: it is dehumanizing. "Every *thing* on the estate is
cherished but *man*" (italics mine).

She goes on to propose a concrete alternative to an aesthetics
rooted in social inequality, contrasting the picturesque palaces and
hovels she saw on her 1785–86 journey to Portugal with English
smallholders' productive if unpicturesque gardens.

Returning once from a despotic country to a part of England well
cultivated, but not very picturesque – with what delight did I not observe
the poor man's garden! – The homely palings and twining woodbine, with
all the rustic contrivances of simple, unlettered taste, was a sight which
relieved the eye that had wandered indignant from the stately palace to
the pestiferous hovel, and turned from the awful contrast into itself to
mourn the fate of man, and curse the arts of civilization!

Why cannot large estates be divided into small farms? these dwellings
would indeed grace our land. Why are huge forests still allowed to stretch
out with idle pomp and all the indolence of Eastern grandeur? Why does
the brown waste meet the traveller's view, when men want work? But
commons cannot be enclosed without *acts of parliament* to increase the
property of the rich! Why might not the industrious peasant be allowed to
steal a farm from the heath? (56–57)

The new kind of pleasure that Wollstonecraft proposes depends on
visible signs of social justice and material prosperity. The traces of
inequality destroy pleasure, leaving nothing but indignation. Her
use of "taste," if somewhat condescending, nonetheless suggests an
impulse toward a conscious redefinition of terms; she puts this
powerful concept in a humble social context directly opposed to its
usual connotations of elite social status and prestige. An explicit
protest against the British government's land use policies
culminates in a plea for reform. To decouple aesthetic pleasure
from oppressive politics and reconnect it with a saner system of
land use, Wollstonecraft attacks the powerful tradition of landscape
aesthetics, which she understood to be shaped by anti-egalitarian
beliefs like Burke's.

Such harsh criticisms of conventional aesthetics do not mean, she assures her reader, that she wants to get rid of aesthetics altogether, "banish all enervating modifications of beauty from civil society" for a Spartan regime of "mortification and self-denial." A different kind of cultural work is in order: a morally motivated reassessment that would empirically test possible sources of pleasure: "But should experience prove that there is a beauty in virtue, a charm in order, which necessarily implies exertion, a depraved sensual taste may give way...to rational satisfactions. Both may be equally natural to man; the test is their moral difference, and that point reason alone can decide" (46). Setting aside the essentialist assumptions that informed mainstream aesthetics' insistence on a universal standard of taste, Wollstonecraft opens aesthetic response to a broad range of possibilities, though her middle-class outlook prefers the active, "rational" pleasures of "exertion" to the passive, "sensual" satisfactions of "enervating...beauty." She adds a caveat, however: "Such a glorious change can only be produced by liberty. Inequality of rank must ever impede the growth of virtue, by vitiating the mind that submits or domineers; that is ever employed to procure nourishment for the body, or amusement for the mind" (46). Unless state and society are organized differently – unless the material conditions of our lives fundamentally change – the overhaul of aesthetic language, practice, and response will remain incomplete. The two are inseparable. A social division of labor that allots only hard work to some and only frivolous leisure to others is wrong in itself and inimical to aesthetics as Wollstonecraft reconceives it, scuttling the standard belief that only the educated and leisured can experience aesthetic pleasure.

Rendered in the terms of the moralist, Wollstonecraft's analysis nonetheless seems closely akin to Marx's belief that capitalist social relations yield alienated senses, so that changing those relations is the only way to achieve "the complete *emancipation* of all human senses and attributes." Aesthetic experience, understood in its root meaning as the sensuous pleasure we take in daily productive life, is inextricable from our broader social being: "The *forming* of the five senses is a labour of the entire history of the world down to the present."[19] As Eagleton puts it, explicating Marx, "If communism is necessary, it is because we are unable to feel, taste, smell and touch as fully as we might." Wollstonecraft shares with Marx (and to some extent Eagleton as well) a Romantic–humanist "expression/repression model" of human capacities, assuming these will unfold in desirable directions when no longer hindered by political and social constraints. Despite such a paradigm's obvious difficulties, it has the advantage of throwing into relief the limitations of conventional aesthetics.[20] Connecting social structure, everyday life, and the quality of aesthetic experience, Wollstonecraft decisively transcends the liberal tradition in search of a cultural politics concerned with the substantive quality of life for everyone.

SCANDINAVIAN SCENES

Letters Written during a Short Residence in Sweden, Norway and Denmark continues to evince an urgent concern with material conditions of existence, especially those of the poorer sort of Scandinavians. Though most critics have focused on its more personal dimension, this epistolary travel report addresses wide-ranging social and political concerns, from overpopulation and environmental destruction to capital punishment.[21] Its preoccupation with aesthetics, especially landscape aesthetics, is inseparable, I will argue, from Wollstonecraft's political engagement. She is still rebutting Burke as she demonstrates the need to represent the relation between human beings and their environment in a manner compatible with a humane politics. In the war between reactionary Europe and post-Terror France, Scandinavia was neutral – conveniently for wartime profiteers like Wollstonecraft's lover Imlay, on whose business she traveled.[22] But these neutral northern countries proved a congenial intellectual setting for her work toward a politically and philosophically grounded reconception of aesthetics.

Written the year before she died, this is in many ways, as Ralph Wardle remarks, Wollstonecraft's "most mature and most delightful book."[23] She achieves a relaxed, engaging style that bespeaks a new level of writerly confidence and control. The book's rhetorical strategy is oblique compared to the full-on polemic of both *Vindications*. This obliqueness is dictated first of all by her need to sell as many books as possible as a means of achieving economic independence from Imlay.[24] Relying on the established popularity of travel literature and the vogue for natural scenery, she could draw in an audience much broader than her immediate political sympathizers on England's beleaguered left.

The genre of the epistolary travel report, with its informal tone and episodic structure, is especially congenial to the kind of experiment Wollstonecraft undertakes. It gives her the freedom to move back and forth between narrative and anecdote, social comment and personal reverie.[25] She weaves these seemingly disparate elements together into a sophisticated texture, one of whose binding threads is a subtly but insistently revisionist presentation of aesthetic experience. "Private" response emerges as inseparable from public or political determinations. To interrogate the nature and content of aesthetic experience, she demonstrates, is one way to speculate about the nature of a desirable civilization. *Letters* explores, by turns and in tandem, the symbolic construction of land as aesthetic object and the construction of the aesthetic subject or perceiver. It presents itself not as a treatise on aesthetics but as a lively and engaging series of personal letters. Nor is it unambiguously utopian. More than *A Vindication of the Rights of Men*, *Letters* is marked by conflicting discourses about class. The egalitarian impulses underlying Wollstonecraft's revision of aesthetics are occasionally contradicted by a reflexive condescension, even revulsion, that marks the limits of her liberal politics.

Letters' daring lies in the way it uses the prestige of aesthetics, that fashionable status symbol, to draw readers into its project of subtly, playfully, but profoundly subverting the world view that informs aesthetic discourse. Early on Wollstonecraft seems to flaunt her command of the nuances of beautiful, sublime, and picturesque in remarks like this vaguely Burkean effusion: "I walked on, still delighted with the rude beauties of the scene; for the sublime often gave place imperceptibly to the beautiful, dilating the emotions which were painfully concentrated" (247). But she soon goes beyond parroting faddish phrases to challenge the accepted authorities of aesthetics, dismissing Hogarth's line of beauty: "I never before admired the beech tree; and when I met stragglers here, they pleased me still less. Long and lank, they would have forced me to allow that the line of beauty requires some curves, if the stately pine, standing near, erect, throwing her vast arms around, had not looked beautiful, in opposition to such narrow rules" (289). The conspicuously feminine pine is reminiscent of the fine or stately woman whom Wollstonecraft in the *Vindication of the Rights of Woman* opposed to Burke's sickly, lisping beauties.[26] Redefining beauty beyond narrow rules will have consequences for people as well as trees.

Letter III challenges basic tenets of estate landscaping. Wollstonecraft uses a type of set piece familiar since Pope's 1731 "Epistle to Burlington," the comparison between two country estates, to question gardening's anti-utilitarianism and its anti-localism – its tendency to "improve" by the rules of painting, with little regard to the actual site. In contrast to *A Vindication of the Rights of Men*, Wollstonecraft here addresses philosophical principles more than political effects. Her preference in garden design is localized and utilitarian. She commends the restraint of the landowner who has done little but put up a "rude" stone table and bench under a cliff: "It requires uncommon taste to...introduce accommodations and ornaments analogous with the surrounding scene" (256). The other estate's expensive, conspicuously un-Scandinavian "italian colonades," "Venuses and Apollos" draw her jeers as "abortions of vanity" (257). A footnote extrapolates localism to an English context. The fashionable "grottoes," she declares, "are absurd in this temperate climate" – English gardens need sun, not shade. Moreover, "the usefulness of a garden ought to be conspicuous":

in order to admit the sun-beams to enliven our spring, autumn and winter, serpentine walks, the rage for the line of beauty, should be made to submit to convenience...a broad straight gravel walk is a great convenience for those who wish to take exercise in all seasons, after rain particularly. When the weather is fine, the meadows offer winding paths, far superior to the formal turnings that interrupt reflection, without amusing the fancy. (256)

In another shot at the serpentine line of beauty, as applied by the famous landscaper "Capability" Brown, Wollstonecraft puts the convenience and comfort of those inhabiting land ahead of aesthetic considerations. To collapse beauty and use in this manner was aesthetic heresy – "uncommon taste" indeed. She flies in the face of mainstream landscaping theory and practice to envision a way of dwelling on land that would integrate aesthetic with practical considerations.

Such straightforward disagreement, however, is the exception in *Letters*. More prevalent is oblique criticism through pointed departures from convention in her own descriptions. Landscape description was an expected element of the travel account, and it occupies considerable space in this one. Wollstonecraft's numerous reviews of travel books for Joseph Johnson's *Analytical Review* pay special attention to descriptive passages, citing those whose style she considers especially good or especially pretentious.[27] Descriptive language, we learn, carried a heavy conceptual burden. Read in light of established conventions, the cumulative effect of *Letters'* landscape descriptions is subtly, unsystematically, but thoroughly to flaunt standard descriptive practice, defying basic principles of mainstream aesthetic theory. Wollstonecraft's explicit and implicit departures from convention critique disinterested contemplation by destroying the distance between a perceiver and a statically framed scene. They attack the autonomy of the aesthetic domain, or the segregation of aesthetic from practical, by rejecting landscape aesthetics' distancing, marginalizing representations of figures in the landscape and challenging its anti-utilitarian bias. This description, for example, begins quite conventionally but ends in playful unorthodoxy:

Advancing towards Quistram, as the sun was beginning to decline, I was particularly impressed by the beauty of the situation. The road was on the declivity of a rocky mountain, slightly covered with a mossy herbage and vagrant firs. At the bottom, a river, straggling amongst the recesses of stone, was hastening forward to the ocean and its grey rocks, of which we had a prospect on the left, whilst on the right it stole peacefully forward into the meadows, losing itself in a thickly wooded rising ground. As we drew near, the loveliest banks of wild flowers variegated the prospect, and promised to exhale odours to add to the sweetness of the air, the purity of which you could almost see, alas! not smell, for the putrifying herrings, which they use as manure, after the oil has been extracted, spread over the patches of earth, claimed by cultivation, destroyed every other. (261)

Wollstonecraft mobilizes the standard vocabulary of the picturesque travelogue ("declivity," "herbage," "prospect," "variegated") to build the aestheticized impression that she then wickedly undercuts with the incongruous stench of rotten fish, signifiers of practical agricultural activity. The incompatibility of aesthetic and practical is exaggerated to the point of burlesque; Gilpin's doctrine that the traces of human industry ruin our pleasure in a picturesque scene is carried out in a way that playfully suggests its ludicrousness. Appealing to the "lower" sense of smell, she undercuts the primacy of the visual. The homely realism of the putrid herrings points out the artifice of an aesthetics that guards against life's bad smells.

A later passage takes as its target the static character of the typical picturesque description, the verbal framing that distanced viewer from scene. Wollstonecraft rejects such framing, presenting the "wild charms" of a Norwegian countryside as a loose, deliberately un-composed collection of objects, incorporating motion and change: "Rocks still enclosed the valleys, whose grey sides enlivened their verdure. Lakes appeared like branches of the sea, and branches of the sea assumed the appearance of tranquil lakes; whilst streamlets prattled amongst the pebbles, and the broken mass of stone which had rolled into them; giving fantastic turns to the trees whose roots they bared" (303). Active verbs – enlivened, prattled, rolled – and ideas of motion or transformation – "fantastic turns," "broken mass," lakes becoming inlets or vice versa – break out of the initial image of enclosure, refusing to permit the distance or self-containment of the conventional aesthetic object and subject.

But Wollstonecraft is not content merely to disrupt. The same description expands, with a seamless transition from aesthetic to practical, into a meditation on the relationship between living beings and their environment. The focus is on the trees, again those anthropomorphized pines.

It is not, in fact, surprising that the pine should be often undermined, it shoots its fibres in such an horizontal direction, merely on the surface of the earth, requiring only enough to cover those that cling to the craggs. Nothing proves to me, so clearly, that it is the air which principally nourishes trees and plants, as the flourishing appearance of these pines. – The firs demanding a deeper soil, are seldom seen in equal health, or so numerous on the barren cliffs. (303)

This concern with the material conditions of everyday life, the ways in which beings adapt to their surroundings, and what, exactly, they live on, extends to people as well as pines: the rural Scandinavians whose meager circumstances she records in a degree of detail incompatible with the conventions of the picturesque tour. Wherever Wollstonecraft goes she inquires after household economics. Her inn in East Riisoer, Norway, is kept by a widow whose daughter is married to a harbor pilot and has three cows, along with a patch of land for growing hay, which must be carried in by boat since the field is two miles away (293). Middle-class values color her approving account of industrious villagers who combine agricultural wage labor with garden cultivation, fishing, spinning and weaving, "so that they may fairly be reckoned independent;

having also a little money in hand to buy coffee, brandy, and some other superfluities" (300).

A vivid description of life on the inhospitable Swedish coast suggests an attempt to empathize with those who eke out their living in harsh conditions – to grasp the relation between the physical circumstances of their life and its subjective or affective quality.

The population of Sweden has been estimated from two millions and a half to three millions; a small number for such an immense tract of country: of which only so much is cultivated, and that in the simplest manner, as is absolutely necessary to supply the necessaries of life; and near the sea-shore, from whence herrings are easily procured, there scarcely appears a vestige of cultivation. The scattered huts that stand shivering on the naked rocks, braving the pitiless elements, are formed of logs of wood, rudely hewn; and so little pains are taken with the craggy foundation, that nothing like a pathway points out the door.

Gathered into himself by the cold, lowering his visage to avoid the cutting blast, is it surprising that the churlish pleasure of drinking drams takes place of social enjoyments amongst the poor, especially if we take into the account, that they mostly live on high-seasoned provisions and rye bread? Hard enough, you may imagine, as it is only baked once a year. (253)

From the traveler's conventional statistics the focus zooms in on the personified huts, shivering in midsummer: synecdoches for their inhabitants, whose isolation, "gathered into [themselves]," and the effort of life in harsh conditions is marked by the absence of door paths. The hostile environment mortifies the senses with cold weather, hard bread, and "high-seasoned provisions," antithetical to pleasure. Emphasizing the continuities between the practical conditions of life and its qualitative dimension suggests we reconceive the aesthetic as embedded in everyday life, rather than sharply separated from it.

A description of the Norwegian coast shows the same empathetic impulse, drawing a more explicit, if more complex connection between material circumstances and affective or aesthetic response.

Approaching the frontiers, consequently the sea, nature resumed an aspect ruder and ruder, or rather seemed the bones of the world waiting to be clothed with every thing necessary to give life and beauty. Still it was sublime.

The clouds caught their hue of the rocks that menaced them. The sun appeared afraid to shine, the birds ceased to sing, and the flowers to bloom; but the eagle fixed his nest high amongst the rocks, and the vulture hovered over this abode of desolation. The farm houses, in which only poverty resided, were formed of logs scarcely keeping off the cold and drifting snow; out of them the inhabitants seldom peeped, and the sports or prattling of children was neither seen nor heard. The current of life seemed congealed at the source: all were not frozen; for it was summer, you remember; but every thing appeared so dull, that I waited to see ice, in order to reconcile me to the absence of gaiety. (262–63)

Wollstonecraft presents the "rude," austere, bare-bones feeling of the coastal landscape, "this abode of desolation," and the overall feeling of the inhabitants' lives as logical consequences of their poverty. This remote corner of European civilization reverses the course of nature, exuding winter in midsummer; its sun is afraid to shine, its birds refuse to sing and its flowers to bloom. Its starkness places it under the category of the sublime, which Wollstonecraft suggestively links to her meliorist view of history. She cherishes a characteristic Enlightenment faith that the "bones of the world," the material foundation of civilization, will gradually and inevitably be "clothed with every thing necessary to give life" (material subsistence, the first step) "and beauty" (art and culture, the culmination of the civilizing process).[28] Assimilated to the grand march of civilization through history, even the stark, impoverished Norwegian coast takes on a hopeful aspect. The language of aesthetics mediates between Wollstonecraft's empathic recreation of how it must feel to live in this particular location in space and time, and her sense of its place in a larger scheme of things.

Letters repeatedly defies convention to place the human beings who live on and from the land at the center of its representation. Often, as in the two passages quoted above, instead of seeing those inhabitants from the outside we see, or rather feel, from their perspective. Wollstonecraft's imaginative re-creation of the materially grounded quality of people's lives – in this case, a vivid sense of their misery – permeates her descriptions and informs their aesthetic quality. The political statement implicit in this approach to landscape description directly contradicts the ethos of mainstream aesthetic theory. Rather than justify social hierarchy and privilege, *Letters* challenges these by representing land according to the perceptions, feelings, and needs of those who live on it, people who did not match the conventional qualifications of the aesthetic subject. Wollstonecraft implicitly attributes aesthetic capacities, at least potentially, to everyone, however socially low. This stands in pointed contrast to mainstream theories that disqualified virtually everyone, only to universalize the judgment of a tasteful elite.

The political dimension of Wollstonecraft's aesthetic experiments clearly emerges in another description which opens by showing her command of, and obvious pleasure in, the principles of aesthetic landscape appreciation: variety, contrast, the play of light and shadow. Soon, however, she disrupts the peaceful scene, as we have often watched her do. The force of her political statement relies on readers' familiarity with picturesque convention. The ruined castle or abbey was a favorite ornament for a picturesque view; I have noted the way conventional treatments of the ruin used it as a formal element whose historical associations were kept deliberately vague, diffusing at most an air of generalized melancholy over the scene. For Wollstonecraft the iconography of the castle has more to do with the Bastille, archetypal symbol of an oppressive *ancien régime*.

The rocks which tossed their fantastic heads so high were often covered with pines and firs, varied in the most picturesque manner. Little woods filled up the recesses, when forests did not darken the scene; and vallies and glens, cleared of the trees, displayed a dazzling verdure which contrasted with the gloom of the shading pines. The eye stole into many a covert where tranquillity seemed to have taken up her abode, and the number of little lakes that continually presented themselves added to the peaceful composure of the scenery. The little cultivation which appeared did not break the enchantment, nor did castles rear their turrets aloft to crush the cottages, and prove that man is more savage than the natives of the woods. I heard of the bears, but never saw them stalk forth, which I was sorry for; I wished to have seen one in its wild state. In the winter, I am told, they sometimes catch a stray cow, which is a heavy loss to the owner. (263)

In keeping with Wollstonecraft's embrace of the useful into aesthetics, signs of cultivation are not what break the "peaceful composure." Rather, in an aggressively anti-aesthetic turn she notes the absence of that standard picturesque element, the castle, glossing its politics so as to disenchant aesthetic contemplation. Burke's reactionary fondness for the castle as a symbol of the feudal–aristocratic past hovers over the passage. The woodland cottages, with their egalitarian aura, supplant the castle-dominated landscape in an overtly revisionist gesture. The seeming digression about the bears carries forward Wollstonecraft's emphasis on the relation between land and its human inhabitants. Her irrepressible wish to see a real, live bear reduces to absurdity the aesthetics of the sublime and its fashionable obsession with the "savage" or "wild." When her curiosity gives place to concern for the farmers whose cows are in danger, conventional aesthetic contemplation of nature is again disrupted by her involvement with people's, especially humble people's, practical needs.

Letter III displays this involvement as Wollstonecraft waxes indignant about the treatment of servants, which "shews how far the swedes are from having a just conception of rational equality"(253). Their wages are too low to buy shoes, their food inferior to their masters', and they can be beaten with impunity. "Still," she adds sarcastically, "the men stand up for the dignity of man, by oppressing the women…In the winter, I am told, they take the linen down to the river, to wash it in the cold water; and though their hands, cut by the ice, are cracked and bleeding, the men, their fellow servants, will not disgrace their manhood by carrying a tub to lighten their burden" (253). But these poignant observations of women servants' double oppression do not lead her to question domestic service as an institution. She moralizes, "We must love our servants, or we shall never be sufficiently attentive to their happiness" (254). Her own Parisian maid becomes a foil for her mistress as Wollstonecraft repeatedly contrasts herself to the stereotypical timidity and frivolity of the uneducated Marguerite.[29] Indeed, her concern for laboring-class inhabitants of the Scandinavian landscape occasionally gives way to attitudes more typical of her middle-class background.

This contradictory mixture of liberal concern and bourgeois condescension disintegrates by Letter XVI. Swindled at a post-house, Wollstonecraft grumbles, "I discovered…that these sluggish peasants had their share of cunning" (313). Unable to find lodging because of a country fair, she cannot persuade her postilion to drive her further. She vents her scorn and flaunts her education with a classical allusion: "Nothing…can equal the stupid obstinacy of some of these half alive beings, who seem to have been made by Prometheus, when the fire he stole from Heaven was so exhausted, that he could only spare a spark to give life, not animation, to the inert clay" (314). As the tired man reluctantly chauffeurs her one more stage, Wollstonecraft depicts roadside revelers in terms that evoke the Bakhtinian grotesque body.[30] She assumes and deplores

the fairgoers' promiscuity: "Hapless nymphs! thy haunts I fear
were polluted by many an unhallowed flame; the casual burst of
the moment!" (314).

An overcrowded inn confronts her with more grotesque bodies as
she picks her way through a room littered with sleeping people,
cats, and dogs. "I entered, and was almost driven back by the
stench...I passed, nothing dreading, excepting the effluvia, warily
amongst the pots, pans, milk-pails, and washing-tubs" on her way
to her private chamber. The next morning "I hastened through the
apartment, I have already described, not wishing to associate the
idea of a pigstye with that of a human dwelling. I do not now wonder that the girls lose their fine complexions at such an early age, or
that love here is merely an appetite...never enlivened by either
affection or sentiment" (314). The historical process of creating a
sublimated bourgeois body emphasized cleanliness and the eradica-
tion of odors, sanctioned by just such visceral disgust. The pig, as
Stallybrass and White have noted, was a preeminent early modern
emblem of corporeal immoderation and offenses against polite
manners. "To have nothing in common with pigs – was not that the
aim of every educated bourgeois subject...?" (52). Wollstonecraft's
phrasing implies she feels guilty at associating the overcrowded
Swedes with pigs, underscoring the conflict between her conscious
politics and her powerful class prejudices.

It is not surprising to those familiar with Wollstonecraft's *oeuvre*
that contradiction erupts around the representation of bodies, their
functions and pleasures. Issues of class are also recurrent sites of
ambivalence and conflict in her writings.[31] The laboring classes,
like women, were traditionally thought of as ruled by their bodies
rather than their minds. Wollstonecraft's deep ambivalence about
such oppressive, essentializing constructions of woman earlier led
her to reject female sexual pleasure in favor of a sublimated,
rational life.[32] Here we uncover a related ambivalence about the
laboring classes, a group to which Wollstonecraft (as she emphasizes) does not belong, but who like women are a focus for her
political concern. *Letters* is working at a very different discursive
conjuncture from *A Vindication of the Rights of Woman* – one that
offers an alternative to the oppressive image of the poor as trapped
in their sluggish, smelly bodies. It is as though the distancing effect
of landscape aesthetics, which Wollstonecraft deplores when it
leads the privileged to ignore the humanity of the poor, opens a

breathing space, so to speak, between her and those bodies, letting her attribute dignity to the rural Scandinavians and validate their corporeally grounded needs. Sometimes (as Mary Wortley Montagu also found) distance can demonstrate respect.

The very next page returns to a more dignified presentation of laboring bodies and their material needs. Again Wollstonecraft revises the canons of scenic description to make a seamless transition from aesthetic to practical; again she places rural dwellers and their subsistence at the center of the landscape.

The purple hue which the heath now assumed, gave it a degree of richness, that almost exceeded the lustre of the young green of spring – and harmonized exquisitely with the rays of the ripening corn. The weather was uninterruptedly fine, and the people busy in the fields cutting down the corn, or binding up the sheaves, continually varied the prospect. The rocks, it is true, were unusually rugged and dreary, yet as the road runs for a considerable way by the side of a fine river, with extended pastures on the other side, the image of sterility was not the predominant object, though the cottages looked still more miserable, after having seen the norwegian farms...The women and children were cutting off branches from the beech, birch, oak, etc., and leaving them to dry – This way of helping out their fodder, injures the trees. But the winters are so long, that the poor cannot afford to lay in a sufficient stock of hay. By such means they just keep life in the poor cows, for little milk can be expected when they are so miserably fed. (315)

Aesthetic considerations of color, harmony, and variety give way to concern for the cottagers' "miserable" standard of living. Wollstonecraft focuses on one activity, cutting branches, to open a window onto these cottagers' bare-subsistence lives. By inserting rural economics into her description, she counteracts the deliberate distancing that marked most landscape description in her day. Like every woman writer I have discussed, Wollstonecraft often displays conflicted, even self-contradictory attitudes toward aesthetics itself and toward the social Others who became aesthetic objects. Nonetheless, *Letters'* revisionist strain is persistent and daring. Laboring bodies and their practical needs break the frame of picturesque convention to make room for a more humane mode of representation.

RE-SITUATING THE AESTHETIC SUBJECT

The *Letters'* playful but pointed revision of the symbolic construction of land as aesthetic object extends to the subject as well. For mainstream theorists, as we saw in Chapter Three, aesthetic contemplation entailed setting aside any kind of investment in particular material things. Aesthetic experience, though rooted in the senses, came to be understood as disinterested and virtually disembodied. The aesthetic subject was nonetheless assumed to be from a particular social segment: upper-class, male, and European. The "Vulgar," thought of as trapped in their bodies, were disqualified from "high" cultural pursuits under the dualistic metaphysics that separates body from mind and valorizes the latter. The subject of the picturesque conforms to this paradigm: the detached viewpoint epitomized by the rigid "Stations" of West's *Guide to the Lakes* makes the viewer into a pure organizing eye, with no physical connection to the landscape. Instead of being in nature, the viewer is positioned as in a picture gallery, opposite a framed, contained scene. As the viewer is cut off from the scene, visual aesthetic satisfaction is correspondingly cut off from other dimensions of experience. The consequences are finally political. The absence of contact between those who view land as connoisseurs and those who must live on and from that land doubtless encouraged the exploitation against which Wollstonecraft's first *Vindication* railed.

She constructs her aesthetic perceiver in resistance to this model. The highly individualized persona of the *Letters* combines intellectual curiosity and political engagement with a consciously deployed emotional vulnerability. Such a traveler flaunted the conventions of travel writing, which prescribed reticence about the self, as well as those of aesthetics.[33] Her Advertisement proclaims, "I found I could not avoid being continually the first person – 'the little hero of each tale.'...I give [readers] leave to shut the book, if they do not wish to become better acquainted with me" (241). Such an approach to travel was not entirely new by 1796. Sterne's quirky sentimental traveler had spawned imitations *ad nauseam*, but the main current of travel writing still tended toward impersonality. Like Sterne, Wollstonecraft uses the episodic structure of the travel narrative as a frame for exploring and describing subjective states of being; her persona builds a complex interiority through her responses to her surroundings. In this sense she takes travel writing closer to genres that twentieth-century critics classify as more "literary," partly because they are genres more preoccupied with individual psychology – the realist novel, as well as lyric poetry. But simply assimilating *Letters* to a Romantic movement conceived as preoccupied with interiority would overlook the polemical philosophical and political elements of its rhetorical strategy. Read against the distancing conventions of landscape aesthetics and travel writing, Wollstonecraft's deliberately personalized, particular interaction with her surroundings transgresses the categorial boundaries of class and nation that circumscribed both these discourses. By giving the aesthetic subject a feminine gender and a corporeal connection to her environment, she subtly but audaciously redefines aesthetic pleasure to make it more inclusive and more humane.

Travel accounts by Wollstonecraft's contemporaries frequently segregate descriptive passages from narration. The picturesque travelogue, preoccupied with its rather formulaic landscape descriptions, keeps narrative to a minimum. Travelers to more exotic destinations almost always describe the landscape as though it were uninhabited, relegating inhabitants' "manners and customs" to separate encapsulated sections.[34] Such practices marginalized and symbolically dispossessed the inhabitants of land. Wollstonecraft's descriptions, by contrast, deliberately include Scandinavian inhabitants. She reaches out to them with an empathy that subverts the distancing conventions of landscape aesthetics and travel writing. In Letter I, as sailors row her ashore for her first landing in a remote Swedish bay, she self-consciously intimates her inappropriateness as a conventional aesthetic subject.

The weather was pleasant, and the appearance of the shore so grand, that I should have enjoyed the two hours it took to reach it, but for the fatigue which was too visible in the countenances of the sailors...Yet, in spite of their good humour, I could not help growing uneasy when the shore, receding, as it were, as we advanced, seemed to promise no end to their toil. This anxiety increased when, turning into the most picturesque bay I ever saw, my eyes sought in vain for the vestige of a human habitation. (244)

The aesthetic terms "grand" (a synonym for "sublime") and "picturesque" are intermingled with practical concerns – compassion for the sailors, anxiety for herself – that are incompatible with the conventional disinterestedness of the aesthetic perceiver.

Aesthetic and practical compete for attention, mingling in the narrative flow of Wollstonecraft's perception. As they row along in search of a pilot's hut she observes, "There was a solemn silence in this scene, which made itself be felt. The sun-beams that played on the ocean, scarcely ruffled by the lightest breeze, contrasted with the huge, dark rocks, that looked like the rude materials of creation forming the barrier of unwrought space, forcibly struck me; but I should not have been sorry if the cottage had not appeared equally tranquil" (245). Practical concerns, in this case the need to find transportation and get on with her journey, supersede tranquil scenic description in a pattern that recurs throughout the *Letters*. Life will not stand still for aesthetic contemplation. To expect it to do so begins to seem disturbingly artificial. A different aesthetics is needed to account for pleasure that is embedded in the practical texture of lived experience.

A remarkable sequence in Letter VIII works in the *Letters'* typically oblique fashion to re-situate the aesthetic subject in her body and aesthetic experience in everyday life. The associative flow of Wollstonecraft's prose establishes these connections; to demonstrate the effect I will need to reproduce several paragraphs in full. She has been unexpectedly detained in Tonsberg, Norway, for three weeks, and uses this scenic town as a kind of spa to recover her temporarily lost physical and psychological equilibrium.

Tonsberg was formerly the residence of one of the little sovereigns of Norway; and on an adjacent mountain the vestiges of a fort remain, which was battered down by the swedes; the entrance of the bay lying close to it.

Here I have frequently strayed, sovereign of the waste, I seldom met any human creature; and sometimes, reclining on the mossy down, under the shelter of a rock, the prattling of the sea amongst the pebbles has lulled me to sleep – no fear of any rude satyr's approaching to interrupt my repose. Balmy were the slumbers, and soft the gales, that refreshed me, when I awoke to follow, with an eye vaguely curious, the white sails, as they turned the cliffs, or seemed to take shelter under the pines which covered the little islands that so gracefully rose to render the terrific ocean beautiful. The fishermen were calmly casting their nets; whilst the seagulls hovered over the unruffled deep. Every thing seemed to harmonize into tranquillity – even the mournful call of the bittern was in cadence with the tinkling bells on the necks of the cows, that, pacing slowly one after the other, along an inviting path in the vale below, were repairing to the cottages to be milked. With what ineffable pleasure have

I not gazed – and gazed again, losing my breath through my eyes – my very soul diffused itself in the scene – and, seeming to become all senses, gilded in the scarcely-agitated waves, melted in the freshening breeze, or, taking its flight with fairy wing, to the misty mountains which bounded the prospect, fancy tript over new lawns, more beautiful even than the lovely slopes on the winding shore before me. – I pause, again breathless, to trace, with renewed delight, sentiments which entranced me, when, turning my humid eyes from the expanse below to the vault above, my sight pierced the fleecy clouds that softened the azure brightness; and, imperceptibly recalling the reveries of childhood, I bowed before the awful throne of my Creator, whilst I rested on its footstool. (279–80)

We notice first of all the unconventional positioning of the observer in this landscape description. Rather than being stationed outside the scene, she places herself physically within the landscape. Strategic sensory details remind us that this is an emphatically embodied perceiver. Wollstonecraft invokes senses other than sight, which mainstream aesthetics privileged as the least corporeal of the senses. We almost feel the softness of the moss on which she lies, the refreshing breeze, and the cool comfort of the shade as we listen to the prattling sea that is her lullaby. Nature embraces and nurtures her like a child. This suggestion subtly connects aesthetic pleasure to another experience that, throughout the *Letters*, emblematizes Wollstonecraft's new-found comfort with her body: the experience of motherhood. References to physical contact with her young daughter, hugging her or watching her "frolick" in a meadow (293, 299), embrace the corporeal self that her earlier writings had treated with suspicion.

The scene to which she awakens from her nap contains elements familiar to readers versed in landscape aesthetics. The boats and fishermen in the bay are reminiscent of a harbor scene by Claude Lorrain; the balance between the beautiful or graceful islands and the sublime or "terrific" ocean is a standard compositional device. There is more motion than we would expect – boats turning, fishermen casting nets, cows pacing the path – but the overall feeling remains tranquil and idyllic. The transition from picturesque scene to transcendent moment ("my very soul diffused itself in the scene…seeming to become all senses") moves away from static framing, but continues the conventional disembodiment of the aesthetic subject. If we stopped reading after this paragraph, Wollstonecraft might seem to be enacting the conventional disembodiment of the aesthetic subject, succumbing to the estrangement from her body that critics find in her earlier writings.

But the context in which Wollstonecraft carefully sets this transcendent moment gives it a very different valence. The next paragraph, in a quietly audacious rhetorical move, yokes aesthetic pleasure with the kind of pleasure from which theorists were most concerned to distinguish it: sexual pleasure.

> You have sometimes wondered, my dear friend, at the extreme affection of my nature – But such is the temperature of my soul – It is not the vivacity of youth, the hey-day of existence. For years have I endeavoured to calm an impetuous tide – labouring to make my feelings take an orderly course. – It was striving against the stream. – I must love and admire with warmth, or I sink into sadness. Tokens of love which I have received have rapt me in elysium – purifying the heart they enchanted. – My bosom still glows. – Do not saucily ask, repeating Sterne's question, "Maria, is it still so warm?" Sufficiently, O my God! has it been chilled by sorrow and unkindness – still nature will prevail – and if I blush at recollecting past enjoyment, it is the rosy hue of pleasure heightened by modesty; for the blush of modesty and shame are as distinct as the emotions by which they are produced. (280)

The euphemistic language ("Tokens of love...have rapt me in elysium") was sufficiently suggestive for alert readers. The reference to her glowing bosom anchors "elysium" in a physical response. Wollstonecraft's letters to Imlay use the characteristic "suffusion" of his body and face to refer to their lovemaking.[35] The blush, topic of a long-standing debate in the literature of female conduct, unconventionally appears here as a sign of neither ignorance nor guilt, but rather a "rosy hue of pleasure" to which a woman is actually entitled. Such a claim, unobtrusive at first glance, comes to seem astonishingly bold in the context of the eighteenth-century sexual double standard.

The allusion to Sterne's Maria, the famous madwoman who appears in both *Tristram Shandy* (1761–65) and *A Sentimental Journey* (1768), adds a significant dimension. Maria, driven mad when her banns were forbidden by a corrupt clergyman, wanders the roads with her flute and goat, the kind of innocent, pathetic victim that Sterne's sensibility cherishes. The immediate context of the allusion is Maria's offer to dry Yorick's handkerchief, with which he has wiped her tears, in her bosom. He responds with one of Sterne's famous sentimental-sexual *double entendres*: "And is your heart still so warm, Maria?"[36] Wollstonecraft's emphatic negation, "Do not saucily ask," rebukes the male addressee's imagined leer as she repudiates the link between herself and this quintessential sexual victim. Modestly but frankly acknowledging her own "warm heart," her sexual desires and disappointments, this female persona refuses to be the butt of dirty jokes – as if to say, "I am not Maria; I do not intend to let my sexuality rob me of my understanding or my dignity." Wollstonecraft declares her entitlement to the sexual pleasure that her culture conspired to deny women, along with the other pleasure to which she implicitly connects it: aesthetic pleasure. Conflating these two pleasures, both interdicted to women, becomes a quietly revolutionary gesture.

The parallel between aesthetic pleasure and sexual pleasure operates at a structural level as well. Both are shown leading to an experience of religious or quasi-religious rapture. But the paragraphs that follow ground these experiences in physical well-being. Transcending the body need not indicate contempt for the corporeal. Rather, both kinds of pleasure are made possible in the first place by the senses. Wollstonecraft posits her recovered health as a necessary precondition of the aesthetic enjoyment she describes.

I need scarcely inform you, after telling you of my walks, that my constitution has been renovated here; and that I have recovered my activity, even whilst attaining a little *embonpoint*. My imprudence last winter, and some untoward accidents just at the time I was weaning my child, had reduced me to a state of weakness which I never before experienced. A slow fever preyed on me every night, during my residence in Sweden, and after I arrived at Tonsberg. By chance I found a fine rivulet filtered through the rocks, and confined in a bason for cattle. It tasted to me like a chalybeat; at any rate it was pure; and the good effect of the various waters which invalids are sent to drink, depends, I believe, more on the air, exercise and change of scene, than on their medicinal qualities. I therefore determined to turn my morning walks towards it, and seek for health from the nymphs of the fountain; partaking of the beverage offered to the tenants of the shade.

Chance likewise led me to discover a new pleasure, equally beneficial to my health. I wished to avail myself of my vicinity to the sea, and bathe; but it was not possible near the town; there was no convenience. The young woman whom I mentioned to you, proposed rowing me across the water, amongst the rocks; but as she was pregnant, I insisted on taking one of the oars, and learning to row. It was not difficult; and I do not know a pleasanter exercise. I soon became expert, and my train of thinking kept time, as it were, with the oars, or I suffered the boat to be carried along by the current, indulging a pleasing forgetfulness, or fallacious hopes. – How fallacious! yet, without hope, what is to sustain life, but the fear of annihilation – the only thing of which I have ever felt a dread – I cannot bear to think of being no more – of losing myself – though existence is often but a painful consciousness of misery; nay, it appears to me impossible that I should cease to exist, or that this active, restless spirit, equally alive to joy and sorrow, should only be organized dust – ready to fly abroad the moment the spring snaps, or the spark goes out, which kept it together. Surely something resides in this heart that is not perishable – and life is more than a dream. (280–81)

More than just preconditions for other, higher varieties of pleasure, fresh air and exercise are pleasures in and of themselves. The structure of the movement toward transcendence is repeated yet again as her excursions in the rowboat lead to musings on death and immortality. All three kinds of pleasure – aesthetic enjoyment, sex, and exercise – are implicitly grouped together, contradicting theories that separate aesthetic experience from other pleasures as something qualitatively different, higher, and distinctively non-corporeal. Aesthetic enjoyment takes its place among the simple physical delights of everyday life. Rather than segregate the aesthetic from the body's needs and desires, Wollstonecraft points toward an aesthetics anchored in and arising from these. She critiques the autonomous aesthetic domain by offering an alternative model.

The theory of pleasure that the *Letters* suggest goes far to reclaim the aesthetic as, in Eagleton's words, "a kind of incipient materialism" (196). To situate aesthetic pleasure this way is to insist on the continuity between the "taste of sense" and the "taste of reflection," the body's needs or compulsions and the spirit's freedom, a continuity that classical or Kantian aesthetics would decisively interrupt. Bourdieu criticizes the "pure pleasure" of Kantian aesthetics as an "ascetic, empty pleasure which implies the renunciation of pleasure, pleasure purified of pleasure." He attributes that renunciation to a social logic: "the antithesis between culture and bodily pleasure (or nature) is rooted in the opposition between the cultivated bourgeoisie and the people."[37] We have observed Wollstonecraft's concern in *Letters* and elsewhere to re-include "the people" in the aesthetic equation, putting working inhabitants back into the landscape from which polite taste would effectively erase them. A similar political impulse accounts for her materialist rejection of the disinterested, disembodied aesthetic subject and his ascetic-aesthetic pleasure.

Wollstonecraft brings her musings full circle with a casual anecdote that can be read as a parable for her approach to aesthetics.

Sometimes, to take up my oar, once more, when the sea was calm, I was amused by disturbing the innumerable young star fish which floated just below the surface: I had never observed them before; for they have not a hard shell, like those which I have seen on the sea-shore. They look like thickened water, with a white edge; and four purple circles, of different forms, were in the middle, over an incredible number of fibres, or white lines. Touching them, the cloudy substance would turn or close, first on one side, then on the other, very gracefully; but when I took one of them up in the ladle with which I heaved the water out of the boat, it appeared only a colourless jelly.

I did not see any of the seals, numbers of which followed our boat when we landed in Sweden; for though I like to sport in the water, I should have had no desire to join in their gambols. (281)

Her attentive description (reminding us of the strong symbiosis between travel writing and natural history in this period) attributes beauty and grace to this humble organism, the "star fish" or jellyfish.[38] But the beauty only appears in its natural environment; the minute it is removed it becomes an unappealing blob. This parable of localism resonates on several levels with the theory of aesthetic pleasure implied in Wollstonecraft's *Letters*, which put people at the center of the landscapes they inhabit, instead of obscuring their material connection to land, and situate aesthetic pleasure among other pleasures rather than setting it apart.

The jellyfish anecdote ties together the water imagery that has unobtrusively permeated the whole sequence, helping us understand that pleasure, like water, is necessary to life – from the "scarcely-agitated waves" of the bay to the "impetuous tide" or "stream" of her emotions and the "chalybeat" spring, symbolizing fresh air and exercise as sources of well-being. Her aside, "I like to sport in the water," reiterates the theme that began the sequence: the most satisfying aesthetic experience places the perceiver in an environment, rather than separating her from what then becomes a lifeless aesthetic object, like a jellyfish out of water.

Letters Written...in Sweden re-constructs both subject and object of aesthetic experience in a manner so sharply opposed to mainstream eighteenth-century aesthetics as to deserve the label "anti-aesthetics." Wollstonecraft offers an alternative to conventional definitions of aesthetic pleasure as qualitatively distinct from other kinds of pleasure, disembodied, and detached or disinterested. Her version of aesthetic response takes its place among other pleasures, involves both body and mind, and openly serves political interests. She offers a reminder – salutary even today – that our pleasures are indeed political, despite the still powerful ideology of an autonomous aesthetic sphere set apart from sordid practical concerns. *Letters* is especially noteworthy as an expression of Wollstonecraft's feminism. Presenting herself as a full-fledged aesthetic subject whose feminine gender, sexuality, and motherhood are not suppressed, but rather incorporated into the specific quality of her aesthetic experience, was a bold move in the masculinist context of eighteenth-century aesthetic theory.

The aesthetic in its modern form is a product of the Enlightenment, exemplifying our legacy of contradiction from that vexed historical conjuncture. Aesthetics can be both repressive and potentially emancipatory, epitomize social hierarchy even as it feeds Utopian aspirations. Wollstonecraft's anti-aesthetics partakes of a Romantic vision shared in some respects (as Eagleton observes) by such unlikely bedfellows as Shaftesbury and Karl Marx, as well as her contemporary Friedrich Schiller: the idea "that human powers and human society are an absolute end in themselves. To live well is to live in the free, many-sided realization of one's capacities, in reciprocal interaction with the similar self-expression of others."[39] *Letters* articulates a vision of civilization centered in the imagination, for Wollstonecraft the primary aesthetic faculty. For her the history of the world is a history of progress toward higher pleasures and toward a social and economic organization more conducive to realizing aesthetic capacities, broadly conceived.

The more I see of the world, the more I am convinced that civilization is a blessing not sufficiently estimated by those who have not traced its progress; for it not only refines our enjoyments, but produces a variety which enables us to retain the primitive delicacy of our sensations. Without the aid of the imagination all the pleasures of the senses must sink into grossness...I never met with much imagination amongst people who had not acquired a habit of reflection; and in that state of society in which the judgment and taste are not called forth, and formed by the cultivation of the arts and sciences, little of that delicacy of feeling and thinking is to be found characterized by the word sentiment. (250–51)

Civilization is a blessing because it refines our enjoyments and connects our senses to the imagination and understanding. This is reminiscent of Kantian faculty psychology's more precise rationale for elevating the aesthetic. Language like "grossness" and "refinement" evokes an elitist aesthetics. But in the context of Wollstonecraft's implicit attribution of aesthetic capacities to everyone, however socially low, it reads with a qualitative difference.[40] Her outlook, inflected by her historical meliorism, is inclusive rather than exclusive. Given the right "state of society," everyone could live aesthetically.

Letters also conveys a distinctly dystopic moment, however. Wollstonecraft perceives a looming threat to the unfolding of humanity's aesthetic capacities in the form of commerce or "traffic," her term for the mercantile capitalism that was the source of England's rapidly rising prosperity. She admits that "England and America owe their liberty to commerce, which created a new species of power to undermine the feudal system. But let them beware," she adds, "of the consequence; the tyranny of wealth is still more galling and debasing than that of rank" (309). Throughout her travels she condemns what she judges to be the corrupting effects of the narrow pursuit of gain. Increasingly she homes in on the wartime speculation practiced by her correspondent, her estranged lover Imlay. When she roundly declares that "an adoration of property is the root of all evil" (325), we remember her critique of Burke's aesthetic politics as corrupted by his worship of property and power. Visiting the commercial center of Hamburg, she compares notes with an American acquaintance. Here, he remarks, "you will not meet with a man who has any calf to his leg; body and soul, muscles and heart, are equally shrivelled up by a thirst of gain" (342).

The image of bodily shriveling resonates with Wollstonecraft's earlier emphasis on the reciprocity between physical health and aesthetic pleasure. We recall from Letter VIII her pride in regaining her "*embonpoint*," joined to her renewed relish for the Swedish landscape. Her rather random, unsystematic, and admittedly ambivalent condemnation of capitalism allies her with Schiller as he decries the division of labor, which leads to "whole classes of human beings developing only a part of their capacities, while the rest of them, like a stunted plant, shew only a feeble vestige of their nature."[41] Marx's theory of *Entfremdung* (alienation or estrangement) more systematically explores the antithesis between capitalism and his version of an aesthetic Utopia. Private property promotes a one-dimensional relation to the object world, "the sheer estrangement of *all* [the] senses – the sense of *having*...The transcendence of private property is therefore the complete *emancipation* of all human senses and attributes...The eye has become a *human* eye, just as its *object* has become a social, *human* object" (87). Presenting capitalism as inherently dystopic, a threat to the development of an aesthetic civilization, Wollstonecraft thus aligns herself with an important tradition encompassing both idealist and materialist aestheticians. The politicized theory of pleasure sketched out in *Letters Written...in Sweden* needs to be weighed along with her other writings as part of her contribution to the still unfinished dialectic of Enlightenment.

CHAPTER 6

Dorothy Wordsworth and the cultural politics of scenic tourism

Scotland is the country above all others that I have seen,
in which a man of imagination may carve out his own
pleasures.[1]

Dorothy Wordsworth is best known not for her travel journals, but
for those she kept at home: at the cottage she shared with her
brother William in Grasmere, in the heart of the scenic Lake
District. The prevalent image of Wordsworth as something of a
homebody, content to cook, clean, and copy poems for her more
publicly ambitious brother, contrasts with Mary Wollstonecraft's
self-assertive, consciously politicized persona.[2] Feminist critics have
been intrigued by the contrast between the habitual, sometimes
distressing self-effacement of the sister's writing and the brother's
expansive Romantic ego.[3] But Wordsworth's treatment of aesthetic
discourse in the journals and in her remarkable travel narrative,
Recollections of a Tour Made in Scotland, A. D. 1803, shares significant
features with Wollstonecraft's anti-aesthetics. Both writers disrupt
and reconceptualize the aesthetic perception of land. Both are
concerned with the practical realities of dwelling in a place and the
ways in which these can or should influence perceptual pleasure,
for those who dwell there and those who travel through.

The *Grasmere Journals* take advantage of a particular conjuncture
of material and cultural conditions to achieve, with understated
grace, a textual integration of aesthetic and practical. Walking in
the hills and enjoying their visual qualities takes its place for
Wordsworth among the practices of housework, gardening,
socializing, almsgiving, reading, and writing. She provisionally circumvents mainstream theorists' segregation of the aesthetic by
reconceiving aesthetic pleasure not as passive contemplation, but
as an activity or practice woven among other activities in the
rhythm or texture of everyday life.

In *Recollections*, too, we notice an alternation between aesthetic and practical perception and we sense an attempt to integrate the two along the same lines as in the *Grasmere Journals*. Wordsworth made the trip narrated in *Recollections* in August and September of 1803, just months after the final entry in the *Journals*, dated January of that year. But uprooting this discursive synthesis from home (as she uprooted the flowers she planted in her Grasmere garden), and transplanting it across the Tweed to the relatively close but still alien Scottish terrain, seems to exacerbate the threats to its fragile textual ecology. As much as Wordsworth is concerned to set herself apart from "prospect-hunters and 'picturesque travellers,'" she is a tourist too (271). The institution of tourism confronts her, inscribed on the face of the country by Scots eager to convert scenic rapture into cash. Aesthetic distance is amplified to a peculiar self-alienation. Like the *Grasmere Journals*, *Recollections* insists that land is inhabited by people with practical needs, feelings, desires, subjectivities, and voices; both texts thus counteract to some extent the dehumanizing tendency of landscape aesthetics. But in *Recollections*, recurrent, oddly intrusive images and tropes trouble the balance that the *Journals* had painstakingly achieved. Travel forces Wordsworth to confront the mediatedness of the natural world with which she had lived in comfortable intimacy at home. Images from the city and its consumer culture, as well as recurrent allusions to the overseas Other of colonial exploration, manifest the intimate fragmentation of this female aesthetic subject.

A "PROSPECT...ALLIED TO HUMAN LIFE"

The writer's intense attachment to a specific place is a central feature of the *Grasmere Journals*. It is well to begin, then, by characterizing that attachment – first by what it is not. Wordsworth's sense of place is not an indigenous localism like that of her contemporary, the laborer poet John Clare. Born and raised in the village of Helpston, until adulthood Clare seldom if ever ventured more than one or two miles from home. Helpston parish was literally the only place he knew. His autobiography describes getting lost as a child: "I eagerly wanderd on & rambled along the furze the whole day till I got out of my knowledge when the very wild flowers seemd to forget me & I imagind they were the inhabitants of new countrys the very sun seemd to be a new one & shining in a different quarter of the sky." The phrase "out of my knowledge," as John Barrell points out, carries a great deal of weight in the context of the deliberate localism of his poetic project. Most of his *oeuvre* is devoted to mourning the loss through enclosure, with its topographical alterations, of the Helpston Clare knew – and thus, in a sense, of everything he knew. His disorientation arises from an epistemological orientation that recognizes only particulars. Thus his nature poetry describes not nature in general, but only nature's particular manifestation in Helpston.[4]

Critics' comments on Clare's poetry are reminiscent of critical assessments of Dorothy Wordsworth's journals. Both writers refuse to go beyond the particular, to superimpose meditation or metaphysics on what they see. Clare's vision, observes John Middleton Murry, cannot "pass beyond itself" in the manner (he implies) of William Wordsworth or Keats.[5] Similarly, Susan Levin finds in Wordsworth's journals a "faithfulness to objects," a commitment to the particularity of her environment to the extent that she "often appears a mere cataloguer of irrelevant detail, a person strangely fixated on the minutiae around her." Combined with this positive commitment Levin observes a "refusal to generalize, refusal to move out of a limited range of vision, refusal to speculate, refusal to reproduce standard literary forms."[6]

Clare's sense of place contrasts strongly with the attitude to land inherent in picturesque aesthetics, which depends precisely on denying particularity. The ability to compare a place with another place, a painting, or a set of compositional rules is a precondition for such an aesthetics. For the purpose of comparison, a degree of mobility – the experience of more than one landscape – is clearly helpful. Mobility in eighteenth-century England was by and large the prerogative of the upper classes, who unlike most of the rural population were not "bound up in...any particular locality which they had no time, no money, and no reason ever to leave."[7] By the 1790s this was changing, however, as the steady stream of itinerants through Wordsworth's Grasmere testifies.

Social status and biographical circumstance combined to prevent Dorothy Wordsworth from developing a relation to any one place comparable to John Clare's roots in Helpston. Born in Cockermouth in the Lake District in 1771, she was uprooted at the age of six by her mother's death. Her next nine years were spent in the village of Halifax with a cousin, Elizabeth Threlkeld. In 1787 economizing measures by her guardians (her father died in 1783) forced her to move to her grandparents' home in Penrith, about twenty-five miles from Cockermouth, fifteen miles from Grasmere, and twenty miles from Hawkshead, where her brothers were raised. In 1788 she accompanied her uncle William Cookson and his new wife to Furncett in Norfolk, where she helped care for their growing family until she moved in with her brother William in 1794. Their first rented home together was Racedown Lodge in Dorset; their second, Alfoxden, was at Nether Stowey near Coleridge's house. Not until 1799, in her twenty-ninth year, did Dorothy Wordsworth finally settle in the village of Grasmere, a location selected by her brother on a walking tour with Coleridge.[8] Their youthful attachment to the Lake District clearly entered into the decision, but the particular site of the siblings' domestic idyll was chosen (the choice dictated in part by the availability of rental property). By then both brother and sister had experienced enough different places to realize the comparative aesthetic value of the one they chose to call home.

That appeal was already evident to most educated Britons. In 1778 Thomas West's *Guide to the Lakes*, the single most popular piece of tourist literature on the region (seven editions by 1800), institutionalized the Lake District tour. His directions, in an autocratic imperative voice, propel the tasteful to a series of "stations" chosen for their picture-perfect views. The "Rage for the Lakes" (Hester Piozzi's phrase) is aptly described by Malcolm Andrews: "In the summer months, coaches of all shapes and sizes rattled along the shores of the Lakes, struggled up steep passes, and now and again, waited at the roadside while passengers jumped out to take a quick sketch of a bewildered shepherd. The Lakes themselves were scarcely less congested. Packed pleasure-boats loitered at viewpoints on Ullswater or Windermere, now and then firing off cannon to enable the tourists to listen to the succession of echoes."[9] Though noisy cannons and prosperous pleasure-seekers' stares may have annoyed inhabitants, tourism made an undeniable contribution to the region's depressed economy. The Lake District's scenic appeal began to change its appearance as well-heeled outsiders bought land, enclosed commons, and built houses commanding scenic views. Dorothy Wordsworth's journal deplores in strong terms the design of one sprung-up estate along Windermere, which had apparently replaced farmland: "They have made no natural glades, it is merely a lawn with a few miserable young trees standing as if they were half-starved. There are no sheep no cattle upon these lawns. It is neither one thing or another – neither *natural* nor wholly cultivated and artificial which it was before. And that great house! Mercy upon us! If it *could* be concealed it *would* be well for all who are not pleased to see the pleasantest of earthly spots deformed by man."[10] The tackier manifestations of the quest for taste did not end with ugly villas and sickly shrubs. For example, Joseph Pocklington, scion of a Nottinghamshire banking family, bought himself an island in Derwentwater and some land along its shores. Pocklington liked to whitewash things: his house, the adjoining rocks, and even an oak tree which he manicured into an obelisk. He built a white castellated hermitage and advertised for a hermit who, for half a crown a day, was to refrain from washing, cutting his nails, or talking for seven years. The position remained unfilled.[11]

The grounds of Wordsworth's objection to the villa are clearly those of taste, rather than concern for dispossessed farmers. Earlier, however, she records a pessimistic prediction by John Fisher, brother of the Wordsworths' servant Molly, who "observed that in a short time there would be only two ranks of people, the very rich and the very poor, for those who have small estates says he are forced to sell, and all the land goes into one hand" (19). Wordsworth also relates the heroic efforts of another Grasmere family, the Ashburners, to keep their "small estate" from falling into the hands of Londoners: Peggy Ashburner "told me with what pains and industry they had made up their taxes interest etc. etc. – how they all got up at 5 o'clock in the morning to spin and Thomas carded, and that they had paid off a hundred pound of the interest" (61). Recording the concerns and voices of those who inhabit this beautiful, tourist-ridden area, Wordsworth fashions a polylogic record of the historical changes affecting her chosen home.

Though Dorothy and William Wordsworth's attitudes toward that home diverged sharply from those of *nouveau riche* intruders like Pocklington, they also differed from those of the Fishers or Ashburners. The Wordsworths were Lake District natives, but not native to Grasmere. Moreover, they shared a mentality, conditioned by their socioeconomic status and education, that was not very compatible with indigenous subsistence farmers' concern for the practical use value of land. Raymond Williams' often-quoted phrase, "a rentier's vision," partly captures this attitude: a sense of the country "not...of the working farmer but of the fortunate resident," bringing money from elsewhere and a sensitivity to scenery fostered through mobility and comparison.[12] During their early Grasmere years the Wordsworths lived on the interest income typical of England's leisured classes, though its meagerness made them depend on gardening and fishing, as well as friends and relatives' generosity, for periodic supplements.[13] They rented Dove Cottage but aspired to the security of property ownership. Spotting a "prospect divinely beautiful" on one of her walks, Wordsworth remarks, "If I had three hundred pounds and could afford to have a bad interest for my money I would buy that estate, and we would build a cottage there to end our days in" (21). Such imaginative appropriation, as we have seen, marked eighteenth-century landscape aesthetics as a cultural expression of Britain's property-owning classes. We recall Alan Liu's observation that the picturesque helped transform feudal notions of property into a new idea of exchangeable property.[14] Dorothy Wordsworth's conversion of scenic value into investment potential, if perhaps ironically edged, nonetheless reveals a deeply held wish depending on the possibility of such "new property" – the same possibility that allowed Pocklington and his ilk to invest in Lake District land.

The mental manipulation typical of the picturesque eye had its correlative in actual physical "improvement." Wordsworth was horrified by the kitsch that some "improving" landowners had introduced, but she was an improver in her own right.[15] Though she and her brother did not own their home, they landscaped its grounds to suit their taste, including Dorothy's terraced garden of transplanted wildflowers and the seat she describes William building in a "cool shady spot" in the orchard (122). Their zeal did not end in their own backyard, but roved the countryside. Happening on "a Bower, the sweetest that was ever seen," covered with ivy, with a view of Grasmere lake and Ambleside vale, they "resolved to go and plant flowers" in it (115). We sense a similar impulse behind their habit of carving their initials in rocks and naming favorite spots after family members. Though leery of the crasser manifestations of the improving mentality and its economic and social effect on the area, Wordsworth seems compelled to reproduce it in her own register. Her journals unfold her in-between situation: more sympathetic with her Grasmere neighbors than with the Pocklingtons, but nonetheless revealing deep affinities to the aesthetic ideology that drove the tourist invasion.

If we bear in mind Wordsworth's position between an indigenous or laboring-class appreciation of the particularity of land, with its practical use value, and a middle-class projection of scenic value upon it, a profound ambivalence emerges from her journal entry for June 9, 1800. The event she records cannot have been unusual: rich scenery-seekers driving past Dove Cottage and pausing to gawk. Wordsworth's typically understated prose does not comment explicitly on the event, but does so indirectly through the context in which she embeds it.

In the morning W. cut down the winter cherry tree. I sowed French Beans and weeded. A coronetted Landau went by when we were sitting upon the sodded wall. The ladies (evidently Tourists) turned an eye of interest upon our little garden and cottage. We went to R. Newton's for pike-floats and went round to Mr. Gell's Boat and on to the Lake to fish. We caught nothing – it was extremely cold. The Reeds and Bulrushes or Bullpipes of a tender soft green, making a plain whose surface moved with the wind. The reeds not yet tall. The lake clear to the Bottom, but saw no fish. In the evening I stuck peas, watered the garden and planted Brocoli. Did not walk for it was very cold. (25)

Kurt Heinzelman reads in this moment Wordsworth's sense of the "ladies'" approval of the evident "labor bestowed and invested in improvement" (71): that is, a shared appreciation for the means of heightening property value. This dimension does seem to be present, especially given the financial overtones of the word "interest" and her previous entry describing the excited ritual of William's homecoming from Yorkshire. "We did not go to bed till 4 o'clock in the morning so he had an opportunity of seeing our improvements" (25). But the other activities Wordsworth records in the entry – work in the orchard and garden, fishing – are those of practical subsistence, the relation to land which the discursive topography of the time categorically opposed to the aesthetic attitude of the picturesque tourist. Elsewhere in the *Journals* Wordsworth self-consciously, even smugly, positions herself against "the rich" with their degenerate manners: "avarice, inordinate desires, and the effeminacy unnaturalness and the unworthy objects of education" (41). The June 9 entry implies a variation on this theme, contrasting Dorothy and William's useful activities with the "inordinate desire" of the touring aristocrats for Lake District scenery. The passage illustrates the ambivalence that runs through the *Journals*, charting their author's middle-class social location between the privileged "rentier's vision" of picturesque aesthetics and the more practical orientation toward land characteristic of the indigenous "estatesman," or small farmer.

But we can also detect an attempt to reconcile this contradiction by reconceptualizing the aesthetic. In the midst of the unsuccessful fishing trip Wordsworth records an aesthetic perception of sorts, but not in a conventional vocabulary: "The Reeds and Bulrushes or Bullpipes of a tender soft green, making a plain whose surface moved with the wind." Embedding her aesthetic response to the plants' color and motion within the practical project of fishing, so that the recognition of beauty arises matter-of-factly amid the narration, she aligns that recognition alongside the other activities of daily life. She goes on to merge aesthetic and practical in a single downward gaze: "The lake clear to the Bottom, but saw no fish." Her understated prose uncouples aesthetic perception from privileged leisure, insisting that the need for beauty is as basic as the need for shelter or food. Contemplation collapses into practice in a move whose critical stance toward conventional aesthetics recalls Marx's critique of Feuerbach: "the thing, reality, sensuousness, is conceived only in the form of the object or of *contemplation*, but not as *human sensuous activity, practice.*"[16]

Breaking out of the passive, framing or objectifying stance typical of landscape aesthetics at the time, Wordsworth finds a different way to appreciate natural beauty. She recasts the detached passivity of aesthetic contemplation as productive action. She does this tactically, opportunistically, lacking (in Michel de Certeau's terms) a "proper" discursive base from which to undertake an explicit critique. De Certeau's discussion of the tactics of the disempowered for appropriating and using the products of a dominant culture helps to illuminate Wordsworth's relation to aesthetic discourse. A strategy, as he defines it, is undertaken by a fully authorized, empowered subject operating from a well-circumscribed, proper (*propre*) discursive "place." "The place of a tactic," by contrast, "belongs to the other. A tactic insinuates itself into the other's place, fragmentarily, without taking it over in its entirety, without being able to keep it at a distance... [The] tactic depends on time – it is always on the watch for opportunities that must be seized 'on the wing.'"[17] The in-betweenness of Wordsworth's sense of place, her relation to Grasmere, amplifies her in-between relation to aesthetic discourse as a middle-class woman. Her class privilege qualifies her as an aesthetic subject, even as her gender keeps her at the margin of the aesthetic sphere. She can neither entirely adopt nor entirely resist this powerful way of seeing, but her journals show her maneuvering creatively in its discursive interstices. The journal form, with its dated entries, seizes timely opportunities to reconfigure or recombine discursive elements in ways that suggest a critical perspective. Never intended for publication, the journals' privacy no doubt made possible a degree of experimentation that would have been more difficult in a published genre.

The June 9 entry exemplifies the *Journals'* continual textual weaving together of the Wordsworths' day-to-day activities into a distinctive texture of habitual practice, a tactic that circumvents the theoretically enshrined segregation of aesthetic from practical. Alan Liu has described, in a different context, the way in which repeated activities structure the *Journals*. The endlessly repetitive cycle of housework – cooking, cleaning, sewing, laundry – is a prominent example of the rhythms of practical activity that anchor Wordsworth's text.[18] We can begin to assess its significance by looking at entries that juxtapose housework with the aesthetic practice of walking and looking in nature. For example, on July 2, 1800, she writes,

> Wm. and Coleridge went to Keswick. John went with them to Wytheburn and staid all day fishing and brought home 2 small pikes at night. I accompanied them to Lewthwaite's cottage and on my return papered Wm.'s room. I afterwards lay down till tea time and after tea worked at my shifts in the orchard. A grey evening. About 8 o'clock it gathered for rain and I had the scatterings of a shower, but afterwards the lake became of a glassy calmness and all was still. I sate till I could see no longer and then continued my work in the house. (32)

Wallpapering and sewing partake of Grasmere's "glassy calmness," a serenity radiating from this still center through even the most mundane chores. The October 29, 1800, entry works similarly: "A very rainy night. I was baking bread in the morning and made a giblet pie. We walked out before dinner to our favourite field. The mists sailed along the mountains and rested upon them enclosing the whole vale. In the evening the Lloyds came. We drank tea with them at Borrick's and played a rubber at whist – stayed supper.

Wm looked very well. A fine moonlight night when we came home" (48–49). The quality of moonlight and mist on the mountaintops is noted as matter-of-factly as baking a pie and socializing over cards. All these activities together comprise the texture of a Dove Cottage day; the evenness of Wordsworth's prose brings out their continuity. Rather than bracket off landscape descriptions from narration, in the picturesque convention, she seems deliberately to efface the frame. She situates the experience of beauty almost offhandedly amid the everyday. Making the aesthetic commonplace, she makes the commonplace aesthetic. This discursive leveling quietly counteracts the elitist tendency of mainstream aesthetic discourse.

The other practical element that Wordsworth often interweaves with aesthetic pleasure is her representation of the poor, Grasmere inhabitants as well as the itinerant homeless or unemployed. Juxtaposing these people's insistent, unfilled needs with descriptions of natural beauty, she populates her landscape in a way antithetical to picturesque convention, whose figures are faceless, voiceless, untroubled by urgencies that could break the idyllic pictorial repose. Wordsworth's journals present people with desires and voices. One of these is the "Cockermouth traveller" (peddler), a hardy woman whose physical vigor is reminiscent of Wordsworth's own. Part of her entry for October 10, 1800, reads,

In the morning when I arose the mists were hanging over the opposite hills and the tops of the highest hills were covered with snow. There was a most lovely combination at the head of the vale – of the yellow autumnal hills wrapped in sunshine, and overhung with partial mists, the green and yellow trees and the distant snow-topped mountains. It was a most heavenly morning. The Cockermouth traveller came with thread hardware mustard, etc. She is very healthy; has travelled over the mountains these thirty years. She does not mind the storms if she can keep her goods dry. Her husband will not travel with an ass, because it is the tramper's badge – she would have one to relieve her from the weary load. She was going to Ulverston and was to return to Ambleside Fair. After I had finished baking I went out with Wm Mrs Jameson and Miss Simpson towards Rydale – the fern among the Rocks exquisitely beautiful. (44)

The "lovely combination" in the early autumn morning suggests a pictorial composition with its spatial elements of hills and trees in the near distance, mountains further off, and the attention paid to effects of light and color. But the debt to the picturesque ends with the traveler's entrance. She has nothing in common with the sanitized quaintness of the picturesque staffage figure. The only reference to her exterior is the comment on her health, which could refer to a feeling on the traveler's part as well as her appearance, since the rest of the passage has us seeing and feeling from the perspective of this hard-working woman. Wordsworth's free indirect discourse gives us an inside view of the traveler's endurance through decades of treks over the Cumberland hills, her prudent care to protect her goods from the weather, and her weariness unrelieved by a husband more concerned with appearances than with his wife's well-being. The transition from aesthetic response to practical concerns is not abrupt; Wordsworth's characteristic evenness effectively integrates elements usually held apart. We are witnessing a reconfiguration of aesthetic discourse, one so subtle it does not seem to disrupt, but rather to restore what is fit.

Such juxtapositions of scenic beauty with human needs are fairly frequent in the *Journals*. I will point out just two more. On June 16, 1800, Dorothy and William take a long walk. "A succession of delicious views from Skelleth to Brathay. We met near Skelleth a pretty little Boy with a wallet over his shoulder – he came from Hawkshead and was going to 'late' a lock [seek a measure] of meal. He spoke gently and without complaint. When I asked him if he got enough to eat he looked surprized and said 'Nay.' He was 7 years old but seemed not more than 5" (28). The boy is "pretty," in keeping with the scenery, but he is needy as well. The intrusion of his poverty, hunger, and stunted growth into the "succession of delicious views" disrupts aesthetic convention. The gustatory adjective "delicious" hints at self-rebuke, contrasting the frivolity of the Wordsworths' aesthetic errand to the boy's desperately practical quest. Wordsworth aligns us with his subjective point of view as she reproduces the quality of his voice. His local, lower-class dialect, its burden of need tempered by childish stoicism, is set in dialogue with the discourse of the picturesque to expose the latter's ideological blind spots. Much like Wollstonecraft's *Letters*, these journals foreground rural inhabitants' material needs in ways that are plainly critical of landscape aesthetics' anti-utilitarian bias.

Perhaps Wordsworth's most striking contextualization of landscape is her account of a woman pauper's funeral in her entry for September 3, 1800.

A fine coolish morning. I ironed till 1/2 past three – now very hot. I then went to a funeral at John Dawson's. About 10 men and 4 women. Bread cheese and ale. They talked sensibly and chearfully about common things. The dead person 56 years of age buried by the parish. The coffin was neatly lettered and painted black and covered with a decent cloth. They set the corpse down at the door and while we stood within the threshold the men with their hats off sang with decent and solemn countenances a verse of a funeral psalm. The corpse was then borne down the hill and they sang till they had got past the Town-end. I was affected to tears while we stood in the house, the coffin lying before me. There were no near kindred, no children. When we got out of the dark house the sun was shining and the prospect looked so divinely beautiful as I never saw it. It seemed more sacred than I had ever seen it, and yet more allied to human life. The green fields, neighbours of the churchyard, were as green as possible and with the brightness of the sunshine looked quite gay. I thought she was going to a quiet spot and I could not help weeping very much. When we came to the bridge they began to sing again and stopped during 4 lines before they entered the churchyard. The priest met us – he did not look as a man ought to do on such an occasion – I had seen him half-drunk the day before in a pot-house. Before we came with the corpse one of the company observed he wondered what sort of cue "our Parson would be in." N.B. it was the day after the Fair. I had not finished ironing till 7 o'clock. The wind was now high and I did not walk – writing my journal now at 8 o'clock. Wm and John came home at 10 o'clock. (38–39)

Alan Liu has argued that it is appropriate for Wordsworth to begin and conclude her narration of the funeral with ironing – part of the mundane cycle of cleansing or purification that is laundry, one of the repetitive activities that help structure her journal. On this day "laundering brackets a passionate story of purgation, of immersion in a spectral 'dark house,' emotional purification, and baptismal emergence into a same/other world of washed 'green,' 'brightness,' and 'sunshine.'"[19] The funeral is a collective ritual in which community standards are at a premium, as we note with her reiterated "decent." Critics have often commented on the importance of community to Dorothy Wordsworth's version of Romanticism.[20] The contrast between the dead woman's aloneness ("no near kindred, no children") and the strong communal bond among those attending the funeral is visually figured by the contrast between the dark room where the corpse has lain and the extreme sunniness of the "prospect" outside, a landscape emphatically "allied to human life" as Wordsworth's language projects human community onto "the green fields, neighbours of the churchyard." The nearly unbearable desolation of dying alone and friendless is cathartically redeemed, first by the funeral ritual with its preliminary communion of bread, cheese, and ale, and then more dramatically by the description of the glowing "prospect," the centerpiece of the passage, mingling the human and the sacral. The disruptive presence of the hung-over curate, with Wordsworth's snide "N.B.," suggests the culpable inadequacy of state institutions like the Church of England and the poor-relief system to allay such suffering. Death and reabsorption into the land with the help of a parish-subsidized funeral are the only release and transcendence available to such as her. This landscape's involvement in human suffering and release sets it decisively apart from the distanced, reposeful landscape of picturesque convention.

Throughout the *Grasmere Journals*, Dorothy Wordsworth works with subtle insistence to integrate the experience of natural beauty into the rhythm of day-to-day activities satisfying practical needs. Besides enjoying scenery, Wordsworth routinely records another kind of aesthetic activity: the production of texts – William's poetic composition with Dorothy's secretarial help – as well as both siblings' reading of Chaucer, Spenser, Shakespeare, and others. These practices form part of the texture of everyday life that these journals weave for their reader. William composes poems in between taking walks, sticking peas, and fishing; his sister copies them, "cleaning up" his messy manuscripts. Textual production becomes a kind of housework, a cottage industry. Occasionally Wordsworth mentions her own production: "I have been writing this journal while Wm has had a nice little sleep" (88). Not all of the textual production and consumption in the *Journals* is what we would call literary. Many entries are punctuated by the reading and writing, sending and receiving of letters. Wordsworth walks long distances in all weather hoping to fetch a letter from William when he is absent, from Mary or Sara Hutchinson or the often woebe-gone Coleridge. Letters or their absence can raise or lower the emotional tenor of a day. Sometimes they bring small amounts of money to augment the meager domestic economy. The letter, Janet Gurkin Altman has argued, attempts to overcome distance and absence, to bring closer someone far away; of course, letters never completely succeed in making themselves unnecessary.[21]

Like the letters that circulate through its pages, Wordsworth's journal seems impelled to overcome distance – the aesthetic distance of the picturesque, the "over-there-ness" of landscape separated from the beholder and from practical life. Wordsworth brings landscape in close by insistently linking beauty with practical activities and needs, her own and those of the people who inhabit the land. Here too, however, as with letters, a stubborn excess remains. Alien intentions cling to the aesthetic vocabulary Wordsworth persists in using, despite the pains she takes to neutralize them through her careful contextualization. The synthesis achieved in her journal is a fragile one, dependent on her particular location "home at Grasmere" and the specific combination of practices available to her. She is able to integrate the aesthetic with the practical in this text because the practices of her everyday life supply a common ground into which she can weave elements conceptually incompatible within the contemporary discursive formation. Her attempt to export her achievement northward over the border in *Recollections of a Tour Made in Scotland, A. D. 1803* exposes its provisional, tenuous nature.

THE AMBIVALENT TOURIST

Wordsworth's travel narrative is a profoundly divided text. It oscillates between distance and closeness, a committed engagement in the aesthetic practice of scenic tourism and a countertouristic concern for rural Scots' material conditions of existence. The behavior of the party (including Dorothy, William, and for part of the trip Coleridge) is certainly not that of ordinary tourists. With their almost ludicrous Irish jaunting-car, balky horse, and habit of venturing into rugged back country in any weather, they did not aspire to the standard of comfort and style set by the Lake Country ladies in their coroneted landau. Nonetheless, the Wordsworths did share, if marginally, in the basic prerequisites of tourism – means, education, and leisure – placing them among a small minority of Britons. These class attributes, which set them apart from their Grasmere neighbors, also condition Wordsworth's representation of her Scottish tour. *Recollections* shares with the *Grasmere Journals* (and with Wollstonecraft's Scandinavian letters) an insistence on the humanity and practical needs of the people who dwell in scenically appealing areas. But Wordsworth cannot reinvent scenic tourism, an institution with a history of its own. As *Recollections* alternates between engagement with and opposition to touristic practice, the dense texture of her writing discloses traces of what we might call alienation: a frustrated sense of being inescapably entangled in a troubling pursuit.[22]

Scotland, like the Lake District, was among the domestic beauty spots enshrined by tourism, which by 1803 was obtrusively inscribed on the Scottish landscape itself as well as in published tours.[23] The Wordsworths had been reading these, including at least Gilpin's;[24] John Stoddart's illustrated *Remarks on Local Scenery and Manners in Scotland during the Years 1799 and 1800* (357); and the journal of William's friend Thomas Wilkinson, later published as *Tours to the British Mountains* (380). Her reading shapes Wordsworth's expectations. Two days after they cross the border, ascending into "steep, bare hills," she declares, "We now felt indeed that we were in Scotland" (205). A ferry-house near Loch Ketterine exudes authenticity: "This was the first genuine Highland hut we had been in" (270).[25]

The party is equipped with a map, which they consult "looking about for something which we might yet see" (351). They see − and Wordsworth records, even dwells on − the forms of mediation inscribed in the face of the land itself, helping deliver Scottish nature to the tourist eye. Though she and her brother find some of these efforts tacky, others win their approval. The instability of the distinction between kitsch and good taste underlines the Wordsworths' complicity in the enterprise of "packaging" Scotland. At the falls of the Clyde, "what Wm. calls an ell-wide gravel walk" conducts tourists from view to view, with benches at each "station." A moss-lined "pleasure-house" is "beautifully wrought," but badly placed; openings along the path are "injudiciously managed" (223–24).[26] To view the cascade at Kenmore they must enter through a fake hermit's cell, "a quaint apartment stuck over with moss, hung about with stuffed foxes and other wild animals, and ornamented with a library of wooden books covered with old leather backs." But the cell's bow window frames waterfall, village, and lake in a "very beautiful prospect" (343). Kitsch and good taste coexist side by side; it is clear that in principle, if not always in practice, Wordsworth endorses the artful packaging of nature.

At the falls of the Bran in Dunkeld they are led into another antechamber, this one decorated with a painting of Ossian[27] which suddenly (we presume with their guide's help) disappears,

> parting in the middle, flying asunder as if by the touch of magic, and lo! we are at the entrance of a splendid room, which was almost dizzy and alive with waterfalls, that tumbled in all directions – the great cascade, which was opposite to the window that faced us, being reflected in innumerable mirrors upon the ceiling and against the walls. We both laughed heartily, which, no doubt, the gardener considered as high commendation; for he was very eloquent in pointing out the beauties of the place. (358–59)

A distinct uneasiness underlies Wordsworth's tongue-in-cheek tone. The burst of laughter marks a moment of extreme "unnaturalness" intruding on the search for natural beauty. It is "almost," her prose reluctantly reveals, sublime – for the split second until they realize it is done with mirrors. The language that represents the parlor-trick sublime unwillingly mimics the language of true sublimity, hinting at a troubling continuity between the kitschy and the tasteful, what the Wordsworths repudiate and what they seek. Even as *Recollections* calls attention to tourism's packaging of the Scottish landscape, it reveals its author's implication in that process. This text confronts us with its dividedness, its ambivalence about its own project.

This sense is amplified by comments that self-consciously distance Wordsworth from her tourist role by historicizing scenic tourism. If "one may judge from the writings of Chaucer and from the old romances, more interesting passions were connected with natural objects in the days of chivalry than now, though going in search of scenery, as it is called, had not then been thought of" (234). Glimpsing possibilities outside the dominant discursive construction of nature, she holds the paradigm momentarily at arm's length. The self-important arrival of "the renowned Miss Waughs of Carlisle" (289) and their entourage at the "celebrated" New Inn of Arrochar (287) spurs a similar reflection. "Twenty years ago, perhaps, such a sight had not been seen here except when the Duke of Argyle, or some other Highland chieftain, might chance to be going with his family to London or Edinburgh" (289). Then rural nobility sought the metropolis; now the metropolitan bourgeoisie invades the countryside. Inflated adjectives from guidebooks or advertising mock the puffery of touristic discourse, but Wordsworth's sarcastic attempt to distance herself from the Miss Waughs calls attention to their shared role as contemporary scenic tourists.

Scenic tourism's favored jargon, the language of landscape aesthetics, is more obtrusive here than in the *Grasmere Journal*. Wordsworth is constantly on the alert for natural "pictures." John R. Nabholtz has noted echoes of Gilpin in her responses to specific scenes as well as her general assessment of Scottish landscape.[28] Views not mentioned by Gilpin also elicit the vocabulary of the picturesque. The "irregularity of the ground" in the mining village of Leadhills leads her to opine, "I should think that a painter might make several beautiful pictures in this village. It straggles down both sides of a mountain glen" (208). Near Tarbet an enthusiasm incongruous to the twentieth-century reader animates the painter's technical language: "We called out with one voice, 'That's what we wanted!' alluding to the frame-like uniformity of the side-screens of the lake for the last five or six miles" (256). We notice the familiar impulse to compare. The country near the Clyde reminds Wordsworth of views on the Thames in Kent, "which, though greatly superior in richness and softness, are much inferior in grandeur" (239). A view of Loch Awe "made us think of the descent from Newlands into Buttermere, though on a wider scale, and much inferior in simple majesty" (300).

An object, like a single sailboat rounding a point on Loch Awe, can lend aesthetic focus to a landscape: "I cannot express what romantic images this vessel brought along with her — how much more beautiful the mountains appeared, the lake how much more graceful" (307). People and animals often serve a similar function. Workers in a field, stopping to observe the tourists, "formed most beautiful groups" (323), and on an "eminence" near Loch Dochart a "groupe of figures...made us feel how much we wanted in not being painters. Two herdsmen, with a dog beside them, were sitting on the hill, overlooking a herd of cattle scattered over a large meadow by the river-side. Their forms, looked at through a fading light, and backed by the bright west, were exceedingly distinct, a beautiful picture in the quiet of a Sabbath evening, exciting thoughts and images of almost patriarchal simplicity and grace" (341). The precisely specified lighting adds to the serenely static, painterly quality of the description. Herdsmen, dog, and cattle, pleasingly grouped, attain a semi-inanimate status.

The resting laborers and herdsmen are not the only examples of aestheticized or objectified human figures, seen from a distance and from the outside. An old woman sitting alone and motionless in a field, "wrapped up in a grey cloak or plaid," touches a chord of sublime melancholy: "there was so much obscurity and uncertainty about her, and her figure agreed so well with the desolation of the place, that we were indebted to the chance of her being there for some of the most interesting feelings that we had ever had from natural objects connected with man in dreary solitariness" (213). The tourists' bafflement at the woman's reasons for sitting as she does invokes the Burkean category of obscurity, in the sense of mystery or inscrutability.[29] Lacking access to her consciousness, Wordsworth renders her as a kind of aesthetic icon rather than a human agent, shifting the focus entirely to her effect on the observer.

In another evocative passage, the sight of a boy calling cattle at dusk concentrates the imaginative appeal of his surroundings:

We had three miles to walk to Tarbet. It rained, but not heavily; the mountains were not concealed from us by the mists, but appeared larger and more grand; twilight was coming on, and the obscurity under which we saw the objects, with the sounding of the torrents, kept our minds alive and wakeful; all was solitary and huge – sky, water, and mountains mingled together. While we were walking forward, the road leading us over the top of a brow, we stopped suddenly at the sound of a half-articulate Gaelic hooting from the field close to us; it came from a little boy, whom we could see on the hill between us and the lake, wrapped up in a grey plaid; he was probably calling home the cattle for the night. His appearance was in the highest degree moving to the imagination: mists were on the hillsides, darkness shutting in upon the huge avenue of mountains, torrents roaring, no house in sight to which the child might belong; his dress, cry, and appearance all different from anything we had been accustomed to. It was a text, as Wm. has since observed to me, containing in itself the whole history of the Highlander's life – his melancholy, his simplicity, his poverty, his superstition, and above all, that visionariness which results from a communion with the unworldliness of nature. (286)

As with the old woman, the boy's aesthetic power is tied to his inscrutable otherness, the differentness of everything about him, as well as the "obscurity" of the surrounding scene. Levin compares the siblings' responses: "Dorothy notes that which is definitely in the world," particular appearances and effects, while William abstracts or generalizes into a "text" (87–88). William's attention to the boy's incomprehensible Gaelic hooting is reminiscent of his poem "The Solitary Reaper," in which the woman's Erse song sets off a chain of romantic associations whose condition of possibility is the very incomprehensibility of her words. Lack of access to what the reaper actually sings or feels is the necessary basis for the process of projection that defines her imaginative value to the poet. Elsewhere in *Recollections* Wordsworth transcribes "The Solitary Reaper," carefully noting that William did not write it in response to an actual incident during their tour. Rather, the poem "was suggested to Wm. by a beautiful sentence in Thomas Wilkinson's *Tour in Scotland*" (380).[30] The textualized reaper migrates from the travel journal of William's friend Wilkinson into his poem, and thence into his sister's text, the words of her own song still uncomprehended. Wordsworth's deliberate attention to the multiple mediation of the Scottish landscape, and the Scots themselves, through aesthetic discourse suggests an incipient critical distance from that discourse.

A series of quite different encounters in the Scottish countryside generates further resistance against the touristic attitude. Besides her eye for beauty and sublimity, Wordsworth also proves alert to signs of prosperity or poverty, traces of the practical connection between people and land. An early passage juxtaposes contrasting perspectives on Scottish country folk. Near the village of Wanlockhead the Wordsworths meet three boys, one carrying a fishing rod: "the hats of all were braided with honeysuckles; they ran after one another as wanton as the wind. I cannot express what a character of *beauty* those few honeysuckles in the hats of the three boys gave to the place: what bower could they have come from?" (206). Coleridge stops the boys, asking where they live and whether they go to school (they do; they are learning Latin and Greek). Shortly afterward they meet another boy about the same age.

I must mention that we met, just after we had parted from them, another little fellow, about six years old, carrying a bundle over his shoulder; he seemed poor and half starved, and was scratching his fingers, which were covered with the itch. He was a miner's son, and lived at Wanlockhead; did not go to school, but this was probably on account of his youth. I mention him because he seemed to be a proof that there was poverty and wretchedness among these people, though we saw no other symptom of it. (207)

Wordsworth sets up a casual but telling contrast between the previous boys' gaiety and this one's misery. His gauntness, crusty fingers, and compulsive scratching are in stark contrast to the romantic image of honeysuckle-garlanded hats, suggesting an effort at balance or correction, a tacit admission that aesthetic discourse presents a socially skewed picture of the countryside. Such an uncommented juxtaposition of aestheticized image with realistic observation recalls the uneven text of Ann Radcliffe's *Journey* and its marks of struggle against aesthetics' ideologically inflected detachment.

Wordsworth's most significant tactic for undercutting the objectifying effect of aesthetic discourse recalls, and perhaps goes beyond, Wollstonecraft's Scandinavian letters. *Recollections* is punctuated by moments of extraordinary empathy with individuals dwelling in this beautiful, barren land. Amid her scenic descriptions Wordsworth inserts evocations of the rural Scots' inner lives and meditations on their multidimensional relationships with the places where they dwell. Unlike Radcliffe's *Journey Through Holland and Germany* (places densely peopled in comparison to Scotland), this is a well-populated travelogue. The Wordsworths seem to notice, and usually strike up a conversation with, everyone who crosses their path. They are curious about Scottish education, agriculture, emigration, and other practical matters. A pastoral description gets an unconventional twist when they pass a shepherd, "sitting upon the ground, reading, with the book on his knee, screened from the wind by his plaid, while a flock of sheep were feeding near him among the rushes and coarse grass" (212). To include the act of reading suggests an independent subjectivity; it de-aestheticizes the shepherd. More than a staffage figure in a pastoral landscape, he becomes a human agent in history, participating in the high level of literacy that the Wordsworths have noticed among Scotland's laboring classes.

Another passage takes its start from a similar sociological observation: Wordsworth notes that people in thinly populated parts of Scotland are willing to travel long distances in order to attend church. She extrapolates this fact to a whole phenomenology, imaginatively reconstructing the churchgoers' sense of the event and its place in their subjective time:

There is something exceedingly pleasing to my imagination in this gathering together of the inhabitants of these secluded districts...If it were not for these Sabbath-day meetings one summer month would be like another summer month, one winter month like another – detached from the goings-on of the world, and solitary throughout; from the time of earliest childhood they will be like landing-places in the memory of a person who has passed his life in these thinly peopled regions; they must generally leave distinct impressions, differing from each other so much as they do in circumstances, in time and place, etc., – some in the open fields, upon hills, in houses, under large rocks, in storms, and in fine weather. (282)

Imagining what it must be like to dwell in this remote Highland area, and how the material conditions of such a location would affect people's mental lives, Wordsworth again presents people in their landscape as human agents living in historical time, involved in complicated relationships with the places they inhabit.

The most striking moments of empathy in *Recollections* are with other women. Susan Levin has noted the frequency with which Wordsworth describes domestic interiors, especially kitchens, the main sites of women's labor (80). As she weaves a practical dimension into her narrative of scenic travel, she adds a gendered slant, a strong emphasis on women and the household labor that fulfills the most basic, universal human needs. The journal is replete with informal, friendly interactions with Scottish women. She chats comfortably with a shop-woman who sends a boy to fetch her thread from another store (210); is lent a dry gown and wool stockings after a rainstorm by two talkative Highland sisters (279–80); and prolongs her stay in an uncomfortably smoky cottage for the pleasure of chatting with its mistress: "My eyes smarted exceedingly, but the woman seemed so kind and chearful that I was willing to endure it for the sake of warming my feet in the ashes and talking to her" (301). Mrs. Macfarlane, the Wordsworths' hostess near remote Loch Katrine, ends a day of generous country hospitality by giving her guest a bunch of eagle feathers: "I was much pleased with the gift, which I shall preserve in memory of her kindness and simplicity of manners, and the Highland solitude where she lived" (269). Wordsworth watches and helps women prepare food, patiently answers their questions, including "the old one over again, if I was married," and listens in turn to the stories of their lives: "she began to tell how long she had been married, that she had had a large family and much sickness and sorrow, having lost several of her children" (382). A web of bonds between women, established through transactions over food and lodging but extending beyond this practical nexus, forms a significant element of Wordsworth's counter-aesthetic textual practice.

Relating at length one encounter with a Scottish woman who is materially and spiritually downtrodden, Wordsworth displays considerable skill at character depiction. In a member of Britain's humblest orders, doubly oppressed by class and gender, she recognizes a full and complex subjectivity. After an exceptionally long day of travel Dorothy and William have been refused lodging at a village inn. Their horse exhausted, they push on, "spiritless, and at a dreary pace." Out of the darkness they are suddenly "greeted by a gentle voice from a poor woman, whom, till she spoke, though we were close to her, we had not seen." The voice in the darkness gives their acquaintance with this woman, from the first, a strangely intimate quality. She offers them shelter in her cottage nearby. As they walk on, Wordsworth speculates, "What sort of countenance and figure shall we see in this woman when we come into the light?" But when they do she remarks ambiguously, "it was an interesting moment," without giving a physical description – as if to emphasize the woman's interiority by eliding her corporeal self (354-55).

In return for their service as gatekeepers on the estate of a Mr. Butler, says the woman, she and her husband live rent-free. She hints at her landlord's arrogance and has the air, Wordsworth observes, of "an injured and oppressed being" (355). The bed she gives her guest is of chaff, but covered with "a pair of very nice strong clean sheets, – she said with some pride that she *had* good linen. I believe the sheets had been of her own spinning, perhaps when she was first married, or before, and she probably will keep them to the end of her life of poverty" (356). The sheets, made from flax possibly grown by the cottagers themselves, are material evidence of their practical connection to the land they live on. These "very nice strong clean sheets" become the focus for a rare moment of pride in a woman rendered apathetic by poverty and bad treatment – a pride that Wordsworth implicitly contrasts with the oppressive arrogance of the landowner. The sheets, the concrete product of the woman's labor, metonymize her dignity. By including such a character in her scenic tour, Wordsworth tacitly questions aesthetics' emphasis on leisure as the precondition for truly valuable experience. She populates her travel narrative with individualized characters, as well as ornamental figures, bridging the distance that is such an essential feature of aesthetic discourse. The poignancy and understated power of her glimpses into the subjectivity of isolated, impoverished Highlanders goes far to undercut the conventions of scenic tourism.

Wordsworth's attempts at empathy with people she sees on her travels are occasionally checked, however, when the people look back. A curious, amused, or even resentful gaze turned on the ambivalent tourist reminds her of her own out-of-placeness and makes her whole endeavor momentarily strange. In the remote and beautiful area called the Trossachs the Wordsworths stop to talk to a group of agricultural workers and their employer in a field. "A laugh was on every face when Wm. said we were come to see the Trossachs; no doubt they thought we had better have stayed at our own homes" (265). The very concept of tourism is absurd to these rural dwellers, casting it in doubt for Wordsworth and her reader as well.

Other encounters in this vein are less light-hearted. One gloomy afternoon Dorothy and William walk to the head of Loch Lomond in pursuit of "a very interesting view back upon the village [Luss] and the lake and islands beyond" (248). Continuing along the shore, they stop to rest at a bark hut. "While we were here a poor woman with a little child by her side begged a penny of me, and asked where she could 'find quarters in the village'. She was a travelling beggar, a native of Scotland...I thought what a dreary waste must this lake be to such poor creatures, struggling with fatigue and poverty and unknown ways!" (249) The lake as "interesting view" and "dreary waste" stand in disturbing contrast. The brief interaction underscores the difference between Wordsworth's carefree delight and the dulled perspective of travelers burdened with practical cares. Her characteristic empathy, in this case, seems to coexist uneasily with an unspoken discomfort in her tourist's role.[31]

On the Inversneyde ferry Wordsworth encounters another family of poor travelers, husband, wife, and child. Comparing their situations more explicitly to her own, she focuses on the woman.

When we parted from this family, they going down the lake, and we up it, I could not but think of the difference in our condition to that poor woman, who, with her husband, had been driven from her home by want of work, and was now going a long journey to seek it elsewhere: every step was painful toil, for she had either her child to bear or a heavy burthen. *I* walked as she did, but pleasure was my object, and if toil came along with it, even *that* was pleasure, – pleasure, at least, it would be in the remembrance.

We were, I believe, nine miles from Glenfalloch when we left the boat. To us, with minds at ease, the walk was delightful. (369)

The involuntary travel of these victims of Scotland's depressed economy again highlights for Wordsworth the voluntary, even capricious nature of her own errand. Her hammering emphasis on "pleasure," repeated three times, holds the concept up for scrutiny and makes it suddenly strange. At the same time, she identifies powerfully, physically, with the poor woman, shifting from "we" to "I": "*I* walked as she did." Middle-class guilt opens a space of incongruity between the italicized, emphatically female "I" and the foregrounded state of aesthetic pleasure. Empathy with another woman across lines of nationality and class becomes a fulcrum for critical insight into the restrictiveness of that pleasure's cultural definition. The aesthetic perceiver and the embodied female self part ways in a moment of acute self-division which, however, quickly subsides as Wordsworth goes on to describe the lakeside in conventional aesthetic terms: "not that sort of variety which leaves distinct separate remembrances, but one impression of solitude and greatness" (370). This insistence on unity protests too much on the heels of her inadvertent exposure of the multiple fissures between toil and pleasure, poverty and ease, physical compulsion and mental freedom.

As it juxtaposes picturesque descriptions with moments of discomfort, critical distance, and self-division, *Recollections* is charged with a palpable incongruity. The dense texture of Wordsworth's writing foregrounds and problematizes the pleasure that, conventionally, is the tourist's object. The writer is no longer comfortably ensconced at Grasmere amid the cycle of housework and the circulation of letters, cultivating her garden and her seemingly effortless intimacy with nature. Crossing the border into a country both close and alien, and stepping into a role laden with as much cultural baggage as scenic tourism had accumulated by 1803, she cannot quite hold her fragile synthesis together. At a different time, in a different place, her tactics lose their effectiveness.

IMAGES OF INAUTHENTICITY

Wordsworth's text's ambivalence about its own project emerges perhaps most strikingly through three recurrent patterns of

8. J. B. Cipriani *del.*, F. Bartolozzi *sculp.*, "A view of the Indians of Tierra del Fuego in their Hut." John Hawkesworth, *An Account of the Voyages Undertaken by the Order of His Present Majesty for Making Discoveries in the Southern Hemisphere* (1773).

metaphor or imagery. The first of these describes Scottish Highlanders in language drawn from Britain's ongoing imperial adventures in remote parts of the world. Like so many of her contemporaries, Wordsworth has been reading the literature of exploration, or at least looking at the pictures: she compares a pleasure-house at the falls of the Clyde to "huts in the prints belonging to Captain Cook's Voyages" (224). The island of Inch-ta-vanach in Loch Lomond overlooks "an outlandish scene – we might have believed ourselves in North America" (252). Nearby dwellings look "like savages' huts" (254); William is quoted as describing a ferryman's house near the Trossachs as "Hottentotish" (259). The Highlanders themselves take on an alien aspect: a traveling tinker near Glencoe emits a "savage cry" in Erse, while a guide's uncanny ability to track "reminded us of what we read of the Hottentots and other savages" (373). It is as if, in this remote corner of Britain, the strange and exotic become the everyday, or the everyday assumes an alien aura. Tierra del Fuegans, Africans, and American Indians, icons of otherness, become interchangeable with the "savage" Highlanders. The tourist's figures of speech draw Scotland as a miniature map of a world whose remote corners, from the Atlantic to the Pacific and back to Loch Lomond, are pulled close together by the imperial project.

Wordsworth imports all this distance into Britain's own internally colonized Celtic backyard. The process of national mod-ernization, well underway by the time she wrote, involved keeping order on the periphery, forcing Scotland, Ireland, and Wales to develop in ways that would benefit the English center of imperial power. Tourists' homage to the scenic attractions of this "fringe," Deidre Lynch has argued, legitimized uneven development by nostalgically celebrating the past and the pastoral, even the "sav-age," at the same time as these were segregated, relegated to a space and time (the vacation) decisively removed from modern daily life. Tourism thus fostered an ideologically convenient "dual-ity of the self," an ambivalent engagement with civilized modernity that provided a fantasy escape from its harshness while reaffirming its necessity in the face of the "savage" Other.[32]

But scenic tourism's institutionalized self-division takes on added complexity as practiced by a middle-class woman, with her already conflicted relation to its aesthetic discourse. Though her gender is not part of the dominant discursive construction of the aesthetic

subject, her social status and educational capital stake her claim to
the privilege of the polite imagination. Representing other Others,
this ambivalent tourist traces her own divided subjectivity. Her
comparisons to Indians and Hottentots collude with the
picturesque to distance the reader from Scottish inhabitants. Mary
Pratt notes the affinity between the framing and distancing of landscape description, its "fantasy of dominance," and the colonial
project of controlling indigenous populations; we have seen how
Janet Schaw's representation of the West Indian plantation masks
domination and coercion with aesthetic appeal.[33] But Wordsworth's
exoticizing language stands in sharp contrast to the empathy and
respect that she accords the laboring-class Scots whom she actually
meets. Her individualized portraits of the poor, I have argued, suggest a critical distance from the objectifying language of aesthetics.
In this context we may venture to read in her colonial metaphors a
self-contradictory double distance: from the "savages" of Africa
and Glencoe, but also from the savagery of scenic tourism itself.

The second pattern of figurative language that hovers at the
edge of a reader's consciousness in *Recollections of a Tour* transports
us from the exotic margins of empire back to its urban center.
Wordsworth imports into her description of rural Scotland tropes
drawn from contemporary popular culture, especially city spectacles like puppet theater and panoramas or peepshows. She had visited London several times before 1803. In 1797 she was given free
tickets to Covent Garden and Drury Lane; in 1802 Charles Lamb
showed her and William around "Bartlemy Fair."[34] A series of
urban images extends this text's oblique commentary on scenic
tourism and the woman writer's complicated relation to this peculiar institution. One such image unexpectedly enters her description of Dumbarton Castle, perched high on massive Dumbarton
Rock – "very grand when you are close...at a little distance, under
an ordinary sky, and in open day, it is not grand, but curiously
wild" (240). Gazing upward from its base she notices some sheep,
including two rams "with twisted horns," and a red-coated sentinel
pacing back and forth. An optical illusion ensues:

The sheep, I suppose owing to our being accustomed to see them in similar situations, appeared to retain their real size, while, on the contrary,
the soldier seemed to be diminished by the distance till he almost looked
like a puppet moved with wires for the pleasure of children...I had never
before, perhaps, thought of sheep and men in soldiers' dresses at the same

time, and here they were brought together in a strange fantastic way...the fearlessness and stillness of those quiet creatures, on the brow of the rock, pursuing their natural occupations, contrasted with the restless and apparently unmeaning motions of the dwarf soldier, added not a little to the general effect of this place, which is that of wild singularity. (240–241)

The perceived disproportion between the looming sheep and the oddly dehumanized, miniaturized soldier, with the contrast between the beasts' repose and the puppet-man's mechanistic twitching, at first diminishes human civilization in the face of a serenely primal nature. Like the figures in a picturesque landscape, the soldier is faceless, deindividuated. But unlike a picturesque scene, Wordsworth's picture is far from reposeful. Its "wild singularity" verges on the surreal as her puppet brings an urban restlessness and artifice to the peaceful countryside. The distorted juxtaposition of soldier and sheep radically fractures the aesthetic conventions that draw nature and human figures together into a harmonious composition. The image is profoundly anti-picturesque. It captures the edgy self-estrangement that marks Wordsworth's involvement in scenic tourism.

Puppets persistently recur in *Recollections*. Near the Glasgow Exchange Wordsworth notices "the largest coffee-room I ever saw...Perhaps there might be thirty gentlemen sitting on the circular bench of the window, each reading a newspaper. They had the appearance of figures in a fantoccine, or men seen at the extremity of the opera-house, diminished into puppets" (237). The cosmopolitan metaphor of fantoccine, or marionettes, is less incongruous in urban Glasgow than juxtaposed with sheep on Dumbarton Rock. "Diminishing" the reading men to puppets carries overtones of mistrust for the expanding print culture represented by newspapers, but also by the proliferating guidebooks and tours that carried the countryside into city print shops to be carried back out in the pockets and minds of sophisticated scenery seekers. These readers, made mechanical by the printed discourse that circulates through them, suggest Wordsworth's building discomfort with the conventions of tourism. The all-male institution of the coffee-house gives a gender to her oblique comment. Mary Wortley Montagu compared the women's Turkish baths to a women's coffee-house in implicit protest against English women's exclusion from the public sphere. This Glasgow coffee-house seems no place that an independent-minded woman like Wordsworth would care to enter.

The puppet metaphor situates her resistance to the gendered language of landscape aesthetics in the context of a profound mistrust of the masculinist institutions of Britain's burgeoning print culture.

Another set of allusions picks up the idea of circulation, this time the circulation of visual images. At an inn she glances into a private parlor where the landlady is having a party. The festive scene reminds her of "the fatted calf in the alehouse pictures of the Prodigal Son" (339). As with picturesque tourism, perception is filtered through a pre-existing image. Here, however, the image is not high art, but popular culture produced for the lowest common denominator of the alehouse. High and low culture, kitsch and good taste, disclose troubling structural similarities. In another inn she evaluates the pictures on the walls: one engraved after Reynolds "in a much better style," along with others "such as may be found in the basket of any Italian image and picture hawker" (200–201). She imagines the circulation of images physically carried out by someone – the Italian peddler – strolling through the countryside. Picture hawking becomes an evocative trope for picturesque tourism. The Italian, an eighteenth-century type of the exotic, amplifies the hint of alienation. The Wordsworths too stroll around Scotland, re-circulating images and language they have absorbed from guidebooks and aesthetic treatises. Could their tasteful pursuit bear a distasteful likeness to the hawker's banal commerce?

Approaching Inverary, Wordsworth again displaces her discomfort with tourism onto a form of mediation beyond the pale of good taste. She notes the town's "festive appearance"; it is "a showy scene…in connexion with its situation, different from any place I had ever seen, yet exceedingly like what I imaged to myself from representations in raree-shows, or pictures of foreign places (Venice, for example) painted on the scene of a play-house, which one is apt to fancy are as cleanly and gay as they look through the magnifying-glass of the raree-show or in the candle-light dazzle of a theatre" (294). The raree-show, according to Richard Altick, was "one of the archetypal forms of post-sixteenth-century popular amusement." The term refers to a peepshow or perspective box that, "framed and artificially lighted, consisted of modeled groups of figures placed against a painted background; they were seen not directly, but as reflected in a slanted mirror on the principle of the camera obscura." "Raree-show" had pejorative connotations, despite the surprising range and delicacy of the effects that could be achieved within such boxes.[35] These effects depended on lighting and its transforming power, a power that also preoccupied theorists of the picturesque. Wordsworth associates the "fancy" that paints Inverary's "showy scene" with flagrantly deceptive artificial lighting – "the candle-light dazzle of a theatre." As she catches herself familiarizing the unfamiliar through the lens of popular spectacle, the "glass of the raree-show," her concern with falsification picks up her earlier references to the trial of the famous forger Hatfield (196). Are her own descriptions a culpable "meddling with pen and ink"?[36]

Her figurative excursions into urban popular culture continue to make strange the aesthetic discourse and practice of scenic tourism. Whether a Scottish country town becomes a raree-show or a "genuine Highland hut" suddenly turns South American, Wordsworth's comparisons tarnish the aura of authenticity that all tourists supposedly desire. Her figures of speech cross the boundaries between high and low, domestic and foreign; she transgresses the very distinctions that discursively construct the aesthetic subject as masculine, propertied, and European. A woman – a member of one group with a dubious claim on the privilege of the polite imagination – laces her scenic tour with references to other such groups, the laboring classes as well as "savages." *Recollections'* disruption of picturesque repose points to a suppressed anxiety on the woman tourist's part, a sense of her own suspect credentials. But these repeated allusions also suggest an incipient critical comprehension of the social logic of aesthetic discourse.

Both this anxiety and this critical impulse seem to inform a third pattern of imagery throughout *Recollections.* This is Wordsworth's housewifely preoccupation with dirt, which seems to leap out at her everywhere she goes.[37] Inverary viewed close up is not "cleanly and gay," but "a doleful example of Scotch filth...the windows and door-steads were as dirty as in a dirty by-street of a large town" (295). Likewise, small farmhouses on Lord Breadalbane's estate "did not look so comfortable when we were near to them as from a distance; but this might be chiefly owing to what the inhabitants did not feel as an evil – the dirt about the doors" (306). Close up, the figures in the Scottish landscape can sometimes evoke the opposite of aesthetic pleasure, an instinctive revulsion or disgust. In

Lanerk she observes "the doors and windows dirty,...the women too seemed to be very dirty in their dress." In the inn parlor "the tables were unwiped, chairs in disorder, the floor dirty, and the smell of liquors was most offensive" (219). Inns at Hamilton (229) and Dumbarton (239) likewise offend her sensibilities. The Glasgow suburbs are "all ugly; and the inhabitants dirty...We were annoyed by carts and dirt" (235). Luss, for a change, offers accommodations "clean for a Scotch inn," she snidely remarks (247). The ferry house at Loch Creran spoils her appetite: "though very much needing refreshment, I had not heart to eat anything there, the house was so dirty, and there were so many wretchedly dirty women and children; yet perhaps I might have got over the dirt (though I believe there are few ladies who would not have been turned sick by it) if there had not been a most disgusting combination of laziness and coarseness in the countenances and manners of the women" (318). A broad-minded lady, but a lady still, Wordsworth links dirt to class prejudice against the coarse and lazy lower orders. Throughout *Recollections*, "Scotch filth" crystallizes the Scots' otherness, their material distance of class and culture from herself. The lady tourist's disgust with dirt offsets her rapture with the beauties of Scottish landscape, and her frequent empathy with its inhabitants, in a densely ambivalent counterpoint between distance and closeness.

Mary Douglas's classic anthropological analysis, *Purity and Danger*, seeks to account for both the danger and the power of dirt. Dirt – things out of place – disrupts a culture's order, flaunting the manner in which that culture symbolizes its world. Dirt is that which cannot be accepted, which must be swept away. At the same time, it represents a glimpse of a possible alternative order.[38] Just such ambivalence, combining intense repulsion with an equally intense fascination, informs Dorothy Wordsworth's representation of Scotland. Her disgust with its dirty buildings and people self-referentially recoils on her own enterprise; her context suggests that we should perhaps displace her labels of "savage" and "Hottentotish" from the Highlanders to the institution of tourism itself. Amid *Recollections'* multiple marks of friction and self-division, her obsessive references to Scottish dirt concentrate the woman writer's sense of scenic tourism as profoundly contaminated and herself as contaminated by it. This sense of a frustrating inadequacy in the available construction of nature seems to propel Wordsworth, in one extraordinary passage, toward an alternative aesthetic.

Most of her allusions to popular culture, as we have seen, evoke feelings of strain or self-estrangement. But one passage bestows a very different valence on the shows of London, the realm of popular illusion. The Wordsworths are lodging at the Loch Katrine ferry house, "the first genuine Highland hut we had been in" (270).

I went to bed some time before the family. The door was shut between us, and they had a bright fire, which I could not see; but the light it sent up among the varnished rafters and beams, which crossed each other in almost as intricate and fantastic a manner as I have seen the under-boughs of a large beech-tree withered by the depth of the shade above, produced the most beautiful effect that can be conceived. It was like what I should suppose an underground cave or temple to be, with a dripping or moist roof, and the moonlight entering in upon it by some means or other, and yet the colours were more like the colours of melted gems. I lay looking up till the light of the fire faded away...I was less occupied by remembrance of the Trossachs, beautiful as they were, than the vision of the Highland hut, which I could not get out of my head. I thought of the Fairyland of Spenser, and what I had read in romance at other times, and then, what a feast would it be for a London pantomime-maker, could he but transplant it to Drury Lane, with all its beautiful colours! (277–78)[39]

Artificial lighting, the firelight on the varnished beams, is now not deceptive, but liberating, releasing the magic of color and the play of fantasy. Natural images like the cave, tree, and gems proliferate, not in a framed and distanced picturesque composition, but fantastically jumbled together and superimposed. Wordsworth's exuberant imagery extrapolates the emphasis by theorists of the picturesque, especially Uvedale Price, on intricacy and the surface play of light and color.[40] She sets aside "real" images of nature, the touted beauties of the Trossachs, in favor of a vision that sparks associations with high culture – Spenser – but also with Drury Lane pantomime. Popular culture's feast of colors evokes not disdain but desire as the woman writer's impolite imagination unapologetically crosses the boundary between "high" and "low," overturning mainstream aesthetics' hierarchical social valence and its limiting visual rules to explore the liberating potential at its margins. This is an exceptional moment in *Recollections*, as innovative as the *Grasmere Journals*, but in a very different vein. A woman writer moves beyond a pattern of disruption to a positive, experimental engagement with the aesthetic – carving out her own pleasures.

Leaving Dove Cottage for a Scotland collectively imagined and materially marked by scenic tourism, Wordsworth left behind the conjunction of circumstance that grounded the achievement of her *Grasmere Journals*. But her record of her Scottish tour displays the same gift for creative tactical maneuver in a different situation. Writing and revising with a mind to publication introduced generic constraints irrelevant to a private journal. The genre of the pic- turesque tour and the practice of scenic tourism confronted her with issues she had been able to smooth over, if not resolve, at home in Grasmere: the mediatedness of "nature" and the social divisiveness of landscape aesthetics' construction of land. Aesthetics' distancing, subtly dehumanizing jargon divides privi- leged lookers from those they look upon, the mobile from the fixed, the polite from the vulgar. Wordsworth's text, much like Radcliffe's *Journey through Holland and Germany*, interrupts its own aestheticizing in ways that both underline these divisions and undermine them. Like Mary Wollstonecraft, Wordsworth breaks the frame to bring the figures in the landscape up close, dwelling on aspects of their lives not representable in the limited language of scenic tourism. She produces a text whose dividedness bespeaks the conflicted sub- jectivity of the middle-class woman – her ambivalent and compro- mised relation to the powerful languages of patriarchal culture. We can recognize this, however, only when we learn to read such divided texts not as deficient or incoherent, but as eloquent witnesses to a particular historical situation.

Travel has a way of making travelers renegotiate their relation to cultural verities easier to take for granted at home. Though they take along their familiar ways of seeing and knowing, these seldom weather the stress of cultural confrontation entirely unscathed. The language of aesthetics, if highly portable, was nonetheless struc- tured by the hierarchical imperatives of British society. British women carried with them into unfamiliar terrain their subordinate position in their own society, epitomized by their marginal relation to aesthetics. Did this dispose them to resist aesthetics' objectifica- tion of other kinds of socially marginal individuals as figures in the landscape? Many twentieth-century feminists have been disposed to seek affinities between women and other oppressed groups, whether laborers, slaves, or "Orientals." Billie Melman, for example, argues that women travelers recognized analogies between their own position and that of women in Middle Eastern cultures, analogies that fostered "self-criticism rather than cultural smugness and sometimes resulted in an identification with the other that cut across the barriers of religion, culture and ethnicity." Moira Ferguson, on the other hand, sees women abolitionists' identification with slaves as displacing their anxiety about their own powerlessness. This led them toward a feminist consciousness; at the same time, however, they helped construct a colonial discourse that "more severely objectified and marginalized" the Africans themselves. Ferguson's research lends weight to Gayatri Spivak's warning against assuming that feminism automatically equals anti-imperialism, or resistance to any other specific category of oppression.[41]

Women travelers' use of aesthetic discourse registers the complexity of their relation to their "travelees." They often seem to identify with Turkish or Scottish women, Scandinavian peasants or French revolutionaries. How much of this is projection or displacement, writing their own cultural exclusion through that of these other Others? The figures of those abjected by mainstream aesthetics – the "vulgar" who served as foils, defining the man of taste by what he was not – become sites of disruption in these women's texts. When Montagu and Williams turn aesthetics to the defense of injured groups, their tactics stretch the limits of this conservative discourse and eventually run up against its most intractable features. For Wollstonecraft and Wordsworth, moments of empathy with rural inhabitants' concrete hardships, indescribable in the limited language of aesthetics, become a fulcrum to pry loose aesthetics' objectifying frame. Janet Schaw endorses both slavery and conventional womanhood. Nonetheless, her text erupts transgressively with the sardonic phrase, "brown beauty," suggestively blurring the boundaries of gender and race and unsettling both these categories' relation to the aesthetic. Schaw offers an extreme instance of the division or self-contradiction that we have noticed in every one of these texts. Even committed radicals like Williams and Wollstonecraft oscillate between distance and closeness, solidarity and disdain for the laboring classes whom they set out to liberate. In different circumstances, women could use aesthetic discourse as an outlet for subversive energy or a defensive bulwark. In every case it becomes a sensitive gauge of the competing determinants and intimate divisions that mark their social identities as privileged women.

Out of these women's divided texts emerge significant contributions to aesthetic thought. Though they do not theorize in conventionally accepted ways and are not accorded the theorist's prestige by their own contemporaries or ours, they offer cogent insights to readers prepared to expand narrow definitions of what counts as theory. We are now in a position to assess their critical reworking of three founding assumptions of modern European aesthetics: the generic perceiver, disinterested contemplation, and the autonomous aesthetic domain. Canonical eighteenth-century aestheticians like Hume, Burke, and Kant were heavily invested in the possibility of one generalizable model of aesthetic reception. They tried to standardize taste by constructing an unmarked position – a subject whose aesthetic judgments would count as universal, who would have the authority to judge for everyone. But their own texts reveal the subject in question as actually quite specific in his social location, as we saw, for example, with Hume. Implicitly or explicitly, theorists set stringent qualifications of gender, rank, and ethnicity for the "man of a polite imagination," the "true judge of taste."

The contradictions of this project come to the fore when unqualified individuals like women undertake to speak as aesthetic subjects. Boldly entering the space of incongruity between their own concrete social identities and the identity that aesthetic discourse projects for its ideal speaker, they send unpredictable consequences rippling, so to speak, through their texts. The very creativity of women's maneuvers to legitimize themselves as aesthetic subjects conveys their sense that they are not really entitled to this position. Women, conventionally positioned as beautiful objects, sidestep their objecthood to speak as aesthetic subjects. Montagu stakes out the aesthetic domain for the woman traveler only to undergo a series of sobering encounters with women whose culturally induced self-objectification rebukes her presumption. When she dons the veil or keeps her dress on in the Turkish bath to establish herself as the gazer, and not the gazed upon, she calls attention to the culturally constructed power asymmetry along the axis of vision. Janet Schaw does the same thing when she flaunts her suntan and abdicates her status as icon of femininity for the privilege of speaking as an aesthetic subject.

This asymmetry of vision troubles the notion of the generic perceiver by raising the discrepancy between universal validity and universal access. If only a few are qualified to judge aesthetically, then everyone else has to live with the standards imposed by this interested minority. This is Wollstonecraft's point when she criticizes the harmful effect of Burke's power-driven concept of beauty on the women whom it objectifies as passive and weak. Women travel writers' entire range of tactics resists an aesthetics that depends on power for its effects, in which a select few monopolize the power of the gaze and grant universality to their own perceptions by discrediting everyone else's. Each woman writer we have considered systematically tampers with this dominant model of aesthetic perception. Their patterns of deviant practice yield telling criticisms of mainstream aesthetics.

Wollstonecraft goes farthest to challenge the possibility or desirability of a generic perceiver when she imagines a situated aesthetic subject whose specific corporeal and social location do not detract from, but rather enhance the quality of her aesthetic experience. Situatedness entails particular relationships to particular objects – the vested interests that inevitably inform aesthetic perception, despite canonical theorists' stake in believing the contrary. Writings by male theorists from Addison to Archibald Alison, we saw in Chapter 3, explicitly divest the aesthetic subject of such interests, while at the same time carefully specifying his social identity. Women's travel writing lays siege to the concept of disinterested contemplation. Montagu turns disinterestedness to rhetorical use, but does not fully exorcize the prurient interest that colors the tradition of nude painting. Later writers put aesthetics to work advancing political ends as diverse as colonial slavery and bourgeois revolution. Helen Maria Williams' partisan use of aesthetics goes far to re-imagine the relation between the aesthetic and the political. Wollstonecraft, while she deplores the specific politics that Burke's aesthetics of the sublime and beautiful underwrites, endorses his belief that aesthetics and politics are inseparable. For her the question is not whether aesthetics advances political interests, but whose interests these will be. Both Wollstonecraft and Wordsworth repeatedly suggest the harm done by a landscape aesthetics that decouples aesthetic value from practical use as they re-insert inhabitants' material and immaterial needs into the sterile, de-particularized landscape of Gilpin's picturesque. Women's travel writing is especially effective at capturing people's multidimensional connection to the land they live on and from. Breaking down aesthetic distance, they break down social distance as well to work toward a pleasure dependent neither on rigid asymmetries of power and agency nor on a fictive detachment.

By detaching the aesthetic object – the framed, composed, packaged scene – from its material environment, the conventions of landscape aesthetics enact modern aesthetics' founding principle of the autonomous aesthetic domain untouched by sordid instrumentality. The autonomy of aesthetics is, of course, closely related to the disinterestedness or detachment of the aesthetic subject. We have seen women writers repeatedly defy the principle of autonomy to re-situate the aesthetic within the practical. Radcliffe's *Journey* and Wordsworth's *Recollections* interrupt scenic descriptions with contrasting or incompatible language in a disconcerting pattern that erodes picturesque detachment. Wordsworth's *Grasmere Journals* and Wollstonecraft's *Letters* work more synthetically to reconceive the aesthetic by reintegrating the perception of beauty into the everyday. These women's disregard for the autonomy of the aesthetic domain amounts to tacit defiance of a discursive system that is founded, as we saw in Chapter 3, on suppressing the particular in all its implications. To erase from the landscape as aesthetic object the particularity of things in the world, and the traces of the needs or desires that draw subjects to them, affirms the dominance of the de-particularized, unmarked aesthetic subject – the Man of Taste – over all of those whose social identities are symbolically entangled with debased particularity, notably women. In this context, restoring the particular and the practical to the representation of land becomes a meaningful gesture.

The systematic departures from convention that mark this group of travel accounts constitute a collective rethinking of the foundations of modern aesthetics. These writers theorize not by assertion, but through meaningful deviations from convention in the ways they apply aesthetic discourse. If I am now in a position, two centuries later, to recognize these departures and grasp their significance, this is in part symptomatic of the massive paradigm shift commonly known as postmodernism. Every representation of a specific historical past is the product of an interaction between that past and an equally specific present, produced by a materially and socially situated subject. Aesthetics formed part of the new division of knowledge that ushered in European modernity at the Enlightenment, and whose founding assumptions are currently under assault by a wide range of critiques. One of postmodernism's pervasive themes is a deep suspicion of any pretense to universality – a suspicion that most feminists certainly share. As Jane Flax puts it, "Perhaps reality can have 'a' structure only from the falsely universalizing perspective of the dominant group. That is, only to the extent that one person or group can dominate the whole will reality appear to be governed by one set of rules or be constituted by one privileged set of social relations."[42] Both feminism and postmodernism urge us to question modes of perceiving that claim universality or disinterestedness and to uncover the structures of dominance that make them possible. My interested readings of women travel writers' critiques of aesthetics have thus taken shape in an intellectual climate receptive to just such challenges. Acknowledging this should not invalidate my work as less than objective, but rather make clear the timeliness of rereading these prescient achievements of aesthetic thought.

Though I have been primarily occupied with travel writing (a genre whose low profile in present-day literary studies belies its popularity and prestige at the time these women wrote), I will conclude by discussing two novels. The novel's emergence is the hallmark of eighteenth-century literary history. Its characteristic dialogism is especially suited, as Ann Radcliffe and Mary Shelley found, to projects of demystification. Both *The Mysteries of Udolpho* and *Frankenstein* bear out Bakhtin's observation that novels "seek to objectivize the struggle with all types of internally persuasive alien discourse that had at one time held sway over the author." The novel, incorporating a variety of "social languages" or "verbal-ideological belief systems," plays them off against one another to unmask the inadequacies of each one.[43] In Radcliffe's long-winded thriller the dialogic tension between incompatible aesthetic categories, the picturesque and the sublime, explores (though it cannot resolve) the intractible conflicts dividing middle-class female subjectivity. Shelley's formally intricate narrative uses Frankenstein's misunderstood creature to expose the inherent violence of a universal standard of taste – its heavy cost not just to those whom it labels grotesque, but to an entire culture. Each novelist finds formal means to develop a kind of double vision that sees aesthetics, simultaneously or by turns, from the perspective of privilege and that of exclusion. It comes as no surprise that patriarchy and empire look different from their privileged center than from the outside looking in. These writers' achievement lies in extending their insights about the specific concepts and categories of aesthetics to encompass their society's entire ordering of knowledge and the violence which that knowledge does to those who know, as well as those who are known.

CHAPTER 7

The picturesque and the female sublime in Ann Radcliffe's Mysteries of Udolpho

> Charming as were all Mrs Radcliffe's works, and charming
> even as were the works of all her imitators, it was not in them
> perhaps that human nature, at least in the midland counties of
> England, was to be looked for.[1]

The Mysteries of Udolpho presented Jane Austen with an irresistible target for parody. Beneath its cheerful sarcasm, however, *Northanger Abbey* pays a darkly ambiguous tribute to Radcliffe's grasp of the cultural politics of gender in late eighteenth-century Britain. Despite her wry disclaimer, Austen shows Radcliffe's fiction to be (taking a phrase from Patricia Spacks) "both profoundly realistic – that is, its plots speak the realities of the culture from which they emerge – and consistently daring in its exploration of formal, psychological, and social possibility."[2] *Northanger Abbey* responds to Radcliffe's treatment of the difficult issue with which all these women writers struggled: women's relation to knowledge as cultural power. Like women travel writers from Mary Wortley Montagu to Dorothy Wordsworth, Radcliffe chose to engage specifically with one body of knowledge, the fashionable language of aesthetics – the language Austen's Henry Tilney teaches to Catherine Morland in a scene that captures women's derivative and conflicted relation to the powerful discourses of the dominant culture.

Radcliffe certainly earned Samuel Holt Monk's epithet, "the landscape novelist of all time."[3] Her protagonists are not just persecuted Gothic heroines but, first of all, scenic tourists. I want to approach Radcliffe's ambivalent obsession with aesthetics through the equally ambivalent fascination that her novels aroused, not just in Austen, but also in another novelist of the 1790s whose travel writing I have already discussed: Mary Wollstonecraft, author of the unfinished feminist Gothic novel *Maria, or the Wrongs of Woman*.

Wollstonecraft suggests in a more serious vein what Austen's parody denies, only to leave lingering in the back of the reader's mind: that the language of Gothic terror which Radcliffe had developed is indeed adequate to important aspects of women's experience in British culture, specifically women's relation to knowledge and to the powerful men who control it. It is peculiarly appropriate that my account of women writers' troubled engagement with aesthetics should culminate with two Gothic novels, *The Mysteries of Udolpho* and *Frankenstein*. Radcliffe and Shelley take advantage of the lurid language of the Gothic and the formal potential of the novel genre to dramatize their pointed critiques of aesthetics' patriarchal structure. In particular, they explore its subjective effects on those – like Radcliffe's heroine, Emily, and Frankenstein's creature – whom this Enlightenment discourse keeps in the dark.

Dorothy Wordsworth's travel journal conveys through metaphors of artifice, distance, and dirt the sense of self-division or alienation engendered by a woman writer's engagement with aesthetics and scenic tourism. This self-division gives *The Mysteries of Udolpho* its divided structure, with Emily's imprisonment in the sublime Castle Udolpho framed at either end by hundreds of pages of picturesque travelogue. Radcliffe's hair-raising tale of suspense is also a philosophical novel – a sustained thought experiment in which the author serializes her heroine's conflicted subjectivity by splitting the narrative into sections under the aegis of incompatible aesthetic categories. The picturesque and the Burkean sublime preside over contrasting realities and contrasting models of female selfhood. Radcliffe uses the language of aesthetics to register the unstable division of the middle-class female subject in a society where her class privilege coexists uneasily with her gendered oppression. At the same time, the very act of creating a female aesthetic subject casts doubt on fundamental premises of eighteenth-century aesthetic thought.

By the 1790s the novel had become the locus of widespread debate over the place of literacy, reading, and knowledge in genteel women's lives. Conduct manuals, though they encouraged women to pursue a carefully censored course of study, warned them against frivolous and tainted reading matter. Even Wollstonecraft voiced doubts about what women were learning from some novels. The knowledge that endangered women was inevitably presented as carnal, violating their modesty, the keystone of current ideologies of femininity.[4] To some extent, however, the sexual emphasis was a red herring. Novels, J. Paul Hunter has argued, served eager readers of both genders as sources of worldly knowledge in a broader sense – how-to manuals for life – taking over this function from a wide variety of didactic and practical reading matter.[5] *Northanger Abbey* gives us a naive reader-heroine who turns to Radcliffe seeking worldly knowledge, only to generate comic embarrassments. But the reader of Austen's novel, who is assumed to be a reader of Radcliffe as well, comes away with something much more troubling than just contempt for the latter's lack of superficial realism.

The divided structure of *The Mysteries of Udolpho*, if we take Radcliffe's narrator at her word, finally privileges the daylight world of the picturesque and not the sublimely gloomy castle as "real." For an alert reader, however, this clear-cut hierarchy does not hold. The orderly, ordinary scenic world comes to feel eerily artificial, while Montoni's castle uncannily captures aspects of women's real life in patriarchal culture. *Northanger Abbey* imitates Radcliffe's twofold structure, divided between "the anxieties of common life" at Bath and "the alarms of romance" at the Abbey (201). On the face of it, Catherine learns to reject the latter and face the former. Read more searchingly, though, Austen too undermines herself. General Tilney is Montoni-esque in his callous manipulation and greedy motives, as many critics have noticed. But another reversal, more subtle and haunting, pays further tribute to Radcliffe's tutelage in gender politics.

As she pursues the imaginary mystery of the dead Mrs. Tilney, boldly exploring forbidden areas of the Abbey, Catherine takes on an appealing assertiveness. By the time Austen renders her flat, anticlimactic account of Catherine and Henry's marriage – "the bells rang and every body smiled" (252) – this female agency has been stifled by a narrow domesticity. The rooms the General insists on showing Catherine, the kitchen and offices, illustrate his idea of her future role as domestic administrator. In the spatially restricted knowledge that the novel metes out as appropriate to a woman, Austen carries through Radcliffe's preoccupation with masculine control of power/knowledge. She makes a joke of the self-induced fears with which Catherine turns Northanger Abbey into a Gothic castle: after dragging out the suspense over the contents of a mysterious chest and cabinet for pages in classic Radcliffean style, Austen unveils their contents as not corpses, or even bones, but a laundry list and "a white cotton counterpane, properly folded" (164). The comic anticlimax carries a serious suggestion. Could it be that for women in this culture, domesticity is the horror?

Maria also takes up the Radcliffean theme of female fears and delusions. Wollstonecraft's political Gothic reconceives the Gothic castle as an insane asylum, foregrounding Radcliffe's preoccupation with women who have difficulty trusting the evidence of their senses – the definition of madness for Radcliffe's Emily, as we will see. Wollstonecraft uses madness as a metaphor to explore women's strained relation to common knowledge, or dominant ideology. Maria, commited to the madhouse by her unscrupulous husband, is the only sane woman in an institution whose inmates include a "lovely maniac" driven out of her mind by a forced marriage to a jealous old man.[6] Marriage, the central event of a woman's life as it is plotted by this society, puts her at risk of madness – or of being treated as mad when she is actually sane. Though she fears for her sanity, Maria does not notice her vulnerability to another female delusion, romantic love, as she begins to fantasize about a fellow inmate (182–83). When the judge in the climactic trial scene questions Maria's sanity for challenging the laws and customs that regulate women's lives (181), the whole world – or at least the British social and legal system – begins to seem a madhouse indeed.

Wollstonecraft exploits the connections that Radcliffe had established between the language of literary terror and the material and psychological conditions of women's lives. At the same time, *Maria* acts out the uncertainty that plagues Radcliffe's Emily, who cannot decide whether to trust the evidence of her senses. Wollstonecraft's novel cannot decide whether or not the Gothic is an appropriate medium for women's experience. Its opening contrasts literary terror with women's real lives: "Abodes of horror have frequently been described, and castles, filled with spectres and chimeras, conjured up by the magic spell of genius to harrow the soul, and absorb the wondering mind. But, formed of such stuff as dreams are made of, what were they to the mansion of despair, in one corner of which Maria sat, endeavouring to recal her scattered thoughts!" The inhabitants' "groans and shrieks were no insubstantial sounds of whistling winds, or startled birds, modulated by a romantic fancy" (85). Maria is in firm contact with reality, able to separate the real from the insubstantial. She can trust her senses and know the certainty they convey. Wollstonecraft's political Gothic begins by self-consciously distinguishing itself – as had Austen's parody – from the Gothic represented in contemporary consciousness by Radcliffe's novels.

But the account of her life that Maria writes for her daughter, culminating with her abduction to the madhouse, unapologetically resorts to lurid Gothic imagery: the "creeking of...dismal hinges," the "gloomy pile" with "mouldering steps" and a "murderous visage" peeping out of the gate. "A candle flaring in the socket, scarcely dispersed the darkness." A "dismal shriek" feeds a "mysterious emotion of terror" until the drugged Maria "almost doubted whether [she] was alive or dead" (169–70). The embedded narrative ends where the novel begins, with Maria's arrival at the asylum. This structural circle invites reflection: is or is not the language of literary terror appropriate to the experience of Maria/Woman? Wollstonecraft's fragment shows impulses in both directions. Like Austen, but in a more self-consciously political way, the author of the *Vindication* was clearly gripped by the connections that Radcliffe posed between Gothic terror and everyday female experience. It is worth examining in detail how the language of aesthetics structures Radcliffe's treatment of women's relation to knowledge as cultural power in her most famous work, *The Mysteries of Udolpho*.

THE USES OF SCENERY

Terry Castle has admonished the many critics who divide *Udolpho* into "two ontologically distinct realms." Most, she complains, all but ignore the "frame-world" of orderly daylight rationality – the opening and closing thirds of the book – in favor of the "Gothic core," the disordered cosmos of Castle Udolpho.[7] It is true that no one has persuasively accounted for the proliferating scenery in the opening and closing sections of the novel. Castle does Radcliffe criticism a service by urging us to read the whole book and question reductive renderings of its structure; she has not, however, taken sufficient note of the ways the text insists on its own dividedness. Emily dwells repeatedly on the contrast between her life at the castle – a "scene of savage discord," "the dream of a distempered imagination" – and her earlier, blissful life with her parents, which she remembers "like the visions of a higher world," serene and orderly as the stars and planets ruled by nature's laws.[8] The traumatized girl cannot comprehend these radically different experiences as parts of one life. Nonetheless, both are hers.

Through Emily's fractured subjectivity Radcliffe poses the central contradiction of upper-class women's identity, the incommensurability that disturbed their relation to aesthetics: privileged by their class, they are paradoxically disempowered by their gender. Emily becomes first one kind of aesthetic subject, the detached and controlling subject of the picturesque, and then quite another, the powerless, overwhelmed subject of the Burkean sublime. This exaggerated disjunction dramatizes privileged women's position in patriarchal class society as a dream split open by a nightmare – a site riven by dissonance, profoundly unstable. But as it marks its own radical division, the novel simultaneously undermines it. The halcyon surface of the picturesque travelogue subtly calls attention to its own artifice, while the castle nightmare works through significant aspects of women's real lives in late eighteenth-century England.

Written two years after Wollstonecraft's *Vindication of the Rights of Woman*, Radcliffe's novel also deals with women whose privilege lures them to cooperate in their own oppression. The enticements of scenery in *The Mysteries of Udolpho* include the security of the father's house, the utopian La Vallée that Emily longs for when she is locked in the dystopic Castle Udolpho. She associates the protective cocoon of La Vallée with the language of landscape aesthetics. Patriarchy wears two faces for her: the gentle, sensitive visage of her father, St. Aubert, and the grimly inscrutable countenance of the villain Montoni.

Radcliffe begins early to establish aesthetics' prominent position in the symbolic universe of her text. Aesthetic sensibility defines character, as we learn when we meet Emily St. Aubert in her greenhouse room at La Vallée, surrounded by the emblems of educated taste: "her books, her drawings, her musical instruments," and the picturesque landscape outside her window (3). As a member of the leisure class and a woman, Emily's primary responsibilities are those of representation. She must live up to her lineage by demonstrating the taste and sensibility that flow from "native genius" (that is, upper-class birth). Characters' taste is bound up with their moral worth. Those who can appreciate scenery are good, while those who cannot, like Montoni, are obviously evil.

Taste binds the good characters together in tight emotional–moral economies.[9] Landscape mediates Emily's primary attachments, which are to men (her mother dies in the first chapter). She and her father bond as they wander through southern France on a protracted scenic tour; the scenery feeds their shared grief. "The scene before them bore some resemblance…to a favourite one of the late Madame St. Aubert," whose "eyes must never, never more open upon this world" (29). After her father dies, Emily again grieves by fetishizing his favorite landscapes (92). Scenery is also indispensable to her romance with the dashing if ineffectual Valancourt, who first appears as a huntsman, "a characteristic figure" in the wooded landscape. The "scenes, amidst which they had first met, had fascinated her fancy, and had imperceptibly contributed to render Valancourt more interesting" (89). Most of their time together is spent talking about landscape; when they are apart, real or imagined scenes keep them present to one another (163).

Dragged through the countryside by her hard-hearted new guardians, her aunt and Montoni, Emily compulsively continues to practice scenic tourism. It is important to appreciate Radcliffe's subtle unorthodoxy in giving aesthetic contemplation distinctly practical functions for her heroine. Throughout Emily's travels with her father, practical concerns intrude on aesthetic enjoyment: his worsening health – he travels south on doctor's orders (25) – and the logistics and dangers of travel, largely ignored by the picturesque travelogues that these sections of the novel otherwise mimic. The travelers get lost in the dark, cannot find lodging, are endangered by reckless drivers (30) and threatened with financial ruin (59). I have argued that picturesque tourism inscribes on the countryside the notion of aesthetic disinterestedness, the segregation of aesthetic contemplation from practical vested interests. Radcliffe's own scenic tour, *A Journey through Holland and Germany*, banishes practical matters from its scenic tableaux; they return to disrupt the narrative and subvert the ideology of aesthetic distance, as we saw in Chapter 3. *The Mysteries of Udolpho* charts the vicissitudes of a female aesthetic subject moving through a viciously practical, interested world. Radcliffe's fiction presses the critique of aesthetic ideology harder than she found possible in the genre of the travel account.

It makes sense that a young woman who feels increasingly out of control of her life should find an escape in picturesque tourism. The picturesque tourist's elaborate framing of landscape combines distance with control – a mental manipulation closely related, as we have seen, to the estate gardener's physical "improvement" of his domain. The less power she has over her own fate, the more urgent becomes Emily's need for scenery. In Montoni's castle, suffering sensory deprivation and extreme disorientation, she turns for reassurance to the landscape outside her window. These moments sharpen the contrast that Radcliffe develops between the two aesthetic categories, the picturesque and the sublime, and their antithetical consequences for the female aesthetic subject.

RADCLIFFE'S FEMALE SUBLIME

The term "sublime" forms part of Radcliffe's aesthetic vocabulary, not just in the castle sequence, but throughout the novel. It is important to differentiate, however, between the sublime scenery that Emily appreciates during her travels and the version of the Burkean sublime that structures her heroine's experience in Castle Udolpho. Contemporary usage did not strictly separate the sublime and the picturesque, or even (despite Burke) the sublime and the beautiful: for example, a picturesque composition could contain sublime elements, as with Radcliffe's pastoral village surrounded by mountains, "a perfect picture of the lovely and the sublime, of 'beauty sleeping in the lap of horror'" (55). However, though her descriptive vocabulary ranges from "grand" and "wild" to "pastoral" or "romantic," the reams of scenic description that ornament the first two volumes of the novel are consistent in privileging the formal or compositional qualities of a landscape over its affective impact. Even as Emily approaches Castle Udolpho, glowering on its mountainside at dusk, "a gloomy and sublime object" (227), she is still able to frame, objectify, and contain its sublimity.

This changes once she enters the castle. The illusion of control carried by the category of the picturesque gives way to the epistemological abjection that characterizes Radcliffe's female sublime.[10] Emily does not call her experience in the castle sublime; nonetheless, it is clearly structured by Burkean criteria. Radcliffe makes of Emily's sojourn in Castle Udolpho an extended meditation on the potential of Burke's aesthetics of sublimity for constructing an imaginative model of eighteenth-century English women's experience. By making a woman the subject of the Burkean sublime, Radcliffe's fictional thought experiment explores the inter-relations between aesthetic response, politics (in the broad sense of power relations between individuals), and gender, a specific site of unequal power relations in patriarchal society.

Burke's aesthetics are fundamentally political in this broad sense, as Wollstonecraft understood. His 1757 treatise on the sublime and beautiful specifies power and fear as fundamental causes of the sublime; his discussion of sublime power seamlessly moves from dangerous animals to "kings and commanders" to the power of God.[11] Burke's commentators have generally recognized the sublime drama of confrontation with that in the universe more power-ful than ourselves as (at least in part) a symbolic enactment of power struggles between human individuals.[12] For Burke, the sub-ject's position in a hierarchy of human power relations determines not only aesthetic response, but the individual's entire experience of the world, encompassing "aesthetic" as well as "practical" aspects – as when he asserts that "we submit to what we admire, but we love what submits to us" (113). Admiration or awe is our aesthetic response to sublime power, love is our aesthetic response to beauty (and as Burke notes in passing, "love approaches much nearer to contempt than is commonly imagined" [67]). The aesthetic emotions of love and awe, in Burke's world, both pivot around the question of power. Castle Udolpho is profoundly Burkean in the intertwinement it displays between aesthetic experi-ence and power relations.

The power relations in Montoni's castle are gendered. Here Radcliffe exploits an aspect of Burke almost ludicrously obvious to post-Freudians. The sublime is hyper-masculine, large, dark, powerful, forbidding, and rugged; the beautiful epitomizes a then-current ideal of the feminine as small, weak, light, rounded, and smooth. Though Burke seems to take the masculine gender of the aesthetic subject for granted, his text presents a significant ambigu-ity in this regard. A subject confronted by the sublime (though he nowhere makes this explicit) is effectively feminized, put in a weak and passive position. For a man this feminized stance is temporary, merely experimental. His powerlessness is cushioned by "certain distances, and...certain modifications" (40): a threat, to be sublime, cannot be immediate or personal. Radcliffe's crucial innovation is to make the subject of the sublime actually feminine – immersed in real, immediate, inescapable powerlessness. Aesthetic distance, the privilege of the man of taste, is not available to this female aesthetic subject.

This feminine version of the Burkean sublime dramatizes women's experience of oppression by the institutionalized power relations between men and women. The marriage between Emily's aunt and Montoni puts both women in his power; his control over people, light and knowledge in his castle is a microcosm of male hegemony in society at large. Radcliffe exploits Burke's category of obscurity literally, as darkness, and metaphorically, as lack of information, uncertainty to the point of disorientation or trauma. Wollstonecraft's *Vindication of the Rights of Woman*, published two years before *Udolpho*, analyzes the ways in which women's lack of education and miseducation perpetuated their oppression. Radcliffe gives us a parable of women kept literally and metaphorically in the dark by a powerful man.[13] We will move through the gathering gloom of her text toward its most debilitating consequence: undermining women's trust in the evidence of their own senses.

Let me begin by recapitulating Burke on obscurity. His psychology divides our passions into two groups, those concerned with self-preservation and with society. The former, our most powerful feelings, produce the sublime: "Whatever is fitted in any sort to excite the ideas of pain, and danger, that is to say, whatever is in any sort terrible, or is conversant about terrible objects, or operates in a manner analogous to terror, is a source of the *sublime;* that is, it is productive of the strongest emotion which the mind is capable of feeling" (39). Obscurity, in turn, is an essential source of terror.

To make any thing very terrible, obscurity seems in general to be necessary. When we know the full extent of any danger, when we can accustom our eyes to it, a great deal of the apprehension vanishes. Every one will be sensible of this, who considers how greatly night adds to our dread, in all cases of danger, and how much the notions of ghosts and goblins, of which none can form clear ideas, affect minds, which give credit to the popular tales concerning such sorts of beings. Those despotic governments, which are founded on the passions of men, and principally upon the passion of fear, keep their chief as much as may be from the public eye. (58–59)

Especially revealing is the easy transition to obscurity as an instrument of political power. Whether governments rule primarily through fear or love, they always depend, for Burke, on an imbalance of knowledge between rulers and ruled, and they use aesthetic effects as ideological weapons to stay in power.

Literal, visual obscurity – darkness – saturates Castle Udolpho. No lamp ever lights a whole chamber: "Annette stood at the door...with the light held up to shew the chamber, but the feeble rays spread through not half of it" (232). Tiptoeing through the dank galleries, Emily is scarcely helped by "the feeble glimmer of the lamp," which "only shewed the gloom around her, and the passing air threatened to extinguish it" (253). The wind-extinguished lamp, of course, is a recurrent Radcliffean motif, which Austen does not forbear to ridicule. The logistical challenge of getting a light often puts Emily in a double bind: "the dismal obscurity of her chamber recalled fearful thoughts, but she remembered, that to procure a light she must pass through a great extent of the castle, and, above all, through the halls, where she had already experienced so much horror" (319). Montoni and his people control both light and knowledge in his castle.

Radcliffe's text keeps up a constant interplay between literal and figurative obscurity. Montoni's systematic withholding of information begins with his sudden decision to take his household to Udolpho. Emily is wakened in the middle of the night; when she asks for an explanation, the servant only knows "that the Signor is just come home in a very ill humour, that he has had us all called out of our beds, and tells us we are all to leave Venice immediately" (222). On their arrival at the castle Emily screws up her courage: "'May I ask, sir, the motive of this sudden journey?'" She is answered with an unjustified rebuke. "'It does not suit me to answer enquiries,' said Montoni, 'nor does it become you to make them; time may unfold them all: but I desire I may be no further harassed, and I recommend it to you to retire to your chamber, and to endeavour to adopt a more rational conduct, than that of yielding to fancies, and to a sensibility, which, to call it by the gentlest name, is only a weakness'" (230). This seeming non sequitur captures the dynamics of Emily's powerless situation.

Montoni's taciturnity leaves no basis for rational assessment of her situation. The anxiety that this causes breeds fancy and superstition, for which Emily is then blamed or ridiculed by Montoni (and by generations of condescending critics).

The longer Emily and her aunt stay in the castle, the more their unanswered questions multiply. How did Montoni actually come to own the place? What happened to Signora Laurentini, the previous owner? Servants' rumors mixed with superstition give Emily disturbing ideas, but nothing conclusive. How did Emily's bedroom door, open one evening when she went to bed, come to be bolted next morning? The wind made the bolts slide, says Montoni – but they are rusted tight. Again he lectures her on sensibility: "No existence is more contemptible than that, which is embittered by fear" (244). Who are those unsavory-looking men arriving at the castle? Why are the fortifications being repaired? Walking on the ramparts, "the only walk, indeed, which was open to her" (287), Emily sees things that she can't and Montoni won't explain.

She bends her hermeneutic powers in his direction, trying to decipher the thought processes that have such influence over her life:

> sometimes the deep workings of his mind entirely abstracted him from surrounding objects, and threw a gloom over his visage that rendered it terrible; at others, his eyes seemed almost to flash fire, and all the energies of his soul appeared to be roused for some great enterprise. Emily observed these written characters of his thoughts with deep interest, and not without some degree of awe, when she considered that she was entirely in his power. (191–92)

But no matter how much energy she invests in her decoding attempts, her captor remains inscrutable. "'O could I know,' said she to herself, 'what passes in that mind; could I know the thoughts, that are known there, I should no longer be condemned to this torturing suspense!'" (243). Montoni initiates a long tradition of powerful men whom heroines attempt to "read": Jane Eyre with Rochester, Lucy Snowe with M. Paul. Tania Modleski's study of mass-produced fantasies for women finds the theme continued today in popular romance fiction, reflecting women readers' special fascination with studies in the ramifications of male power.[14]

When Montoni's wife demands an explanation for the bustle, he counters by demanding that she sign her estates in France over to him – apparently his motive for marrying her in the first place. "Sign the writings...and you shall know more" (305). Information becomes an article of barter in an unequal power struggle that erupts into open contention, threat, and violence as the feisty Madame Montoni accuses her husband of leading a gang of robbers. "Montoni looked at her for a moment with a steady and stern countenance; while Emily trembled, and his wife, for once, thought she had said too much. 'You shall be removed, this night,' said he, 'to the east turret: there, perhaps, you may understand the danger of offending a man, who has an unlimited power over you'" (305). Montoni tears himself from Emily, who pleads at his feet: "as he burst from Emily, leaving his cloak, in her hand, she fell to the floor, with a force, that occasioned her a severe blow on the forehead" (305). Madame goes into convulsions, her eyes rolling, and falls likewise to the floor. It is only when Emily and her maid have wrestled her onto the bed that Annette's screams alert Emily to the blood dripping down her own face. When women demand information, violence erupts, exposing the violence latent in masculine control of power/knowledge. The scene alludes to Richardson's *Clarissa*, humiliated by her father as physical abasement completes a pattern of psychological abuse.[15] Radcliffe's allusion invokes the claustrophobic atmosphere of Richardson's realistic fable of patriarchal control, pointing toward the kind of realism that undergirds her melodramatic version of woman's estate.

The increasing fear and uncertainty that Montoni imposes on Emily and her aunt affects the two women's relationship as shared powerlessness draws them together. The tough, domineering Madame Montoni shows a new side on their first evening at Castle Udolpho: "'Good night, madam,' said [Emily] to her aunt, with an assumed composure, that could not disguise her emotion. 'Good night, my dear,' said Madame Montoni, in a tone of kindness, which her niece had never before heard from her; and the unexpected endearment brought tears to Emily's eyes" (230). The sound of Madame weeping behind her closed door and the sight of her tear-stained face are ominous reminders of the consequences of a false step in love and marriage. Madame still practices petty harassment, but a new solidarity emerges. When she disappears, Emily actively seeks her, venturing alone to the isolated east turret. This enterprise shows that critics who view Radcliffe's heroine as a passive, naive victim of Montoni and of her own sensibility are reading selectively at best. Much of the time Emily – like Austen's Catherine – takes a surprisingly active role. If we take her danger and her disorienting uncertainty seriously, her bouts of dread scarcely seem exaggerated.[16]

"THAT I MAY NOT LOSE MY SENSES"

Radcliffe's female sublime diverges most sharply from its Burkean model when we consider the cause of Emily's deepest fears in Castle Udolpho. This divergence is eloquent about women's vexed relation to patriarchal knowledge. Where Burke founds all aesthetic judgment, empirically, on common sense experience, Radcliffe derives her sublimest effects at the brink of exclusion from the social compact of the senses. His "Introduction on Taste" in *A Philosophical Enquiry* proclaims, "If we suffer ourselves to imagine, that their senses present to different men different images of things, this sceptical proceeding will make every sort of reasoning on every subject vain and frivolous...Thus the pleasure of all the senses, of the sight, and even of the Taste, that most ambiguous of the senses, is the same in all, high and low, learned and unlearned" (13, 16). The will to believe in an empirically based universal standard of taste was shared with Burke's contemporaries, notably Hume. Such a standard, I have argued, falsely universalizes the tastes of a few privileged men at the expense of those (peasants, Indians, women) from whom the man of taste distinguishes himself.

Radcliffe, by contrast, tests the possibility that different individuals in different material and social circumstances – at various positions in the hierarchical power relations that structured her society – might actually have different sense experiences. In particular, the novel asks whether oppression and intimidation may radically affect aesthetic response. Radcliffe's female sublime explores the connection between aesthetics and exclusion, specifically women's exclusion from experiences that dominant ideology took for granted as common or universal. This stands in direct contrast to the aesthetics that Emily espouses outside the castle: the picturesque, which standardizes nature through predetermined patterns and rules.

One important scene, Emily's reunion with her aunt after her protracted search, explicitly connects the two women's fear of

isolation in the menacing castle to the deeper fear of exclusion
from shared sensory experience. Emily has climbed seemingly
endless stairs to the gloomy, gaping turret chamber that is
Madame's prison and sickroom. The former battleaxe is "pale and
emaciated," changed almost beyond recognition; Montoni's cal-
lousness has engraved itself on his wife's body.

She was still alive, and, raising her heavy eyes, she turned them on her
niece.
  "Where have you been so long?" said she, in the same hollow tone, "I
thought you had forsaken me."
  "Do you indeed live," said Emily, at length, "or is this but a terrible
apparition?" She received no answer, and again she snatched up the
hand. "This is substance," she exclaimed, "but it is cold – cold as
marble!" She let it fall. "O, if you really live, speak!" said Emily, in a
voice of desperation, "that I may not lose my senses – say you know me!"
  "I do live," replied Madame Montoni, "but – I feel that I am about to
die." (364)

The scene dramatizes the feelings of isolation that torment both
women in the castle, where Montoni has assigned them widely
separated rooms (231). But the isolation Emily dreads is more than
merely physical. When she begs her aunt to supplement sight with
two additional senses, hearing and touch, to prove she is not a
ghost, she gives voice to her deepest fear: the fear of losing her
connection to the shared sensory universe. In the terms of
Radcliffe's aesthetic microcosm, such isolation from common sense
experience, or common knowledge, amounts to madness. It bor-
ders on death, the ultimate sublime. When Emily says she is afraid
of losing her senses, she is really afraid – like Wollstonecraft's
Maria – of losing her mind.
  Radcliffe's heroines are notorious for "losing their senses" by
fainting. Emily faints at moments when her senses deceive her into
thinking she is face to face with an image of her own death: the
moments when she lifts the veil from the mysterious "painting"
(249) and draws the curtain in the portal chamber to glimpse a
luridly disfigured corpse (348). Each time she thinks she sees the
body of a woman murdered by Montoni; she believes (mistakenly,
as she later finds out) that the wax dummy behind the veil is the
remains of Signora Laurentini and the dead soldier is Madame
Montoni. She is afraid she will be next. Emily's reaction at each

moment of horror mimics death, but it also acts out her own definition of madness as sensory shutdown. The second incident actually drives her temporarily mad. For fear of Montoni's vengeance, she cannot tell anyone what she has seen, cannot verify the testimony of her senses. "Thus compelled to bear within her own mind the whole horror of the secret, that oppressed it, her reason seemed to totter under the intolerable weight" (350).

Throughout her stay at the castle Emily totters under the burden of trying to distinguish between real and imaginary fears, both of which abound. Her position is that of woman in a culture where women's access to common knowledge is mediated by the men who produce and control that knowledge. Women hover at the margin between inclusion and isolation, certainty and madness. Wollstonecraft takes Radcliffe's female sublime a step further when she reconceives the Gothic castle as a lunatic asylum whose only sane inmate risks succumbing to the madness that orders her culture. No longer does madness consist of exclusion from the dominant paradigm; the dominant paradigm is mad. But Wollstonecraft's very ambivalence toward Radcliffe's language of terror reenacts the paralyzing, culturally induced uncertainty that is the central feature of that language.

SUBLIME AND PICTURESQUE

In Montoni's obscure stronghold Emily increasingly becomes the powerless, overwhelmed subject of the Burkean sublime. But the picturesque does not drop out of Radcliffe's repertoire while her heroine is locked in the castle. Emily's bouts of terror are punctuated by interludes of looking out of her window at the spectacular mountain scenery around the castle; she composes herself as she composes the scenes she views.[17] Her beleaguerment intensifies the emotional pull that the picturesque holds for her. Radcliffe pointedly, repeatedly juxtaposes the two aesthetic categories and the contrasting models of the female self that they elaborate. Testing each against the other – the exaggerated nightmare of gendered oppression inside the castle, the dream of benevolent patriarchy on the outside – the novel presents a radically disjunctive vision of privileged female subjectivity.

In Venice, as Montoni pressures her to marry an aggressive Italian count, Emily consoles herself with memories of her childhood home at La Vallée. "The ideal scenes were dearer, and more soothing to her heart, than all the splendour of gay assemblies; they were a kind of talisman that expelled the poison of temporary evils, and supported her hopes of happy days: they appeared like a beautiful landscape, lighted up by a gleam of sunshine, and seen through a perspective of dark and rugged rocks" (191). Landscape mediates the connections to loved individuals, now distant or dead, that emotionally fortify the girl against Montoni's onslaughts. The scenes of La Vallée are ideal, in the sense of being mental images; but also idealized, "improved" by the picturesque mind's eye. The simile of a landscape with the conventional dark foreground and brightly lit distance explicitly connects the framing effect of picturesque aesthetics with the hope and comfort that Emily needs, transposing her temporal distance from her happy past and hoped-for future into the manageable spatial distance of pictorial perspective. Radcliffe yokes emotional sustenance to distance and control in the "talismanic" function that picturesque aesthetics assumes for Emily. It is a function of her membership in the social class whose view of land this aesthetics codified. The ideal order of the picturesque scene evokes a political and social order in which she naively trusts. In effect, the privileged woman looks to her class status for protection from the consequences of being a woman – but in vain.

The morning after Emily arrives at Castle Udolpho we get an elaborate instance of scenery as normalizing force. "She rose, and, to relieve her mind from the busy ideas, that tormented it, compelled herself to notice external objects. From her casement she looked out upon the wild grandeur of the scene" (241). The rest of the paragraph describes in exhaustive detail a picturesque "vista" of a pastoral valley stretching to a distant blue horizon, framed by a dark foreground of mountains and woods. The "external objects" that distract Emily from her unhealthy brooding are mediated by a discourse with a strong class identification. Again, the framed and distanced order of the picturesque scene – and its established connection to the benevolent patriarchy of her childhood – mentally fortifies her in her powerless situation.

Repeatedly Emily comes back to the window. Each interlude builds the contrast between her nightmare present and her idealized past. Taking refuge from the fighting and chaos that follows a mysterious attempt to poison Montoni, she "sat down, near one of the casements, and, as she gazed on the mountain-view beyond, the deep repose of its beauty struck her with all the force of contrast, and she could scarcely believe herself so near a scene of savage discord" (318). The window becomes an ambivalent icon: the view outside it is a source of strength, but the frame itself, set in the castle's thick walls, reminds her she is a prisoner. One evening Emily goes to her casement, tormented by anxiety about her missing aunt. The night scene is "an image of repose"; the motions of the planets evoke the laws of the universe, which her father explained to her long ago. She remembers "all the strange and mournful events, which had occurred since she lived in peace with her parents. And to Emily, who had been so tenderly educated, so tenderly loved, who once knew only goodness and happiness – to her, the late events and her present situation – in a foreign land – in a remote castle – surrounded by vice and violence – seemed more like the visions of a distempered imagination, than the circumstances of truth" (329). Her bitten-off phrases and pauses are eloquent of bewilderment. She cannot encompass within a single reality the two models of female experience that Radcliffe's narrative uneasily yokes. Is the father a protector or a persecutor? Is women's world orderly or lawless? Emily's sessions at her window are the moments when the novel insists most strongly on its schizophrenic division into picturesque dream and sublime nightmare.

This fundamental disjunction between two aesthetic categories, two antithetical visions of bourgeois female experience, is rich in implications. While Radcliffe's female sublime explores the structure and consequences of gendered oppression, her treatment of the picturesque suggests the seductions of privilege that reconcile women to patriarchy. She asserts the reality of the picturesque vision, but gives the sublime castle far more vividness and charisma. The novel tests each paradigm against its opposite but does not resolve its ambivalence in favor of one or the other, suggesting a historically conditioned reluctance on the woman writer's part to put the female self into narrative as unified and coherent.

The double vision of the castle sequence, its oscillating counterpoint between the threat of the sublime and the security of the picturesque, approaches a crisis when the castle is threatened with a siege and Montoni packs Emily off for a brief "vacation" at a cottage in Tuscany. The odd solicitude of his gesture suggests a curious blurring of the novel's fundamental opposition between good and bad fathers presiding over picturesque and sublime spheres. The characteristic features of Radcliffe's female sublime – Montoni's withholding of information and Emily's anxiety – are exaggerated in the pages leading up to her departure, crowned by her terror as his two thugs escort her through the woods on a stormy night (409). She thinks she is done for. Instead she is installed in a hyper-picturesque "bower of sweets" (414), complete with perfect fruit, flowers, and cream-colored cows, a patently artificial idyll marred only by the henchman who guards her promenades through the too-perfect scenery. This final, forced juxtaposition between exaggerated scenic appeal and extreme fear underscores the disjunctiveness of Radcliffe's narrative. Though the narrator tells us Emily feels at home in "her pleasant embowered chamber" (418), by this point the reader no longer feels at home in either one of the narrative's aesthetic/existential modes. We are left with a sense of transcendental homelessness (to misapply Lukács' phrase), a kind of double alienation. At Castle Udolpho, the sublime is under siege; in Tuscany, the picturesque is under guard. Each paradigm erodes under pressure from the other, exposing the instability of the novel's peculiar double vision.

FIGURES OF RETREAT

The rapid disintegration of Montoni's regime soon after Emily's return from Tuscany is the first step in the narrative's protracted, disorderly retreat from its fractured vision, with the unresolvable tensions that have energized it. Earlier she has fantasized about escaping into a picturesque scene: "Emily almost wished to become a peasant of Piedmont...and to pass her careless hours among these romantic landscapes. To the hours, the months, she was to pass under the dominion of Montoni, she looked with apprehension" (167–68). Now she gets her wish, slipping improbably out of the "dreadful gates" into the scenic countryside (451). She forgets her hat and replaces it with a straw one "such as was worn by the peasant girls of Tuscany" (455).[18] Something resembling the static timelessness of the picturesque tableau supersedes the agonizing suspense of Castle Udolpho as the narrative meanders through hundreds of pages of confusing subplots and dragged-out misunderstandings to its anticlimactic close. The Villefort subplot gives us another well-born girl, another castle harboring a mystery. But instead of a villain, Chateau-le-Blanc is ruled by a benevolent patriarch, a sterner St. Aubert. Radcliffe is rewriting Montoni before we even know he is dead (or as Emily puts it, "his life was vanished like a shadow!" [580]). Emily's faded double, Blanche Villefort, is protected and not oppressed by the men in charge of her life.

The very protractedness of this last section, Radcliffe's apparent difficulty in bringing the novel to a close, bespeaks the difficulty of effacing the impression she has made. These anxious attempts at erasure confirm the transgressiveness of her vision. The ravings of Sister Agnes, or Signora Laurentini, represent another attempt at damage control. The fate of Udolpho's former owner marks the limits of female sensibility, a term whose ambiguities have troubled the novel from its beginning. Celebrating one kind of sensibility – aesthetic sensibility, in particular sensitivity to scenic landscapes – it condemns another, the kind that leads to forbidden sexuality. Laurentini's severe punishment for her sexual transgression illustrates Radcliffe's fear that the two kinds of sensibility might actually have a great deal in common. When the female aesthetic subject appropriates a prestigious body of knowledge, she risks a transgression that is predictably figured as sexual. St. Aubert's dark warnings to his daughter about the dangers of sensibility warn Radcliffe's reader of the risks run by women who know too much.[19] When Emily and her husband finally retreat to the site of her secure, sexless bourgeois childhood, the picturesque La Vallée, she seems permanently to have evaded the consequences of adult womanhood represented by Radcliffe's female sublime. But her "favourite haunts" (671) are haunted by linguistic hints of death and the supernatural. The narrative stubbornly refuses to leave Castle Udolpho and its terrors entirely behind.[20]

The self-consciously escapist veneer of Radcliffe's novels signals the intensity of the conflict that divides the woman writer against herself. She gravitates to the language and categories of aesthetics as a means to explore aspects of upper-class women's experience too threatening to articulate directly. But aesthetics also gives her a convenient means to distance herself from her own insights. The harrowing adventures of Radcliffe's female aesthetic subject in her interest-driven fictional world discredit the concept of aesthetic disinterestedness. At the same time, the novelist exploits this central feature of the Enlightenment division of knowledge; her novels' self-conscious artifice – their elaborately aestheticized surface, rife with allusions to painting and poetry – insists on its own escapism, the autonomy of the aesthetic domain. They have convinced generations of readers. In another sign of the radical ambivalence that pervades her writings, their critique subjects itself to that "creative repression or amnesia" which Terry Eagleton identifies as the most powerful feature of the ideology of aesthetics.[21]

The Mysteries of Udolpho cannot be declared a successful novel by standards of formal unity or psychological consistency. Its success must be measured in other terms.[22] Radcliffe's realism is not the realism of "human nature" in midland England or the Pyrenees, as Jane Austen knew. Like so many women's attempts to write the language of aesthetics, this one bears the marks of struggle. Like women travel writers from Montagu to Wordsworth, Radcliffe seems caught between categories, pulled in different directions by incommensurable aspects of her social self. She situates the female subject uneasily between aesthetics' seductive appeal and its threat to those not really entitled to wield its privileged knowledge. Her Gothic effects – like those of Wollstonecraft's *Maria* – circle around the pain and terror of realizing one's arbitrary exclusion from the culture one had believed to be one's own. Mary Shelley's *Frankenstein* renders the predicament of another outsider, this time not a beautiful woman but a monster. Both Radcliffe and Shelley use Gothic terror to assault the fundamental assumptions of aesthetics.

CHAPTER 8

Aesthetics, gender, and empire in Mary Shelley's
Frankenstein

His limbs were in proportion, and I had selected his features
as beautiful.
Beautiful! – Great God![1]

Mary Shelley was well acquainted with the growing tradition of
women writing the language of aesthetics. She records in her
journal reading Radcliffe's *Mysteries of Udolpho* and *The Italian*. Like
Radcliffe, Shelley was a traveler and the author of a scenic tour,
*History of a Six Weeks' Tour through a part of France, Switzerland,
Germany, and Holland* (1817), in which she refers to the castle of
Nimeguen, "mentioned in the letters of Lady Mary Montague."[2] In
Paris she and Percy sought her parents' friend Helen Maria
Williams, hoping for a loan.[3] And, of course, she knew the writings
of both her famous parents. In *History of a Six Weeks' Tour* Mary,
Percy, and Claire Clairmont float down the Rhine: "the sun shone
pleasantly, S[helley] read aloud to us Mary Wollstonecraft's Letters
from Norway, and we passed our time delightfully" (61–62). Amid
the picturesque scenes of the Rhine, the daughter pays tribute to
her dead mother's revisionist aesthetics.

Shelley carries forward Wollstonecraft's and her fellow women
travelers' subversive insistence on representing the voices and subjectivities of those normally objectified by aesthetic discourse.
Frankenstein's creature, that memorable character, combines a
hideous exterior with an eloquent voice.[4] His relation to the communities that exclude him, beginning with the Frankenstein and
De Lacey families, has the charged ambivalence of women writers'
relation to aesthetics. For him the seductions of the dominant
culture coexist uneasily with its oppressions, as they had for women
like Montagu, Radcliffe, and Wordsworth. *Frankenstein* offers
another double vision, seeing that culture from inside and outside

at once. The little communities in the novel are bonded together by shared tastes and aesthetic practices; their attractiveness is marred by troubling flaws that indict oppressive aspects of nineteenth-century British culture – a culture whose ideals are undeniably alluring, and yet corrupt, because founded on structural violence.

The creature's surreptitious, closeted education initiates him into Western culture, only to teach him his inevitable exclusion. His aesthetic education reinforces the lesson. Obsessively watching the handsome De Laceys, he internalizes their appearance as an unacknowledged standard of taste; hence his shocked self-loathing when he sees his own face in the pool. This crucial moment alludes to Part IV of *Gulliver's Travels,* an earlier work concerned with the psychological dynamics of colonization – for this is, in part, what I believe we are seeing in the creature's conflicted relation to European culture. In the years before she wrote *Frankenstein* Mary Shelley read widely in the literature of travel and exploration; she was especially fascinated with colonial and Oriental destinations like the West Indies, India, and China. Another favorite genre, not coincidentally, was the Oriental tale.[5] Frankenstein's creature is a colonized being whose pathetic adherence to the aesthetic standards that label him a monster epitomizes his relation to the culture that both forms and rejects him.

Critical attention to *Frankenstein* has increased as concerns with exclusion and oppression have moved to the center of theoretical debates. Much of this work is feminist, often reading the creature as an honorary woman who vents the woman writer's suppressed rage at her cultural exclusion.[6] But a narrow feminism, as Gayatri Spivak insists, diminishes the scope and power with which Shelley mythologizes her historical moment.[7] Poised between First and Second Empires, on the threshold of large-scale colonial expansion abroad and intensifying class conflict at home, she weaves into her creature's indeterminate identity Britain's collective anxieties about otherness of more than one kind. By constructing him as a "position of nameless, fetishized lack," in Zohreh T. Sullivan's phrase, she points toward the active interdependence between "hierarchies of race and class, ideologies of empire, and gender oppositions."[8] More than any writer we have yet considered, Shelley explores the common ground between women and aesthetics' other figures of abjection.

She pushes to the limit Wollstonecraft's project and that of the other women who rewrote aesthetic discourse. Reading *Frankenstein* in the light of everything we have learned from them allows us to recognize the radical character of Shelley's critique and the implications of this entire tradition for the nineteenth-century culture of empire. *Frankenstein* uses the nightmare fantasy of a creature who is created a blank slate, but made a monster, to explore the latent violence of a master discourse constructed on principles of detachment and exclusion. In the concept of monsterhood, appearance – that is, aesthetics – stands in for the social and moral dimensions of deformity. Negative aesthetic reactions of horrified disgust at the creature's unearthly ugliness warp his relations with others and drive the plot toward destruction. He grotesquely embodies all of those, including but not limited to women, whose suppression or exclusion is aesthetics' condition of possibility. His relation to aesthetic value becomes a synecdoche for his relation to an imperial culture that needs its vilified others.

AESTHETICS AND EMPIRE

Like Ann Radcliffe, Shelley is preoccupied with the power of knowledge; both associate it with the aesthetics of the sublime.[9] A chilly sublimity presides over Shelley's treatment of Victor Frankenstein's masculine Prometheanism, with key scenes set in the Arctic ice fields or on the glacial heights of Mont Blanc. She exploits the Burkean opposition between the solitary experience of the sublime and the social character of beauty. The sublime quest isolates the quester, rending the social ties that stabilize someone like Victor's childhood friend Henry Clerval – ties the novel associates with the enjoyment of beauty, and especially natural scenery. Both Victor and the explorer Walton let "the enticements of science" lead them into isolation from family and friends (46). Given all of this, it might seem fitting to seek an antidote to these dangerous tendencies in the human connection or "domestic affection" that binds the little community from which the heroic individual exiles himself. But Shelley is not content to criticize the Enlightenment division of knowledge for letting pure reason operate in isolation from morality and taste. She turns a suspicious lens on the latter as well, exposing the aestheticized ties that bind the Frankenstein circle as deeply compromised. Henry Clerval, in particular – handsome, affectionate, and accomplished – comes to embody a vision of European civilization as both irresistibly attractive and deeply flawed.

Aesthetics is woven into the bonds among the members of the Frankenstein circle, beginning with their shared appreciation of natural beauty and Shelley's choice of scenic Geneva as their home. At the center of this circle is the lovely Elizabeth, Victor's surrogate sister and later bride, a woman devoted to both aesthetics and interpersonal bonds. As a child Victor is attracted to factual, empirical knowledge, while Elizabeth loves poetry and drawing (30).[10] Her aesthetic aptitude persists into adulthood; for example, after her wedding to Victor (and just before her murder), as the newlyweds cross the lake for their honeymoon, she points out "the beauty of the scene" to take his mind off his premonitions (190). But this female aesthetic subject makes a poor showing in contrast to Wollstonecraft's vigorous, corporeal version. Her passivity and colorlessness are heightened in the 1831 revision, but already apparent in the 1818 text.[11] Other-directed, "forgetful of herself" (39), Elizabeth meets the standards of conservative arbiters of female behavior like Thomas Gisborne; she is much too boring and superficial to be, in Kate Ellis's words, "a real force in the novel."[12] Her character is especially unsatisfying compared to Safie, who embodies Wollstonecraft's feminist teachings. Safie leaves her tyrannical father and travels alone through a foreign country in search of her lover; Elizabeth sees Victor and Henry off on their travels and stays at home. The contrast between the two women, heightened in 1831, seems intended to emphasize Elizabeth's relative passivity.[13] The Frankensteins' aesthetic community subtly emerges as less than ideal. It can accommodate women, but only in a supporting role – the marginal position that eighteenth-century aesthetics generally assigned them.

The other pillar of this little community is Henry, who also shows his aesthetic proclivities early. From childhood he loves "books of chivalry and romance" (30); he is "no natural philosopher," but a poet and linguist who finally convinces his father to let him go to Ingolstadt and study languages (64). Coincidentally, he arrives on the "dreary night of November" when Victor brings the creature to life. He finds Victor wandering the streets, physically sapped and mentally deranged after the traumatic event. His scientific obsession has led him to neglect both natural beauty and social bonds. "It was a most beautiful season...but my eyes were insensible to the charms of nature. And the same feelings which made me neglect the scenes around me caused me also to forget those friends who were so many miles absent" (50). Now Victor is delighted to see his old friend, whose "presence brought back to my thoughts my father, Elizabeth, and all those scenes of home so dear to my recollection...I felt suddenly, and for the first time during many months, calm and serene joy" (55). The novel insists on connecting aestheticized nature with family or community bonds, offering both as balm for the physical and psychological dis-ease of hypertrophied reason. When Henry nurses his friend through his "nervous fever," the first sign of Victor's recovery is his renewed pleasure in the signs of spring (57).

Henry is also an avid scenic tourist who organizes first a walking tour around Ingolstadt and later a trip down the Rhine and over to England. Scenic tourism is part of Victor's therapy. "Clerval called forth the better feelings of my heart; he again taught me to love the aspect of nature, and the cheerful faces of children. Excellent friend!" (65). Victor's "better feelings" are both social and aesthetic; the picturesque tour brings out the connection between aesthetics and social bonds. Indeed, there seems no other way to account for the length of this sequence and its conspicuous staging in the vocabulary of scenic tourism, with Henry as guide and Victor as the distracted tourist whose preoccupation with his research (now that he has agreed to stitch up a female creature) once again precludes aesthetic response (151–52).[14] Henry Clerval is the quintessential Man of Taste, representing all that is finest in European civilization. He has the sensitivity of Radcliffe's St. Aubert and Valancourt without their spinelessness, good looks, intelligence, and a nurturing side. He is almost too good to be true.

As with Elizabeth, however, the 1831 revision heightens a troubling tendency in Henry's character, one that is already evident in the 1818 text. From an idealistic student of Oriental languages he evolves into a full-fledged colonial entrepreneur. "He came to the university with the design of making himself complete master of the oriental languages, as thus he should open a field for the plan of life he had marked out for himself. Resolved to pursue no inglorious career, he turned his eyes toward the East, as afford-ing scope for his spirit of enterprise" (243–44). More specifically, "His design was to visit India, in the belief that he had in his knowledge of its various languages, and in the views he had taken of its society, the means of materially assisting the progress of European colonisation and trade" (253). Why is it precisely this exemplary figure whom Shelley endows with imperial ambitions?

We might conclude that she shared the enthusiasm of so many of her contemporaries for Britain's global projects. But other references to colonization in the novel are less sanguine. For example, as the creature listens to Felix De Lacey instruct his "sweet Arabian" from Volney's *Ruins of Empires,* he "heard of the discovery of the American hemisphere, and wept with Safie over the hapless fate of its original inhabitants" (115). Mary Favret has called attention to the novel's formal intricacy – its shifting perspectives, or "multiple competing voices," including the narratives of Walton, Victor, and the creature, but also the various social languages that Shelley ventriloquizes by turns, among them Miltonic, scientific, Orientalist, political, ethical, and aesthetic discourse. A common thread weaving through this heteroglossia is her preoccupation with power and its effects.[15] A closer look at her handling of aesthetic discourse – a language structured, as I have shown, by multiple asymmetries of social power – can help make sense of the seeming inconsistency in the narrative's attitude toward empire.

Let us begin with a close look at one remarkable passage: Victor's retrospective meditation on the relation between the pursuit of knowledge, social relationships, and aesthetic pleasure. Significantly, his musings lead him into another colonial allusion. He takes a measured tone that sets this passage apart from his other, more histrionic self-condemnations; its position just before the climactic bringing-to-life scene lends it additional weight. Telling his story to Walton, Victor proposes a moral-psychological ideal of balance or harmony, regulated by social affection and aesthetic pleasure, which he now understands that he has dangerously disregarded. He begins with his father's assumption that if Victor doesn't write home, he is probably neglecting his other duties as well.

I then thought that my father would be unjust if he ascribed my neglect to vice, or faultiness on my part; but I am now convinced that he was justified in conceiving that I should not be altogether free from blame. A human being in perfection ought always to preserve a calm and peaceful mind, and never to allow passion or a transitory desire to disturb his tranquillity. I do not think that the pursuit of knowledge is an exception to this rule. If the study to which you apply yourself has a tendency to weaken your affections, and to destroy your taste for those simple pleasures in which no alloy can possibly mix, then that study is certainly unlawful, that is to say, not befitting the human mind. If this rule were always observed; if no man allowed any pursuit whatsoever to interfere with the tranquillity of his domestic affections, Greece had not been enslaved; Caesar would have spared his country; America would have been discovered more gradually; and the empires of Mexico and Peru had not been destroyed. (50–51)

The "human being in perfection" turns out to be a man of taste. Victor's nostalgic celebration of the "taste for...simple pleasures" surely includes the aesthetic pleasure in nature that he cannot feel during his scientific research. The state of "tranquillity," undisturbed by "passion or a transitory desire," paraphrases eighteenth-century theorists' definitions of disinterested aesthetic contemplation. One passion that is incompatible with this ideal state is Victor's hunger for knowledge, which he describes in phrases like "a kind of transport" (46) and "a resistless, and almost frantic impulse" (49).

Victor believes his hard-won experience has earned him the right to advance a vision of the aesthetic as an ideal regulating the development of civilization. This vision is reminiscent of the utopian strain in Wollstonecraft's aesthetic thought, in which the imagination presides over the progress of humankind. If pure reason, instead of operating in isolation from morality (or "domestic affection") and aesthetic judgment, would be ruled by these, then progress could be humanely managed and monstrosity contained.[16] Victor pointedly connects his dark scientific urge to the destructive hunger for discovery, conquest, and colonization that led to genocide in the Americas. He poses an antithesis between aesthetics and empire: a more tasteful, tranquil civilization would never have done these horrible things.

Here as elsewhere, however, Victor turns out to advocate a flawed perspective. Shelley's ambitious novel does not rest content with a critique of reason's excesses, but broadens its scope to include the very aspect of Enlightenment culture that it first seemed to offer as a remedy: the aesthetic. If Victor the scientist and Walton the explorer are dangerously misled, so is Shelley's third incarnation of Enlightenment Man – Henry Clerval, the man of taste. We have already seen Shelley hint at distasteful aspects of the Frankensteins' aesthetic community: it represses women and promotes colonialism, even genocide. Western civilization, viewed from the inside, has not got its parts put together quite right. The suspicion is confirmed when we see this disproportion reflected from the outside, blown up in the monstrous mirror that is Frankenstein's creature.

His character pushes to the limit the tactic, used by women travel writers since Montagu, of representing with independent subjectivities and voices types of people who were denied these by demeaning conventions of representation, from Orientalism to the aesthetics of the picturesque. Earlier writers disrupted aesthetic detachment by inviting readers to recognize the needs and feelings of the figures in the landscape. Shelley endows with feelings and needs a being whom aesthetic judgment can only label grotesque. Her novel extends the critical strain in Wollstonecraft and other women travel writers; like them, she reveals aesthetics as a socially divisive discourse which, in order to "civilize" some members of a society, needs to devalue the rest. The creature's boundless pain and rage at his treatment by the human race stand as Shelley's indictment of forms of language or knowledge whose insistence on detachment ends up promoting inhumanity.

THE AESTHETIC EDUCATION OF A MONSTER

The voice beneath the creature's frightening exterior is eloquent indeed. Telling his story, he generates a sympathy which casts doubt on the values that condemn him, in particular the aesthetic values that label him an object of disgust. His exclusion from the Frankenstein and De Lacey families causes him a degree of anguish that reflects disturbingly on these happy microcosms of Western culture. We realize that the comfort and beauty of their way of life feeds on the violence their civilization does to its outsiders. The creature's incongruous combination of repulsiveness and dignity, menace and pain, exposes aesthetics as imperialist in its very structure: beauty is violence.

His story dramatizes the conflicted relation of women and other marginal groups to the powerful knowledges of the culture that is and is not theirs. As he sits in his hovel absorbing the lessons intended for Safie, the process of internalizing a sexist and racist ordering of the world is punctuated by moments of resistance. The two of them, separated by the wall, join in mourning the genocide of the native Americans right after hearing De Lacey compare the "slothful Asiatics" to the "stupendous genius…of the Grecians" (115). Safie's ironic in-between status as part "slothful Asiatic" (half Arab Christian, half Turk) helps us interpret their outpouring as part of the identity crisis undergone, if differently, by both these colonized beings. Like so many of the women writers I have considered, Safie and the creature are both of the dominant culture and not of it, in it and outside it, its aspiring participants but just as much its victims and scapegoats.

The psychological and physical violence that people do to the creature is triggered by their aesthetic reactions to his appearance. The aesthetics of the beautiful, as we have seen, circumscribes the Frankenstein and De Lacey families; by this criterion the creature falls blatantly outside their pale. Despite Victor's good intentions, "the wretch" is hideous, as Shelley's famous first description testifies.

His limbs were in proportion, and I had selected his features as beautiful. Beautiful! – Great God! His yellow skin scarcely covered the work of muscles and arteries beneath; his hair was of a lustrous black, and flowing; his teeth of a pearly whiteness; but these luxuriances only formed a more horrid contrast with his watery eyes, that seemed almost of the same colour as the dun white sockets in which they were set, his shrivelled complexion, and straight black lips. (52)

She parodies an aesthetic vocabulary of "proportion" and "contrast"; decorative "luxuriances" mock the self-subversion of the creature's design. Listing these ornaments of flowing hair and pearly teeth, the description burlesques the poetic blazon, the conventional part-by-part praise of woman as aesthetic object. Aesthetic unity has eluded Victor as he stitched together his carefully chosen collection of body parts. The creature's skin (in Frances Ferguson's phrase) is too tight, highlighting the incoherence of the composition beneath.[17] So badly has Victor botched his work that he achieves exactly the opposite of what he had hoped. Instead of beautiful, the creature is so ugly children shriek and women faint at the sight. His appearance alone is enough to provoke vicious attacks (101). When the creature approaches little William Frankenstein, hoping he is too young to have learned his elders' prejudices, even the child shares this apparently primal reaction: "As soon as he beheld my form, he placed his hands before his eyes, and uttered a shrill scream" (139).

This universal recoil seems to affirm the standard of taste defended by eighteenth-century aestheticians like Hume and Burke: the idea that aesthetic standards are a uniform part of human nature, like sense perception itself, and thus universal or absolute, rather than culturally relative. As Hume puts it, "Some particular forms or qualities, from the original structure of the internal fabric, are calculated to please, and others to displease; and if they fail of their effect in any particular instance, it is from some apparent defect or imperfection in the organ."[18] What is beautiful to one must necessarily be beautiful to all, unless some contingent factor gets in the way of judgment. Conversely, what is disgusting to anyone must be so to everyone. I argued in Chapter 3 that these theorists construct a generic aesthetic perceiver through a process of disqualification that defines the "true judge" against the "peasant or Indian," the figures of abjection whose aesthetic incompetence provides a necessary contrast to the true judge's refinement. Such theories generate value through systems of hierarchical classification sanctioned by "nature" – a procedure tellingly congruent with the racial classification that rationalized European expansion. Deficient as aesthetic subjects, non-Europeans are judged deficient objects as well. More insidious, with the proper education they may come to judge themselves that way. A Eurocentric aesthetics of human appearance reinforces the European gentleman's entitlement to dictate value of every kind, but only with the cooperation of imperial subjects who accede to standards that condemn them.

Frankenstein's creature is a tragic example. The universal standard of taste seems to be confirmed once again by his own horrified reaction in the pivotal scene when he glimpses his face in a pool. His account of his development from an eight-foot infant into a fully sentient being leads up to this key scene with the gradual awakening of his aesthetic sensibility. He progresses from simple sensory pleasures like moonlight and birdsongs to more complex responses. By the time he arrives at the De Laceys' cottage he is ready for a fairly sophisticated appreciation of beauty. The sentimental genre piece of old M. De Lacey playing the violin to his daughter is "a lovely sight, even to me, poor wretch! who had never beheld aught beautiful before" (103). An aesthetic vocabulary describes the tableau of father and son walking in the garden: "Nothing could exceed in beauty the contrast between these two excellent creatures" (104).

The lonely voyeur's emotional investment in these domestic scenes prepares us for his startled self-loathing.

I had admired the perfect forms of my cottagers – their grace, beauty, and delicate complexions: but how was I terrified, when I viewed myself in a transparent pool! At first I started back, unable to believe that it was indeed I who was reflected in the mirror; and when I became fully convinced that I was in reality the monster that I am, I was filled with the bitterest sensations of despondence and mortification. Alas! I did not yet entirely know the fatal effects of this miserable deformity. (109)

His soliloquy takes the elusive "I" through a fatal progression, beginning with aesthetic contemplation and ending in death. The cottagers' beauty, their "perfect forms," ground the shocking contrast that generates his seemingly instinctive terror when "I" comes face to face with "myself." Instead of a moment of constitutive integration, as in Lacanian psychology – the necessary illusion of wholeness that allows a fundamentally fractured self to function – this mirror scene sets off a poisonous process of self-division. The movement from incredulity to conviction is a movement into "despondence and mortification," a profound self-hatred that can only culminate in death. The creature's sensibility, his aesthetic capacity, gives him more misery than pleasure.

Is this Shelley's ironic way of condemning Victor's research as unnatural, as Harold Bloom suggests?[19] I think there is more to it than that. Critics have noted the parallel between the creature's development and Rousseau's writings on primitive man.[20] At least as relevant is the keen interest that both Shelley's parents took in education: their faith in its power to mold individuals and shape the political fate of whole societies, since (as Godwin entitles a key chapter of *Political Justice*) "The Characters of Men Originate in their External Circumstances."[21] But the creature's narrative of his early life implicitly counters Godwin's extreme rationalism with a very different theory of education, premised on the child's need for acceptance by those in his immediate environment. The childlike creature attributes beauty to those from whom he desires acceptance – the only other beings he knows – and then condemns himself by this emotionally colored standard. If his own aesthetic response to his appearance is contingent rather than necessary, then, quite probably, so is everyone else's. Shelley subtly reveals the supposedly visceral disgust provoked by the creature's unearthly ugliness as a second nature that is really a cultural construction. Her treatment of aesthetic value partakes of Godwin's and Wollstonecraft's willingness to consider even the most seemingly natural human qualities as cultural artifacts.

Exposing the constructedness of aesthetic response, Shelley follows in the footsteps of women travel writers since Montagu. Each in her own way refuses to take for granted aesthetics' contradictory combination of universal pretensions and exclusionary assumptions. Their fractured texts trace the fault lines of a discourse whose claim to universality could only be sustained at the expense of subjects like themselves: figures of abjection symbolically identified with body rather than mind, matter as opposed to form, and the particular, rather than the general or universal. Writing from the paradoxical position of someone both included and excluded by aesthetics' ambiguous criteria, these literate, privileged women collectively demolish the fiction of the generic perceiver, the condition of possibility for any universal standard. A standardized, monolithic aesthetics fails to account for every perceiver's particular material and social location. As a woman, Mary Wortley Montagu cannot regard the spectacle of woman with the same eyes as could a man. Helen Maria Williams' political investment emotionally colors the spectacle of Revolution, making her aesthetic response to it very different from, for example, Burke's; Mary Wollstonecraft's experience of landscape is likewise informed by her experiences as a political radical and a woman. None of these women's texts maintains the detachment prescribed by mainstream aesthetic theorists. All of them write in and through the multiple, often conflicting investments that color their authors' aesthetic experience.

All of my analyses have stressed the divided, conflicted character of the female consciousness whose formation these writings trace. Shelley's novel explores most fully the correspondence between women's position and that of a colonized being like Frankenstein's creature. Staring into his pool, he captures the bitter pain of those who internalize values that demean them. His colonized consciousness renders a tragic double vision of Western culture from inside and outside at once. He is frequently on the outside looking in, peering through the bed-curtains at his creator or peeping through the one-way chink in the De Laceys' wall to experience their happiness and his loneliness, their civilization and his exclusion. His agonized self-hatred measures the scarring, warping effect of ways of knowing that are grounded in detachment and exclusion.

Women's travel writing registers the cost of such knowledge to both objects and subjects – to the figures in the landscape, reduced to facelessness, and to women themselves as they struggle to adopt a perspective that both is and cannot be their own. Shelley indicts aesthetics as imperial knowledge that arrogantly universalizes one very particular point of view. Her daring subversion of eighteenth-century aestheticians' favorite fantasy, the universal standard of taste, extends women travel writers' critiques to cast doubt on the universality of the other ruling-class values that Europeans exported to colonized peoples around the globe. *Frankenstein* impugns the missionary assumption that most powerfully rational-ized nineteenth-century imperialism: since our values are self-evidently universal, we are justified in imposing them on those too benighted to recognize the truth by themselves. The language of aesthetics, grounded in an imperial symbolic, distinguishes between categories of subjects. It anaesthetizes some and dehumanizes others; an entire civilization pays the price.

A WORLD OF OTHERS

Shelley's meditation on aesthetics and empire is enriched by a pointed allusion, sure to stand out for readers in 1818. The mirror scene in *Frankenstein* bears a striking similarity to a moment in Book IV of *Gulliver's Travels*, which Shelley records reading in November 1816 as she worked on her novel.[22] The allusion draws into Shelley's frame of reference Swift's familiar context of travel and exploration – relevant settings, in 1818 as well as 1726, for encoun-ters with seemingly monstrous Others. Gulliver arrives among the Houyhnhnms and Yahoos with a colonizer's arrogance, but gradu-ally takes on the caricatured humility and self-loathing of the colonized in relation to the noble horses. Admiring their virtues, desiring their approval, he adopts their aesthetics as well.

When I happened to behold the reflection of my own form in a lake or fountain, I turned away my face in horror and detestation of myself, and could better endure the sight of a common yahoo, than of my own person. By conversing with the Houyhnhnms, and looking upon them with delight, I fell to imitate their gait and gesture, which is now grown into a habit, and my friends often tell me in a blunt way that I "trot like a horse."[23]

Gulliver has absorbed Houyhnhnm standards that monsterize him to himself and trigger an intense self-loathing. Though Swift makes a joke of it, his satire offers a complex precedent for the reaction of Shelley's creature confronted with the contrast between his appearance and the De Laceys'.

The creature's aesthetic experience is an experience of exclusion that engenders not just self-hatred, but also a misanthropy that is profoundly Swiftian. Like Gulliver, he undergoes a protracted identity crisis that moves him inexorably toward confronting his own monsterhood. Both protagonists are at the same time profoundly human and profoundly alien. Gulliver's process of realizing that "I was a real Yahoo in every limb and feature" (215) is punctuated by specular moments: not just seeing himself in a mirror, but seeing himself in others – the Yahoos – or in others' reaction to seeing him. The young female Yahoo's lust for Gulliver is the equivalent of the loathing that Frankenstein's creature evokes in everyone who looks at him: it is evidence of monsterhood. The whole Yahoo species, like the creature, lives by aesthetic values that breed a pervasive hatred, which comes down to self-hatred. They "were known to hate one another more than they did any different species of animals; and the reason usually assigned was the odiousness of their own shapes, which all could see in the rest, but not in themselves" (209). This phantasmic "odiousness" suggests an instability in its own construction: now you see it, now you don't. As Shelley reimagines the narrative of monsterhood, the value-laden distinction between self and other, beautiful and repulsive, does not hold up under scrutiny. Self and other collapse into one another, leading us to question not the humanness of the creature, but the humaneness of a culture that relies on the abjection of Others to construct its selves.

The creature, that elusive figure, cannot recognize himself anywhere in the versions of civilization that his education delivers to him. "When I looked around, I saw and heard of none like me. Was I then a monster...?" (116). But the novel repeatedly associates him with a whole world of excluded Others. The allusion to *Gulliver's Travels* is part of this pattern. The Yahoos are a precedent for the way in which Shelley's creature amalgamates multiple dimensions of difference. Swift's descriptions of them echo contemporary discourses of "race," but also epitomize the "hideous corporeality" of the misogynist version of woman found in his scatological poetry, as Laura Brown has shown.[24] This allusion is part of a pattern of reference throughout the novel linking the creature to a whole world of excluded Others. Walton's first remark about Victor is to distinguish him from the creature, sledding away in the distance: "He was not, as the other traveller seemed to be, a savage inhabitant of some undiscovered island, but an European" (18). Certainly the creature's yellow skin carries racial overtones, whether Chinese, Japanese, or East Indian.[25] Victor's excuse for destroying the female creature is racist as well as viscerally misogynist: " a race of devils would be propagated upon the earth" (163).

Sandra Gilbert and Susan Gubar long ago taught us to see in the creature's distorted silhouette, dancing around the De Laceys' burning cottage, "a woman in the shape of a monster/ A monster in the shape of a woman," a combination of self-loathing and sublimated rage.[26] But the political discourse of the French Revolution period, monsterizing the revolutionary crowd, also contributes to Shelley's synthetic myth. Fear of England's laboring class as a collective monster ready to rend its chains must have been visceral for the early nineteenth-century middle classes.[27] The creature's charismatic power derives from his status as a quintessential outsider. His character conflates multiple dimensions of otherness with a purposeful density of reference. This is perhaps most jarring in the end that the remorse-torn creature projects for himself (but has not carried out by the novel's close).

He commemorates his bizarre homosocial bond to his creator by pledging to "collect [his] funeral pile, and consume to ashes this miserable frame" (220). Fire is no longer the instrument of destructive revenge, but the suicidal weapon of self-hatred. The image of the pyre contains a double allusion whose disjunctiveness is an oddly appropriate emblem for the self-division experienced by women writing the language of aesthetics. It alludes to the death of the mythical strongman Hercules, whose massive power aptly symbolizes imperial Europe, heir to the Greek and Roman empires.[28] But it also calls to mind the Indian widow whose self-immolation, or *sati*, was the topic of heated debate by India's colonial rulers at the time Shelley wrote.[29] This curious double exposure superimposes a classical masculine icon of empire on the figure of empire's humblest subaltern, fusing them in mutual self-destruction. Allusively, *Frankenstein* insists on the unstable hybridity of selves in a world of complex global interdependence where a long history of border crossings – "the imbrication of...various pasts and presents, the ineluctable relationships of shared and contested meanings, values, material resources" – has made cultural purity long obsolete, if it ever existed.[30] Between cultures and within them, selves depend on their opposites and include them: I embrace multitudes.

Such a self is wholly foreign to the distanced, de-particularized aesthetic subject proposed by mainstream theorists like Sir Joshua Reynolds, whose suppression of details in painting symbolically defends the polite imagination against the messy encroachment of base matter, low faculties, and vulgar minds. Aesthetic distance strives to protect the imperial self from impure influences. Women writers from Montagu to Shelley insisted on the heavy cost of such detachment in its anaesthetized response to human suffering. The British Hercules will not escape the consequences of the psychic self-immolation sponsored by imperial knowledge at home and abroad. Aesthetics epitomizes a system of power/knowledge whose sterile universality is founded on keeping its Others at arm's length. The tradition of women rewriting the language of aesthetics culminates with Frankenstein's creature, whose eloquent voice brings a world of Others in close before his monstrous figure is finally "lost in darkness and distance."[31]

Notes

INTRODUCTION

1 Austen, *Northanger Abbey*, in *The Novels of Jane Austen*, ed. R. W. Chapman, third edition, vol. V (London: Oxford University Press, 1965), pp. 110–11. Though published in 1818, the first version of the novel was written in 1798–99.

2 I paraphrase Nancy K. Miller: "the irreducibly complicated relationship women have historically had to the language of the dominant culture." "Emphasis Added: Plots and Plausibilities in Women's Fiction," in *Subject to Change* (New York: Columbia University Press, 1988), p. 29.

3 Claudia L. Johnson has taught us to understand *Northanger Abbey* as a deeply political book, continuous with the Gothic novels that it parodies in its mistrust of patriarchy. *Jane Austen: Women, Politics, and the Novel* (University of Chicago Press, 1988), pp. xxiv, 32–48.

4 Austen, *Northanger Abbey*, pp. 107, 108, 111. Eleanor Tilney's ambiguous role in this scene as the defender of history and Henry is typical of Austen's elusive approach to social criticism, which gives with one hand what it takes away with the other.

5 *The Works of the Right Honorable Lady Mary Wortley Montagu including her correspondence, poems, and essays, in five volumes* (London, 1803), vol. IV, p. 185, and see *Complete Letters of Lady Mary Wortley Montagu*, ed. Robert Halsband (Oxford: Clarendon Press, 1967), vol. III, p. 22. Austen continues bitingly, "The advantages of natural folly in a beautiful girl have been already set forth by the capital pen of a sister author…I will only add in justice to men, that though to the larger and more trifling part of the sex, imbecility in females is a great enhancement of their personal charms, there is a portion of them too reasonable and too well informed themselves to desire any thing more in woman than ignorance." The "sister author" is Frances Burney in *Camilla*, referring to the character of Indiana.

6 The single exception I have found is Frances Reynolds' treatise, *An Enquiry concerning the Principles of Taste, and of the Origin of our Ideas of Beauty* (London, 1785). It is discussed by Peter De Bolla, *The Discourse of the Sublime: History, Aesthetics, and the Subject* (Oxford: Basil Blackwell, 1989), pp. 48–54.

7 Carl Paul Barbier, *William Gilpin* (Oxford: Clarendon Press, 1963), p. 149. Timothy Reiss argues for a similar model of women's participation in the Enlightenment discourse of reason: marginal incorporation was a better method of control than total exclusion. "Revolution in Bounds: Wollstonecraft, Women, and Reason," in *Gender and Theory: Dialogues on Feminist Criticism*, ed. Linda Kauffman (Oxford: Basil Blackwell, 1989), pp. 12–13.

8 *The Spectator*, ed. Donald Bond (Oxford: Clarendon Press, 1965), no. 10 (March 12, 1711), Vol. I, pp. 46–47.

9 John Bender, "A New History of the Enlightenment?" *Eighteenth-Century Life*, 16 (1992), p. 17, n. 8.

10 For example, Judith Lowder Newton, *Women, Power, and Subversion: Social Strategies in British Fiction, 1778–1860* (Athens: University of Georgia Press, 1981); Mary Poovey, *The Proper Lady and the Woman Writer: Ideology as Style in the Works of Mary Wollstonecraft, Mary Shelley, and Jane Austen* (University of Chicago Press, 1984); Kristina Straub, *Divided Fictions: Fanny Burney and Feminine Strategy* (Lexington: University Press of Kentucky, 1987); and Claudia Johnson, *Jane Austen.*

11 Carolyn Korsmeyer, "Introduction," in *Aesthetics in Feminist Perspective*, eds. Hilde Hein and Carolyn Korsmeyer (Bloomington: Indiana University Press, 1993), p. ix. The term "aesthetics" itself was Anglicized largely after the period with which I am concerned. Though the OED lists "aesthetic" as an adjective in 1798 ("of or pertaining to sensuous perception"), the noun "aesthetics" is not found until 1832, when it is rather disdainfully identified as a German import. Resistance to the term continued until at least mid-century. My use of "aesthetics" as an inclusive category is a matter of convenience, and must be understood as both retrospective and heuristic.

12 Barrell, *The Political Theory of Painting from Reynolds to Hazlitt* (New Haven: Yale University Press, 1986), p. 222. Barrell notes briefly at the outset of his discussion that "women are denied citizenship, and denied it absolutely, in the republic of taste as well as in the political republic" (p. 66). Nowhere does he consider the possibility that women may have disputed this state of affairs. His article, "'The Dangerous Goddess': Masculinity, Prestige, and the Aesthetic in Early Eighteenth-Century Britain," *Cultural Critique*, 12 (1989), pp. 101–31, investigates the gendering of the aesthetic but ignores women's contribution to aesthetic thought. Gender enters Eagleton's *The Ideology of the Aesthetic* (Oxford: Basil Blackwell, 1990), on pp. 16, 49–50, 55–59, and 115. He contends that aesthetics is gendered feminine in opposition to "the masculine regime of reason" or the moral law, whether this is seen as an advantage, as by British moral sense philosophers and Burke, or a disadvantage, as by Hume and Schiller. Though he agrees with Wollstonecraft that Burke's politicized aesthetics deploys the feminine in a manner that would exclude women from the domain of

truth and morality (p. 59), he shows no awareness that she developed a counter-aesthetics of her own.

13 Diane Macdonell, *Theories of Discourse: An Introduction* (Oxford: Basil Blackwell, 1986), pp. 1–2 and *passim*. My methods are obviously influenced by Foucault, although I do not adopt his unworkably narrow and technical definition of the discursive formation. *The Archaeology of Knowledge,* trans. A. M. Sheridan Smith (New York: Pantheon, 1972), pp. 37–38 and *passim*.

14 Bender surveys the problem of defining "Enlightenment" in "A New History of the Enlightenment?" pp. 5–6. I use the term in a provisional sense like the one he suggests, "not to define a strict historical period but rather as a marker to signify a large, somewhat rough-edged phase in European culture." He identifies four enduring "foundational presumptions" dating to the Enlightenment, the first one being the "invention of the aesthetic as an autonomous discursive realm" (p. 9). See also Peter Gay, *The Enlightenment: An Interpretation* (New York: Alfred A. Knopf, 1969), vol. I, pp. 3–4, 16–18.

15 See, for example Katharine Everett Gilbert and Helmut Kuhn, *A History of Esthetics* (Bloomington: Indiana University Press, 1954), which does not record a woman theorist until the twentieth century (Suzanne Langer).

16 Joan Kelly-Gadol, "Did Women Have a Renaissance?" in *Becoming Visible: Women in European History,* eds. Renate Bridenthal and Claudia Koonz, (Boston: Houghton Mifflin, 1977), pp. 137–64. Joan B. Landes, *Women and the Public Sphere in the Age of the French Revolution* (Ithaca: Cornell University Press, 1988) and Rita Goldberg, *Sex and Enlightenment: Women in Richardson and Diderot* (Cambridge University Press, 1984) point out regressive tendencies in Enlightenment gender ideology and in the cultural politics of the French Revolution.

17 Joan Wallach Scott, *Gender and the Politics of History* (New York: Columbia University Press, 1988), p. 2; see also Chapter 2, "Gender: A Useful Category of Historical Analysis," pp. 28–50. Little scholarly work existed until quite recently on the significance of gender to the history of aesthetics. Besides the essays in Hein and Korsmeyer, *Aesthetics in Feminist Perspective,* see Martha Woodmansee, *The Author, Art, and the Market: Rereading the History of Aesthetics* (New York: Columbia University Press, 1994), ch. 5; Anne K. Mellor, *Romanticism and Gender* (New York: Routledge, 1993), chs. 5 and 6; Christine Battersby, *Gender and Genius: Towards a Feminist Aesthetics* (Bloomington: Indiana University Press, 1989); Naomi Schor, *Reading in Detail: Aesthetics and the Feminine* (New York: Methuen, 1987) and "Rereading in Detail: Or, Aesthetics, the Feminine, and Idealism," *Criticism,* 32 (1990), pp. 309–23; Barrell, "'The Dangerous Goddess'"; Paul Mattick, Jr., "Beautiful and Sublime: Gender Totemism and the Constitution of Art," *Journal of Aesthetics and Art Criticism* 48:4 (1990), pp. 293–303; and Ronald Paulson, *Representations of Revolution (1789–1820)* (New Haven: Yale University

Press, 1983), esp. pp. 79–87. Feminist art historians address related issues; see for example, Rozsika Parker and Griselda Pollock, *Old Mistresses: Women, Art and Ideology* (London and Henley: Routledge & Kegan Paul, 1981) and Linda Nochlin, *Women, Art, and Power and Other Essays* (New York: Harper & Row, 1988).

18 John W. Draper, *Eighteenth-Century English Aesthetics: A Bibliography* (New York: Octagon Books, 1968) contains more than 1,200 entries. De Bolla claims to have seen an unpublished bibliography of over 6,000 items (*Discourse of the Sublime*, p. 29). On Kant's relation to British thought, see Jerome Stolnitz, "On the Origins of 'Aesthetic Disinterestedness,'" *Journal of Aesthetics and Art Criticism*, 20 (1961–62), pp. 131–43.

19 Korsmeyer, "Introduction," *Aesthetics in Feminist Perspective*, p. viii.

20 Feminist film theorists have wrestled with the paradox of woman as spectator (or director) in a medium structured around a masculine subjectivity. My enterprise, broadly considered, bears significant analogies to theirs. See for example, Laura Mulvey, "Visual Pleasure and Narrative Cinema" and "Afterthoughts on 'Visual Pleasure and Narrative Cinema' inspired by *Duel in the Sun*," in *Feminism and Film Theory*, ed. Constance Penley (New York: Routledge, 1988), pp. 57–68 and 69–79.

21 *The Spectator*, no. 411 (June 21, 1712), Vol. III, p. 538. Addison implies a view of eighteenth-century British society that will be my premise throughout this study. Of the many perceived gradations in socioeconomic status, Harold Perkin asserts, by far the most significant (though not easy to quantify) was "one horizontal cleavage of great import": the distinction between gentlemen — persons not obliged to work for a living, with "polite" breeding and manners — and "mechanics," including tradesmen as well as the laboring classes per se. Women's social status derived from that of their fathers or husbands. *Origins of Modern English Society* (New York: Routledge, 1969), p. 24. See also J. C. D. Clark, *English Society 1688–1832: Ideology, Social Structure and Political Practice During the Ancien Regime* (Cambridge University Press, 1985), pp. 93–118. I use the term "class" in the heuristic manner that E. P. Thompson endorses, aware that during the eighteenth century "class was not available within people's own cognitive system." "Eighteenth-Century English Society: Class Struggle Without Class?" *Social History*, 3 (1978), pp. 151, 148.

22 Addison, *The Spectator*, Vol. III, p. 538.

23 Paul Mattick, Jr., "Introduction," in *Eighteenth-Century Aesthetics and the Reconstruction of Art*, ed. Paul Mattick, Jr., (Cambridge University Press, 1993), p. 5.

24 Bourdieu, *Distinction: A Social Critique of the Judgement of Taste*, trans. Richard Nice (Cambridge, Mass.: Harvard University Press, 1984), p. 5 and *passim*. Bourdieu's is one useful approach to the historicist analysis of aesthetics. Until recently aesthetics seemed oddly immune to

such historicizing. But see Timothy Dykstal, "The Politics of Taste in the *Spectator*," *The Eighteenth Century: Theory and Interpretation*, 35 (1994), pp. 46–63; Woodmansee, *The Author, Art, and the Market*; Mattick, ed., *Eighteenth-Century Aesthetics*; Ronald Paulson, *Breaking and Remaking: Aesthetic Practice in England, 1700–1820* (New Brunswick: Rutgers University Press, 1989); De Bolla, *Discourse of the Sublime*; Eagleton, *Ideology of the Aesthetic*; Howard Caygill, *Art of Judgement* (Oxford: Basil Blackwell, 1989); Barrell, *Political Theory of Painting*; and Michael McKeon, "The Origins of Aesthetic Value," *Telos*, 57 (1983), pp. 63–82. I encountered three important new books dealing with the history of aesthetics too late to engage them here: Luc Ferry, *Homo Aestheticus*, trans. Robert De Loaiza (University of Chicago Press, 1993); Tom Furniss, *Edmund Burke's Aesthetic Ideology: Language, Gender, and Political Economy in Revolution* (Cambridge University Press, 1993); and W. J. T. Mitchell, ed., *Landscape and Power* (University of Chicago Press, 1994).

25 Shaftesbury, *Characteristics*, ed. J. M. Robertson (London, 1900), vol. II, pp. 126–27.

26 Robert Halsband, *The Life of Lady Mary Wortley Montagu* (New York: Oxford University Press, 1960), pp. 194–95.

27 Another unsubtle instance is Edmund Burke on the beautiful, giving a woman's neck and breasts as an example of "gradual variation." *A Philosophical Enquiry into the Origin of our Ideas of the Sublime and Beautiful*, ed. James T. Boulton (Notre Dame, Ind.: University of Notre Dame Press, 1968), p. 115.

28 P. O. Kristeller, "The Modern System of the Arts" (1951), in *Renaissance Thought and the Arts* (Princeton University Press, 1990), p. 165. See Mattick, "Introduction" to *Eighteenth-Century Aesthetics*. I agree with Mattick, Kristeller, and Eagleton that "something new is indeed afoot" in the eighteenth century, though not in the sense of an absolute newness or metaphysical break; Eagleton, *Ideology of the Aesthetic*, p. 4. On possible seventeenth-century antecedents see, for example, Michael McKeon, "Politics of Discourses and the Rise of the Aesthetic in Seventeenth-Century England," in *The Politics of Discourse*, eds. Kevin Sharpe and Steven Zwicker (Berkeley: University of California Press, 1987), pp. 35–51, and Patricia Fumerton, *Cultural Aesthetics* (University of Chicago Press, 1992).

29 See, for example, the section entitled "Formalism, Philosophy, and Contemporary Plastic Arts" in *Aesthetics: A Critical Anthology*, eds. George Dickie and Richard C. Sclafani (New York: St. Martin's Press, 1977), pp. 423–69, and Alan Liu, "The Power of Formalism: The New Historicism," *ELH*, 56 (1989), pp. 721–71.

30 Eagleton, *Ideology of the Aesthetic*, p. 13.

31 *Sexual Suspects: Eighteenth-Century Players and Sexual Ideology* (Princeton University Press, 1992), pp. 3–23.

32 This is Laura Brown's insight in *Ends of Empire: Women and Ideology in*

Early Eighteenth-Century Literature (Ithaca: Cornell University Press, 1993), p. 174.

33 Mary Louise Pratt, *Imperial Eyes: Travel Writing and Transculturation* (New York: Routledge, 1992), p. 138.

34 Louis Althusser, "Ideology and Ideological State Apparatuses," in *Lenin and Philosophy and Other Essays*, trans. Ben Brewster (New York: Monthly Review Press, 1971), pp. 132–33, and Macdonell, *Theories of Discourse*, pp. 30–31.

35 Beauty, "where it is highest in the female sex, almost always carries with it an idea of weakness and imperfection. Women are very sensible of this; for which reason, they learn to lisp, to totter in their walk, to counterfeit weakness, and even sickness. In all this, they are guided by nature. Beauty in distress is much the most affecting beauty." "The beauty of women is considerably owing to their weakness, or delicacy, and is even enhanced by their timidity, a quality of mind analogous to it." Burke, *Philosophical Enquiry*, pp. 110, 116.

36 *A Vindication of the Rights of Men*, in *The Works of Mary Wollstonecraft*, eds. Janet Todd and Marilyn Butler (New York University Press, 1989), Vol. v, p. 45. The emotion evoked by the beautiful in Burke's scheme is love; we respond to the sublime with astonishment, admiration or respect; *Philosophical Enquiry*, p. 57. *A Vindication of the Rights of Woman*, in *Works*, Vol. v, p. 76.

37 *The Sublime: A Study of Critical Theories in XVIII-Century England* (New York: Modern Language Association, 1935), pp. 212, 215–16.

38 Poovey, *The Proper Lady and the Woman Writer*, pp. 26–27.

39 Theresa M. Kelley, *Wordsworth's Revisionary Aesthetics* (Cambridge University Press, 1988).

40 James Clifford, "Traveling Cultures," in *Cultural Studies*, eds. Lawrence Grossberg, Cary Nelson, and Paula A. Treichler (New York: Routledge, 1992), p. 105. On women travelers, see Marie E. McAllister, *Woman on the Journey: Eighteenth-Century British Women's Travel in Fact and Fiction*, diss. Princeton University 1988, and Sara Mills, *Discourses of Difference: An Analysis of Women's Travel Writing and Colonialism* (New York: Routledge, 1991).

41 Mikhail Bakhtin describes the "social atmosphere of the word" as "filled with…alien words, value judgments and accents," the "dialogic play of verbal intentions." "Discourse in the Novel," in *The Dialogic Imagination*, trans. Caryl Emerson and Michael Holquist (Austin: University of Texas Press, 1981), p. 277. Bakhtin's influence should be obvious throughout my discussion, especially his insistence on the concrete social and historical specificity of language use and its necessarily dialogic character: every utterance is also a response to a previous utterance or utterances, as these women writers respond to previous aesthetic theorists and travel writers.

42 For the useful distinction between the subject, a discursive or ideological construct, and the concrete subject or individual, living in a

particular place and time, who is constituted as a subject in discourse and by ideology, see Althusser, "Ideology and Ideological State Apparatuses," p. 171.

43 John Frow, *Marxism and Literary History* (Cambridge, Mass.: Harvard University Press, 1986), p. 61.

44 Teresa de Lauretis, *Alice Doesn't: Feminism, Semiotics, Cinema* (Bloomington: Indiana University Press, 1984), p. 159. I am using "experience" in the sense for which Joan Scott argues in "The Evidence of Experience," *Critical Inquiry,* 17 (1991).

45 Scott, "The Evidence of Experience," p. 793.

46 Frow, *Marxism and Literary History* , p. 73.

47 Miller, "Emphasis Added," p. 29; "Arachnologies: The Woman, the Text, and the Critic," in *Subject to Change,* p. 83. Neely, "Constructing the Subject: Feminist Practice and the New Renaissance Discourses," *English Literary Renaissance,* 18 (1988), p. 15.

48 Newton, *Women, Power, and Subversion,* p. 40; Straub, *Divided Fictions,* p. 3.

49 See, for example, Hein and Korsmeyer, *Aesthetics in Feminist Perspective;* Paul Gilroy, "Cultural Studies and Ethnic Absolutism," pp. 187–98, and Ian Hunter, "Aesthetics and Cultural Studies," pp. 346–67, in Grossberg *et al.,* eds., *Cultural Studies;* Eagleton, *Ideology of the Aesthetic;* Tony Bennett, *Outside Literature* (London: Routledge, 1990), chs. 5–7; Hal Foster, ed., *The Anti-Aesthetic: Essays on Postmodern Culture* (Port Townsend, Wash.: Bay Press, 1983); and Stephen Greenblatt, "Towards a Poetics of Culture," in *The New Historicism,* ed. H. Aram Veeser (New York: Routledge, 1989), pp. 1–14.

50 See Paul Mattick, Jr., "Arts and the State: The NEA Debate in Perspective," *The Nation,* vol. 251, no. 10 (October 1, 1990), pp. 348–58.

1 AESTHETICS AND ORIENTALISM IN MARY WORTLEY MONTAGU'S LETTERS

1 Mary Astell's preface to Montagu's Turkish Embassy letters, written when Montagu loaned her the manuscript in 1724. Astell urged publication, but Montagu declined. *The First English Feminist: Reflections Upon Marriage and Other Writings,* ed. Bridget Hill (New York: St. Martin's Press, 1986), p. 234.

2 Her play *Simplicity* remained unproduced and unpublished, along with much of her early poetry and, during her lifetime, her letters. She published some items anonymously or under a pseudonym, such as her letter from a "Turkey merchant" defending the Turkish practice of smallpox inoculation, which she introduced into England, and her periodical essays in *The Non-sense of Common Sense.* Pirated versions of some of her poetry were also in print; this led to a painful misunderstanding with an Italian cardinal who requested a copy of her "Works" and was incredulous when she replied, "upon my word I had

never printed a single line in my Life." To her daughter she commented heatedly, "Sure no body ever had such various provocations to print as my selfe." *Complete Letters of Lady Mary Wortley Montagu,* ed. Robert Halsband (Oxford: Clarendon Press, 1967), vol. III pp. 38–39. References in the text are to this edition by volume and page; I have retained original spelling. Montagu, *Essays and Poems and Simplicity, a Comedy,* eds. Isobel Grundy and Robert Halsband (Oxford: Clarendon Press, 1977).

3 Robert Halsband, *The Life of Lady Mary Wortley Montagu* (New York, Oxford University Press, 1960), pp. 288–92; Mary Shelley, *History of a Six Weeks' Tour through a part of France, Switzerland, Germany, and Holland* (London, 1817), p. 75.

4 Marie E. McAllister, *Woman on the Journey: Eighteenth-Century British Women's Travel in Fact and Fiction,* diss. Princeton University, 1988, p. 133.

5 Edward W. Said, *Orientalism* (New York: Random House, 1978), esp. pp. 6, 186–88, 206, and see "Orientalism Reconsidered," in *Europe and Its Others: Proceedings of the Essex Conference on the Sociology of Literature,* eds. Francis Barker *et al* (Colchester: University of Essex, 1985), p. 23, on the connection between Orientalism and patriarchy.

6 Many of the letters I cite, notably that describing the women's baths, are addressed to women. However, Montagu revised the Embassy letters after her return with an eye toward publication, and thus an audience of both genders. See Billie Melman, *Women's Orients: English Women and the Middle East, 1718–1918* (Ann Arbor: University of Michigan Press, 1992), pp. 78–81, and Joseph W. Lew, "Lady Mary's Portable Seraglio," *Eighteenth-Century Studies,* 24 (1991), p. 436.

7 *The Rhetoric of English India* (University of Chicago Press, 1992), pp. 3, 1, 4.

8 *Women's Orients,* pp. 1–3, 18. I do not intend to claim that "women's Orients" are necessarily different from men's; male travelers could also cultivate limited reciprocity with non-Europeans. An example is Mungo Park's *Travels in the Interior Districts of Africa* (London, 1799). See Mary Louise Pratt, *Imperial Eyes: Travel Writing and Transculturation* (New York: Routledge, 1992), pp. 69–85, and "Scratches on the Face of the Country; or, What Mr. Barrow Saw in the Land of the Bushmen," in *"Race," Writing, and Difference,* ed. Henry Louis Gates (University of Chicago Press, 1986), p. 160. I believe, like Melman, that far from presenting a separate, coherent view, women's representations of the Orient are in a constant "dynamic interchange" with "hegemonic orientalist culture" (p. 10) – much like women's versions of the language of aesthetics.

9 Sara Mills, *Discourses of Difference: An Analysis of Women's Travel Writing and Colonialism* (London, Routledge, 1991), p. 58.

10 Robert Withers, *A Description of the Grand Signour's Seraglio, or Turkish Emperour's Court* (London, 1653); Paul Rycaut, *The Present State of the*

Ottoman Empire (London, 1668); Aaron Hill, *A Full and Just Account of the Present State of the Ottoman Empire* (London, 1709); Jean Dumont, *A New Voyage to the Levant*, fourth edition (London, 1705). References in the text are to pages in these editions.

11 On Western fascination with harem fantasies, see Malek Alloula, *The Colonial Harem*, trans. Myrna Godzich and Wald Godzich (Minneapolis: University of Minnesota Press, 1986). Hollywood has perpetuated the quasi-pornographic harem up to Elvis Presley's *Harum Scarum* (1965) and beyond; Ella Shohat, "Gender and Culture of Empire: Toward a Feminist Ethnography of the Cinema," *Quarterly Review of Film and Video*, 13 (1991), esp. pp. 71–74.

12 Pope, *Correspondence*, ed. George Sherburn (Oxford: Clarendon Press, 1956), Vol. I, p. 368, quoted in Rana Kabbani, *Europe's Myths of Orient* (Bloomington: Indiana University Press, 1986), p. 30; see also pp. 26ff. on seventeenth-century stereotypes of Oriental women.

13 Melman, *Women's Orients*, p. 91.

14 For readers alert to this dimension of Montagu's polemic it is ironic that the journalist and pornographer John Cleland, creator of Fanny Hill, is credited with editing the letters and fabricating an additional volume in 1767. Halsband, *Life of Lady Mary*, pp. 288–89.

15 Melman, *Women's Orients*, pp. 99–100, 132. Victorian women travelers do not represent the bathers as "stark naked," but cover them with strategic towels. Their manifest disgust for Turkish women's corporeality begins with Elizabeth Craven's roomful of sallow, obese females in her *Journey through the Crimea to Constantinople* (London, 1789), pp. 263–64; see Melman, pp. 112, 130–36.

16 See Elizabeth V. Spelman, "Woman as Body: Ancient and Contemporary Views," *Feminist Studies*, 8 (1982), pp. 109–31.

17 John Berger *et al.*, *Ways of Seeing* (New York: Penguin, 1972), p. 54.

18 See Judith Brown, "Lesbian Sexuality in Medieval and Early Modern Europe," pp. 67–75, and James M. Saslow, "Homosexuality in the Renaissance: Behavior, Identity, and Artistic Expression," esp. p. 95, both in *Hidden From History: Reclaiming the Gay and Lesbian Past*, eds. Martin Duberman, Martha Vicinus, and George Chauncey, Jr. (New York: Penguin, 1989).

19 Jürgen Habermas, *The Structural Transformation of the Public Sphere*, trans. Thomas Burger and Frederick Lawrence (Cambridge, Mass.: MIT Press, 1989), pp. 32–42; Peter Stallybrass and Allon White, *The Politics and Poetics of Transgression* (Ithaca: Cornell University Press, 1986), pp. 80–84.

20 Lew, "Portable Seraglio," pp. 445–46. Leila Ahmed points out the ambiguity of the harem: "The harem can be defined as a system that permits males sexual access to more than one female. It can also be defined, and with as much accuracy, as a system...which enables women to have frequent and easy access to other women in their community...[I]t was its second aspect, that of women being freely

and continuously together...which Western men viewed with considerable fascination." "Western Ethnocentrism and Perceptions of the Harem," *Feminist Studies,* 8 (1982), p. 524.

21 Lew, "Portable Seraglio," pp. 441–43. Lew discusses the cultural significance of Montagu's corset, as does Jill Campbell, "Lady Mary Wortley Montagu and the Historical Machinery of Female Identity," in *History, Gender and Eighteenth-Century Literature,* ed. Beth Fowkes Tobin (Athens: University of Georgia Press, 1994), pp. 64–85.

22 Lew, "Portable Seraglio," pp. 447–50, and see Terry Castle, *Masquerade and Civilization: The Carnivalesque in Eighteenth-Century English Culture and Fiction* (Stanford University Press, 1986).

23 On Islamic law regarding women's property, see John L. Esposito, *Women in Muslim Family Law* (Syracuse University Press, 1982), pp. 24, 36 and *passim,* and Ian C. Dengler, "Turkish Women in the Ottoman Empire: The Classical Age," in *Women in the Muslim World,* eds. Lois Beck and Nikki Keddie (Cambridge, Mass.: Harvard University Press, 1978), p. 237; on privacy, see Ahmed, "Western Ethnocentrism," pp. 528–29. This oversimplifies the legal history of married women's property in Britain; see Susan Staves, *Married Women's Separate Property in England, 1660–1833* (Cambridge, Mass.: Harvard University Press, 1990).

24 Dengler, "Turkish Women," pp. 230–31.

25 Campbell, "Historical Machinery of Female Identity," p. 81, and personal communication.

26 James Clifford, "Introduction: Partial Truths," in *Writing Culture: The Poetics and Politics of Ethnography,* eds. James Clifford and George E. Marcus (Berkeley: University of California Press, 1986), p. 23.

27 I refer to Spivak's well-known formulation, "white men are saving brown women from brown men." "Can the Subaltern Speak? Speculations on Widow-Sacrifice," *Wedge* 7/8 (1985), p. 121. See also Spivak "Three Women's Texts and a Critique of Imperialism," *Critical Inquiry,* 12 (1985), pp. 243–61, and Aihwa Ong, "Colonialism and Modernity: Feminist Re-presentations of Women in Non-Western Societies," *Inscriptions,* 3/4 (1988), pp. 79–93.

28 Ong, "Colonialism and Modernity," pp. 87–88.

2 JANET SCHAW AND THE AESTHETICS OF COLONIALISM

1 Jamaica Kincaid, *A Small Place* (New York: Farrar Straus Giroux, 1988), p. 77. Kincaid's description of her native island (written in Vermont) trenchantly connects tourism with neo-colonialism.

2 "Contact zone" is Mary Pratt's phrase in *Imperial Eyes: Travel Writing and Transculturation* (New York: Routledge, 1992), pp. 4, 6–7.

3 [Schaw, Janet,] *Journal of a Lady of Quality; Being the Narrative of a Journey from Scotland to the West Indies, North Carolina, and Portugal, in the years 1774 to 1776,* eds. Evangeline Walker Andrews and Charles McLean

Andrews, second edition (New Haven: Yale University Press, 1934). Schaw accompanied one brother, who had taken a job in the St. Kitts customs office, and later went on to visit another, a North Carolina planter; she stopped in Portugal on her way home. The journal was not published during its author's lifetime, though apparently circulated in manuscript. At least three copies remain, including the British Library copy from which the Andrews worked. References in the text are to this edition.

4 Rev. William Smith, *Natural History of Nevis and the rest of the English Leeward Charibee Islands in America* (London, 1745); Rev. Griffith Hughes, *Natural History of Barbados* (London, 1750); Edward Long, *History of Jamaica* (London, 1774); Maria Nugent, *Journal*, ed. Philip Wright (Kingston: Institute of Jamaica, 1966) covering the years 1801 to 1805 (she was the governor's wife); John Stewart, *An Account of Jamaica* (London, 1808, reprinted Freeport, N.Y.: Books for Libraries Press, 1971) (he was a plantation bookkeeper). References in the text are to these editions.

5 Sara Suleri, *Rhetoric of English India* (University of Chicago Press, 1992), links colonialism, aesthetics, and gender. See esp. chs. 2, "Edmund Burke and the Indian Sublime," and 4, "The Feminine Picturesque."

6 "The Romance of Empire: *Oroonoko* and the Trade in Slaves," *The New Eighteenth Century*, eds. Felicity Nussbaum and Laura Brown (New York: Methuen, 1987), pp. 41–61; Aphra Behn, *Oroonoko, or the Royal Slave*, 1688 (New York: W. W. Norton & Co., 1973), for example p. 2. Going back further, we might view Shakespeare's *The Tempest*, for example, as aestheticizing early exploration and colonialism.

7 Addison, *The Spectator*, ed. Donald Bond (Oxford: Clarendon Press, 1965), no. 69 (May 19, 1711), vol. I, p. 296.

8 Quoted in Laura Brown, *Alexander Pope* (New York: Basil Blackwell, 1985), p. 13. See also Louis A. Landa, "Pope's Belinda, the General Emporie of the World, and the Wondrous Worm," in *Pope: Recent Essays by Several Hands*, eds. Maynard Mack and James A. Winn (Hamden, Conn.: Archon Books, 1980), pp. 177–200.

9 Alexander Pope, *The Rape of the Lock*, 1:129–136. *Poems*, third edition, ed. Geoffrey Tillotson (London: Methuen, 1962), vol. II, pp. 155–56.

10 J. H. Parry, Philip Sherlock and Anthony Maingot, *A Short History of the West Indies*, fourth edition (New York: St. Martin's Press, 1987), pp. 56, 64, 83.

11 *Distinction: A Social Critique of the Judgement of Taste*, trans. Richard Nice (Cambridge, Mass.: Harvard University Press, 1984), p. 47; he is speaking not of landscape aesthetics in particular but aesthetics in general.

12 Henry Home (Lord Kames), *Elements of Criticism*, 1762 (New York, 1860); his distinction between emotions and passions, pp.29–30, helps to develop the concept of aesthetic disinterestedness.

13 Laura Brown notes similarities between Swift's Yahoos and eighteenth-century descriptions of Africans. *Ends of Empire: Women and*

Ideology in Early Eighteenth-Century Literature (Ithaca: Cornell University Press, 1993), pp. 188–97.

14 *Spectator*, no. 412 (June 23, 1712), vol. III, p. 540.

15 Parry *et al.*, *Short History*, p. 88; Gordon K. Lewis, *The Growth of the Modern West Indies* (New York: Monthly Review Press, 1968), p. 50. For the history of the islands' indigenous inhabitants, culminating in the First and Second Carib Wars of 1772–73 and 1795–96 on St. Vincent, see Peter Hulme, *Colonial Encounters: Europe and the Native Caribbean, 1492–1797* (London: Routledge, 1992), esp. ch. 6.

16 Compare Long, *History of Jamaica*, II:205: "the fertile glade called King's Valley…exhibits a lively and picturesque scene. Though not above half a mile across, it is inimitably contrasted throughout…it is decorated with some handsome plantation-houses; at one of which (called Glasgow) situated on a rising ground, is a battery which was of great use in protecting the estates here during the Negroe rebellion."

17 Homi Bhabha, "The Other Question: Difference, Discrimination and the Discourse of Colonialism," in *Literature, Politics and Theory*, eds. Francis Barker *et al.* (New York: Methuen, 1986), pp. 171–72, 165–66. Bhabha, like myself, is especially interested in tracing the "multiple, cross-cutting determinations" of race and gender in the "processes of subjectification" made possible through such discourse (pp. 150, 149), though his orientation toward these processes is more heavily inflected by psychoanalysis and deconstruction than is my own.

18 Gilpin lists figures among such ornaments in *Three Essays: on Picturesque Beauty; on Picturesque Travel; and on Sketching Landscape* (London, 1792), pp. 66, 77.

19 Smith, *Natural History of Nevis*, pp. 22–23. See also, for example pp. 37–38, 87–88 and 308–9. Long, *History of Jamaica*, I:343; Nugent, *Journal*, p. 54; see also pp. 8, 10, 17, 25 ff., 61, 65, 70–77, 83, 115, 145, and Stewart, *Account*, pp. 7–10, 17, 121 ff.

20 Stewart, *Account*, pp. 98, 105–6; Nugent, *Journal* pp. 26, 67, 94.

21 Pratt, *Imperial Eyes*, pp. 31, 38, and see pp. 24–68. Pratt summarizes the varieties of Homo sapiens accepted by natural historians circa 1758, commenting, "One could hardly ask for a more explicit attempt to 'naturalize' the myth of European superiority": the Wild Man, the American, the European, the Asiatic, and lastly "African. Black, phlegmatic, relaxed. Hair black, frizzled; skin silky; nose flat, lips tumid; crafty, indolent, negligent. Anoints himself with grease. Governed by caprice" (p. 32).

22 Raymond Williams, *The Country and the City* (New York: Oxford University Press, 1973), p. 32.

23 Londa Schiebinger, "The Anatomy of Difference: Race and Sex in Eighteenth-Century Science," *Eighteenth-Century Studies* 23 (1990), p. 394.

24 Brown, *Ends of Empire*, p. 189. Nugent also refers to black boys as "monkeys" (*Journal*, p. 42).

25 Compare Stewart's *Account:* "The negroes are crafty, artful, and plausible...they are avaricious and selfish, obstinate and perverse, giving all the plague they can to their white rulers; little ashamed of falsehood, and strongly addicted to theft. Some of these dispositions doubtless originate in, and are fostered by, the nature of their situation and treatment; and would probably spring up in an European breast, if sunk and degraded by a state of servile bondage. The negro has, however, some good qualities mingled with his unamiable ones. He is patient, cheerful, and commonly submissive..." (p. 234).

26 Michael Taussig, *Shamanism, Colonialism and the Wild Man: A Study in Terror and Healing* (University of Chicago Press, 1986), p. 134.

27 The other writers' views on slavery range along a spectrum from Long, on the conservative end, to Maria Nugent at the liberal extreme. Smith, a clergyman, discourages baptizing slaves (*Natural History of Nevis*, p. 230). Hughes, another clergyman, dispassionately notes the large number of slave deaths from overwork, whence "we are obliged...to have a yearly Supply from Africa" (*Natural History of Barbados,* p. 14). Curiously ambivalent, he admits that the "Capacities of their Minds in the common Affairs of Life are but little inferior, if at all, to those of the Europeans" (p. 16), but mounts a full-scale argument to justify slavery. Stewart's defense runs similarly to Long's, mitigated by assertions that treatment of slaves is far more humane than formerly (*Account*, pp. 226–31). On abolition, see Herbert S. Klein, *African Slavery in Latin America and the Caribbean* (Oxford University Press, 1986), pp. 243ff. Nugent believes and tries to persuade others that blacks are human beings with souls (*Journal*, p. 98); she works actively towards baptism for her own slaves (p. 38) and dances with an elderly slave man at a ball she gives for slaves' entertainment, shocking other white ladies (p. 156). She is "disgusted" at hearing details of the slave trade (p. 55). Nonetheless, she calls slaves "blackies" and assumes they are childlike, easily gratified by simple pleasures (pp. 48–49, 84, 98). Though she calls for reforms, she nowhere suggests abolishing slavery as an institution.

28 On slaves' Christmas festivities, see Nugent, *Journal*, pp. 48 and 218–19, and Stewart, *Account*, pp. 262–63.

29 Orlando Patterson, *The Sociology of Slavery* (Rutherford, N.J.: Fairleigh Dickinson University Press, 1967), pp. 236, 247.

30 On the intersection between patterns of racial and sexual difference in eighteenth-century texts, see Brown, *Ends of Empire*, and Carol Barash, "The Character of Difference: The Creole Woman as Cultural Mediator in Narratives about Jamaica," *Eighteenth-Century Studies*, 23 (1990), pp. 406–24.

31 Klein points out that the highly efficient organization of plantation labor did not differentiate by gender, except in skilled occupations; the typical field gang, like the one Schaw observed, was over half women. *African Slavery*, pp. 60–64.

32 See, for example, Janaki Nair, "Uncovering the Zenana: Visions of Indian Womanhood in Englishwomen's Writings, 1813–1940," *Journal of Women's History*, 2 (1990), p. 10, and Ann Laura Stoler, "Carnal Knowledge and Imperial Power: Gender, Race, and Morality in Colonial Asia," in *Gender at the Crossroads of Knowledge: Feminist Anthropology in the Postmodern Era*, ed. Micaela di Leonardo (Berkeley: University of California Press, 1991), p. 56. The feminization of "Oriental" males described by Said's *Orientalism* (New York: Random House, 1978) functions similarly.

33 Stoler documents the uses of the "politics of sexual peril" in colonial Africa, India, and Indonesia. She observes that "the rhetoric of sexual assault and the measures used to prevent it had virtually no correlation with actual incidences of rape of European women by men of color." See "Carnal Knowledge," esp. pp. 67–70.

34 Long (*History of Jamaica*, II:280) and Stewart (*Account*, pp. 157 ff.) praise the creole ladies' virtues, especially their temperance.

35 Adam Smith, *The Theory of Moral Sentiments*, eds. A. L. Macfie and D. D. Raphael (Indianapolis: Liberty Classics, 1982), pp. 190–91.

36 Bhabha, "The Other Question," p. 78.

37 Burke's definition of beauty comes to mind; see *A Philosophical Enquiry into the Origin of our Ideas of the Sublime and Beautiful*, ed. James T. Boulton (Notre Dame, Ind.: University of Notre Dame Press, 1968), pp. 98, 108–110.

38 Pratt, *Imperial Eyes*, p. 105.

39 Brown, *Ends of Empire*, p. 174. Both Swift's misogyny and his anti-colonialism are controversial. The Stella poems obviously complicate the former, while the latter is called into question by Swift's role as a spokesman for the Church of Ireland – a major apparatus of internal colonialism – despite his reputation as "the Hibernian Patriot." See Rick Canning, "Colonial Shorthand: Swift, the Ascendancy, and Internalized Colonialism," diss. University of Illinois, Urbana Champaign, 1994. Perhaps no other literary figure so well justifies poststructuralists' questioning of the unified self.

40 Caryl Phillips' novel *Cambridge* (New York: Alfred A. Knopf, 1992) draws extensively on Schaw's journal and other period writings as it brings "a European consciousness face to face with Europe's global perpetrations" in the setting of the West Indian sugar plantation (Graham Swift, interview with Phillips, *Bomb*, Winter 1992, p. 32). Phillips, born on St. Kitts but brought up in England, juxtaposes narratives in the voices of Emily, the daughter of an absentee owner who travels to her father's plantation to avoid a forced marriage, and Cambridge, a literate displaced African who has lived free in England before being re-enslaved and shipped to the Caribbean. Emily's complex response to the aestheticized aura of island life becomes a powerful catalyst in Phillips' re-vision of the colonial legacy.

3 LANDSCAPE AESTHETICS AND THE PARADOX OF THE FEMALE PICTURESQUE

1 Frances Burney, *The Wanderer; or, Female Difficulties,* eds. Margaret Anne Doody, Robert L. Mack, and Peter Sabor (Oxford University Press, 1991), pp. 700–701.

2 Malcolm Andrews' selected bibliography of about 115 tours in *The Search for the Picturesque* (Stanford University Press, 1989) includes ten by women, five of them published (a fairly representative proportion), as well as eighteen anonymous.

3 Teresa de Lauretis, *Alice Doesn't: Feminism, Semiotics, Cinema* (Bloomington: Indian University Press, 1984), p. 8: "the position of woman in language and in cinema is one of non-coherence; she finds herself only in a void of meaning, the empty space between the signs."

4 Mattick, "Arts and the State: The NEA Debate in Perspective," *The Nation,* vol. 251, no. 10 (October 1, 1990). p. 353. In the field of ceramics, for example, debate among artists and critics over the relation of ceramics to "art" is ongoing. See Jeff Kelley, "Upward Mobility," *American Ceramics,* 9 (Summer 1991), pp. 34–39 and John Perreault, "The Eloquent Object, Crafts Is Art," *Ceramics Monthly,* 36 (March 1988), pp. 39–45.

5 See Hal Foster, ed., *The Anti-Aesthetic: Essays on Postmodern Culture* (Port Townsend, Wash: Bay Press, 1983), and Andreas Huyssen, "Mapping the Postmodern," in *Feminism/Postmodernism,* ed. Linda J. Nicholson (New York: Routledge, 1990), esp. pp. 242–45.

6 Jerome Stolnitz, "On the Origins of 'Aesthetic Disinterestedness,'" *Journal of Aesthetics and Art Criticism,* 20 (1961–62), pp. 131–43. For Kames' distinction between passions, which are followed by desire, and emotions, the "quiescent" adjuncts of aesthetic experience, see Henry Home (Lord Kames), *Elements of Criticism,* 1762 (New York, 1860) vol. I, pp. 29–30. See also M. H. Abrams, "From Addison to Kant: Modern Aesthetics and the Exemplary Art," in *Studies in Eighteenth-Century British Art and Aesthetics,* ed. Ralph Cohen (Berkeley: University of California Press, 1985), pp. 16–48.

7 Addison, *The Spectator,* ed. Donald Bond (Oxford: Clarendon Press, 1965), no. 411 (June 21, 1712), vol III, pp. 538, 537.

8 *Essays on the Nature and Principles of Taste,* 1790 (Hildesheim: Georg Olms, 1968), pp. 6, 62.

9 *A Treatise of Human Nature,* ed. P. H. Nidditch (Oxford: Clarendon Press, 1978), pp. 472, 581–82 (italics Hume's).

10 Smith suggests that "the power of Hume's temperamental skepticism and cosmopolitan personal history continuously conspired to subvert, but was in turn subverted by, both the momentum of…axiological logic and also his perspectives and interests as an eighteenth-century man of letters and member of polite society." *Contingencies of Value: Alternative Perspectives for Critical Theory* (Cambridge, Mass.: Harvard

University Press, 1988), pp. 63, 64. See also Tony Bennett, *Outside Literature* (London: Routledge, 1990), pp. 154–57; Richard Shusterman, "Of the Scandal of Taste: Social Privilege as Nature in the Aesthetic Theories of Hume and Kant," in *Eighteenth-Century Aesthetics and the Reconstruction of Art*, ed. Paul Mattick, Jr. (Cambridge University Press, 1993), pp. 96–119; and W. B. Carnochan's entry on Hume in *The Johns Hopkins Guide to Literary Theory and Criticism*, eds. Michael Groden and Martin Kreiswirth (Baltimore: Johns Hopkins University Press, 1993).

11 "Of the Standard of Taste" in *Essays Moral, Political, and Literary*, eds. T. H. Green and T. H. Grose (London, New York, Bombay and Calcutta: Longmans, Green, and Co., 1875), pp. 278–79. References in the text are to this edition.

12 "Cultural Studies and Ethnic Absolutism," in *Cultural Studies*, eds. Grossberg *et al.* (New York: Routledge, 1992), p. 188.

13 Hume, "Of National Characters," in *Essays Moral, Political, and Literary*, p. 252. Cited in Henry Louis Gates, "Introduction: Writing 'Race' and the Difference it Makes," in *"Race," Writing, and Difference*, ed. Henry Louis Gates (University of Chicago Press, 1986), pp. 10–11.

14 Edward Long, *History of Jamaica* (London, 1774), vol. II, p. 353.

15 Quoted in P. J. Marshall and Glyndwr Williams, *The Great Map of Mankind: Perceptions of New Worlds in the Age of Enlightenment* (Cambridge, Mass.: Harvard University Press, 1982), pp. 245–46.

16 Edmund Burke, *A Philosophical Enquiry into the Origin of our Ideas of the Sublime and Beautiful*, ed. James T. Boulton (Notre Dame, Ind.: University of Notre Dame Press, 1968), p. 144. Quoted in Gilroy, "Cultural Studies and Ethnic Absolutism," p. 189.

17 On the problems of defining "neoclassicism," see Robert Rosenblum, *Transformations in Late Eighteenth Century Art* (Princeton University Press, 1967), pp. 1–49, and Hugh Honour, *Neo-Classicism* (New York: Penguin, 1968).

18 Reynolds' views on painting by no means enjoyed unchallenged hegemony. His long-standing rivalry with Gainsborough, whose less idealized style found favor in George III's court, is discussed by Edgar Wind in *Hume and the Heroic Portrait: Studies in Eighteenth-Century Imagery* (Oxford: Clarendon Press, 1986), esp. p. 31. In this context the *Discourses* may be understood as a polemic for the high or heroic style in a society whose interest in it was perceived to be flagging. Reynolds' own income, of course, came from portraiture, which he considered an inferior genre, though he often elevated his portraits by adding mythological elements reminiscent of history painting. If we were to scrutinize his practice of the art of painting, we might not always find it consistent with his strict theoretical doctrine. However, despite the waning popularity of history painting itself, with its outmoded heroic trappings, the de-particularized mode of perception that grounds Reynolds' argument for history painting persisted in the increasingly prestigious genre of landscape painting and the aesthetics of the picturesque.

19 *Discourses on Art*, ed. Robert R. Wark (New Haven: Yale University Press, 1975), p. 44. References in the text are to this edition.

20 Naomi Schor, *Reading in Detail: Aesthetics and the Feminine* (New York: Methuen, 1987), p. 16.

21 Quoted in Michael Macklem, "Reynolds and the Ambiguities of Neo-Classical Criticism," *Philological Quarterly*, 31 (1952), p. 383.

22 Barrell, *The Political Theory of Painting from Reynolds to Hazlitt* (New Haven, Yale University Press, 1986), pp. 1–162.

23 *The Machiavellian Moment: Florentine Political Thought and the Atlantic Republican Tradition* (Princeton University Press, 1975).

24 *The Function of Criticism* (London: Verso, 1984), p. 16.

25 J. G. A. Pocock, *Virtue, Commerce, and History: Essays on Political Thought and History, Chiefly in the Eighteenth Century* (Cambridge University Press, 1985), pp. 48–49, 68–71, 103–23, and see P. G. M. Dickson, *The Financial Revolution in England: A Study in the Development of Public Credit* (London: Macmillan, 1967).

26 *Discourses*, for example pp. 48, 57, 93, 117 and 170–71.

27 Shaftesbury, as Barrell points out, was an earlier proponent of civic humanist aesthetics. See his analysis of Shaftesbury's plan for a painting of the "Judgment of Hercules," *Political Theory of Painting*, pp. 27–33.

28 Some also point out anti-Platonic features, such as his ridicule of a vatic theory of artistic inspiration. See for example W. J. Hipple, Jr., *The Beautiful, the Sublime, and the Picturesque in Eighteenth-Century British Aesthetic Theory* (Carbondale: Southern Illinois University Press, 1957), pp. 133–48; Macklem, "Reynolds and the Ambiguities of Neo-Classical Criticism"; and Wark's introduction to the *Discourses*, p. xix.

29 *The Republic* in Plato, *Works*, trans. Benjamin Jowett (Cambridge, Mass.: Riverside Press, 1871), vol. II, pp. 259–72, Sections 434–48. References in the text are to this edition by Renaissance page.

30 See Barrell, *Political Theory of Painting*, p. 13.

31 *Ibid.*, p. 16.

32 On the centrality of the mind–body duality to Plato, his "somatophobia," and his association of women (as well as slaves, children, and animals) with the body and the lower, body-oriented faculties of the mind, see Elizabeth V. Spelman, "Woman as Body: Ancient and Contemporary Views," *Feminist Studies*, 8 (1982).

33 Schor, *Reading in Detail*, p. 16.

34 For the standard view, see, for example, Tzvetan Todorov, *Theories of the Symbol* (Ithaca: Cornell University Press, 1982), esp. pp. 114–16 on Batteux's "neoclassical" concept of beautiful nature, and M. H. Abrams, "From Addison to Kant," 18–21.

35 Pierre Bourdieu, *Distinction: A Social Critique of the Judgement of Taste*, trans. Richard Nice (Cambridge, Mass: Harvard University Press, 1984), p. 5 and *passim*. However, Bourdieu confines himself to stratifi-

cation by class and class fraction, ignoring gender, and pays too little attention to the role of language in aesthetic practice.

36 See, for example, Bennett, *Outside Literature*, esp. chs. 6 and 7, and Ian Hunter, "Aesthetics and Cultural Studies," in *Cultural Studies*, eds. Grossberg *et al.* Bennett defines aesthetics more narrowly than I do, since I take women writers who criticize aesthetics' hegemonic or universalist claims (for him the defining feature of aesthetics, p. 152) as nonetheless participating in aesthetic debate. "Ideology" is a less useful designation for aesthetics to the extent that it retains overtones of mystification or misapprehension, thus implying the possibility of a non-distorted or more fully "human" mode of subject formation, as Bennett's discussion of Eagleton, pp. 173–75, suggests.

37 *The Politics and Poetics of Transgression* (Ithaca: Cornell University Press, 1986), pp. 5–6.

38 "Contingent Foundations: Feminism and the Question of 'Postmodernism,'" in *Feminists Theorize the Political*, eds. Judith Butler and Joan W. Scott (New York: Routledge, 1992), pp. 12–13.

39 "Disinterestedness and Denial of the Particular: Locke, Adam Smith, and the Subject of Aesthetics," in *Eighteenth-Century Aesthetics*, ed. Mattick, pp. 16–51.

40 Adam Smith, *The Theory of Moral Sentiments*, eds. A. L. Macfie and D. D. Raphael (Indianapolis: Liberty Classics, 1982), pp. 28, 190. See also John B. Bender, *Imagining the Penitentiary: Fiction and the Architecture of Mind in Eighteenth-Century England* (University of Chicago Press, 1987), pp. 201–28.

41 "Impartiality and the Civic Public: Some Implications of Feminist Critiques of Moral and Political Theory," in *Feminism as Critique*, eds. Seyla Benhabib and Drucilla Cornell (Minneapolis: University of Minnesota Press, 1987), p. 67.

42 *The Great Arch: English State Formation as Cultural Revolution* (Oxford: Basil Blackwell, 1985), p. 4.

43 *On the Landed Property of England.* Quoted in Harold Perkin, *Origins of Modern English Society* (1969. London and New York: Ark Paperbacks, 1986), pp. 41–42.

44 *Married Women's Separate Property in England, 1660–1833* (Cambridge, Mass.: Harvard University Press, 1990), pp. 4, 226–27. The historian Staves cites is A. P. W. Malcomson, *The Pursuit of the Heiress: Aristocratic Marriage in Ireland, 1750–1820* (1982).

45 Alexander Pope, "Epistle IV: To Richard Boyle, Earl of Burlington," in *Poems*, ed. F. W. Bateson (London: Methuen, 1951), vol. III. ii, pp. 137–38, lines 47–56. Citations in the text are from this edition by line. This poem became a *locus classicus* for the century's characteristic concern with distinguishing true from false taste, especially in gardening. Mary Wollstonecraft, as late as 1796, approvingly adapts Pope's satire of the pretentious, statue-strewn "Timon's Villa" to an estate she visits near Göteborg. The only redeeming feature of such

tasteless extravagance, both writers point out, is the employment it provides for local laborers. Wollstonecraft's comment, "It requires uncommon taste...to introduce accommodations and ornaments analogous with the surrounding scene," echoes Pope's directive, "Consult the Genius of the place in all" (line 57). *Letters Written During a Short Residence in Sweden, Norway, and Denmark*, in *The Works of Mary Wollstonecraft*, eds. Marilyn Butler and Janet Todd (New York University Press, 1989), vol. VI, p. 257.

46 John Dixon Hunt, *The Figure in the Landscape: Poetry, Painting, and Gardening during the Eighteenth Century* (Baltimore: Johns Hopkins University Press, 1976), p. 63. See also the anthology *The Genius of the Place: The English Landscape Garden 1620–1820*, eds. John Dixon Hunt and Peter Willis (Cambridge, Mass.: MIT Press, 1988); John Barrell, *The Idea of Landscape and the Sense of Place, 1730–1840: An Approach to the Poetry of John Clare* (Cambridge University Press, 1972), pp. 45–50; and Ronald Paulson, *Emblem and Expression: Meaning in English Art of the Eighteenth Century* (Cambridge, Mass.: Harvard University Press, 1975), pp. 19–34.

47 "Binding and Dressing Nature's Loose Tresses: The Ideology of Augustan Landscape Design," *Studies in Eighteenth-Century Culture*, 8 (1979), pp. 111, 110, 117. Further references in parentheses in the text.

48 Quoted in Fabricant, "Binding and Dressing," p. 112.

49 *The History of the Modern Taste in Gardening*, in *Genius of the Place*, eds. Hunt and Wills, pp. 313–14; quoted in Fabricant, "Binding and Dressing," pp. 111–12.

50 Fabricant, "Binding and Dressing," p. 112. She cites Walpole's list of the paintings of Salome, Dido, Helen, Venus, Andromeda, and Cleopatra in the great salon at Stourhead, site of one of England's most famous landscape gardens. Young, *A Six Weeks Tour through the Southern Counties of England and Wales*, second edition (Dublin, 1771) and *A Six Months Tour through the North of England*, 4 vols., second edition (London, 1771).

51 *Spectator*, no. 411 (June 21, 1712), vol. III, p. 538.

52 Quoted in Fabricant, "Binding and Dressing," p. 115; see also John Berger *et al.*, *Ways of Seeing* (New York: Penguin, 1972), pp. 83–112.

53 Berger, *Ways of Seeing*, p. 16.

54 This despite Walter Benjamin's contrast between the "auratic" medium of oil painting and the supposedly liberatory, anti-auratic photographic technologies. Taking gender into account destabilizes this opposition. "The Work of Art in the Age of Mechanical Reproduction," in *Illuminations*, ed. Hannah Arendt, trans. Harry Zohn (New York: Schocken Books, 1969), pp. 217–52. On film theory see Introduction, note 20. Donna Haraway's analysis of "the persistence of vision" is of interest in this connection: "Situated Knowledges: The Science Question in Feminism and the Privilege of Partial Perspective," *Feminist Studies*, 14 (1988), pp. 581–83.

55 Bermingham, *Landscape and Ideology: The English Rustic Tradition, 1740–1860* (Berkeley: University of California Press, 1989), pp. 13–14, and see pp. 63–85, esp. 66, 75. See also Raymond Williams, *The Country and the City* (Oxford University Press, 1973), pp. 96–107 and 124–25; W. E. Tate, *The English Village Community and the Enclosure Movements* (London: Victor Gollancz, Ltd., 1967); and G. E. Mingay, *English Landed Society in the Eighteenth Century* (London: Routledge and Kegan Paul, 1963).

56 Ann Radcliffe, *The Romance of the Forest*, ed. Chloe Chard (Oxford University Press, 1986), p. 156. References in the text are to this edition.

57 Dr. John Brown's letter on the Lakes, probably written in 1753 and partially published in 1767, is usually cited as "the first distinct evidence of a romantic and Picturesque response" to this region, though Malcolm Andrews reminds us that Gilpin pays tribute to the Lakes as early as 1748 in his *Dialogue upon the Gardens of the Right Honourable the Lord Viscount Cobham, at Stow in Buckinghamshire; The Search for the Picturesque*, p. 159. Thomas West's phenomenally successful *Guide to the Lakes in Cumberland, Westmorland and Lancashire* (1778, seven editions by 1800) marks the start of the flood of tours and guidebooks that continued well into the nineteenth century.

58 John A. Dussinger, "Hester Piozzi, Italy, and the Johnsonian Aether," *South Central Review* 9.4 (Winter 1992), p. 49. Dussinger notes the first recorded usage of the word "tourist" in the 1780s.

59 West, *Guide to the Lakes*, facsimile of third edition 1784 (Oxford: Woodstock Books, 1989), p. 1.

60 Wordsworth, letter to the Editor of the *Morning Post*, Dec. 9, 1844, reprinted in Wordsworth, *Guide to the Lakes*, ed. Ernest de Selincourt (Oxford University Press, 1977), p. 150.

61 Kim Ian Michasiw, "Nine Revisionist Theses on the Picturesque," *Representations*, 38 (1992), pp. 76–100; Fabricant, "The Literature of Domestic Tourism and the Public Consumption of Private Property," in *The New Eighteenth Century*, eds. Felicity Nussbaum and Laura Brown (New York: Methuen, 1987), pp. 254–75.

62 Dorothy Wordsworth, *Journals*, ed. Mary Moorman, second edition (Oxford University Press, 1971), p. 25.

63 Pratt, *Imperial Eyes*, pp. 38–68, esp. 51, 59–61. A similar erasure of indigenous inhabitants to imagine pure landscape was often applied by explorers and frontiersmen to the "virgin land" of America; see, for example, Annette Kolodny, *The Lay of the Land: Metaphor as Experience and History in American Life and Letters* (Chapel Hill: University of North Carolina Press, 1975).

64 *Man and the Natural World: Changing Attitudes in England 1500–1800* (New York: Pantheon Books, 1983), p. 301.

65 Bermingham, *Landscape and Ideology*, pp. 83–85. She restricts this observation to the "popular picturesque," as opposed to "the exclu-

siveness written into the picturesque by Price and Knight." I understand the creation and possession of distinctive aesthetic commodities as precisely a mark of exclusiveness. Rosalind E. Krauss locates the modernity – or actually post-modernity – of the picturesque in its integration of the copy as a condition of possibility for the "original": "what allows a given moment of the perceptual array to be seen as singular is precisely its conformation to a multiple" – a truth that the aesthetic ideology of modernity strove desperately to conceal, while postmodernity forces it into the foreground. "The Originality of the Avant-Garde," in *The Originality of the Avant-Garde and Other Modernist Myths* (Cambridge, Mass.: MIT Press, 1986), pp. 162–66.

66 *Wordsworth: The Sense of History* (Stanford University Press, 1989), p. 94.

67 Barrell, *Idea of Landscape,* pp. 1–3; Nikolaus Pevsner, "Genesis of the Picturesque," in *Studies in Art, Architecture and Design* (New York: Walker and Company, 1968), vol. I, p. 86.

68 Richard Payne Knight, *The Landscape, a Didactic Poem, in Three Books* (London, 1794), lines 193–96.

69 Gilpin, *Observations on the River Wye and several parts of South Wales, &c. relative chiefly to Picturesque Beauty; made in the Summer of the Year 1770,* fifth edition (London, 1800), p. 1. See also *Three Essays* (London, 1792); *Observations, relative chiefly to Picturesque Beauty, Made in the Year 1772, on Several Parts of England; particularly the Mountains, and Lakes of Cumberland, and Westmoreland* (London, 1786); *Observations, relative chiefly to Picturesque Beauty, Made in the Year 1776, on Several Parts of Great Britain; particularly the High-Lands of Scotland* (1789). In addition to Andrews' *Search for the Picturesque,* standard discussions include Christopher Hussey, *The Picturesque: Studies in a Point of View* (London: Frank Cass 1927; reprinted 1967, 1983); W. J. Hipple, *The Beautiful, the Sublime, and the Picturesque,* pp. 185–283; and Carl Paul Barbier, *William Gilpin* (Oxford: Clarendon Press, 1963). Elizabeth Wheeler Manwaring, *Italian Landscape in Eighteenth-Century England* (New York: Oxford University Press, 1925), presents the picturesque in the context of connoisseurship. See also Martin Price, "The Picturesque Moment," in *From Sensibility to Romanticism: Essays Presented to Frederick A. Pottle,* eds. Frederick W. Hilles and Harold Bloom (New York: Oxford University Press, 1965), pp. 259–92; Nikolaus Pevsner, "Genesis of the Picturesque," "Richard Payne Knight," and "Uvedale Price," in *Studies in Art, Architecture and Design,* vol. I, pp. 78–101, 108–25 and 126–37 respectively; Luke Herrmann, *British Landscape Painting of the Eighteenth Century* (New York: Oxford University Press, 1974), pp. 91–132; Bermingham, *Landscape and Ideology,* pp. 9–14 and 57–85; Barrell, *Idea of Landscape,* pp. 1–63; Thomas, *Man and the Natural World,* pp. 254–269; Liu, *Wordsworth,* pp. 61–137; and Michasiw, "Nine Revisionist Theses."

70 Gilpin, qtd. in Barbier, *William Gilpin,* p. 102. Later theorists like Knight were impatient with Gilpin for his hybrid term "picturesque beauty," which did not clearly distinguish between the beautiful, understood in the Burkean sense of smoothness and regularity, and the picturesque

proper, which accentuated roughness and interesting textures. Theoretical inexactitude is a hallmark not only of Gilpin but also of other scenic tourists' opportunistic application of landscape aesthetics; these are best read not logically, but ideologically.

71 Austen, *Northanger Abbey*, p. 111.

72 Barbier, *William Gilpin*, p. 99; Liu, *Wordsworth*, p. 92.

73 Gilpin, *Three Essays*, p. 49.

74 Gilpin, *Observations on the River Wye*, p. 131. Further citations in the text are to this edition.

75 Michasiw, "Nine Revisionist Theses," p. 93.

76 Hipple, *The Beautiful, the Sublime, and the Picturesque*, p. 292.

77 *The Search for the Picturesque*, pp. 49, 64.

78 Hussey, *The Picturesque*, p. 5; Bourdieu, *Distinction*, p. 47.

79 Gilpin, first draft of his *Poem on Landscape Painting*, quoted in Barbier, *William Gilpin*, p. 146; Barbier, *William Gilpin*, p. 144; Gilpin, *Three Essays*, p. 44; Gilpin, quoted in Barbier, *William Gilpin*, p. 144.

80 An occasional exception in Gilpin's doctrine would be figures in a picture positioned where they can see parts of the landscape not visible to the viewer, thus stimulating him to identify with them by imagining unseen vistas. Barbier, *William Gilpin*, pp. 136–37.

81 E. P. Thompson, *Customs in Common* (New York: The New Press, 1991), p. 45.

82 Fabricant, "The Aesthetics and Politics of Landscape in the Eighteenth Century," in *Studies in Eighteenth-Century British Art and Aesthetics*, ed. Ralph Cohen (Berkeley: University of California Press, 1985), p. 65. On the ideologically charged representation of the poor in eighteenth-century landscape painting, see John Barrell, *The Dark Side of the Landscape: The Rural Poor in English Painting 1730–1840* (Cambridge University Press, 1980).

83 "Moral economy" is Thompson's term; see *Customs in Common*, pp. 185–351.

84 Andrews, *The Search for the Picturesque*, pp. 41–50, esp. pp. 45–46.

85 Barbier, *William Gilpin*, pp. 115–21.

86 Liu, *Wordsworth*, pp. 61–84, 85.

87 G. J. Barker-Benfield, *The Culture of Sensibility: Sex and Society in Eighteenth-Century Britain* (University of Chicago Press, 1992), pp. 23–29. R. F. Brissenden discusses the relation between medical and literary discourses of sensibility or sentiment, but does not attend to its gender ambiguities. *Virtue in Distress: Studies in the Novel of Sentiment From Richardson to Sade* (New York: Barnes & Noble, 1974), pp. 11–55.

88 Hume, "Of the Delicacy of Taste and Passion," in *Essays Moral, Political and Literary*, p. 92, quoted in Barker-Benfield, *Culture of Sensibility*, p. 27; see Eagleton, *The Ideology of the Aesthetic* (Oxford: Basil Blackwell, 1990), pp. 41–43.

89 Hume, "Of the Rise and Progress of the Arts and Sciences," in *Essays Moral, Political and Literary*, p. 194; Barker-Benfield, *Culture of Sensibility*,

pp. 105–41, esp. pp. 133–37, 140; Eagleton, *Ideology of the Aesthetic,* pp. 16, 58–59.

90 Bridget Hill, *Women, Work, and Sexual Politics in Eighteenth-Century England* (Oxford: Basil Blackwell, 1989), pp. 47–68.

91 Barker-Benfield, *Culture of Sensibility,* pp. 159–213.

92 *Ends of Empire: Women and Ideology in Early Eighteenth-Century Literature* (Ithaca: Cornell University Press, 1993), pp. 112–21.

93 Ann Radcliffe, *The Mysteries of Udolpho,* ed. Bonamy Dobrée (Oxford University Press, 1980), p. 3; Barker-Benfield, *Culture of Sensibility,* p. 206.

94 Barker-Benfield, *Culture of Sensibility,* pp. 199, 202, 205.

95 *A Journey made in the Summer of 1794, through Holland and the Western Frontier of Germany, with a Return down the Rhine, to which are added Observations during a Tour to the Lakes of Lancashire, Westmoreland, and Cumberland* (London 1795), p. 122. References in the text are to this edition.

96 Jerome McGann's historical interpretations of Romantic nature poetry find similar patterns in complex and ambiguous literary forms. *The Romantic Ideology: A Critical Investigation* (University of Chicago Press, 1983), pp. 59–92.

97 This may also reflect opposition to British involvement in Continental wars. Radcliffe's husband, a lawyer, was known to oppose such overseas commitments. Aline Grant, *Ann Radcliffe* (Denver: Alan Swallow, 1951), pp. 54–55.

4 HELEN MARIA WILLIAMS' REVOLUTIONARY LANDSCAPES

1 Helen Maria Williams, *Letters From France,* ed. Janet M. Todd (Delmar, N.Y.: Scholars' Facsimiles and Reprints, 1975), 1.2.23. The first volume was published in 1790, the second in 1792, the third and fourth in 1793, and the remaining four in 1795–96. The reprint is in two volumes, each including four volumes of the original; citations in the text will be by reprint volume, original volume, and page, for example, 1.1.34. I have chosen to discuss these eight volumes, leaving aside the two additional volumes that Williams wrote during her sojourn in Switzerland in 1794: *A Tour of Switzerland; or, a View of the present State of the Governments and Manners of those Cantons, with comparative Sketches of the present State of Paris* (London, 1798). Her previous publications include the novel *Julia* (1790), as well as poetry including *Ode on the Peace* (1783), *Peru* (1784), and *The Slave Trade* (1788). Little has been written on her life and work; see Lionel D. Woodward, *Une Anglaise Amie de la Révolution Française* (Paris: Librairie Ancienne Honoré Champion, 1930), the only biography besides the brief reference in the *Dictionary of National Biography;* John G. Alger, *Englishmen in the French Revolution* (London, 1889); and M. Ray Adams, "Helen Maria Williams and the French Revolution," in *Wordsworth and Coleridge: Studies in Honor of*

George McLean Harper, ed. Earl Leslie Griggs (New York: Russell & Russell, 1962), pp. 87–117.

2 *The English Novel in the Magazines, 1740–1815* (Evanston, Ill: Northwestern University Press, 1962), p. 259.

3 "Helen Maria Williams and the French Revolution," pp. 88–91; see Alger, *Englishmen*, p. 70, and Woodward, *Une Anglaise Amie*, pp. 60ff. On Barère, see Williams, *Letters*, II.1.170–73.

4 For example, *Gentleman's Magazine* proclaimed that Williams had "debased her sex, her heart, her feelings," Horace Walpole denounced her as a "scribbling trollop," and the Rev. Richard Polwhele's *The Unsex'd Females*, a polemic against women radicals, called her "an intemperate advocate of Gallic licentiousness." All cited in Janet Todd's Introduction to *Letters From France*.

5 *The Dictionary of National Biography*, for example, perpetuates the *Anti-Jacobin* legacy, describing Williams' letters as "impressions frequently formed on very imperfect, one-sided, and garbled information, travestied by the enthusiasm of a clever, badly educated woman, and uttered with the cocksureness of ignorance." Hedva Ben-Israel, *English Historians on the French Revolution* (Cambridge University Press, 1968), calls her "an English example of that revolutionary mentality which various and incompatible ideals were firing with a restless and muddled enthusiasm during the early years of the Revolution," p. 12. Marilyn Butler is similarly dismissive in her editorial introduction: "Her attitudes are the naive ones of literary sentimentalism at its most simple and popular." *Burke, Paine, Godwin, and the Revolution Controversy* (Cambridge University Press, 1984), p. 80. For Chris Jones, "As a commentator on historical events she is easy to criticize, over-partial towards her Girondin friends and naive in her enthusiasms, with her sensibility often obtrusively on display" (p. 5). Jones seems most interested in Williams' influence on "more major figures, especially Wordsworth" (p. 5), men whom he refers to by their surnames while Williams is "Helen." "Helen Maria Williams and Radical Sensibility," *Prose Studies*, 12 (1989), pp. 3–24.

6 Favret, *Romantic Correspondence: Women, Politics and the Fiction of Letters* (Cambridge University Press, 1993), pp. 53–95; Bray, "Helen Maria Williams and Edmund Burke: Radical Critique and Complicity," *Eighteenth-Century Life*, 16:2 (1992). pp. 1–24. See also Julie Ellison, "Redoubled Feeling: Politics, Sentiment, and the Sublime in Williams and Wollstonecraft," *Studies in Eighteenth-Century Culture*, 20 (1990), pp. 197–215.

7 Lynn Hunt, *Politics, Culture, and Class in the French Revolution* (Berkeley: University of California Press, 1984), pp. 19–20, and 74–86 on dress. On the calendar, see Mona Ozouf, *Festivals and the French Revolution*, trans. Alan Sheridan (Cambridge, Mass: Harvard University Press, 1988), pp. 158ff., and Ronald Paulson, *Representations of Revolution (1789–1820)* (New Haven: Yale University Press, 1983), pp. 15–18 (also on playing cards).

8 Keith Michael Baker, *Inventing the French Revolution: Essays on French Political Culture in the Eighteenth Century* (Cambridge University Press, 1990), pp. 4, 10. Historians like Baker and Hunt have applied the methods of literary criticism to analyzing Revolutionary political culture, while literary critics like Ronald Paulson and Alan Liu have contributed to writing the cultural history of the Revolution on both sides of the Channel.

9 Ozouf, *Festivals*, pp. 84, 160, 116, 195. Ozouf, like Liu, skillfully probes the relation between Nature and History as the Revolution is put into discourse. Williams' redaction of historical crisis through the lens of an aestheticized Nature presents another version of this vexed relation.

10 On the historical phenomenology of the guillotine, see Regina Janes, "Beheadings," *Representations*, 35 (1991), pp. 21–51.

11 *Reflections on the Revolution in France*, ed. Thomas H. D. Mahoney (Indianapolis: Bobbs-Merrill, 1955), pp. 37–39, 44, 56, 59. References in the text are to this edition.

12 Ronald Paulson surveys British observers' figurative language in *Representations of Revolution*, pp. 37–56, esp. 42, 55.

13 *Rights of Man*, ed. Eric Foner (New York: Penguin, 1984), p. 273. See Paulson, *Representations of Revolution*, pp. 73–74, on this passage. Paulson, pp. 49–51, also points out that the word "revolution" itself was in the process of changing its primary meaning from that of a regular, cyclical process, like the natural cycles of heavenly bodies and seasons, to that of one-directional, irreversible change, or absolute innovation. From 360 degrees, in other words, to 180 degrees. Supporters of the Revolution, like Paine, made rhetorical use of the former sense; Burke was the first English writer to use the word in the new sense of a violent political upheaval culminating in a fundamentally restructured society.

14 Quoted in Paulson, *Representations of Revolution*, p. 44. The euphoria of these early tributes gave way to a very different "Nature" with the September Massacres, the execution of Louis XVI, and France's declaration of war on Britain in 1793. Alan Liu best summarizes later British conceptualizations of French violence as a savage, barbaric, bestial, cannibalistic, and parricidal Nature whose key attribute is to be uncivilized, and thence essentially different from civilized England. *Wordsworth: The Sense of History* (Stanford University Press, 1989), 139–41.

15 Quoted in Paulson, *Representations of Revolution*, p. 43.

16 Wollstonecraft, *A Vindication of the Rights of Men*, in *The Works of Mary Wollstonecraft*, eds. Marilyn Butler and Janet Todd (New York University Press, 1989), vol. V, p. 56.

17 Alphabetical order, Ozouf points out, was intended as a tactic against the hierarchical order of social rank that had structured *ancient régime* society and its processions (though she points out that "the democracy

was more apparent than real," since all the deputies were "notables," men of a certain social class). *Festivals*, p. 41.

18 Ozouf's section entitled "Boredom and Disgust" shows historians divided between seeing revolutionary festivals as too orchestrated, unspontaneous and boring, or too licentious and Bacchanalian. *Festivals*, pp. 27–32. Janes comments, "Burke deprives the crowd of any motivation – ideological, political, or economic – for its violence. The violence stands alone, isolated, irreducible, and incomprehensible." "Beheadings," p. 22. Though this first volume of letters was published by November 23, 1790, just weeks after Burke's *Reflections*, and does not refer to him by name, Williams' specific response to points he makes, especially in her last letter, convinces me that she is consciously responding, if not to *Reflections* itself, then to points Burke had made in well-publicized speeches previous to its publication. See Bray, "Helen Maria Williams and Edmund Burke," p. 3 and notes 9 and 10.

19 Contra Bray's attempt to extract a philosophical consistency from Williams' use of the sublime in "Helen Maria Williams and Edmund Burke." See Ellison, "Redoubled Feeling," pp. 198, 203.

20 On other writers' use of the Gothic in representing the Revolution, see Paulson, *Representations of Revolution*, pp. 215–47.

21 Compare Williams' presentation of these events with Burke's famously melodramatic description of the "Theban and Thracian orgies" of "ruffians and assassins" threatening the Queen with their phallic "poniards"; *Reflections*, pp. 81–83. Paine gives a contesting version in *Rights of Man*, pp. 60–64.

22 Ian Ousby, *The Englishman's England: Taste, Travel, and the Rise of Tourism* (Cambridge University Press, 1990), p. 126.

23 Wollstonecraft, *Vindication of the Rights of Men*, vol. V, p. 10.

24 See Ozouf, *Festivals*, pp. 232–61, on the complicated history of the Liberty Tree as a revolutionary symbol evolving in part from the traditional popular ritual of the maypole.

25 As Julie Ellison points out, the vocabulary of sentiment had both male and female variants. "Redoubled Feeling," pp. 197–98.

26 Mayo, *English Novel in the Magazines*, p. 260.

27 Joan B. Landes, *Women and the Public Sphere in the Age of the French Revolution* (Ithaca, N.Y: Cornell University Press, 1988), pp. 40, 43, 44–45.

28 *Ibid.*, pp. 23–31, 45, 93–151.

29 The Advertisement reads as follows:

Though, for particular reasons, the author's name could not be prefixed to these Letters, the reader will, on the perusal of them, be at no loss to determine from what quarter they proceed.

It is only fair, however, to premise, that they are not all the production of the same pen. The Letters, Nos. 2, 3, 4, 5, 6, in Vol. III.

which contain a history of the campaign of 1792, are by another hand; but the public will easily perceive that they are written by a person who has had the *best* information on the subject that France can afford.

The concluding letter is by a third person; but as it contained a very interesting disquisition concerning the popular topics of the times, the publisher conceived he could not render a more acceptable service to the purchasers of these volumes than to insert it.

In letter 2 of vol. 1.4, Williams alerts her reader to collaborative authorship in this volume as well: "The friend who favoured me [in Vol. 1.3] with the account you have read of Dumourier's campaign, has written the history of his desertion of the popular cause in a manner so clear and interesting, that, instead of attempting to trace the event myself, which I should do very imperfectly, I shall subjoin my friend's letter" (p. 60).

Williams probably chose anonymity at this point because of an "increasingly harsh reception" of her earlier work in England, as well as to protect herself "from legal reprisals on both sides of the channel," according to Favret, *Romantic Correspondence*, pp. 81–82; see pp. 83–85 on multiple authorship and the disappearance of the privileged individual spectator.

30 Favret, *Romantic Correspondence*, p. 95.
31 Julie Ellison notes that Williams is insensitive to issues of class. "Redoubled Feeling," p. 201. The Legislative Assembly was the successor body to the National Assembly from October 1791.
32 See J. M. Thompson, *The French Revolution* (Oxford, Basil Blackwell, 1966), pp. 324–25 on the changing class composition of the commune from middle to lower bourgeoisie, and the difficulty of defining the revolutionary "People."
33 *The Melodramatic Imagination* (New York: Columbia University Press, 1985), p. 21.
34 See II. 1.173–74, Favret, *Romantic Correspondence*, p. 88, and Woodward, *Une Anglaise Amie*, p. 189, for details of how the letters came to Robespierre's attention.
35 See Ozouf, *Festivals*, on the Festival of the Supreme Being, esp. pp. 110–18.
36 The architects of the revolutionary festival shared Williams' tendency to set aside historical causality in their aesthetic presentation of the Revolution. According to Ozouf, their staging of the history of the present "did not manage to imagine…episodes with a causal connection"; *Festivals*, p. 157.

5 MARY WOLLSTONECRAFT'S ANTI-AESTHETICS

1 Terry Eagleton, *The Ideology of the Aesthetic* (Oxford: Basil Blackwell, 1990), p. 207.

2 Richard Polwhele, *The Unsex'd Females* (1798), ed. Gina Luria (New York: Garland, 1974); Horace Walpole cited in Ralph Wardle, *Mary Wollstonecraft: A Critical Biography* (Lawrence: University of Kansas Press, 1951), p. 159.

3 Three Wollstonecraft biographies appeared in the early 1970s: Eleanor Flexner's *Mary Wollstonecraft* (New York: Coward, McCann & Geoghegan, 1972); Claire Tomalin's *The Life and Death of Mary Wollstonecraft* (London: Weidenfeld and Nicolson, 1974); and Emily W. Sunstein, *A Different Face: The Life of Mary Wollstonecraft* (New York: Harper and Row, 1975). Reviews of these are listed in Janet Todd, *Mary Wollstonecraft: An Annotated Bibliography* (New York: Garland, 1976). Homage to Wollstonecraft is ubiquitous in feminist classics like Betty Friedan's *The Feminine Mystique* and Germaine Greer's *The Female Eunuch*. Recent reconsiderations include Mary Poovey, *The Proper Lady and the Woman Writer, Ideology as Style in the Works of Mary Wollstonecraft, Mary Shelley, and Jane Austen* (University of Chicago Press, 1984), pp. 48–81; Cora Kaplan, "Wild Nights: Pleasure/Sexuality/Feminism" and "Pandora's Box: Subjectivity, Class and Sexuality in Socialist Feminist Criticism," in *Sea Changes: Essays on Culture and Feminism* (London: Verso, 1986), pp. 31–56, 147–76; Landes, *Women and the Public Sphere in the Age of the French Revolution* (Ithaca, N.Y.: Cornell University Press, 1988), pp. 127–38; Timothy J. Reiss, "Revolution in Bounds: Wollstonecraft, Women, and Reason," in *Gender and Theory: Dialogues on Feminist Criticism*, ed. Linda Kauffman (Oxford: Basil Blackwell, 1989), pp. 11–50. Further references appear in the text.

4 Landes, *Women and the Public Sphere in the Age of the French Revolution*, and Rita Goldberg, *Sex and Enlightenment: Women in Richardson and Diderot* (Cambridge University Press, 1984) point out regressive tendencies in gender ideology of the period. The classic discussion of the Enlightenment's ambivalent legacy is Max Horkheimer and Theodor W. Adorno, *Dialectic of Enlightenment,* trans. John Cumming (New York: Herder and Herder, 1972).

5 Frances Ferguson, "Wollstonecraft Our Contemporary," in *Gender and Theory,* ed. Kauffman, p. 58.

6 *A Vindication of the Rights of Men in The Works of Mary Wollstonecraft,* eds. Marilyn Butler and Janet Todd (New York University Press, 1989), vol. V, p. 7. References in the text are to this edition by page only. Quoted and discussed in Virginia Sapiro, *A Vindication of Political Virtue: The Political Theory of Mary Wollstonecraft* (University of Chicago Press, 1992), pp. 198 ff. Sapiro's indispensable interpretation of Wollstonecraft's political thought is the first book-length study on the

topic, 200 years after the publication of *A Vindication of the Rights of Woman.*

7 *A Vindication of the Rights of Woman in Works,* vol. V, pp. 74–75, and see Sapiro, *Vindication of Political Virtue,* pp. 91–92, 95–96. Sapiro elsewhere discusses Wollstonecraft's affinities with republican versions of civic humanism, like those espoused by her friends William Blake and Henry Fuseli, despite her frequent association by twentieth-century critics with the liberal language of rights and possessive individualism identified with Locke. In fact she was heavily influenced by both idioms and would not have understood them as mutually exclusive. There is no space to take up this complicated question here, but see Sapiro, pp. xx, 208–16.

8 Sapiro, *Vindication of Political Virtue,* p. xiv and *passim.*

9 Alison M. Jaggar, *Feminist Politics and Human Nature* (Totowa, N.J.: Rowman & Allanheld, 1983), p. 28.

10 *Ideology of the Aesthetic,* pp. 196, 201–202.

11 See Poovey, *Proper Lady,* and Kaplan, "Pandora's Box" and "Wild Nights."

12 Interpretations of the first *Vindication* include James T. Boulton, *The Language of Politics in the Age of Wilkes and Burke* (London: Routledge & Kegan Paul, 1963), pp. 167–76; Mitzi Myers, "Politics from the Outside: Mary Wollstonecraft's First Vindication," *Studies in Eighteenth-Century Culture,* 6 (1977), pp. 113–32; Ronald Paulson, *Representations of Revolution (1789–1820)* (New Haven: Yale University Press, 1983), pp. 79–87; and Poovey, *Proper Lady,* pp. 56–68. Further references appear in the text.

13 Burke, *Reflections on the Revolution in France* ed. Thomas H. D. Mahoney (Indianapolis: Bobbs-Merrill, 1955), pp. 86–87. References in the text are to this edition.

14 Boulton, *Language of Politics,* p. 86n; Burke, Reflections, p. 89n.

15 Burke attempts to tie British liberty to property, metaphorically equating them by referring to liberty as an "entailed inheritance" or "estate" (p. 37). Wollstonecraft's attack aims to separate the two and reveal them as actually opposed: aristocratic property deprives working people of their liberty. She gives the example of the government press gangs that legally kidnapped able-bodied men into naval service, a practice that continued through the Napoleonic wars, as well as the notorious British penal code with over 200 capital offenses, including minor crimes against property: "Our penal laws punish with death the thief who steals a few pounds; but to take by violence, or trepan, a man, is no such heinous offence" when committed by a press gang (p. 15).

16 See Paulson, *Representations of Revolution,* p. 68.

17 The problem, as Paulson astutely notes (*Representations of Revolution,* pp. 80–87), is Burke's category of the beautiful. As long as women are defined, and define themselves, as aesthetic objects, they will risk

becoming as morally bankrupt as "the fair ladies, whom, if the voice of rumour is to be credited, the captive negroes curse in all the agony of bodily pain, for the unheard of tortures they invent...But these ladies may have read your Enquiry concerning the origin of our ideas of the Sublime and Beautiful...You may have convinced them that *littleness* and weakness are the very essence of beauty; and that the Supreme Being, in giving women beauty in the most supereminent degree, seemed to command them, by the powerful voice of Nature, not to cultivate the moral virtues that might chance to excite respect, and interfere with the pleasing sensations they were created to inspire" (*Vindication of the Rights of Men*, p. 45). *A Vindication of the Rights of Woman* pursues this idea at length, see, for example, Wollstonecraft, *Works*, vol V, pp. 76–77, 88–98, 109.

18 Pierre Bourdieu argues in his postscript on Kant that pure taste is "purely negative in its essence," founded on disgust for the facile or vulgar. *Distinction: A Social Critique of the Judgement of Taste*, trans. Richard Nice (Cambridge, Mass.: Harvard University Press, 1984) p. 486.

19 Karl Marx, *Economic and Philosophic Manuscripts of 1844*, in *The Marx–Engels Reader*, second edition, ed. Robert C. Tucker (New York: W. W. Norton, 1978), pp. 87, 89. Eagleton's comment on Marx applies to Wollstonecraft as well: "the goal of human life, for Marx as for Aristotle, is not truth, but happiness or well-being. His work is an extensive enquiry into what material conditions would be necessary for this goal to be realized as a general human condition, and thus belongs to the discourse of classical morality. Marx is a moralist in the most traditional sense of the term, which is to say that he is concerned with the political determinations of the good life. His morality thus stands opposed to that withered modern sense of the 'moral', impoverished to interpersonal relations and 'spiritual' values alone" (p. 227).

20 Eagleton, *Ideology of the Aesthetic*, pp. 201, 219–21. Eagleton himself points out the main problem with the repression/expression paradigm: assuming that "human capacities become morbid only by virtue of their alienation, repression, dissociation or one-sidedness" is "surely a dangerous illusion; we must count among our capacities the power to torture and wage war" (p. 221). A Foucaultian perspective would understand such a repression hypothesis as part of a disciplinary technology of person formation; see, for example, Tony Bennett, *Outside Literature* (London: Routledge, 1990), pp. 173–81.

21 For this emphasis on the personal, see, for example, Wardle, *Mary Wollstonecraft*, pp. 250–57; Carol H. Poston, "Introduction" to Wollstonecraft, *Letters Written...in Sweden* (Lincoln: University of Nebraska Press, 1976); Mitzi Myers, "Mary Wollstonecraft's *Letters Written...in Sweden*: Toward Romantic Autobiography," *Studies in Eighteenth-Century Culture*, 8 (1979), pp. 165–85; Poovey, *Proper Lady*,

pp. 83–94; and Jeanne Moskal, "The Picturesque and the Affectionate in Wollstonecraft's *Letters from Norway*," *Modern Language Quarterly* 52 (1991), pp. 263–94. Mary A. Favret calls attention to this culturally conditioned tendency to focus on the "personal," "sentimental" and "womanly" features of *Letters*, arguing persuasively that such interpretations are inevitably misleading. *Romantic Correspondence: Women, Politics and the Fiction of Letters* (Cambridge University Press, 1993), pp. 100 ff.

22 Her business concerned Imlay's venture in the wartime currency trade with a Norwegian partner, who had mysteriously "lost" a ship containing £3,500 in silver ingots. Wollstonecraft was commissioned to investigate, to negotiate a settlement, or if that was impossible to file a legal claim for damages. The ship was not found, and it is not known whether Imlay recovered any of his money. Per Nyström, *Mary Wollstonecraft's Scandinavian Journey* (Göteborg: Kungl. Vetenskaps- och Vitterhets-Samhället, 1980). Imlay probably encouraged the trip for personal reasons as well, as a kind of therapy for Wollstonecraft following her depression and unsuccessful suicide attempt, and to keep her occupied while he continued his affair with another lover. Sunstein, *A Different Face*, chapter 13.

23 Wardle, *Mary Wollstonecraft*, p. 256.

24 *Ibid.*, p. 257; Favret, *Romantic Correspondence*, p. 124; and see Wollstonecraft's prickly letter to Imlay dated July 18, 1795: "I have begun — [Letters] which will, I hope, discharge all my obligations of a pecuniary kind. – I am lowered in my own eyes, on account of my not having done it sooner." *Letters to Imlay* in Wollstonecraft, *Works*, vol. VI, p. 422.

25 Wollstonecraft, *Letters Written during a Short Residence in Sweden, Norway and Denmark*, in *Works*, vol. VI, p. 241. Further references appear in the text by page only; title abbreviated as *Letters*.

26 *A Vindication of the Rights of Woman* in Wollstonecraft, *Works*, vol. V, p. 116. Ironically, Hogarth, far from defending the status quo, advocated and practiced an aesthetics of iconoclasm, raising a "world of variety, liberty, and subculture above the old doctrines based on unity and order," as Ronald Paulson has shown. *Breaking and Remaking: Aesthetic Practice in England, 1700–1820* (New Brundswick: Rutgers University Press, 1989), pp. 202, 149–202.

27 *Contributions to the Analytical Review 1788–1797*, in Wollstonecraft, *Works*, vol. VII. For example, she approves of the "interesting and beautiful" scenic descriptions in Charlotte Smith's novel *Emmeline* (p. 27) and in Hester Thrale Piozzi's travels in France, Italy, and Germany (p. 109), while the style of Hassell's tour of the Isle of Wight (p. 279) and the Rev. Shaw's to the west of England strikes her as "weak and affected" (p. 182). These reviews document her familiarity with the works of Gilpin on the picturesque, three of which she reviews – his tours of Scotland (p. 196) and of the New Forest (p. 386) and *Three Essays* (p. 455) – as well as with the literature of landscape gardening. See her 1790 review of the Abbé de Lille's *The Garden; or the Art of laying out*

Grounds, in which she comments, in a vein reminiscent of the first *Vindication*, on "the fopperies of modern taste, or the idle luxury of endeavouring to give eastern charms to a temperate climate, whilst welcome sunshine is shut out. – Equally absurd likewise appears the vain parade of making waters spring in dry places, and a sober flat assume a wild aspect...An English garden is seldom susceptible of improvements calculated to raise sublime ideas, and when they are introduced they look like the fustian rant of impotence" (pp. 302–3).

28 On this characteristic optimism or meliorism, see, for example, Peter Gay, *The Enlightenment: An Interpretation* (New York: Alfred A. Knopf, 1969), vol. II, pp. 3–55.

29 For example, *Letters*, pp. 244, 249, 333, and see Favret, *Romantic Correspondence*, p. 117.

30 Mikhail Bakhtin, *Rabelais and His World*, trans. Hélène Iswolsky (Bloomington: Indiana University Press, 1984). Peter Stallybrass and Allon White apply Bakhtin's description to the grotesque bodies of Britain's early modern populace, whose exaggerated, unruly physical needs and pleasures are "the antithesis of order, civility and decorum." The *Politics and Poetics of Transgression* (Ithaca: Cornell University Press, 1986), p. 32. Further references in parentheses in the text.

31 See Kaplan, "Wild Nights," pp. 48–49 on the intersection of class and gender in *A Vindication of the Rights of Woman*; another example is the character of the ex-prostitute Jemima in Wollstonecraft's unfinished novel *Maria, or the Wrongs of Woman* (1798), whose manifest heroism cannot entirely overcome the edge of condescension with which she is portrayed.

32 Kaplan, "Wild Nights" and "Pandora's Box"; Poovey, *Proper Lady*, esp. pp. 74–78; and see Wollstonecraft's *Vindication of the Rights of Woman*, for example p. 119, on the heroic widow who "forgets her sex."

33 Charles L. Batten, Jr., *Pleasurable Instruction: Form and Convention in Eighteenth-Century Travel Literature* (Berkeley: University of California Press, 1978), p. 13.

34 Mary Louise Pratt, *Imperial Eyes: Travel Writing and Transculturation* (New York: Routledge, 1992), pp. 51, 63.

35 *Letters to Imlay* in Wollstonecraft, *Works*, for example vol. VI, pp. 383, 385; and see Sunstein, *A Different Face*, p. 260; Poovey, *Proper Lady*, p. 82.

36 Laurence Sterne, *Tristram Shandy*, ed. Howard Anderson (New York: W. W. Norton, 1980), vol. IX, chapter 24, pp. 444–46; Sterne, *A Sentimental Journey*, ed. Ian Jack (Oxford University Press, 1984), pp. 113–16.

37 Bourdieu, *Distinction*, pp. 491, 490.

38 On travel and natural history, see Pratt, *Imperial Eyes*, chapter 2, and Barbara Maria Stafford, *Voyage into Substance: Art, Science, Nature, and the Illustrated Travel Account, 1760–1840* (Cambridge, Mass.: MIT Press, 1984).

39 Eagleton, *Ideology of the Aesthetic*, p. 226. Aesthetics' self-contradictory potential is a central point of Eagleton's book; for example pp. 2–3.

40 Here I disagree with Favret, who argues that Wollstonecraft sets herself and her work of imagination apart from the laboring classes (*Romantic Correspondence*, p. 125), though as we have seen the issue is not without ambiguity.

41 Friedrich Schiller, *On the Aesthetic Education of Man*, trans. Reginald Snell (New York: Frederick Ungar, 1965), p. 38. However, Martha Woodmansee uncovers a distinctly undemocratic cultural politics in Schiller's aesthetics. "'Art' as a Weapon in Cultural Politics: Rereading Schiller's *Aesthetic Letters*," in *Eighteenth-Century Aesthetics and the Reconstruction of Art*, ed. Paul Mattick, Jr. (Cambridge University Press, 1993), pp. 178–209.

6 DOROTHY WORDSWORTH AND THE CULTURAL POLITICS OF SCENIC TOURISM

1 Dorothy Wordsworth, *Recollections of a Tour Made in Scotland, A. D. 1803*, in *Journals of Dorothy Wordsworth*, ed. Ernest de Selincourt (New York: Macmillan, 1941), vol. I, p. 214. References in the text are to this edition.

2 I will refer to Dorothy Wordsworth by her surname and her brother, when he is mentioned, as William, reversing the prevalent practice among critics of both writers. Susan M. Levin qualifies Wordsworth's reputation as a homebody by pointing out that the bulk of her writings were travel journals, displaying considerable energy and independence; *Dorothy Wordsworth and Romanticism* (New Brunswick: Rutgers University Press, 1987), pp. 73–74. One example of this is her second trip to Scotland, accompanied only by her friend Joanna Hutchinson without a male escort, a daring venture in 1822. De Selincourt reprints the brief and unpolished record of this trip as *Journal of my Second Tour in Scotland* (58 pages). In addition to the two Scottish tours (the first 214 pages long), he includes five travel journals: *Journal of Visit to Hamburgh and of Journey from Hamburgh to Goslar (1798)* (16 pages); *Excursion on the Banks of Ullswater (November 1805)* (10 pages); *Excursion up Scawfell Pike (October 1818)* (6 pages); *Journal of a Tour on the Continent (1820)* (329 pages); and *Journal of a Tour in the Isle of Man (1828)* (19 pages).

3 Levin, *Dorothy Wordsworth and Romanticism;* Margaret Homans, *Women Writers and Poetic Identity: Dorothy Wordsworth, Emily Brontë, and Emily Dickinson* (Princeton University Press, 1980); and James Holt McGavran, Jr., "Dorothy Wordsworth's Journals: Putting Herself Down," in *The Private Self*, ed. Shari Benstock (Chapel Hill: University of North Carolina Press, 1988), pp. 230–53. William's Romantic imagination is most satisfied, he declares in Book XI of the 1805 *Prelude*, in moments when he has the "deepest feeling that the mind /

Is lord and master, and that outward sense / Is but the obedient servant of her will" (lines 221–23). Most of Dorothy Wordsworth's critics have extensively discussed her relationship with her brother, a relationship obviously important to both siblings' artistic development. For my purposes, I have chosen to leave this relationship in the background and treat Wordsworth's writing on its own terms.

4 Clare is quoted in John Barrell, *The Idea of Landscape and the Sense of Place, 1730–1840: An Approach to the Poetry of John Clare* (Cambridge University Press, 1972), p. 120, and see pp. 119–21.

5 Quoted in Barrell, *Idea of Landscape,* p. 130. Barrell remarks that "we should be wary of the assumptions behind criticism of this kind; and particularly the assumption that for a descriptive poem to have content, it must pass beyond itself, into meditation or whatever."

6 Levin, *Dorothy Wordsworth and Romanticism,* p. 4. Levin's feminist analysis values these qualities; she finds in Wordsworth's writing "an equipoise of self and the phenomenal world that challenges the notion of assertive self advanced by so many romantic writers" (p. 5). My main disagreement with Levin's valuable work, grounded in Carol Gilligan's and Nancy Chodorow's models of feminine psychological development, concerns its essentialist tendencies. She sometimes implies, misleadingly I believe, that Wordsworth's textual selflessness correlates with a gain in immediacy or linguistic transparency – that the relative absence of an "appropriating self" allows her really to achieve what her brother calls "wise passiveness," a truer receptiveness to "nature" (p. 7). Such an interpretation risks moving in the direction of oppressive, essentialist links between Woman and Nature.

7 Barrell, *Idea of Landscape,* p. 63.

8 See Robert Gittings and Jo Manton, *Dorothy Wordsworth* (Oxford: Clarendon Press, 1985).

9 Malcolm Andrews, *The Search for the Picturesque* (Stanford University Press, 1990), p. 153, and see Chapter 2 above. On the Lake District, see Andrews, pp. 152–95, esp. 158–59. The first published description of the Lake District's scenic beauties was a 1754 poem by Dr. John Dalton; in 1767 Dr. John Brown, William Gilpin's tutor and drawing master, published his famous letter on the Lakes. Gilpin himself made the tour in 1772, though his description did not appear in print until 1786 as *Observations, relative chiefly to Picturesque Beauty, Made in the Year 1776 on Several Parts of Great Britain; particularly the High-Lands of Scotland* (London, 1786).

10 *Journals of Dorothy Wordsworth,* second edition, ed. Mary Moorman (Oxford University Press, 1971), p. 133. References to the *Grasmere Journals* in the text will be to this edition.

11 Andrews, *Search for the Picturesque,* pp. 182, 190–91.

12 *The Country and the City* (Oxford University Press, 1973), pp. 46–47.

13 See Gittings and Manton, *Dorothy Wordsworth.*

14 *Wordsworth: The Sense of History* (Stanford University Press, 1989), pp. 91–92, and see Chapter 3 above.

15 Kurt Heinzelman, "The Cult of Domesticity: Dorothy and William Wordsworth at Grasmere," in *Romanticism and Feminism*, ed. Anne K. Mellor (Bloomington: Indiana University Press, 1988), p. 54. Further references will appear in the text.

16 "Theses on Feuerbach," in *The Marx–Engels Reader*, ed. Robert C. Tucker, second edition (New York: W. W. Norton, 1978), p. 143. See also Raymond Williams: "Signification, the social creation of meanings through the use of formal signs, is...a practical, material activity; it is indeed, literally, a means of production." *Marxism and Literature* (Oxford University Press, 1977), p. 38.

17 Michel de Certeau, *The Practice of Everyday Life*, trans. Steven Rendall (Berkeley: University of California Press, 1984), p. xix.

18 "On the Autobiographical Present: Dorothy Wordsworth's *Grasmere Journals*," *Criticism*, 26 (1984), esp. pp. 117–18, 123 ff.

19 Liu, "Autobiographical Present," pp. 124–25.

20 See, for example, Susan J. Wolfson, "Individual in Community: Dorothy Wordsworth in Conversation with William," in *Romanticism and Feminism*, ed. Anne K. Mellor (Bloomington, Indiana University Press, 1988), pp. 139–66, and Levin, *Dorothy Wordsworth and Romanticism*, esp. pp. 41–52.

21 *Epistolarity: Approaches to a Form* (Columbus: Ohio State University Press, 1982). For another historical and theoretical perspective on letters in Romantic literature see Mary A. Favret, *Romantic Correspondence: Women, Politics, and the Fiction of Letters* (Cambridge University Press, 1993).

22 Wordsworth wrote her account of her journey between 1803 and 1805. De Selincourt points out that "it was not jotted down, like a diary, from day to day, but written at leisure after her return"; she says in a letter that *"we took no notes"* (*Journals*, vol I, p. vii–viii). Wordsworth first wrote for circulation among a few friends, but then apparently decided to try for publication; "she revised the work extensively, producing five manuscript versions" (Levin, *Dorothy Wordsworth and Romanticism*, p. 79). The idea of publication was dropped, then revived after her second trip to Scotland in 1822. Once again, however, *Recollections* was withheld from print. According to Levin, p. 79, "William finally decided public authorship would be too much strain on his sister's delicate health. The publication history and certain comments in *Recollections* evidence both Dorothy's general anxieties about writing and the difficulties she associates with travel writing." This seems very likely, as we shall see.

23 See Andrews, *Search for the Picturesque*, pp. 196–240.

24 John R. Nabholtz, "Dorothy Wordsworth and the Picturesque," *Studies in Romanticism*, 3 (1964), pp. 122–23.

25 Wordsworth's frequent use of "we" instead of "I" to record her

impressions of Scotland can be off-putting, recalling everything critics
have said about her suppression of self (note 2 above). Throughout
Recollections, "we" often (though not always) seems to appear in more
conventional observations, while "I" tends to mark departures from
the conventions of scenic tourism, as we will see.

26 Private property also intervenes in Wordsworth's scenic pleasure at the
Clyde: "I was grieved to hear that the Falls of the Clyde were shut up
in a gentleman's grounds, and to be viewed only by means of lock and
key. Much, however, as the pure feeling with which one would desire
to visit such places is disturbed by useless, impertinent, or even unnecessary interference with nature, yet when I was there the next morning
I seemed to feel it a less disagreeable thing than in smaller and more
delicate spots, if I may use the phrase" (219–20). One "more delicate
spot" she may be thinking of is Rydal Lower Falls back in the Lake
District; see Liu, *Wordsworth*, pp. 81 ff., on this picturesque scene's ownership by a local baron and the ways its various representations testify
to the "supervision" of landscape by the institution of scenic tourism.

27 See Andrews, *Search for the Picturesque*, pp. 202–6, for a short account of
the late eighteenth-century craze for the Celtic bard Ossian, based on
the much-reconstructed translations in the 1760s by James
Macpherson, and its contribution to scenic tourism in the Highlands.
Andrews also records several other tourists' reactions to this popular
attraction, dubbed "The Hermitage," pp. 214–16.

28 Nabholtz, "Dorothy Wordsworth," pp. 118–28.

29 Edmund Burke, *A Philosophical Enquiry into the Origin of our Ideas of the
Sublime and Beautiful*, ed. James T. Boulton (Notre Dame, Ind.:
University of Notre Dame Press, 1958), pp. 58–64.

30 Wilkinson's journal was later published as *Tours to the British Mountains*
(1824); the sentence in question reads as follows: "Passed a female who
was reaping alone: she sung in Erse as she bended over her sickle; the
sweetest human voice I ever heard: her strains were tenderly melancholy, and felt delicious, long after they were heard no more." Quoted
in Andrews, *Search for the Picturesque*, p. 228.

31 Another possible dimension of Wordsworth's reaction is an insecurity
about her own privilege. Will she and her brother be able to maintain
their tenuous membership in the middle class in uncertain economic
times, given his unlucrative dedication to poetry? Gary Lee Harrison
makes a similar point about William's sublime vagrants in
"Spec(tac)ular Reversals: The Politics of the Sublime and
Wordsworth's Transfiguration of the Rustic Poor," *Criticism*, 34 (1992),
esp. pp. 564, 576.

32 Deidre Lynch, "'Beating the Track of the Alphabet': Samuel Johnson,
Tourism, and the ABCs of Modern Authority," *ELH*, 57 (1990), pp.
369–72. She cites the Scottish Society for the Propagation of Christian
Knowledge on modernizing the Celtic fringe: "nothing can be more
effectual for reducing these counties to order...than teaching them

their duty to God, their King and Country, and rooting out their Irish Language" (p. 398, note 20).

33 Mary Louise Pratt, *Imperial Eyes: Travel Writing and Trasculturation* (New York: Routledge, 1992), p. 60; this fantasy is mediated through a pose of passivity and powerlessness in the complicated transaction Pratt terms "the anti-conquest." See Chapter 2 above.

34 Gittings and Manton, *Dorothy Wordsworth,* pp. 75, 136.

35 Richard D. Altick, *The Shows of London* (Cambridge, Mass.: Harvard University Press, 1978), p. 56. Scotland also made its way into London popular culture; Andrews mentions the production of *Harlequin in Hebrides* during the 1790s at Sadler's Wells: "The lavish sets included 'A *Highland Laird's* Chamber,' 'A *Highland* Village,' and 'A dark, rocky Cavern on the Coast of Scotland.'" *Search for the Picturesque,* p. 206.

36 Levin, *Dorothy Wordsworth and Romanticism,* p. 77: "It seems more than coincidence that Dorothy's first Scottish tour opens as she, William and Coleridge arrive at Carlisle on the very day that John Hatfield, the forger, was condemned."

37 On dirt in the *Grasmere Journals,* see Liu, "Autobiographical Present," esp. pp. 123–27. Other tourists in Scotland, like the poet Gray and Hester Thrale Piozzi, also commented on its dirtiness; see Andrews, *Search for the Picturesque,* pp. 201, 207.

38 *Purity and Danger: An Analysis of the Concepts of Pollution and Taboo,* 1966 (New York: Routledge, 1991).

39 Levin, *Dorothy Wordsworth and Romanticism,* discusses this passage, pp. 79–80.

40 *An Essay on the Picturesque, as Compared with the Sublime and the Beautiful; and, on the Use of Studying Pictures, for the Purpose of Improving Real Landscape,* second edition (London, 1796), esp. pp. 9–16, 36–46.

41 Billie Melman, *Women's Orients: English Women and the Middle East, 1718–1918* (Ann Arbor: University of Michigan Press, 1992), p. 8; Moira Ferguson, *Subject to Others: British Women Writers and Colonial Slavery, 1670–1834* (New York: Routledge, 1992), p. 4; Gayatri Chakravorty Spivak, "Three Women's Texts and a Critique of Imperialism," *Critical Inquiry,* 12 (1985), and see Chapter 1, Note 28 above.

42 Jane Flax, "Postmodernism and Gender Relations in Feminist Theory," in *Feminism/Postmodernism,* ed. Linda J. Nicholson (New York: Routledge, 1990), p. 49.

43 M. M. Bakhtin, "Discourse in the Novel," in *The Dialogue Imagination,* trans. Caryl Emerson and Michael Holquist (Austin: University of Texas Press, 1981), pp. 348, 311–12.

7 THE PICTURESQUE AND THE FEMALE SUBLIME IN
ANN RADCLIFFE'S *MYSTERIES OF UDOLPHO*

1 Jane Austen, *Northanger Abbey,* in *The Novels of Jane Austen,* ed. R. W. Chapman, third edition, vol. V (London: Oxford University Press, 1965), p. 200. References in the text are to this edition.

2 Patricia Meyer Spacks, *Desire and Truth: Functions of Plot in Eighteenth-Century English Novels* (University of Chicago Press, 1990), p. 3.

3 Samuel Holt Monk, *The Sublime: A Study of Critical Theories in XVIII-Century England* (New York: Modern Language Association, 1935), p. 217.

4 Rev. James Fordyce, for example, approves of Richardson, but thunders, "What shall we say of certain books, which we are assured (for we have not read them) are in their nature so shameful, in their tendency so pestiferous…that she who can bear to peruse them must be in her soul a prostitute, let her reputation in life be what it will." *Sermons to Young Women,* fourth edition, 2 vols., (London, 1767), vol. I, 148. See also "An Unfortunate Mother's Advice to her Absent Daughters" in *Instructions to a Young Lady, in every Sphere and Period of Life* (Edinburgh, 1770), pp. 36–37; Dr. John Gregory, *A Father's Legacy to His Daughters,* third edition (Dublin, 1774), pp. 31–32; and Thomas Gisborne, *An Enquiry into the Duties of the Female Sex* (London, 1797), pp. 214–17. Wollstonecraft sternly condemns "the reveries of the stupid novelists, who, knowing little of human nature, work up stale tales, and describe meretricious scenes, all retailed in a sentimental jargon, which equally tend to corrupt the taste, and draw the heart aside from its daily duties." *A Vindication of the Rights of Woman,* in the *Works of Mary Wollstonecraft,* eds. Marilyn Butler and Janet Todd, 7 vols. (New York University Press. 1989), vol. V, p. 256.

5 *Before Novels: The Cultural Contexts of Eighteenth-Century English Fiction* (New York: W. W. Norton & Co., 1990), pp. 90–95 and passim.

6 Mary Wollstonecraft, *The Wrongs of Woman, or, Maria,* in *Works,* vol. I, p. 95. References in the text are to this edition.

7 Terry J. Castle, "The Spectralization of the Other in *The Mysteries of Udolpho,*" in *The New Eighteenth Century,* eds. Felicity Nussbaum and Laura Brown (New York: Methuen, 1987), pp. 231–53. Castle's essay suggests one way in which these oppositions break down as the supernatural atmosphere of Castle Udolpho infiltrates the "daylight" world. Spacks sees both *Udolpho* and *The Italian* as divided along gendered lines, with "double plots that imply two different principles of action": "sublime" masculine ambition and aggression, and "beautiful" feminine affiliation or nurturance. *Desire and Truth,* pp. 151–52 and *passim.*

8 Ann Radcliffe, *The Mysteries of Udolpho,* ed. Bonamy Dobrée (Oxford University Press, 1980), pp. 318, 296, 329. References in the text are to this edition. Aspects of Radcliffe's landscape descriptions are addressed by Rhoda L. Flaxman, "Radcliffe's Dual Modes of Vision," in *Fetter'd or Free? British Women Novelists 1670–1815,* eds. Mary Anne Schofield and Cecelia Macheski (Athens: Ohio University Press, 1986);

Jean Hagstrum, "Pictures to the Heart: the Psychological Picturesque in Ann Radcliffe's *The Mysteries of Udolpho,*" in *Greene Centennial Studies,* eds. Paul J. Korshin and Robert R. Allen (Charlottesville: University of Virginia Press, 1984), pp. 434–41; Charles Kostelnick, "From Picturesque View to Picturesque Vision: William Gilpin and Ann Radcliffe," *Mosaic,* 18 (1985), pp. 31–48; and Daniel Cottom, *The Civilized Imagination: A Study of Ann Radcliffe, Jane Austen and Sir Walter Scott* (Cambridge University Press, 1985).

9 Kostelnick, "From Picturesque View to Picturesque Vision."

10 The transition between the two contrasting models of aesthetic experience is actually not quite this neat. When Emily leaves France for Venice with Montoni at the beginning of Volume II she enters a liminal stage: the function of looking at landscape evolves from a positive bond to loved others toward an increasingly solipsistic and defensive reaction. As she crosses the Alps the stability of earlier scenic tableaux comes loose. Descriptions focus on abstract elements of light, color, and "fantastic forms" (171); "a world of chaos" (165), Emily's description of Alpine clouds, takes on an emotional resonance that continues in Venice with the "fantastic diversity" of Carnival masquerade (174). Her imaginative life in this transitional period betrays a morbid fascination with the consequences of letting go. Like Hannibal, whose soldiers and elephants she imagines "tumbling headlong down the...precipices" (166), the traveler in her occasional poem plunges to his death from a "doubtful bridge" (165); watching Neptune and his nymphs in a Carnival parade, she "almost wished to...plunge into the green wave" (178). All this plunging anticipates Emily's plunge from the lofty detachment of the scenic tourist into the abyss of obscurity that is Montoni's castle.

11 Edmund Burke, *A Philosophical Enquiry into the Origin of our Ideas of the Sublime and Beautiful,* ed. James T. Boulton (Notre Dame Ind.: University of Notre Dame Press, 1968), pp. 64–70. References in the text are to this edition.

12 Thomas Weiskel, *The Romantic Sublime: Studies in the Structure and Psychology of Transcendence* (Baltimore: Johns Hopkins University Press, 1976), p. 5; Frances Ferguson, *Solitude and the Sublime* (New York: Routledge, 1992), esp. pp. 37–53; and Ronald Paulson, *Representations of Revolution (1789–1820)* (New Haven: Yale University Press, 1983), pp. 57–73. As Burke's aesthetics are politicized, his politics are also highly aestheticized; Wollstonecraft's *Vindication of the Rights of Men,* discussed in Chapter 5 above, attacks him for this. Also see Neal Wood, "The Aesthetic Dimension of Burke's Political Thought," *Journal of British Studies,* 4 (1964), pp. 41–64.

13 Radcliffe's suspense, for which she is renowned (and often reviled by readers impatient with the disproportion of apprehension to bodily harm) can also be read as a byproduct of this elaborate thought experiment.

14 *Loving With a Vengeance: Mass-Produced Fantasies for Women* (New York: Methuen, 1982), p. 34.

15 Clarissa is demanding to speak with her father, who is in the next room; her brother holds the door shut as she presses against it, kneeling and pleading. "The door was endeavoured to be opened on the inside, which made my brother let go the key on a sudden; and I pressing against it (all the time remaining on my knees) fell flat on my face into the other parlour; however without hurting myself. But everybody was gone..." Samuel Richardson, *Clarissa* (London: Dent/Everyman's Library, 1962), vol. I, p. 390.

16 Radcliffe and her heroines have seldom been taken seriously in their 200-year critical history. Terry Castle remarks, "No English writer of such historic importance and diverse influence has been so often trivialized by her critics" ("Spectralization of the Other," p. 232.) William Ruff, for example, comments snidely, "She certainly wrote trash, and yet good critics have praised her...Reputation Ann Radcliffe certainly has to this day, and one adds that if she had talent as well she would indeed be the fortunate novelist." "Ann Radcliffe, or, The Hand of Taste," in *The Age of Johnson*, ed. F. W. Hilles (New Haven: Yale University Press, 1949), p. 183. Robert Kiely refuses to take Emily's danger seriously: "the reader is never for a moment allowed to believe that Emily could be raped." By reading her fears as "the projections of hysteria," he is able to ignore the correspondence between Emily's situation and the legal, economic, and social indignities of eighteenth-century womanhood. *The Romantic Novel in England* (Cambridge, Mass.: Harvard University Press, 1972), pp. 73, 75.

17 Marilyn Butler, "The Woman at the Window: Ann Radcliffe in the Novels of Mary Wollstonecraft and Jane Austen," in *Gender and Literary Voice*, ed. Janet Todd, *Women and Literature*, new series, vol. I (New York and London: Holmes and Meier, 1980), pp. 128–48.

18 As Cora Kaplan points out, the hat is a signifier that links class and sexuality, affirming Emily's status as both a lady and sexually pure. "Pandora's Box: Subjectivity, Class and Sexuality in Socialist Feminist Criticism," in *Sea Changes: Essays on Culture and Feminism* (London: Verso, 1986), p. 169.

19 Nelson C. Smith affirms patriarchal common sense by commending St. Aubert in "Sense, Sensibility and Ann Radcliffe," *SEL*, 13 (1973), pp. 577–90, while a feminist critic like Nina da Vinci Nichols views

him as enforcing male fear of female sexuality. "Place and Eros in Radcliffe, Lewis and Brontë," in *The Female Gothic,* ed. Juliann Fleenor (Montreal: Eden Press, 1983), pp. 187–206.

20 Castle, "Spectralization of the Other," p. 234.

21 "The Ideology of the Aesthetic," *Poetics Today,* 9 (1988), p. 329.

22 Kiely's *Romantic Novel in England* argues that Radcliffe tries but fails to achieve unity or balance in both characterization and narrative form, though her exploration of the irrational leads toward a higher, "Romantic" synthesis. Elizabeth Napier condemns Radcliffe less ambiguously for failure to create psychologically realistic characters and a "complex inability to confront both moral and aesthetic responsibilities" whose "feverish search after sensation is puzzlingly joined with a deliberate retreat from meaning." *The Failure of Gothic: Problems of Disjunction in an Eighteenth-Century Literary Form* (Oxford University Press, 1987), p. 39.

8 AESTHETICS, GENDER, AND EMPIRE IN MARY SHELLEY'S *FRANKENSTEIN*

1 Mary Shelley, *Frankenstein, or, The Modern Prometheus,* 1818 text, ed. James Rieger (University of Chicago Press, 1974), p. 52. References in the text are to this edition.

2 Mary Shelley, *History of a Six Weeks' Tour through a part of France, Switzerland, Germany, and Holland* (London, 1817), p. 75. References in the text are to this edition.

3 They apparently did not find her. Emily W. Sunstein, *Mary Shelley: Romance and Reality* (Boston: Little, Brown and Co., 1989), p. 85.

4 My choice to designate Victor Frankenstein's artificial being with the more neutral "creature," rather than "monster," is a conscious one that I share with many of Shelley's recent critics. A shift from "monster" to "creature" can be observed, for example, between the landmark anthology *The Endurance of* Frankenstein: *Essays on Mary Shelley's Novel,* ed. George Levine and U. C. Knoepflmacher (Berkeley: University of California Press, 1979) and the more recent *Approaches to Teaching Shelley's* Frankenstein, eds. Stephen C. Behrendt and Anne K. Mellor (New York: Modern Language Association, 1990).

5 Shelley's reading during the years 1814–17 included such works as Mungo Park, *Travels in the Interior Districts of Africa* (1799); Thomas Pennant, *A View of Hindoostan* (1798–1800); Sir John Barrow's account of the British Embassy to China under Lord Macartney in 1792–94; Anson's *Voyage Round the World;* William Robertson's *History of America;* and Bryan Edwards' *History of the West Indies* (1793–94). This interest in

the faraway or exotic, which Shelley shared with numerous British readers of her day, extended to imaginative works like Johnson's *Rasselas*, Beckford's *Vathek*, Montesquieu's *Lettres persanes*, Voltaire's *Candide* and *Zadig*, Southey's *Thalaba the Destroyer* and *The Curse of Kehama*, Mme. de Graffigny's *Lettres d'une Péruvienne*, Marmontel's *Les Incas*, Thomas Moore's *Lalla Rookh: an Oriental Romance*, and Lady Morgan's *The Missionary: An Indian Tale*. *The Journals of Mary Shelley 1814–1844*, eds. Paula R. Feldman and Diana Scott-Kilvert (Oxford: Clarendon Press, 1987), vol. I, pp. 5–189. Relatively few critics address issues of empire in *Frankenstein*. See Gayatri Chakravorty Spivak, "Three Women's Texts and a Critique of Imperialism," *Critical Inquiry*, 12 (1985); Zohreh T. Sullivan, "Race, Gender, and Imperial Ideology in the Nineteenth Century," *Nineteenth-Century Contexts*, 13 (1989), pp. 19–32; Joseph W. Lew, "The Deceptive Other: Mary Shelley's Critique of Orientalism in *Frankenstein*," *Studies in Romanticism*, 30 (1991), pp. 255–83, and H. L. Malchow, "Frankenstein's Monster and Images of Race in Nineteenth-Century Britain," *Past and Present*, 139 (1993), pp. 90–130.

6 Feminist criticism of *Frankenstein* includes Sandra M. Gilbert and Susan Gubar, *The Madwoman in the Attic* (New Haven: Yale University Press, 1979), pp. 213–47; Ellen Moers, "Female Gothic," pp. 77–87 (reprinted from *Literary Women*), U. C. Knoepflmacher, "Thoughts on the Aggression of Daughters," pp. 88–119, and Kate Ellis, "Monsters in the Garden: Mary Shelley and the Bourgeois Family," pp. 123–42, all in Levine and Knoepflmacher, eds., *The Endurance of Frankenstein*; Mary Jacobus, "Is There a Woman in This Text?" *New Literary History*, 14 (1982), pp. 117–41; Barbara Johnson, "My Monster/My Self," *Diacritics*, 12 (1982), pp. 2–10; Devon Hodges, "*Frankenstein* and the Feminine Subversion of the Novel," *Tulsa Studies in Women's Literature*, 2 (1983), pp. 155–64; Mary Poovey, *The Proper Lady and the Woman Writer: Ideology as Style in the Works of Mary Wollstonecraft, Mary Shelley, and Jane Austin* (University of Chicago Press, 1984), pp. 114–42; Anne K. Mellor, *Mary Shelley: Her Life, Her Fiction, Her Monsters* (New York: Routledge, 1988); and Susan Winnett, "Coming Unstrung: Women, Men, Narrative, and Principles of Pleasure," *PMLA*, 105 (1990), pp. 505–18. Bette London shifts the focus to men in "Mary Shelley, *Frankenstein*, and the Spectacle of Masculinity," *PMLA*, 108 (1993), pp. 253–67.

7 "Three Women's Texts," pp. 243–45 and 254–59.

8 "Race, Gender, and Imperial Ideology," p. 21.

9 Though they have been interested in Shelley's handling of the sublime, critics have not connected *Frankenstein's* treatment of

aesthetics to its preoccupation with empire. See Mary A. Favret, *Romantic Correspondence: Women, Politics and the Fiction of Letters* (Cambridge University Press, 1993), pp. 192–94; Anne K. Mellor, "*Frankenstein* and the Sublime," in *Approaches to Teaching*, eds. Behrendt and Mellor, pp. 99–104, and "Possessing Nature: The Female in *Frankenstein*," in *Romanticism and Feminism*, ed. Mellor, pp. 220–32; Barbara Freeman, "*Frankenstein* with Kant: A Theory of Monstrosity, or the Monstrosity of Theory," *SubStance*, 52 (1987), pp. 21–31; Fred V. Randel, "*Frankenstein*, Feminism, and the Intertextuality of Mountains," *Studies in Romanticism*, 24 (1985), pp. 515–32; and Frances Ferguson, "The Nuclear Sublime," *Diacritics*, 14 (1984), pp. 4–10.

10 This suggestion is amplified in the 1831 revision: "She busied herself with following the aerial creations of the poets; and in the majestic and wondrous scenes which surrounded our Swiss home...she found ample scope for admiration and delight" (236).

11 I disagree with those who view the 1831 text as fundamentally different from and inferior to the earlier version. Mary Poovey, for example, takes the change in Elizabeth's character as a symptom of Shelley's deepening conservatism; Anne K. Mellor attributes "greater internal philosophical coherence" to the 1818 text. "Choosing a Text of *Frankenstein*," in *Approaches to Teaching*, eds. Behrendt and Mellor, p. 31. Kate Ellis agrees with me that the later edition's more angelic Elizabeth actually presents a sharper criticism of conservative ideals of femininity ("Monsters in the Garden," pp. 131–35); James O'Rourke contends that Shelley "in fact maintained a lifelong allegiance to leftist political ideals" ("'Nothing More Unnatural': Mary Shelley's Revision of Rousseau," *ELH*, 56 [1989], p. 544).

12 Ellis, "Monsters in the Garden," p. 135.

13 *Ibid.*, pp. 139, 141.

14 The language of the scenic descriptions reinforces the counterpoint between destructive individualism and the moral-aesthetic ideal of community, as when Henry contrasts the picturesque Rhine Valley with the Swiss mountains, the setting of Victor's confrontation with the creature. The mountaintops are "more majestic and strange; but there is a charm in the banks of this divine river, that I never before saw equalled...Oh, surely, the spirit that inhabits and guards this place has a soul more in harmony with man, than those who pile the glacier, or retire to the inaccessible peaks of the mountains of our own country" (153).

15 *Romantic Correspondence*, p. 178 and *passim*: "heteroglossia" is Mikhail Bakhtin's term in "Discourse in the Novel," in *The Dialogic Imagination*, trans. Caryl Emerson and Michael Holquist (Austin: University of Texas Press, 1981), pp. 263ff.

16 Spivak suggests the analogy to the Kantian subject, ("Three Women's Texts," p. 256). Barbara Freeman traces eruptions of the sublime into the monstrous through the novel ("Frankenstein with Kant").

17 "The Nuclear Sublime," p. 8.

18 Hume, "Of the Standard of Taste," in *Essays*, p. 271.

19 "Afterword" to *Frankenstein*, ed. Harold Bloom (New York: New American Library, 1965), pp. 218–19.

20 For example, O'Rourke, "'Nothing More Unnatural.'"

21 William Godwin, *Enquiry Concerning Political Justice*, ed. Isaac Kramnick (Harmondsworth: Penguin, 1976), Book I, Chapter IV.

22 Her list of books read that year places *Gulliver's Travels* directly above *Paradise Lost* (whose image of Eve staring at her reflection is of course another antecedent for *Frankenstein's* mirror scene, as Gilbert and Gubar note, *Madwoman in the Attic*, p. 240). During the same period she mentions Percy reading aloud to her from Plutarch and Montaigne; the latter's "Of Cannibals" was an early example of the cultural-relativist strain in Enlightenment thought. *Journals*, pp. 96, 145–47. Interestingly, Godwin cites *Gulliver's Travels*, Book IV, Chapter V, on the causes of war, early in *Political Justice* – calling Swiftian satire to his aid in presenting a grim vision of society as it has historically existed. See pp. 86–87.

23 Jonathan Swift, *Travels into Several Remote Nations of the World*, in *Gulliver's Travels and Other Writings*, ed. Louis A. Landa (Boston: Houghton Mifflin, 1960), p. 225.

24 *Ends of Empire: Women and Ideology in Early Eighteenth-Century Literature* (Ithaca: Cornell University Press, 1993), pp. 170–200.

25 Lew suggests his yellow skin is specifically reminiscent of the Bengalis, by 1818 already suffering from several generations of British misrule resulting in a horrendous famine (1770) and the destruction of the cottage textile industry that became a symbol in India's twentieth-century struggle for independence. "The Deceptive Other," p. 273. Zohreh Sullivan suggests the Burmese ("Race, Gender, and Imperial Ideology"). See Malchow, "Frankenstein's Monster and Images of Race," on Shelley's allusions to racial discourse about Africans and the debate about abolishing slavery in the West Indies.

26 Adrienne Rich, "Planetarium," qtd. in Gilbert and Gubar, *The Madwoman in the Attic*, pp. 240–41.

27 Lee Sterrenburg, "Mary Shelley's Monster: Politics and Psyche in *Frankenstein*," in *Endurance of* Frankenstein, eds. Levine and Knoepflmacher, pp. 143–71. In Sterrenburg's view, both Burkean or anti-Jacobin portraits of the revolutionary crowd as inherently evil, and republican versions of the desperate monsters that a despotic

government can produce, contribute to Shelley's synthetic myth. Wollstonecraft and Godwin were certainly monsters to the generation of the French Wars. "The most extravagant and demonic pictures of mass insurrectionary violence in both Wollstonecraft and Burke concern female rebels," he also points out, p. 163. The image of Frankenstein's monster circulated during later political crises: the reform agitation of the early 1830s, 1848–49 with Chartism, the late 1860s, and the Irish troubles of the 1880s. Conservative writers and cartoonists used it "to dwell on the dangers of animating social monsters through hopes of political reform" – that is, to monsterize the lower classes, pp. 166–70.

28 Edith Hamilton summarizes the story of Hercules: his jealous wife sends him a poisoned robe and he kills himself to end his agony. "A fearful pain seized him, as though he were in a burning fire...He could still slay others, but it seemed that he himself could not die...He ordered those around him to build a great pyre on Mount Oeta and carry him to it." *Mythology* (New York: New American Library, 1942), pp. 171–72.

29 Debate on *sati* by India's colonial rulers was active at least from 1813 until the official abolition of the practice in 1829. Lata Mani, "Contentious Traditions: The Debate on *Sati* in Colonial India," in *The Nature and Context of Minority Discourse,* eds. Abdul R. JanMohamed and David Lloyd (Oxford University Press, 1990), pp. 319–56, and see Spivak, "Can the Subaltern Speak? Speculations on Widow-Sacrifice," *Wedge,* 7/8 (1985). Thomas Pennant's four-volume compilation, *The View of Hindoostan* (London, 1798), which Shelley's journal records her reading, mentions a powerful Indian queen who "exempted herself from the cruel rite of burning with the body of her husband, in the manner that the affectionate spouses of her subjects were accustomed to do," vol. I, p. 119. Pennant also refers to the "Hindoo" custom of burning the dead, saying that some inhabitants of the Maldive Islands practice it, "but...our best authority, says, that the poor only inter; the rich commit them to the funeral pile," vol. I, p. 153.

30 S. P. Mohanty, quoted in Sara Suleri, *The Rhetoric of English India* (University of Chicago Press, 1992), p. 14.

31 The final words of the novel, p. 221.

Select bibliography

Abrams, M. H., "From Addison to Kant: Modern Aesthetics and the Exemplary Art," in *Studies in Eighteenth-Century British Art and Aesthetics,* ed. Ralph Cohen (Berkeley: University of California Press, 1985).

Adams, M. Ray, "Helen Maria Williams and the French Revolution," in *Wordsworth and Coleridge: Studies in Honor of George McLean Harper,* ed. Earl Leslie Griggs (New York: Russell & Russell, Inc., 1962).

Addison, Joseph, *The Spectator,* ed. Donald Bond, 5 vols. (Oxford: Clarendon Press, 1965).

Ahmed, Leila, "Western Ethnocentrism and Perceptions of the Harem," *Feminist Studies,* 8 (1982).

Alger, John G., *Englishmen in the French Revolution* (London, 1889).

Alison, Archibald, *Essays on the Nature and Principles of Taste,* 1790 (Hildesheim: Georg Olms, 1968).

Alloula, Malek, *The Colonial Harem,* trans. Myrna Godzich and Wald Godzich (Minneapolis: University of Minnesota Press, 1986).

Althusser, Louis, "Ideology and Ideological State Apparatuses," in *Lenin and Philosophy and Other Essays,* trans. Ben Brewster (New York: Monthly Review Press, 1971).

Altick, Richard D., *The Shows of London* (Cambridge, Mass.: Harvard University Press, 1978).

Altman, Janet Gurkin, *Epistolarity: Approaches to a Form* (Columbus: Ohio State University Press, 1982).

Andrews, Malcolm, *The Search for the Picturesque* (Stanford University Press, 1990).

Austen, Jane, *Northanger Abbey,* in *The Novels of Jane Austen,* ed. R. W. Chapman, 1933, vol. V (London: Oxford University Press, 1965).

Baker, Keith Michael, *Inventing the French Revolution: Essays on French Political Culture in the Eighteenth Century* (Cambridge University Press, 1989).

Bakhtin, M. M., *The Dialogic Imagination,* trans. Caryl Emerson and Michael Holquist (Austin: University of Texas Press, 1981).

Rabelais and His World, trans. Hélène Iswolsky (Bloomington: Indiana University Press, 1984).

Barash, Carol, "The Character of Difference: The Creole Woman as

Cultural Mediator in Narratives about Jamaica," *Eighteenth-Century Studies*, 23 (1990).

Barbier, Carl Paul, *William Gilpin* (Oxford: Clarendon Press, 1963).

Barker-Benfield, G. J., *The Culture of Sensibility: Sex and Society in Eighteenth-Century Britain* (University of Chicago Press, 1992).

Barrell, John, "'The Dangerous Goddess': Masculinity, Prestige, and the Aesthetic in Early Eighteenth-Century Britain," *Cultural Critique*, 12 (1989).

   The Dark Side of the Landscape: The Rural Poor in English Painting 1730–1840 (Cambridge University Press, 1980).

   The Idea of Landscape and the Sense of Place, 1730–1840: An Approach to the Poetry of John Clare (Cambridge University Press, 1972).

   The Political Theory of Painting from Reynolds to Hazlitt (New Haven: Yale University Press, 1986).

Batten, Charles L., Jr., *Pleasurable Instruction: Form and Convention in Eighteenth-Century Travel Literature* (Berkeley: University of California Press, 1978).

Battersby, Christine, *Gender and Genius: Towards a Feminist Aesthetics* (Bloomington: Indiana University Press, 1989).

Behrent, Stephen C., and Anne K. Mellor, eds., *Approaches to Teaching Shelley's* Frankenstein (New York: Modern Language Association, 1990).

Ben-Israel, Hedva, *English Historians on the French Revolution* (Cambridge University Press, 1968).

Bender, John B., *Imagining the Penitentiary: Fiction and the Architecture of Mind in Eighteenth-Century England* (University of Chicago Press, 1987).

   "A New History of the Enlightenment?" *Eighteenth-Century Life*, 16 (1992).

Bennett, Tony, *Outside Literature* (London: Routledge, 1990).

Berger, John, *et al.*, *Ways of Seeing* (New York: Penguin, 1972).

Bermingham, Ann, *Landscape and Ideology: The English Rustic Tradition, 1740–1860* (Berkeley: University of California Press, 1989).

Bhabha, Homi, "The Other Question: Difference, Discrimination and the Discourse of Colonialism," in *Literature, Politics and Theory*, eds. Francis Barker *et al.* (New York: Methuen, 1986).

Bohls, Elizabeth A., "Disinterestedness and Denial of the Particular: Locke, Adam Smith, and the Subject of Aesthetics," in *Eighteenth-Century Aesthetics and the Reconstruction of Art*, ed. Paul Mattick, Jr. (Cambridge University Press, 1993).

Boulton, James T., *The Language of Politics in the Age of Wilkes and Burke* (London: Routledge & Kegan Paul, 1963).

Bourdieu, Pierre, *Distinction: A Social Critique of the Judgement of Taste*, trans. Richard Nice (Cambridge, Mass.: Harvard University Press, 1984).

Bray, Matthew, "Helen Maria Williams and Edmund Burke: Radical Critique and Complicity," *Eighteenth-Century Life*, 16 (1992).

Brissenden, R. F., *Virtue in Distress: Studies in the Novel of Sentiment From Richardson to Sade* (New York: Barnes & Noble, 1974).

Brooks, Peter, *The Melodramatic Imagination* (New York: Columbia University Press, 1985).

Brown, Judith, "Lesbian Sexuality in Medieval and Early Modern Europe," in *Hidden From History: Reclaiming the Gay and Lesbian Past,* eds. Martin Duberman, Martha Vicinus, and George Chauncey, Jr. (New York: Penguin, 1989).

Brown, Laura, *Alexander Pope* (New York: Basil Blackwell, 1985).

Ends of Empire: Women and Ideology in Early Eighteenth-Century Literature. (Ithaca,: Cornell University Press, 1993).

Burke, Edmund, *A Philosophical Enquiry into the Origin of our Ideas of the Sublime and Beautiful,* ed. James T. Boulton (Notre Dame, Ind.: University of Notre Dame Press, 1968).

Reflections on the Revolution in France, ed. Thomas H. D. Mahoney (Indianapolis: Bobbs-Merrill, 1955).

Butler, Judith, "Contingent Foundations: Feminism and the Question of 'Postmodernism,.'" in *Feminists Theorize the Political,* eds. Judith Butler and Joan W. Scott (New York: Routledge, 1992).

Butler, Marilyn, ed., *Burke, Paine, Godwin, and the Revolution Controversy* (Cambridge University Press, 1984).

"The Woman at the Window: Ann Radcliffe in the Novels of Mary Wollstonecraft and Jane Austen," in *Gender and Literary Voice,* ed. Janet Todd, *Women and Literature,* new series, vol. 1 (New York and London: Holmes and Meier, 1980).

Campbell, Jill, "Lady Mary Wortley Montagu and the Historical Machinery of Female Identity," in *History, Gender and Eighteenth-Century Literature,* ed. Beth Fowkes Tobin (Athens: University of Georgia Press, 1994).

Canning, Rick, "Colonial Shorthand: Swift, the Ascendancy, and Internal Colonialism," diss. University of Illinois, Urbana-Champaign, 1994.

Castle, Terry J., *Masquerade and Civilization: The Carnivalesque in Eighteenth-Century English Culture and Fiction* (Stanford University Press, 1986).

"The Spectralization of the Other in *The Mysteries of Udolpho,*" in *The New Eighteenth Century,* ed. Felicity Nussbaum and Laura Brown (New York: Methuen, 1987).

Clark, J. C. D., *English Society 1688–1832: Ideology, Social Structure and Political Practice During the Ancien Regime* (Cambridge University Press, 1985).

Clifford, James, "Introduction: Partial Truths," in *Writing Culture: The Poetics and Politics of Ethnography,* eds. James Clifford and George E. Marcus (Berkeley: University of California Press, 1986).

"Traveling Cultures," in *Cultural Studies,* eds. Lawrence Grossberg, Cary Nelson, and Paula A. Treichler (New York: Routledge, 1992).

Cooper, Anthony Ashley (Lord Shaftesbury), *Characteristics,* ed. J. M. Robertson, 2 vols. (London, 1900).

Corrigan, Philip, and Derek Sayer, *The Great Arch: English State Formation as Cultural Revolution* (Oxford: Basil Blackwell, 1985).

Cottom, Daniel, *The Civilized Imagination: A Study of Ann Radcliffe, Jane Austen and Sir Walter Scott* (Cambridge University Press, 1985).

Craven, Elizabeth, *Journey through the Crimea to Constantinople* (London, 1789).

de Bolla, Peter, *The Discourse of the Sublime: History, Aesthetics, and the Subject* (Oxford: Basil Blackwell, 1989).

de Certeau, Michel, *The Practice of Everyday Life*, trans. Steven Rendall (Berkeley: University of California Press, 1984).

de Lauretis, Teresa, *Alice Doesn't: Feminism, Semiotics, Cinema* (Bloomington: Indiana University Press, 1984).

Dengler, Ian C., "Turkish Women in the Ottoman Empire: The Classical Age," in *Women in the Muslim World*, eds. Lois Beck and Nikki Keddie (Cambridge, Mass.: Harvard University Press, 1978).

Dickie, George, and Richard C. Sclafani, eds., *Aesthetics: A Critical Anthology* (New York: St. Martin's Press, 1977).

Dickson, P. G. M., *The Financial Revolution in England: A Study in the Development of Public Credit* (London: Macmillan, 1967).

Douglas, Mary, *Purity and Danger: An Analysis of the Concepts of Pollution and Taboo*, 1966 (New York: Routledge, 1991).

Dumont, Jean, *A New Voyage to the Levant*, fourth edn. (London, 1705).

Dussinger, John A., "Hester Piozzi, Italy, and the Johnsonian Aether," *South Central Review*, 9.4 (Winter 1992).

Dykstal, Timothy, "The Politics of Taste in the *Spectator*," *The Eighteenth Century: Theory and Interpretation*, 35 (1994).

Eagleton, Terry, *The Function of Criticism* (London: Verso, 1984).
    The Ideology of the Aesthetic (Oxford: Basil Blackwell, 1990).
    "The Ideology of the Aesthetic," *Poetics Today*, 9 (1988).

Ellison, Julie, "Redoubled Feeling: Politics, Sentiment, and the Sublime in Williams and Wollstonecraft," *Studies in Eighteenth-Century Culture*, 20 (1990).

Esposito, John L., *Women in Muslim Family Law* (Syracuse University Press, 1982).

Fabricant, Carole, "The Aesthetics and Politics of Landscape in the Eighteenth Century," in *Studies in Eighteenth-Century British Art and Aesthetics*, ed. Ralph Cohen (Berkeley: University of California Press, 1985).
    "Binding and Dressing Nature's Loose Tresses: The Ideology of Augustan Landscape Design," *Studies in Eighteenth-Century Culture*, 8 (1979).
    "The Literature of Domestic Tourism and the Public Consumption of Private Property," in *The New Eighteenth Century*, eds. Felicity Nussbaum and Laura Brown (New York: Methuen, 1987).

Favret, Mary A., *Romantic Correspondence: Women, Politics and the Fiction of Letters* (Cambridge University Press, 1993).

Ferguson, Frances, "The Nuclear Sublime," *Diacritics*, 14 (1984).
    Solitude and the Sublime (New York: Routledge, 1992).
    "Wollstonecraft Our Contemporary," in *Gender and Theory: Dialogues on Feminist Criticism*, ed. Linda Kauffman (New York: Basil Blackwell, 1989).

Ferguson, Moira, *Subject to Others: British Women Writers and Colonial Slavery, 1670–1834* (New York: Routledge, 1992).

Flax, Jane, "Postmodernism and Gender Relations in Feminist Theory," in *Feminism/Postmodernism*, ed. Linda J. Nicholson (New York: Routledge, 1990).

Flaxman, Rhoda L., "Radcliffe's Dual Modes of Vision," in *Fetter'd or Free? British Women Novelists 1670–1815*, eds. Mary Anne Schofield and Cecelia Macheski (Athens: Ohio University Press, 1986).

Foster, Hal, ed., *The Anti-Aesthetic: Essays on Postmodern Culture* (Port Townsend, Wash.: Bay Press, 1983).

Foucault, Michel, *The Archaeology of Knowledge*, trans. A. M. Sheridan Smith (New York: Pantheon, 1972).

Freeman, Barbara, "*Frankenstein* with Kant: A Theory of Monstrosity, or the Monstrosity of Theory," *SubStance*, 52 (1987).

Frow, John, *Marxism and Literary History* (Cambridge, Mass.: Harvard University Press, 1986).

Gates, Henry Louis, ed., *"Race," Writing, and Difference* (University of Chicago Press, 1986).

Gay, Peter, *The Enlightenment: An Interpretation*, 2 vols. (New York: Alfred A. Knopf, 1969).

Gilbert, Katharine Everett, and Helmut Kuhn, *A History of Esthetics* (Bloomington: Indiana University Press, 1954).

Gilbert, Sandra M., and Susan Gubar, *The Madwoman in the Attic* (New Haven: Yale University Press, 1979).

Gilpin, William, *Observations on the River Wye and several parts of South Wales, &c. relative chiefly to Picturesque Beauty; made in the Summer of the Year 1770*, fifth edn. (London, 1800).

Observations, relative chiefly to Picturesque Beauty, Made in the Year 1772, on Several Parts of England; particularly the Mountains, and Lakes of Cumberland, and Westmoreland (London, 1786).

Observations, relative chiefly to Picturesque Beauty, Made in the Year 1776, on Several Parts of Great Britain; particularly the High-Lands of Scotland (London, 1789).

Three Essays: on Picturesque Beauty; on Picturesque Travel; and on Sketching Landscape: to which is added a Poem, on Landscape Painting (London, 1792).

Gilroy, Paul. "Cultural Studies and Ethnic Absolutism," in *Cultural Studies*, eds. Lawrence Grossberg, Cary Nelson, and Paula A. Treichler (New York: Routledge, 1992).

Gittings, Robert, and Jo Manton, *Dorothy Wordsworth* (Oxford: Clarendon Press, 1985).

Godwin, William, *Enquiry Concerning Political Justice*, ed. Isaac Kramnick (Harmondsworth: Penguin, 1976).

Goldberg, Rita, *Sex and Enlightenment: Women in Richardson and Diderot* (Cambridge University Press, 1984).

Grant, Aline, *Ann Radcliffe* (Denver: Alan Swallow, 1951).

Greenblatt, Stephen, "Towards a Poetics of Culture," in *The New Historicism*, ed. H. Aram Veeser (New York: Routledge, 1989).

Habermas, Jürgen, *The Structural Transformation of the Public Sphere*, trans. Thomas Burger and Frederick Lawrence (Cambridge, Mass.: MIT Press, 1989).

Hagstrum, Jean, "Pictures to the Heart: the Psychological Picturesque in Ann Radcliffe's *The Mysteries of Udolpho*," in *Greene Centennial Studies*, eds. Paul J. Korshin and Robert R. Allen (Charlottesville: University of Virginia Press, 1984).

Halsband, Robert, *The Life of Lady Mary Wortley Montagu* (New York: Oxford University Press, 1960).

Hamilton, Edith, *Mythology* (New York: New American Library, 1942).

Haraway, Donna, "Situated Knowledges: The Science Question in Feminism and the Privilege of Partial Perspective," *Feminist Studies*, 14 (1988).

Harrison, Gary Lee, "Spec(tac)ular Reversals: The Politics of the Sublime and Wordsworth's Transfiguration of the Rustic Poor," *Criticism*, 34 (1992).

Hein, Hilde, and Carolyn Korsmeyer, eds., *Aesthetics in Feminist Perspective* (Bloomington: Indiana University Press, 1993).

Heinzelman, Kurt, "The Cult of Domesticity: Dorothy and William Wordsworth at Grasmere," in *Romanticism and Feminism*, ed. Anne K. Mellor (Bloomington: Indiana University Press, 1988).

Herrmann, Luke, *British Landscape Painting of the Eighteenth Century* (New York: Oxford University Press, 1974).

Hill, Aaron, *A Full and Just Account of the Present State of the Ottoman Empire* (London, 1709).

Hill, Bridget, *Women, Work, and Sexual Politics in Eighteenth-Century England* (Oxford: Basil Blackwell, 1989).

ed., *The First English Feminist: Reflections Upon Marriage and Other Writings* (New York: St. Martin's Press, 1986).

Hipple, W. J., Jr., *The Beautiful, the Sublime, and the Picturesque in Eighteenth-Century British Aesthetic Theory* (Carbondale: Southern Illinois University Press, 1957).

Hodges, Devon, "*Frankenstein* and the Feminine Subversion of the Novel," *Tulsa Studies in Women's Literature*, 2 (1983).

Homans, Margaret, *Women Writers and Poetic Identity: Dorothy Wordsworth, Emily Brontë, and Emily Dickinson* (Princeton University Press, 1980).

Home, Henry (Lord Kames), *Elements of Criticism*, 1762 (New York, 1860).

Honour, Hugh, *Neo-Classicism* (New York: Penguin, 1968).

Hughes, Griffith, *Natural History of Barbados* (London, 1750).

Hulme, Peter, *Colonial Encounters: Europe and the Native Caribbean, 1492–1797* (London: Routledge, 1992).

Hume, David, *A Treatise of Human Nature*, eds P. H. Nidditch (Oxford: Clarendon Press, 1978).

Essays Moral, Political, and Literary, eds. T. H. Green and T. H. Grose (London, New York, Bombay and Calcutta: Longmans, Green, and Co., 1875).

Hunt, John Dixon, *The Figure in the Landscape: Poetry, Painting, and Gardening during the Eighteenth Century* (Baltimore: Johns Hopkins University Press, 1976).

and Peter Willis, eds., *The Genius of the Place: The English Landscape Garden 1620–1820* (Cambridge, Mass.: MIT Press, 1988).

Hunt, Lynn, *Politics, Culture, and Class in the French Revolution* (Berkeley: University of California Press, 1984).

Hunter, Ian, "Aesthetics and Cultural Studies," in *Cultural Studies,* eds. Lawrence Grossberg, Cary Nelson and Paula A. Treichler (New York: Routledge, 1992).

Hunter, J. Paul, *Before Novels: The Cultural Contexts of Eighteenth-Century English Fiction* (New York: W. W. Norton & Co., 1990).

Hussey, Christopher, *The Picturesque: Studies in a Point of View* (London: Frank Cass 1927; reprinted 1967, 1983).

Huyssen, Andreas, "Mapping the Postmodern," in *Feminism/Postmodernism,* ed. Linda J. Nicholson (New York: Routledge, 1990).

Jacobus, Mary, "Is There a Woman in This Text?" *New Literary History,* 14 (1982).

Jaggar, Alison, *Feminist Politics and Human Nature* (Totowa, N. J.: Rowman & Allanheld, 1983).

Janes, Regina, "Beheadings," *Representations,* 35 (1991).

Johnson, Barbara, "My Monster/My Self," *Diacritics,* 12 (1982).

Johnson, Claudia L., *Jane Austen: Women, Politics, and the Novel* (University of Chicago Press, 1988).

Jones, Chris, "Helen Maria Williams and Radical Sensibility," *Prose Studies,* 12 (1989).

Kabbani, Rana, *Europe's Myths of Orient* (Bloomington: Indiana University Press, 1986).

Kant, Immanuel, *Critique of Judgement,* trans. Werner S. Pluhar, 1790 (Indianapolis: Hackett, 1987).

Kaplan, Cora, *Sea Changes: Essays on Culture and Feminism* (London: Verso, 1986).

Kelley, Theresa M., *Wordsworth's Revisionary Aesthetics* (Cambridge University Press, 1988).

Kelly-Gadol, Joan, "Did Women Have a Renaissance?" in *Becoming Visible: Women in European History,* eds. Renate Bridenthal and Claudia Koonz (Boston: Houghton Mifflin, 1977).

Kiely, Robert, *The Romantic Novel in England* (Cambridge, Mass.: Harvard University Press, 1972).

Klein, Herbert S., *African Slavery in Latin America and the Caribbean* (Oxford University Press, 1986).

Knight, Richard Payne, *The Landscape, a Didactic Poem, in Three Books* (London, 1794).

Kolodny, Annette, *The Lay of the Land: Metaphor as Experience and History in American Life and Letters* (Chapel Hill: University of North Carolina Press, 1975).

Kostelnick, Charles, "From Picturesque View to Picturesque Vision: William Gilpin and Ann Radcliffe," *Mosaic,* 18 (1985).

Krauss, Rosalind E., *The Originality of the Avant-Garde and Other Modernist Myths* (Cambridge, Mass.: MIT Press, 1986).

Kristeller, P. O., "The Modern System of the Arts," 1951, in *Renaissance Thought and the Arts* (Princeton University Press, 1990).

Landa, Louis A., "Pope's Belinda, the General Emporie of the World, and the Wondrous Worm," in *Pope: Recent Essays by Several Hands,* eds. Maynard Mack and James A. Winn (Hamden, Conn.: Archon Books, 1980).

Landes, Joan B., *Women and the Public Sphere in the Age of the French Revolution* (Ithaca: Cornell University Press, 1988).

Levin, Susan M., *Dorothy Wordsworth and Romanticism* (New Brunswick: Rutgers University Press, 1987).

Levine, George, and U. C. Knoepflmacher, eds., *The Endurance of Frankenstein: Essays on Mary Shelley's Novel* (Berkeley: University of California Press, 1979).

Lew, Joseph W., "Lady Mary's Portable Seraglio," *Eighteenth-Century Studies,* 24 (1991).

"The Deceptive Other: Mary Shelley's Critique of Orientalism in *Frankenstein,*" *Studies in Romanticism,* 30 (1991).

Lewis, Gordon K., *The Growth of the Modern West Indies* (New York: Monthly Review Press, 1968).

Liu, Alan, "On the Autobiographical Present: Dorothy Wordsworth's *Grasmere Journals,*" *Criticism,* 26 (1984).

"The Power of Formalism: The New Historicism," *ELH,* 56 (1989).

Wordsworth: The Sense of History (Stanford University Press, 1989).

London, Bette, "Mary Shelley, *Frankenstein,* and the Spectacle of Masculinity," *PMLA,* 108 (1993).

Long, Edward, *History of Jamaica* (London, 1774).

Lynch, Deidre, "'Beating the Track of the Alphabet': Samuel Johnson, Tourism, and the ABCs of Modern Authority," *ELH,* 57 (1990).

Macdonell, Diane, *Theories of Discourse: An Introduction* (Oxford: Basil Blackwell, 1986).

Macklem, Michael, "Reynolds and the Ambiguities of Neo-Classical Criticism," *Philological Quarterly,* 31 (1952).

MacPherson, C. B., *The Political Theory of Possessive Individualism: Hobbes to Locke* (New York: Oxford University Press, 1962).

Malchow, H. L., "Frankenstein's Monster and Images of Race in Nineteenth-Century Britain," *Past and Present,* 139 (1993).

Mani, Lata, "Contentious Traditions: The Debate on *Sati* in Colonial India," in *The Nature and Context of Minority Discourse,* eds. Abdul R. JanMohamed and David Lloyd (Oxford University Press, 1990).

Manwaring, Elizabeth Wheeler, *Italian Landscape in Eighteenth-Century England* (New York: Oxford University Press, 1925).

Marshall, P. J., and Glyndwr Williams, *The Great Map of Mankind:*

Perceptions of New Worlds in the Age of Enlightenment (Cambridge, Mass.: Harvard University Press, 1982).

Marx, Karl, *Economic and Philosophic Manuscripts of 1844,* in *The Marx–Engels Reader,* ed. Robert C. Tucker, second edition. (New York: W. W. Norton, 1978).

Mattick, Paul, Jr., "Arts and the State: The NEA Debate in Perspective," *The Nation,* vol. 251, no. 10 (October 1, 1990).

"Beautiful and Sublime: Gender Totemism and the Constitution of Art," *Journal of Aesthetics and Art Criticism,* 48: 4 (1990).

 ed., *Eighteenth-Century Aesthetics and the Reconstruction of Art* (Cambridge University Press, 1993).

Mayo, Robert D., *The English Novel in the Magazines, 1740–1815* (Evanston, Ill.: Northwestern University Press, 1962).

McAllister, Marie E., *Woman on the Journey: Eighteenth-Century British Women's Travel in Fact and Fiction,* diss. Princeton University, 1988.

McGann, Jerome J., *The Romantic Ideology: A Critical Investigation* (University of Chicago Press, 1983).

McGavran, James Holt, Jr., "Dorothy Wordsworth's Journals: Putting Herself Down," in *The Private Self,* ed. Shari Benstock (Chapel Hill: University of North Carolina Press, 1988).

McKeon, Michael, "Politics of Discourses and the Rise of the Aesthetic in Seventeenth-Century England," in *The Politics of Discourse,* eds. Kevin Sharpe and Steven Zwicker (Berkeley: University of California Press, 1987).

"The Origins of Aesthetic Value," *Telos,* 57 (1983).

Mellor, Anne K., *Mary Shelley: Her Life, Her Fiction, Her Monsters* (New York: Routledge, 1988).

 ed., "Possessing Nature: The Female in *Frankenstein,*" in *Romanticism and Feminism,* (Bloomington: Indiana University Press, 1988).

Romanticism and Gender (New York: Routledge, 1993).

Melman, Billie, *Women's Orients: English Women and the Middle East, 1718–1918* (Ann Arbor: University of Michigan Press, 1992).

Michasiw, Kim Ian, "Nine Revisionist Theses on the Picturesque," *Representations,* 38 (1992).

Miller, Nancy K., *Subject to Change* (New York: Columbia University Press, 1988).

Mills, Sara, *Discourses of Difference: An Analysis of Women's Travel Writing and Colonialism* (London: Routledge, 1991).

Mingay, G. E., *English Landed Society in the Eighteenth Century* (London: Routledge and Kegan Paul, 1963).

Modleski, Tania, *Loving With a Vengeance: Mass-Produced Fantasies for Women* (New York: Methuen, 1982).

Monk, Samuel Holt, *The Sublime: A Study of Critical Theories in XVIII-Century England* (New York: Modern Language Association, 1935).

Montagu, Mary Wortley, *Complete Letters*, ed. Robert Halsband, 3 vols. (Oxford: Clarendon Press, 1965–67).

Essays and Poems and Simplicity, a Comedy, eds. Isobel Grundy and Robert Halsband (Oxford: Clarendon Press, 1977).

Mulvey, Laura, "Afterthoughts on 'Visual Pleasure and Narrative Cinema' inspired by *Duel in the Sun,*" in *Feminism and Film Theory,* ed. Constance Penley (New York: Routledge, 1988).

"Visual Pleasure and Narrative Cinema," in *Feminism and Film Theory,* ed. Constance Penley (New York: Routledge, 1988).

Myers, Mitzi, "Mary Wollstonecraft's *Letters Written ...in Sweden*: Toward Romantic Autobiography," *Studies in Eighteenth-Century Culture,* 8 (1979).

"Politics from the Outside: Mary Wollstonecraft's First *Vindication,*" *Studies in Eighteenth-Century Culture,* 6 (1977).

Nabholtz, John R., "Dorothy Wordsworth and the Picturesque," *Studies in Romanticism,* 3 (1964).

Nair, Janaki, "Uncovering the Zenana: Visions of Indian Womanhood in Englishwomen's Writings, 1813–1940," *Journal of Women's History,* 2 (1990).

Napier, Elizabeth, *The Failure of Gothic: Problems of Disjunction in an Eighteenth-Century Literary Form* (Oxford University Press, 1987).

Neely, Carol Thomas, "Constructing the Subject: Feminist Practice and the New Renaissance Discourses," *English Literary Renaissance,* 18 (1988).

Newton, Judith Lowder, *Women, Power, and Subversion: Social Strategies in British Fiction, 1778–1860* (Athens: University of Georgia Press, 1981).

Nichols, Nina da Vinci, "Place and Eros in Radcliffe, Lewis and Brontë," in *The Female Gothic,* ed. Juliann Fleenor (Montreal: Eden Press, 1983).

Nochlin, Linda, *Women, Art, and Power and Other Essays* (New York: Harper & Row, 1988).

Nugent, Maria, *Journal,* ed. Philip Wright (Kingston: Institute of Jamaica, 1966).

Nyström, Per, *Mary Wollstonecraft's Scandinavian Journey* (Göteborg: Kungl. Vetenskaps- och Vitterhets-Samhället, 1980).

Ong, Aihwa, "Colonialism and Modernity: Feminist Re-presentations of Women in Non-Western Societies," *Inscriptions,* 3/4 (1988).

O'Rourke, James, "'Nothing More Unnatural': Mary Shelley's Revision of Rousseau," *ELH,* 56 (1989).

Ousby, Ian, *The Englishman's England: Taste, Travel, and the Rise of Tourism* (Cambridge University Press, 1990).

Ozouf, Mona, *Festivals and the French Revolution,* trans. Alan Sheridan (Cambridge, Mass.: Harvard University Press, 1988).

Paine, Thomas, *The Rights of Man,* ed. Eric Foner (New York: Penguin, 1984).

Parker, Rozsika, and Griselda Pollock, *Old Mistresses: Women, Art and Ideology* (London and Henley: Routledge & Kegan Paul, 1981).

Parry, J. H., Philip Sherlock, and Anthony Maingot, *A Short History of the West Indies,* fourth edition. (New York: St. Martin's Press, 1987).

Patterson, Orlando, *The Sociology of Slavery* (Rutherford, N. J.: Fairleigh Dickinson University Press, 1967).

Paulson, Ronald, *Breaking and Remaking: Aesthetic Practice in England, 1700–1820* (New Brunswick: Rutgers University Press, 1989).

Emblem and Expression: Meaning in English Art of the Eighteenth Century (Cambridge, Mass.: Harvard University Press, 1975).

Representations of Revolution (1789–1820) (New Haven: Yale University Press, 1983).

Pennant, Thomas, *The View of Hindoostan*, 4 vols. (London, 1798).

Perkin, Harold, *Origins of Modern English Society* (New York: Routledge, 1969).

Pevsner, Nikolaus, *Studies in Art, Architecture and Design* (New York: Walker and Company, 1968).

Plato, *The Republic*, in *Works*, trans. Benjamin Jowett (Cambridge, Mass., 1871).

Pocock, J. G. A., *The Machiavellian Moment: Florentine Political Thought and the Atlantic Republican Tradition* (Princeton University Press, 1975).

Virtue, Commerce, and History: Essays on Political Thought and History, Chiefly in the Eighteenth Century. (Cambridge University Press, 1985).

Poovey, Mary, *The Proper Lady and the Woman Writer: Ideology as Style in the Works of Mary Wollstonecraft, Mary Shelley, and Jane Austen* (University of Chicago Press, 1984).

Pope, Alexander, *Correspondence*, ed. George Sherburn (Oxford: Clarendon Press, 1956).

Pratt, Mary Louise, *Imperial Eyes: Travel Writing and Transculturation* (New York: Routledge, 1992).

"Scratches on the Face of the Country; or, What Mr. Barrow Saw in the Land of the Bushmen," in *"Race," Writing, and Difference*, ed. Henry Louis Gates (University of Chicago Press, 1986).

Price, Martin, "The Picturesque Moment," in *From Sensibility to Romanticism: Essays Presented to Frederick A. Pottle*, eds. Frederick W. Hilles and Harold Bloom (New York: Oxford University Press, 1965).

Price, Uvedale, *An Essay on the Picturesque, as Compared with the Sublime and the Beautiful; and, on the Use of Studying Pictures, for the Purpose of Improving Real Landscape* (London, 1810).

Radcliffe, Ann, *A Journey made in the Summer of 1794, through Holland and the Western Frontier of Germany, with a Return down the Rhine, to which are added Observations during a Tour to the Lakes of Lancashire, Westmoreland, and Cumberland* (London, 1795).

The Mysteries of Udolpho, ed. Bonamy Dobrée (Oxford University Press, 1980).

The Romance of the Forest, ed. Chloe Chard (Oxford University Press, 1986).

Randel, Fred V., "*Frankenstein*, Feminism, and the Intertextuality of Mountains," *Studies in Romanticism*, 24 (1985).

Reiss, Timothy J., "Revolution in Bounds: Wollstonecraft, Women, and

Reason," in *Gender and Theory: Dialogues on Feminist Criticism,* ed. Linda Kauffman (Oxford: Basil Blackwell, 1989).

Reynolds, Frances, *An Enquiry concerning the Principles of Taste, and of the Origin of our Ideas of Beauty* (London, 1785).

Reynolds, Joshua, *Discourses on Art,* ed. Robert R. Wark (New Haven: Yale University Press, 1975).

Richardson, Samuel, *Clarissa,* 4 vols. (London: Dent/Everyman's Library, 1962).

Rosenblum, Robert, *Transformations in Late Eighteenth Century Art* (Princeton University Press, 1967).

Ruff, William, "Ann Radcliffe, or, The Hand of Taste," in *The Age of Johnson,* ed. F. W. Hilles (New Haven: Yale University Press, 1949).

Rycaut, Paul, *The Present State of the Ottoman Empire* (London, 1668).

Said, Edward W., "Orientalism Reconsidered," in Francis Barker *et al.,* eds., *Europe and Its Others: Proceedings of the Essex Conference on the Sociology of Literature* (Colchester: University of Essex, 1985).

Orientalism (New York: Random House, 1978).

Sapiro, Virginia, *A Vindication of Political Virtue: The Political Theory of Mary Wollstonecraft* (University of Chicago Press, 1992).

Saslow, James M., "Homosexuality in the Renaissance: Behavior, Identity, and Artistic Expression," in *Hidden From History: Reclaiming the Gay and Lesbian Past,* ed. Martin Duberman, Martha Vicinus, and George Chauncey, Jr. (New York: Penguin, 1989).

[Schaw, Janet,] *Journal of a Lady of Quality; Being the Narrative of a Journey from Scotland to the West Indies, North Carolina, and Portugal, in the years 1774 to 1776,* eds. Evangeline Walker Andrews and Charles McLean Andrews, second edition. (New Haven: Yale University Press, 1934).

Schiebinger, Londa, "The Anatomy of Difference: Race and Sex in Eighteenth-Century Science," *Eighteenth-Century Studies,* 23 (1990).

Schiller, Friedrich, *On the Aesthetic Education of Man,* trans. Reginald Snell (New York: Frederick Ungar, 1965).

Schor, Naomi, *Reading in Detail: Aesthetics and the Feminine* (New York: Methuen, 1987).

"Rereading in Detail: Or, Aesthetics, the Feminine, and Idealism," *Criticism,* 32 (1990).

Scott, Joan Wallach, *Gender and the Politics of History* (New York: Columbia University Press, 1988).

"The Evidence of Experience," *Critical Inquiry,* 17 (1991).

Shelley, Mary, *Frankenstein,* ed. Harold Bloom (New York: New American Library, 1965).

Frankenstein, or, The Modern Prometheus, 1818 text, ed. James Rieger (University of Chicago Press, 1974).

History of a Six Weeks' Tour through a part of France, Switzerland, Germany, and Holland (London, 1817).

The Journals of Mary Shelley 1814–1844, ed. Paula R. Feldman and Diana Scott-Kilvert, 2 vols (Oxford: Clarendon Press, 1987).

Shohat, Ella, "Gender and Culture of Empire: Toward a Feminist Ethnography of the Cinema," *Quarterly Review of Film and Video,* 13 (1991).

Shusterman, Richard, "Of the Scandal of Taste: Social Privilege as Nature in the Aesthetic Theories of Hume and Kant," in *Eighteenth-Century Aesthetics and the Reconstruction of Art,* ed. Paul Mattick, Jr. (Cambridge University Press, 1993).

Smith, Adam, *The Theory of Moral Sentiments,* eds. A. L. Macfie and D. D. Raphael (Indianapolis: Liberty Classics, 1982).

Smith, Barbara Herrnstein, *Contingencies of Value: Alternative Perspectives for Critical Theory* (Cambridge, Mass.: Harvard University Press, 1988).

Smith, Nelson C., "Sense, Sensibility and Ann Radcliffe," *SEL,* 13 (1973).

Smith, William, *Natural History of Nevis and the rest of the English Leeward Charibee Islands in America* (London, 1745).

Spacks, Patricia Meyer, *Desire and Truth: Functions of Plot in Eighteenth-Century English Novels* (University of Chicago Press, 1990).

Spelman, Elizabeth V., "Woman as Body: Ancient and Contemporary Views," *Feminist Studies,* 8 (1982).

Spivak, Gayatri Chakravorty, "Can the Subaltern Speak? Speculations on Widow-Sacrifice," *Wedge,* 7/8 (1985).

"Three Women's Texts and a Critique of Imperialism," *Critical Inquiry,* 12 (1985).

Stafford, Barbara Maria, *Voyage into Substance: Art, Science, Nature, and the Illustrated Travel Account, 1760–1840* (Cambridge, Mass.: MIT Press, 1984).

Stallybrass, Peter, and Allon White, *The Politics and Poetics of Transgression* (Ithaca: Cornell University Press, 1986).

Staves, Susan, *Married Women's Separate Property in England, 1660–1833* (Cambridge, Mass.: Harvard University Press, 1990).

Sterne, Laurence, *A Sentimental Journey,* ed. Ian Jack (Oxford University Press, 1984).

Tristram Shandy, ed. Howard Anderson (New York: W. W. Norton, 1980).

Sterrenburg, Lee, "Mary Shelley's Monster: Politics and Psyche in *Frankenstein,*" in *The Endurance of* Frankenstein: *Essays on Mary Shelley's Novel,* eds. George Levine and U. C. Knoepflmacher (Berkeley: University of California Press, 1979).

Stewart, John, *An Account of Jamaica,* London 1808 (Freeport, N.Y.: Books for Libraries Press, 1971).

Stoler, Ann Laura, "Carnal Knowledge and Imperial Power: Gender, Race, and Morality in Colonial Asia," in *Gender at the Crossroads of Knowledge: Feminist Anthropology in the Postmodern Era,* ed. Micaela di Leonardo (Berkeley: University of California Press, 1991).

Stolnitz, Jerome, "On the Origins of 'Aesthetic Disinterestedness,'" *Journal of Aesthetics and Art Criticism,* 20 (1961–62).

Straub, Kristina, *Divided Fictions: Fanny Burney and Feminine Strategy* (Lexington: University Press of Kentucky, 1987).

Sexual Suspects: Eighteenth-Century Players and Sexual Ideology (Princeton University Press, 1992).

Suleri, Sara, *The Rhetoric of English India* (University of Chicago Press, 1992).

Sullivan, Zohreh T., "Race, Gender, and Imperial Ideology in the Nineteenth Century," *Nineteenth-Century Contexts,* 13 (1989).

Sunstein, Emily W., *Mary Shelley: Romance and Reality* (Boston: Little, Brown and Co., 1989).

Swift, Jonathan, *Travels into Several Remote Nations of the World,* in *Gulliver's Travels and Other Writings,* ed. Louis A. Landa (Boston: Houghton Mifflin, 1960).

Tate, W. E., *The English Village Community and the Enclosure Movements* (London: Victor Gollancz, Ltd., 1967).

Taussig, Michael, *Shamanism, Colonialism and the Wild Man: A Study in Terror and Healing* (University of Chicago Press, 1986).

Thomas, Keith, *Man and the Natural World: Changing Attitudes in England 1500–1800* (New York: Pantheon Books, 1983).

Thompson, E. P., *Customs in Common* (New York: The New Press, 1991).

"Eighteenth-Century English Society: Class Struggle Without Class?" *Social History,* 3 (1978).

Thompson, J. M., *The French Revolution* (Oxford: Basil Blackwell, 1966).

Todorov, Tzvetan, *Theories of the Symbol* (Ithaca: Cornell University Press, 1982).

Wardle, Ralph, *Mary Wollstonecraft: A Critical Biography* (Lawrence: University of Kansas Press, 1951).

Weiskel, Thomas, *The Romantic Sublime: Studies in the Structure and Psychology of Transcendence* (Baltimore: Johns Hopkins University Press, 1976).

West, Thomas, *Guide to the Lakes in Cumberland, Westmorland and Lancashire,* third edition, 1778 (Oxford: Woodstock Books, 1989).

Williams, Helen Maria, *Letters From France,* ed. Janet M. Todd (Delmar, N.Y.: Scholars' Facsimiles and Reprints, 1975).

Williams, Raymond, *The Country and the City* (Oxford University Press, 1973).

Marxism and Literature (Oxford University Press, 1977).

Wind, Edgar, *Hume and the Heroic Portrait: Studies in Eighteenth-Century Imagery* (Oxford: Clarendon Press, 1986).

Winnett, Susan, "Coming Unstrung: Women, Men, Narrative, and Principles of Pleasure," *PMLA,* 105 (1990).

Withers, Robert, *A Description of the Grand Signour's Seraglio, or Turkish Emperour's Court* (London, 1653).

Wolfson, Susan J., "Individual in Community: Dorothy Wordsworth in Conversation with William," in *Romanticism and Feminism,* ed. Anne K. Mellor (Bloomington: Indiana University Press, 1988).

Wollstonecraft, Mary, *The Works of Mary Wollstonecraft,* eds. Marilyn Butler and Janet Todd, 7 vols. (New York University Press, 1989).

Wood, Neal, "The Aesthetic Dimension of Burke's Political Thought," *Journal of British Studies,* 4 (1964).

Woodmansee, Martha, "'Art' as a Weapon in Cultural Politics: Rereading Schiller's *Aesthetic Letters*," in *Eighteenth-Century Aesthetics and the Reconstruction of Art*, ed. Paul Mattick, Jr. (Cambridge University Press, 1993).

The Author, Art, and the Market: Rereading the History of Aesthetics (New York: Columbia University Press, 1994).

Woodward, Lionel D., *Une Anglaise Amie de la Révolution Francaise* (Paris: Librairie Ancienne Honoré Champion, 1930).

Wordsworth, Dorothy, *Journals of Dorothy Wordsworth*, ed. Mary Moorman, second edition (Oxford University Press, 1971).

Recollections of a Tour Made in Scotland, A. D. 1803, in *Journals of Dorothy Wordsworth*, ed. Ernest de Selincourt, 2 vols (New York: Macmillan, 1941).

Wordsworth, William, *Guide to the Lakes*, ed. Ernest de Selincourt, 1906 (Oxford University Press, 1977).

Young, Arthur, *A Six Months Tour through the North of England*, 4 vols., second edition (London, 1771).

A Six Weeks Tour through the Southern Counties of England and Wales, second edition (Dublin, 1771).

Young, Iris Marion, "Impartiality and the Civic Public: Some Implications of Feminist Critiques of Moral and Political Theory," in *Feminism as Critique*, eds. Seyla Benhabib and Drucilla Cornell (Minneapolis: University of Minnesota Press, 1987).

Index

Adams, M. Ray, 109
Addison, Joseph: *The Spectator*, 2–3, 8, 48, 50, 69
aesthetics: and civic humanism, 73–79; and colonialism, 47–48, 50–60, 231, 234–42; aesthetic distance, 183; aesthetic unity, 21, 115, 229; autonomous aesthetic sphere, 9–10, 68–69, 79, 151, 152, 153, 165, 167, 178, 206, 229; defining aesthetics, 5–6; disinterested contemplation, 8–9, 31, 35, 68–70, 79–80, 95, 124, 151, 159, 161, 167, 170, 177, 215, 229, 236; emergence of modern aesthetics, 7; generic perceiver, 10, 27, 79, 204–205, 239, 241; neoclassical, 73, 79; Romantic, 79
Alison, Archibald, 69–70
Altick, Richard, 198–99
Altman, Janet Gurkin, 182
ambivalence, 21, 176, 183–93, 202–204, 210, 230, 241
Andrews, Malcolm, 95, 99, 173
Aristotle, 78
Astell, Mary, 252n1
Atlantic Triangle Trade, 48
Austen, Jane: *Northanger Abbey*, 1–2, 66, 94, 209, 211–12, 229

Baker, Keith Michael, 110
Bakhtin, Mikhail, 156, 207, 251n41
Barash, Carol, 258n30
Barbauld, Letitia, 112
Barker-Benfield, G. J., 100–102
Barrell, John, 5, 74–75, 172
Bastille, the, 116–17, 155
beautiful, the, 14, 63, 232, 238
Behn, Aphra, 47–48
Berger, John, 35, 87
Bermingham, Ann, 88, 93
Bhabha, Homi, 51
Blackmore, Richard, 48
"Blue Stockings," 14

Bourdieu, Pierre, 8, 48, 80, 95, 165
Bray, Matthew, 109–10
Brooks, Peter, 130
Brown, "Capability," 82–83, 150
Brown, Laura, 47, 64, 102, 244
Buffon, Georges Louis Leclerc, 55, 72
Burke, Edmund: *A Philosophical Enquiry into the Origin of our Ideas of the Sublime and Beautiful*, 60, 72, 116, 144, 187, 216–19; *Reflections on the Revolution in France*, 120, 126–27, 135, 142–46
Butler, Judith, 80

Campbell, Jill, 255n21
Castle, Terry, 213
Christie, Thomas, 128
cinema, 87
civic humanism, 74–75
Clare, John, 171–72
Claude glass, 93–94
Clifford, James, 42, 251n40
coffee-houses, 36, 197
conduct manuals, 210–11
Cooper, Anthony Ashley, *see* Shaftesbury, Lord
Corrigan, Philip, 82

David, Jacques-Louis, 121, 134
De Certeau, Michel, 177–78
De Gouges, Olympe, 126
Dengler, Ian C., 40
denial of the particular, 13, 67, 81, 95, 124, 206
Douglas, Mary, 200
Dumont, Jean, 29–30
Dussinger, John, 265n58

Eagleton, Terry, 5, 10, 74, 147–48, 165, 167, 229
Ellis, Kate, 233
Ellison, Julie, 116, 123
enclosure, of common lands, 88, 145

306

CAMBRIDGE STUDIES IN ROMANTICISM

Titles published